THE BREAD BIBLE

THE BREAD BIBLE

beth hensperger's
300 FAVORITE RECIPES

ILLUSTRATIONS BY HARRY BATES

CHRONICLE BOOKS
SAN FRANCISCO

Library of Congress Cataloging-in-Publication Data:
Hensperger, Beth.
        The bread bible: Beth Hensperger's 300 favorite recipes.
            p.   cm.
        Includes index.
        ISBN 0-8118-1686-9 (hc)
        1. Bread.   I. Title
        TX769.H442   1999
        641.8'15—dc21   98-22374
                        CIP

    PRINTED IN THE UNITED STATES OF AMERICA

    DESIGNED BY JILLY SIMONS, KELLY SIMPSON,
    AND JENNIFER CULLEN, CONCRETE, CHICAGO
    TYPESETTING BY JAIME ROBLES

Distributed in Canada by Raincoast Books
8680 Cambie Street
Vancouver, British Columbia V6P 6M9

        10 9 8 7 6 5 4 3 2

    CHRONICLE BOOKS
    85 SECOND STREET
    SAN FRANCISCO,
    CALIFORNIA 94105

    WWW.CHRONICLEBOOKS.COM

ACKNOWLEDGMENTS

Many thanks to my editor, Bill LeBlond, who put this book together and oversaw all aspects of the project with great patience and a discerning eye; assistant editor, Sarah Putman, who took care of the little details; Susan Derecskey, who organized and copyedited the mountain of material; Lisa Howard, our ever-diligent word processor; Roberta "Bobbe" Torgerson, who generously retested recipes with great efficiency; my friends Lynn Alley, Carole Cesario, Jesse Cool, Mary Anne McCready, Johanna Miller, and Suzanne Rosenblum for their thoughtful opinions and for boosting my spirits; and Martha Casselman, my loyal agent, to whom I owe heartfelt thanks and appreciation for her literary acumen, professional insights, and never-wavering moral support.

FOR STEVE

CONTENTS

13 THE ART AND SCIENCE OF GOOD BAKING

17 THE BAKING PROCESS:
ESSENTIAL METHODS AND TECHNIQUES

34 THE ELEMENTS OF A LOAF: INGREDIENTS

42 BACK TO BASICS: WHITE BREADS
White Mountain Bread
French Bread
Tuscan Peasant Bread
Homestyle White Bread with Poppy Seeds
Buttermilk Honey Bread
Farm-Style White Bread with Cardamom
Honey and Seed Bread

62 THE BAKER'S APEX:
EGG BREADS AND BRIOCHE
Jewish Egg Braid
Sweet Vanilla Challah
*Lemon Whole-Wheat Egg Bread with
Nasturtium Butter*
Brioche
Marzipan Brioche with Apricot Brandy Glaze
Cornmeal Brioche
Brie in Brioche

79 ABUNDANT GRAIN: WHOLE-GRAIN BREADS
Sesame Whole-Wheat Bread
Old-fashioned 100 Percent Whole-Wheat Bread
Italian Walnut-Raisin Whole-Wheat Bread
Cracked Wheat Bread
Graham Bread
Bran-Molasses-Sunflower Bread
Oatmeal-Potato Bread
Oatmeal-Bulgur Bread
Rain and Sun
Swedish Rye Bread
Black Russian Rye Bread
Potato and Rye Vienna Twist
Squaw Bread
Anadama Bread with Tillamook Cheddar Cheese
Brown Rice Bread with Dutch Crunch Topping

Wild Rice–Molasses Bread
Seven-Grain Honey Bread

116 TRADITIONAL ROOTS:
COUNTRY HEARTH BREADS
Farmstead Sourdough Bread
Italian Olive Oil Bread
Semolina Sesame Seed Twist
Vienna Bread
Pain de Campagne
Pain de Campagnard
Pain de Seigle
Sour Poppy Seed Rye

136 NATURE'S BOUNTY: VEGETABLE, HERB,
CHEESE, AND NUT BREADS
Seeded Dill Rye
Buttermilk Potato Bread
Whole-Wheat Basil Bread
Cheddar Cheese Bread with Toasted Sesame Seeds
Gruyère Pullman Loaf
Olive Bread
French Nut Bread
California Walnut Bread
Pain Hawaiian
Roasted Chestnut Bread
Celeste's Sunflower-Oatmeal Bread

157 THE ROLL BASKET: DINNER ROLLS,
SANDWICH BUNS, BREAD STICKS, AND BAGELS
My Favorite Buttermilk Dinner Rolls
French-Style Mexican Hard Rolls
Squash Cloverleafs
Petits Pains au Lait
Black Bread Rolls
Water Rolls
Sesame Burger Buns
Sesame Whole-Wheat Long Rolls
California Olive Rolls
Italian Bread Sticks
Wild Rice Bread Sticks
Egg Bagels

181 THE GOLDEN CRUST: BISCUITS,
SHORTCAKES, SCONES, AND SODA BREADS
Classic Buttermilk Biscuits
Sweet Potato Biscuits
Cornmeal-Orange Biscuits
Old-fashioned Shortcake Biscuits
Lemon Cream Scones
Fig-Walnut Scones
Graham Scones with Pine Nuts and Raisins
Irish Soda Bread with Caraway and Drambuie
Whole-Wheat Irish Herb Bread
Whole-Wheat Bran Bread with Dates

194 SAVORY SPECIAL OCCASIONS:
PICNIC BREADS
Sausage Bread
Shallot and Poppy Seed Braid
Crescia al Formaggio
Pancetta-Onion Gruyère Ring
Garlic and Mozzarella Stromboli
Italian-Style Herb Bread
Torta d'Erbe
Eggplant, Pepper, and Artichoke Pie
Onion Tart

212 ARTISTIC PALATE:
PIZZA, CALZONE, AND FOCACCIA
Basic Pizza Dough
Deep Dish Pizza with Sausage and Mozzarella
Pizza Pie with Cheese
Spinach Calzone
Olive Focaccia
Herbed Focaccia

227 FIRST LOAVES:
TORTILLAS, FLATBREADS, AND FRY BREADS
Corn Tortillas
Blue Corn Tortillas
Indian Fry Bread
Flour Tortillas
Country-Style Whole-Wheat Pita

236 A FLASH IN THE PAN: PANCAKES,
WAFFLES, CRÊPES, AND POPOVERS
Old-fashioned Buttermilk Pancakes
Buttermilk Waffles
Sourdough Pancakes and Waffles
Blue Cornmeal Pancakes
Whole-Wheat Blueberry Buttermilk Pancakes
Buckwheat Pancakes
Beer Waffles
Vanilla Belgian Waffles
Crêpes
Cottage Cheese Blintzes
Cornmeal Blini
Savory Wild Rice Pancakes
Old-fashioned Potato Pancakes
Zucchini Pancakes
Baked Pancake with Cucumber Salsa
Baked Apple and Pear Oven Pancake
Mile-High Popovers
The Best Yorkshire Pudding

259 SWEET THINGS: MORNING BREADS,
SWEET ROLLS, AND CROISSANTS
Old-fashioned Raisin Bread with Molasses Glaze
Honey-Prune Bread
Fresh Apple-Walnut Loaf
Cashew-Date Bread
Traditional English Muffins
Cinnamon Rolls with Irish Cream Glaze
Mexican Morning Buns
Yeasted Sopaipillas
Danish Pastries
Whole-Wheat Croissants
Pumpkin Brioche

287 THE CAKE OF BREAD: COFFEE CAKES
Spiced Brown Sugar–Pecan Coffee Cake
Fresh Fruit Cobbler
Pear Spice Coffee Cake

Blueberry Buttermilk Coffee Cake
Vanilla Sour Cream Coffee Cake
Sweet Yeast Dough
Fresh Apple Coffee Cake
Raspberry Braid
Maple-Blueberry Whole-Wheat Braid
Orange Cinnamon Swirl
Golden Italian Coffee Cake
Babka
Cinnamon-Walnut Sweet Bread
Plum Crumb Cake

309 SPUR-OF-THE-MOMENT BAKER:
QUICK BREADS
Lemon–Poppy Seed Bread
Dried Apricot–Pecan Bread
Whole-Wheat Prune Bread
Orange–Date Tea Bread
Banana Bread
Mango Bread
Cranberry-Orange Bread
Carrot and Tangerine Bread
Cream Sherry–Pumpkin Bread
Glazed Zucchini Bread
Steamed Pecan Corn Bread
Steamed Brown Bread with Dried Blueberries

326 PURE AMERICANA: MUFFINS
Fresh Lemon Muffins
Fresh Berry Muffins
Sour Cream Apple Muffins
Old-fashioned Prune Muffins
Banana-Pecan Muffins
Spiced Applesauce Muffins
Everyday Maple Bran Muffins
Raspberry Cornmeal Muffins
Zucchini Madeleines
Bacon–Blue Corn Sticks
Santa Fe Blue Corn Muffins
Quinoa Whole-Wheat Muffins

340 RED, WHITE, AND BLUE: CORN BREADS
Buttermilk Corn Bread
Yogurt Corn Bread
Savory Corn Bread Stuffing
Blue Corn Bread
Green and Red Pepper Corn Bread
Maple Whole-Wheat Johnnycake with Blueberries

349 SUGAR AND SPICE: GINGERBREAD
Gingerbread with Lemon and Raspberry Sauces
Peach Upside-Down Ginger Cake
Blueberry Gingerbread
Fresh Apricot Gingerbread

356 A SLICE OF DIVINITY:
CELEBRATION AND DESSERT BREADS
Pernod Panettone
Stollen with Dried Cherries and Pineapple
Saffron Bread with Scented
  Geranium Powdered Sugar
Bohemian Sweet Rolls
Portuguese Sweet Bread with Honey
Italian Anise Easter Bread
Hungarian Nut Rolls
Alpine Easter Bread
Byzantine Easter Bread
Kulich with Almonds and Ginger
American Chocolate Bread
Hot Cross Buns with Dried Fruit and Two Glazes
Golden Rum Babas
Orange Savarin with Berries
Hungarian Sweet Cheese Bread
Bread with Three Chocolates

394 FAST AND BEAUTIFUL:
FOOD PROCESSOR BREADS
Sesame White Bread
Buttermilk Whole-Wheat Bread
French Bread Made in the Food Processor
Pain de Campagne Made in the Food Processor

Italian *Whole-Wheat Bread*
Sour Rye Bread
Four-Seed *Whole-Wheat Bread*
Rosemary Raisin Bread
Multi-Grain *Wild Rice Bread*
Pepper Cheese Bread
Sour Cream Braid
Alsatian Kugelhopf

415 ROBOTIC KNEADS: THE BREAD MACHINE
Cuban Bread
Cottage Cheese–Dill Bread
Sweet Swirled Breads
Egg Bread
Challah Made in the Bread Machine
Buttermilk Honey Bread Made in the Bread Machine
Brioche with Cheese and *Walnuts*
Honey *Whole-Wheat Bread*
100 Percent *Whole-Wheat Bread Made*
  in the Bread Machine
Sesame Semolina Bread
Cracked *Wheat Bread Made in the Bread Machine*
Bran-Molasses-Sunflower Bread Made
  in the Bread Machine
Graham Granola Bread
Old-fashioned Oatmeal Bread
Country Bread
Narsai's Light Rye Bread
Black Russian Rye Bread Made
  in the Bread Machine

Cornmeal-Millet Bread
Squaw Bread Made in the Bread Machine
Italian Olive Oil Bread Made
  in the Bread Machine
Tuscan Peasant Bread Made
  in the Bread Machine
Buttermilk Potato Bread Made
  in the Bread Machine
Wild Rice–Molasses Bread Made
  in the Bread Machine
Sourdough Farm Bread
Pain de Campagne Made in the Bread Machine
Basic Pizza Dough Made in the Bread Machine
Cinnamon-Raisin-Currant Bread
Maple Pecan Bread
Pernod Panettone Made in the Bread Machine
Mexican Chocolate Bread
Saffron Bread Made in the Bread Machine
Grand Baba

467 BAKING EQUIPMENT

470 HIGH-ALTITUDE BAKING GUIDE

471 MAIL-ORDER SOURCES

474 INDEX

496 TABLE OF EQUIVALENTS

THE ART AND SCIENCE
of Good Baking

Bread baking has somehow taken on a mysterious quality, making it seem an intimidating act for many people. The secret to making good bread is that there is no secret. Let your imagination help you break any rules you imagine exist to daunt you.

JACQUELINE DEVAL, *Reckless Appetites*
(Ecco Press, 1993)

The simple pleasure of savoring homemade fresh bread reminds us of how wonderful the basic integrity of premium-quality ingredients is. Of all the cooking processes, baking bread is regarded with greatest love by its practitioners as well as with the greatest anxiety by the uninitiated. Successful baking combines the elements of a balanced recipe, proper equipment, and good ingredients with skilled hands and a dash of imagination.

After decades of teaching baking bread, I have noticed how seriously home bakers take their skills. They are eager to give their breads a personal touch and expand their skills, yet need to be innovative and playful at the same time. I wanted to create a sourcebook for serious home bakers that would, in addition, be a good place for occasional holiday bakers who are in the process of slowly building their technical expertise to find a recipe as well. I wanted to present a text that is readable, yet infused with my own passion for baking.

In a way, I have returned to my roots here. These are truly my best recipes culled from my earliest to my most recent bread books: from good old-fashioned white breads, the mainstay of the American diet, to time-saving food processor doughs; information on sour starters; popular pizza and flatbreads, the easiest breads to make; the best homemade croissants; and a guide for adapting recipes to the bread machine for the connoisseur who doesn't want to get flour on his counter.

Also in this book the baker will find extravagant celebration breads; lots of flavorful, healthful daily loaves; savory main-dish breads; and breakfast rolls. There are lots of American-style breads, baked in the familiar rectangular-loaf shape and tending to be a bit sweeter and richer than their free-form, crusty

European ancestors. There are many best-of-the-best quick breads, very much like cakes in that they demand precise amounts of liquid, leavening, flour, fat, and flavorings. Yet they offer something modern bakers value: ease of preparation in a short period of time.

You'll also find the imaginative use of whole grains, cereals, and flours in many of these loaves, contributing to the new flavors, aromas, and textures modern bakers crave. At the same time all the recipes reflect a natural way to provide your diet with more dietary fiber, a key element in health. Baking your own bread is an easy avenue toward a healthy, well-balanced diet.

My repertoire has always included as many classic yeasted breads solidly based in traditional technique, no matter how exotic or humble the ingredients. Each recipe in this book is designed to stimulate a renewed interest in the art of baking. Do you think that making yeast bread is too time consuming or too difficult? Do such baker's terms as proofing, fermenting, sponge, and second rise seem like a foreign language? This book can answer your questions. Detailed instructions are given for mixing and kneading by hand, by heavy-duty electric mixer, with a food processor, and with a bread machine.

There are no trick recipes or bewildering complicated techniques in this book. There are, on the other hand, lots of little tips, things often omitted precisely because they are so simple. Detailed information also includes comprehensive mixing and baking techniques, notes detailing dough makeup and assembly, as well as helpful information on ingredients. I care as much about the understanding that goes into the bread making craft as the disciplined performance necessary to get a loaf in and out of the oven. A good baker doesn't need to master a great many recipes to be proficient; one good unpretentious, yet well-executed white bread recipe is the basis for everything from wholesome loaves to dinner rolls, hamburger and hot dog buns, and sweet breads.

I want you, as a reader, to let go of the feeling that you have to bake. You can also enjoy reading or browsing in this book, then head out to your favorite bakery or market for an appetizing bread, muffin, biscuit, croissant, or flatbread to satisfy your urge. Small artisanal bakeries and even some larger scale commercial firms produce breads that are as nutritious and delicious as any home-made loaf. It defeats the purpose to bake under pressure or with a feeling of impending doom. But to enjoy on the spot your own baby brioche hot from the oven, a perfect biscuit, crusty country loaf, or a spice-scented breakfast bread or coffee cake, you must bake yourself.

So often I have been asked how I learned to bake. I really started baking in my late teens for my boyfriend, Steve; he encouraged me by happily eating absolutely everything I baked. Baking for someone you love is the core of a home baker's impetus; a sometimes difficult task is turned into a nourishing labor of love when the care you put into it is appreciated. But it was the repetitive baking daily for seven years in a small restaurant that taught me my trade; that is how I built my confidence as a baker. I went from being unable to control a large mass of dough on the work table and wondering what to do with a dough that did not rise in time to be baked for lunch to being very confident with a repertoire of two dozen loaves of my own invention. I was able to develop my skills directly from the experience of baking the same recipe repeatedly over the years, some well over a thousand times.

In response to requests, I began teaching workshops out of the bakery at night. Later, and for the next thirteen years, I taught at local cooking schools. This was an excellent testing ground for finding the best recipes and techniques through the feedback of hundreds of students.

Writing and sharing these recipes was a natural evolution of a skill that was bounded only by my own interest. Some master bakers practice secret-keeping with their recipes and methods, while other professionals are willing to share theirs—the failures, the successes, the on-going internal processes that are an integral part of baking bread. I was fortunate to learn baking from Barbara Hiken, my first real teacher, who taught me the value of sharing a recipe. She believed that if a person was interested enough to ask, it was an honor to share it. Every baker infuses his work with his own individuality; no one can steal your art from you. The loaves you bake will always be a direct reflection of your personal skill.

One winter when I was unemployed, I took out my copies of the first edition of the *Tassajara Bread Book* and *A World of Bread* by Dolores Casella, published in 1966, and started baking loaves and rolls on page one straight on through to the end. I became secure with the six basic steps in constructing every yeast dough: the mixing, kneading, rising, scaling (dividing the portions of dough), shaping, the second rising, and baking. Without realizing it, I became aware of the variables. I paid attention to the weather, the temperature of the flour, even the conditions in my kitchen. It was through this repetition that I began to understand the craft of bread baking.

I had learned how to make croissants at Gayle's, a popular bakery in Capitola, California. There the construction of the croissant was divided into three separate tasks: first, the mixing, working the butter package, and the rolling in; second, the cutting and shaping; and third, the period of rest followed by baking off. Each of these tasks was executed by different people working in different areas of the bakery. Using that experience as a springboard, I tested eight different recipes over a month. I still have the research notes detailing everything from manipulating the dough with crash kneading to balancing liquid/flour ratios in recipes as diverse as Julia Child's, Narsai David's, Bernard Clayton's, and *Cuisine* magazine's. I felt like an explorer: I understood nothing; I wasn't even sure I was on the right track; I just baked.

As my skill and interest in bread baking grew, I began to find and collect images of bread baking in history and travel books, classical painting, photography, and literature to share in my classes. I searched out the works of photographers like the New York–based Michael Geiger, whose stunning overhead shots of loaves for glossy magazines are remarkable in their sophisticated simplicity.

During my travels, I took the time to study the local breads, loaves baked in thin birch bread pans, which would give a unique scent after baking, or a pretty fluted mold. A baker in Oaxaca offered me her soft giant loaves straight out of a centuries-old wood-fire oven. French bakers still make the crustiest loaves I have ever seen, often so rustic looking they were like an oversized field stone. Bakeries in Britain still sell pan loaves embossed with a trademark like Hovis, a brown bakery bread marketed in Britain since the early 1900s. In Alaska I tasted the best sourdough pancakes ever, and in Baja California, the best flour tortillas.

The world of the bread baker is marked by a sense of innocence, being peaceful, creative, and life-giving. It also calls for the power of observation, scientific techniques, and a flair for combining precious flavors, all infused with a traditional respect for quality. Bread making is a skill that connects the baker with the rich heritage of bread and all the communities of the world.

THE BAKING PROCESS:
Essential Methods and Techniques

I made a study of the ancient and indispensable art of breadmaking, consulting such authorities as offered, going back to the primitive days and first invention of the unleavened kind, when from the wildness of nuts and meats men first reached the mildness and refinement of this diet, and traveling gradually down in my studies through that accidental souring of the dough which, it is supposed, taught the leavening process, and through the various fermentations thereafter, till I came to "good, sweet, wholesome bread," the staff of life. Leaven, which some deem the soul of bread, the spirit of which fills its cellular tissue, which is religiously preserved like the vestal fire . . . some precious bottleful, I suppose, first brought over in the Mayflower, did the business for America, and its influence is still rising, swelling, spreading, in cerealian billows over the land.

HENRY DAVID THOREAU, writing
of the overlapping of the mystery and
science of bread in *On Walden Pond*

Breadmaking is nothing more than a series of steps executed in a systematic order. Practice, and it will become second nature to you. In some ways, it is like learning a new language. Use this section to answer questions about the baking process and as an all-purpose guide to breadmaking techniques.

The yeast bread recipes contained within this book all follow the outline below. Quick breads are far simpler and are explained in their own chapters. From the first basic loaf of bread, these recipes focus on the three indispensable basics—white, whole-wheat, and rye—as well as twisted egg breads, whole-grain breads, and free-form French and Italian country breads and rolls; there is something here for every taste. There are also sections on flatbreads, first loaves, stuffed savory breads, rolls in a variety of beguiling shapes, and finally a repertoire of sweet yeast breads with fillings and simple icing finishes. Before you know it, you will be serving and eating your own homemade bread.

- Select a recipe and calculate the preparation time
- Find a work space
- Assemble the equipment and ingredients
- Measure out the ingredients
- Activate the yeast or prepare a sponge starter
- Mix (by hand, electric mixer, food processor, or bread machine)
- Knead
- Allow first rise
- Divide and shape the dough
- Allow second rise
- Prepare the oven
- Bake
- Cool
- Store

LEAVENING AND FERMENTATION

Three methods are used to create yeast breads. One involves mixing commercial yeast with a bit of sugar and a small amount of warm water and allowing it to stand a few minutes until it activates, or "proofs." It is then mixed with the remaining liquid and dry ingredients to form a dough. Most of the recipes in this book use this procedure, known as the direct method.

An offshoot of this method, the quick-rise method, calls for the yeast and a portion of the dry ingredients to be mixed with warm liquid, then the remaining flour is added to form a dough. This method is used a few times in the book.

Some breads are made using the sponge method, which involves making an initial batter with yeast, some liquid, and a small amount of flour to start fermentation. Salt is never added to a sponge starter. Doughs that are constructed from sponge starters are known for being easy to handle and have a firm, yet supple consistency. The prefermentation evenly distributes the yeast and moistens the gluten, thus beginning the process that will be completed by hand during kneading. A basic sponge can double in volume in 30 to 45 minutes, but some recipes require the sponge to stand up to 6 hours. Some sponges are allowed to rise once, while others rise and fall back upon themselves. This method creates a full-flavored and even-textured bread.

The sourdough method, or natural starter, is the most ancient of mixing techniques for making yeast breads. A combination of flour and water is left to stand at room temperature to attract airborne wild yeasts. No commercial yeast is used; the wild yeast feed on the starch in the flour, resulting in fermentation. The starter can be left to ripen for many days depending on the desired degree of sourness.

MIXING THE DOUGH

Bread can be made by hand, in a heavy-duty electric mixer, in a food processor, or in an automatic bread machine. Mixing by hand takes about ten minutes, the electric mixer takes about 5 minutes, and the food processor takes about one minute. Automated bread machines are programmed. Most of the recipes in this book give instructions for mixing the dough both by hand or a heavy-duty electric mixer, which is particularly recommended for whole-grain doughs. Any traditional bread recipe can be adapted easily to be mixed in a heavy-duty electric mixer.

Mixing by Hand

To mix a dough by hand, place the dry ingredients in a large bowl or directly on the work surface and make a well in the center of the mound. Pour the liquid ingredients into the center and beat vigorously with a large whisk or your hand, slowly incorporating the dry ingredients, for about 3 minutes to create a smooth and creamy batter. Add more flour slowly, about 1/4 cup at a time for the most thorough and controlled incorporation, switching to a wooden spoon when the dough gets too stiff. When ready to knead, the dough will just clear the sides of the bowl or make a sticky mound. Turn the dough out onto a lightly floured work surface to knead if using a bowl.

Mixing by Heavy-Duty Electric Stand Mixer

It is important to use a heavy-duty electric stand mixer for mixing and kneading yeast doughs; hand-held mixers do not have enough power. Heavy-duty mixers make mixing enjoyable and they can efficiently handle small, medium, and large batches of dough with ease. The bowl capacity usually ranges from 5 to 8 quarts.

Place the portion of the dry ingredients specified by the recipe in the large bowl of a heavy-duty mixer fitted with the paddle attachment. (The dough hook can be used at the very end of mixing, but is not recommended in the early stages because it cannot blend thoroughly and the batter will remain lumpy.) Add the liquids and beat at the lowest speed for about 1½ minutes to create a smooth, creamy batter. This is also how to make a sponge batter. Switch to the dough hook if your mixer has one; keep the paddle attachment on if it does not (the new machine kneading arm on heavy-duty mixers has been improved and mixes more efficiently). Add the flour slowly on low speed, ½ cup at a time, until a soft dough is formed. When ready to knead, the dough will just clear the sides of the bowl and begin to work itself up the paddle or dough hook.

If kneading by hand, with a plastic dough scraper or spatula, remove the dough from the paddle and bowl onto a lightly floured work surface for kneading. Include the dry bits collected on the bottom of the bowl and knead by hand on a lightly floured surface to even the dough out (or you can just toss the very dry bits).

If kneading by machine, switch from the paddle to the dough hook, if you haven't already, and knead for 3 to 10 minutes, as indicated in each recipe, or until the dough is smooth and springy; it will spring back when pressed. Remove the dough from the bowl and transfer to a lightly floured work surface and knead briefly by hand to finish shaping.

Mixing in a Food Processor
This fast method of mixing dough is completely different from the previous methods. Check the manufacturer's instructions for specifics on your machine—some processors have motors too weak for bread dough. Small processors can handle about 3 cups total of flour and 1½ cups of liquid. The standard, or larger, processor can handle 6 to 8 cups total of flour and 2½ cups of liquid.

In the work bowl, dissolve the yeast and sugar in half the total amount of liquid called for in the recipe. Add the remaining amount of cool (80° to 90°F) liquid and half the total flour (the processor itself will heat up the dough). Using the plastic yeast blade or steel blade, process for the time directed and then add the remaining flour; the batter should just form a ball of dough. Adjust the dough consistency, if necessary, by adding more flour or liquid. On a lightly floured work surface, give the dough a few kneads by hand to check and even out the dough's consistency. For more information and recipes, see the chapter on Food Processor Breads, page 394.

Mixing in a Bread Machine
Before baking your first loaf of bread, read the manufacturer's manual for your machine carefully. There are models that not only have a 4 cup flour capacity, but 6 cups as well, making traditionally proportioned bread recipes as easy to use as layering your ingredients in the pan as directed.

Layer the ingredients in the pan according to the manufacturer's instructions. Set crust on light and program for the appropriate cycle. Press Start. If using the basic bread cycle for a light whole-grain dough, after the first rise cycle reset the controls, and allow the dough to rise a second time. After the baking cycle ends, immediately remove the bread from the pan, and place on a rack to cool to room temperature before slicing. For more information and recipes, see the chapter on The Bread Machine, page 415.

KNEADING A YEAST DOUGH
Kneading, which can be done by hand or in a heavy-duty mixer using the dough hook, transforms dough from a rough, shaggy mass to a soft and pliable ball. Two of the proteins in wheat flour, called glutenin and guaden, combine with water to form gluten, which becomes stretchy when worked. Glutens create a structure strong enough to contain the expanding carbon dioxide gases that are a by-product of the yeast's reproduction.

Kneading by Hand
Beating, whether by hand, or with an electric mixer, forms the initial batter. When the dough has absorbed close to its limit of flour, it will be stiff and sticky and just clear the sides of the work

bowl. It is then ready for kneading. Techniques for kneading are unique to each baker: Some push, some press, some squeeze, some slam. Some are gentle, others vigorous. If you are happy with the consistency of your dough and satisfied with the finished loaves, then you are doing a good job.

For kneading, be certain your work surface is at a height that allows your arms easy movement at the elbows. Sprinkle the work surface (marble, wood, or plastic) with a light dusting of flour, one to two tablespoons, just enough to prevent sticking. If the dough sticks to the work surface, this will inhibit smooth, easy kneading motions. A light dusting of the palms is also helpful.

Scrape the shaggy dough mass out of the bowl with a spatula or plastic scraper, a universal baker's tool that acts as a hand extension, onto the floured surface. This first step of incorporating small amounts of flour may be done by manipulating the dough with a plastic scraper until the dough automatically picks up enough flour to eliminate very sticky patches and you can take over with your hands.

Place your feet slightly apart, keep your knees flexed, and bend a bit at the waist toward the work surface. Place one hand gently on the dough surface. Using large, fluid movements, slowly push the dough away from your body with the heel of the hand. Remember to breathe with the pushing motion. This motion, which uses the whole body rather than just the arms and shoulders, has been likened to tai chi exercises. As you pull back, use your fingers to lift the farthest edge of the dough and give it a quarter turn, then fold the dough in half towards you and push away again.

Repeat the sequence rhythmically: Push, turn, and fold. Use pressure equal to the resistance felt. The dough will at first be quite soft, needing gentle motions. The kneading process can take anywhere from two to ten minutes, with hand-mixed dough taking more time and machine-mixed dough taking less. If too much dough sticks to your hands, simply rub them together to flake off the excess. Scrape up any large dry slabs of sticky dough from the work surface using the dough scraper and discard. As you work, add additional flour only 1 tablespoon at a time as needed to prevent sticking by sprinkling it on the work surface. Wait until the flour has been absorbed before adding more.

The amount of flour to be incorporated varies from bread to bread; the main point is not to add too much. Every batch of dough is unique in this respect. Whole-wheat and rye doughs, for example, tend to be denser, wetter, and stickier to the touch than white doughs. The level of humidity, the amount of moisture in the flour, and the length of the initial beating all make a difference. You will soon develop a feel for how much flour to add. As it is kneaded, the dough will turn into a smooth ball with tiny blisters forming under the skin.

When to stop kneading depends on the type of bread. Each recipe gives specific directions. If you cut the dough at this point, you will notice a very sticky section which is called the wound. Pinch the wound closed. The dough is now ready to be fermented, or proofed, during the rising period.

BAKER'S WISDOM
Different Types of Dough

Soft dough: For breads containing a large proportion of fat, such as batter bread, yeast coffee cake, and brioche. Requires an exact measure of flour, tends to be sticky, and may not be able to retain its shape. Chilling the dough is required for handling. Soft doughs are never kneaded.

Medium dough: For sweet breads and whole-grain breads. The moisture in such dough contributes to a moist, tender, light-textured baked bread. When kneaded, whole-grain doughs have a definite tacky, even grainy or nubby quality. It is important that the dough not be worked far beyond this point. Refer to the recipes for sweet breads and whole-grain breads for specific pointers for perfect loaves.

Stiff dough: Usually for white bread. The dough is firm, smooth, and has a resistant, yet resilient tension. Whole-grain doughs kneaded to this point, however, will be dry and crumbly. White doughs with eggs will tend to have a soft, translucent quality.

Lean dough: A dough with little or no fat added, such as for French bread and country breads.

Rich dough: A dough with fat and sugar, used to make sweet bread and savory batter bread.

FREEZING DOUGH

Raw doughs are more perishable than baked doughs, but they can be frozen—after mixing, kneading, or after shaping—with excellent results. Some bakers add a bit more yeast to the recipe if planning on long storage to compensate for some loss of activity. Oil the kneaded dough and place immediately in a freezer bag, leaving some space for the swelling that will occur while the dough freezes solid. Loaves of dough can also be placed in disposable aluminum loaf pans, placed in a large freezer bag, and frozen. Place shaped free-form loaves or dinner rolls on a nonstick, disposable aluminum, or parchment-lined baking sheet that will fit into your freezer. Cover the baking sheet tightly with plastic wrap and freeze until firm. Remove the frozen rolls to plastic freezer bags. After freezing, squeeze out any excess air and tightly seal. Store for 3 to 4 weeks, or up to 2 months if you have a very efficient freezer.

RISING THE DOUGH

Rising, also referred to as the fermentation period or proofing, allows the gluten to become smooth and elastic. The dough will transform from a firm, heavy mass to a large, puffy one. Peeking is allowed! Rising times vary with the temperature of the dough (the temperature of the ingredients affect this), its richness, the surrounding atmospheric conditions, and the amount and type of flour and yeast used. Grease the surface of the dough lightly to allow for easy stretching as it swells. Cover the dough loosely with plastic wrap to prevent drying.

Place the dough in a deep container. I use 3- and 4-quart plastic containers with lids for rising dough, although almost any large bowl, but not metal, will do. Grease the container by brushing with oil or melted butter, or use a cooking spray, and place the ball of dough in it, turning it once to grease the top to prevent drying. Plastic wrap is good as a cover, since it helps to retain moisture and to inhibit the formation of a skin; a moist, clean tea towel may be used instead. Mentally note or mark on the container where the dough will be when risen to double. Place the container in a warm draft-free place.

The longer the rise, the better the flavor and texture, but a dough should not rise higher than two-and-one-half to three times its original volume. If the dough must be left for more than 3 hours, it can be deflated repeatedly and/or refrigerated to prevent overrising, which breaks the strands of gluten. Generally, a dough with 1 tablespoon or cake of yeast and 2 cups of liquid rises in 1 to 3 hours, with each subsequent rise requiring about half the initial time. Gently deflate the dough (do not punch it down) to release the trapped carbon dioxide. If your dough overrises and collapses, knead it briefly, form the loaf, and bake immediately.

It is difficult to predict exact rising times, which depend on the temperature of the dough, the amount of yeast used, and general atmospheric conditions. Whole-grain breads and doughs high in fats and such embellishments as dried fruits take longer to rise than lean white-flour doughs. Generally, a dough will take one to two hours to rise to the classic "doubled in bulk" stage at room temperature, about 75°F. Sponges sit for 30 minutes to 2 hours, sour starters, from eight hours to three days. Subsequent risings are faster. Test a risen dough by poking two fingers into it. If the indentations remain, the dough is adequately risen. If not, re-cover the bowl and let the dough sit a while longer before testing it again.

If you have the time, remember that a longer, slower rise always makes for a tastier loaf. Many lean doughs call for rising until triple in bulk. I rise my dough either at cool room temperature for however long it takes, or I leave it overnight in an unheated kitchen. To slow a dough further, rise it in the refrigerator for 8 hours or overnight, covered tightly with plastic wrap to retain moisture. Dough that has been refrigerated must come back to room temperature to complete its rising process; count on about four hours for the dough to return to room temperature.

If you are having trouble finding a good place to rise your dough or you have a particularly cold kitchen, consider some of the following alternatives:

- Turn the oven to the lowest setting for three minutes. Turn off the heat and allow the dough to sit in the oven with the door ajar.

- Allow the dough to rise over a gas pilot on the stovetop or on top of the dryer while drying clothes.

- Place the bowl in or over a pan of warm water away from drafts.

- Rinse a large earthenware bowl with warm water and invert the bowl over the ball of dough.

- Take the dough for a ride around town in the back of the car. Dough loves the gentle motion and warmth of the automobile.

Slow Rising

Any yeast dough may benefit from a slow rise in the refrigerator. It improves flavor and texture. The low temperature, from about 40° to 45°F, of home refrigerators is perfect for retarding the action of yeast. During this cold period, the dough will continue to rise, although over a longer period of time than if at room temperature. This method allows the baker to prepare the dough one day and bake it the next. Yeast doughs may be refrigerated at any point in their rising phase to slow down the fermentation process.

Mix and knead the dough and let it rest, loosely covered with plastic wrap, for about 30 minutes. Divide and shape the dough. Place it in a container that has plenty of room for the dough to expand to double to triple its bulk. Grease the top surface of the dough thoroughly and tightly cover with a double thickness of plastic wrap, with room for expansion, to prevent a crust from forming. (Plastic wrap is best for retaining moisture in doughs.)

Refrigerate for 2 to 24 hours. The dough will continue to rise as the internal temperature drops, to about 1 inch above the rim of the pan. The chilled dough will be ready at any time, up to 4 days, to be formed, risen, and baked.

Plan on triple the rising time for doughs to come completely back to room temperature. While the dough is returning to room temperature, the yeast will resume activity and the dough will continue to rise. The dough will still be slightly cold as it goes into the oven.

This method can be used with any bread recipe. It is especially nice for sweet rolls that can be conveniently prepared ahead and baked just before serving with no extra labor.

DEFLATING THE DOUGH

When the dough is sufficiently risen, it will be light and delicately domed. Turn it out onto a lightly floured work surface. The act of turning out the dough will naturally deflate it. A specific "punching down," isn't always necessary, although this gratifying old ritual is sometimes needed for a very large batch. There are schools of hard deflating and gentle deflating, so choose what you prefer. No more kneading is required at this point, in fact, it will activate the gluten and give the dough a springy tension that can make it difficult to shape.

FORMING THE LOAF

Pat a portion of dough into a rough rectangle with the heel of your hand and your fingertips. Tightly roll the dough towards you, rotating it to make a rectangle, oval, or round shape. Many bread experts give complicated instructions for forming a loaf, but the main objective is to produce a tight surface tension and a smooth top however you do it. Pinch all seams together to close. (Once a loaf is formed and the gluten is activated, it has to sit about 15 minutes for the dough to relax before it can be reshaped.) Place the loaves in the pan, as designated in the recipes, seam side down. The dough should fill a pan halfway to two-thirds.

Divide the dough into equal portions and shape into the desired shape loaves. If the dough resists forming, cover it and let it rest for 10 minutes on the work surface before continuing.

Add any embellishments at this time by patting the dough into a large rectangle, sprinkling it with fruits and nuts as directed in the recipe, and folding the dough into thirds. Knead the dough gently to distribute. This technique quickly and efficiently incorporates any heavy ingredients not added to the dough during mixing.

THE SECOND RISE

Cover the shaped dough with plastic wrap loosely draped over it, and let it rise in a warm place. The dough is ready when doubled in bulk, or about one inch above the pan rim. This usually takes half the time of the initial rises, usually about 30 to 45 minutes.

Before being placed in the oven, many loaves are glazed and most are slashed decoratively. Slashing serves the purpose of allowing the dough to expand during baking. The cuts should be no deeper than ¼ inch. They are made with a quick motion with a blade with a very sharp edge, such as a serrated knife. Some patterns are traditional, but you can choose your own trademark.

GLAZING

A glaze is used when a loaf needs a finishing touch. A glaze is an optional embellishment when appearance is a priority. Although most home-style breads look beautiful to me au naturel, there are appropriate glazes and embellishments for most every kind of loaf, including sprinkles and seeds or grains to reflect the ingredients inside, or a dusting of flour before rising for an earthy look.

* Use a soft brush, reserved exclusively for glazing, to gently apply egg glazes to the risen loaf just before baking, or as directed in the recipe, and take care not to puncture or deflate the loaf before baking.

* A baker's varnish of egg beaten with water, called *dorure* in French, produces a shiny crust and acts as a glue for nuts, seeds, herbs, and flakes of grain. Using just the yolk rather

than the whole egg produces a darker crust; such a glaze is often used on breads rich in fat and sugar. The white alone makes a shiny finish appropriate for a lean dough such as French bread. Egg beaten with milk or cream gives a dark, shiny finish.

* Fats, such as melted butter and oils, can be brushed on a loaf at any point before, during, or after baking, to keep the crust soft, tender, and shiny. Use a warm oil infused with herbs or garlic for extra flavor.

* French or Italian loaves get a very crisp crust when brushed with plain water just before being placed in the oven and a few times during baking. I find this more effective than misting with an atomizer.

* Sweet doughs usually are brushed while hot with a clear gloss for sparkle or drizzled with a sweet glaze.

BAKING OFF

If you are using a baking stone (see page 121), place it on the lowest rack, and preheat the oven to 450°F.

Place the pans in the preheated oven, on the center to lowest shelf unless the recipe states otherwise for the most even baking and well-browned bottom crust. Leave at least two inches of space between the pans for best heat circulation. Breads on baking sheets are best baked on the baking stone or in the center of the oven, one sheet at a time.

Baking stops the fermentation of the yeast by raising the internal temperature of the dough past 140°F and evaporating the alcohol. Within the first ten minutes, the rapidly expanding gas reaches its maximum, a stage known as oven spring, and the shape of the finished loaf is set. After that time, except for allowing heat to escape, you can open the oven door without affecting the finished shape. Check the bread at least ten minutes earlier than the recipe specifies for doneness, to look for signs of early or uneven browning.

If the dough didn't rise long enough before baking, the loaf will be small and compact. If it rose too much, the loaf may collapse in the oven. Every baker I know has seen both of these classic mistakes at least once.

Generally, lean doughs such as French bread and Vienna bread are baked at high temperatures of 400° and 425°F; whole-grain doughs and rich, more cakelike doughs with a high percentage of butter and other embellishments are baked at 350°F. Each recipe specifies baking times.

Use all your senses to determine when a loaf is done: your sense of smell to know when all the alcohol is evaporated; sight to tell if a crust is browned enough; hearing to verify the hollow sound a finished loaf makes when it is tapped. And remember to appreciate irregularities. Homemade bread is supposed to look homemade!

Ovens

It is essential that your oven thermostat be calibrated to the proper temperature. Also, for some reason, a clean oven bakes best. Whichever pans are used, especially if they are placed on baking sheets, there should always be a minimum of one inch of space around them to allow for heat circulation around all sides for even baking.

Always preheat the oven for 20 minutes before baking, since doughs and batters react poorly in cool ovens. Use an auxiliary oven thermometer to be sure your thermostat is accurate. Use heavy-duty insulated oven mitts for secure handling of hot pans. I especially like larger mitts designed for barbecue cookery for the best protection of the wrists and lower arms.

Many bakers prefer convection ovens for baking, which circulate the heat with a fan, providing an even temperature throughout the oven without the heat variables common in a standard oven. These are popular in professional bakeries, but the professional models bake differently than home models, and bake much more evenly. If you bake in a convection oven, note that quick breads (see pages 309–325) are apt to bake more quickly and dry out, so reduce the oven temperature by 25° to 50°F and reduce baking times by 10 to 15 minutes. Consult the manufacturer's literature accompanying your oven for precise directions.

Bread will rise, but not brown, when baked in a microwave oven, and baking times will vary according to the power of the oven.

COOLING, SLICING, AND STORING BREAD

Remove the bread immediately from the pans, unless otherwise directed, and cool completely on racks before slicing. Technically bread has not finished baking until it is cool and the excess moisture has evaporated. French breads and rolls are best eaten when still warm, but richer whole-grain and cake-like breads should be cooled completely and then reheated if desired. A serrated bread knife is designed for slicing bread without squashing or tearing it. Slice the loaves on a bread board with a sawing motion.

Homemade bread has no preservatives, so freeze loaves that will not be eaten within three days. Store bread in the refrigerator, especially sweet or cheese-filled loaves, or at room temperature in a plastic, paper or cloth bag, or in a bread box.

Reheating Bread

Bread may be reheated in a 350°F oven. Place an unsliced loaf, as is or wrapped in aluminum foil, in the preheated oven for 15 to 20 minutes to crisp the crust and heat through. Sliced bread and rolls reheat best wrapped.

To reheat bread in a microwave oven, place an unwrapped loaf or slice on a paper towel. Microwave on High only until slightly warm, about 15 seconds. If bread or rolls are overheated, they will become hard and tough as they cool.

FREEZING BREAD

Although fresh is best when it comes to yeast and quick breads, frozen baked goods are good to have on hand. The freezer compartment of a refrigerator, however, is intended only for short-term storage or a few months. For long-term storage, you need to freeze at 0°F or below. Wrapping bread properly is of the utmost importance. The goal is to create an airtight package to avoid that "freezer" taste. Don't wrap bread just in aluminum foil to avoid freezer burn (see below). And always cool bread before freezing; never put a loaf directly from the oven into the freezer.

Yeast Breads and Dinner Rolls

To freeze yeast breads and dinner rolls, completely bake according to the recipe. Let cool to room temperature on a rack. Wrap whole or presliced loaves first in heavy plastic wrap, then in aluminum foil or in a double layer of heavy-duty freezer bags. Some bakers use airtight plastic containers for freezing rolls. Label and date. Maximum storage time is about 3 months, but for the best flavor and texture, store no longer than 1 month.

To thaw, let the loaf stand at room temperature for about three hours, completely wrapped to preserve moisture. Bread may be refreshed, or thawed, in a 325°F oven. Remove the plastic and place the unsliced loaf, as is or wrapped in aluminum foil, in a preheated oven for fifteen to thirty minutes to heat it through. For a crisp crust, heat the loaf unwrapped. I especially like refreshing a whole loaf using the old-fashioned method of placing it in a damp brown paper bag (it is important that the bag is not made from recycled material or printed with inks that might contain heavy metals) and reheating. This method also works for refreshing a loaf that is a bit stale. Place the loaf in the bag, close with a twist tie or kitchen twine, run tap water over the top of the bag to just moisten, and reheat in a 300°F preheated oven until soft.

Frozen sliced bread may be refreshed in a toaster, or by microwaving 10 to 15 seconds. Rolls reheat best wrapped, as they dry out quickly. Always serve immediately.

Coffee Cakes, Sweet Rolls, Bagels, and Croissants

To freeze coffee cakes, bake according to the recipe. Cool to room temperature, wrap, first in heavy plastic wrap, then in aluminum foil or in heavy-duty freezer bags. Store as for yeast bread.

To freeze sweet rolls, bagels, and croissants, place each roll in a sandwich-size plastic freezer bag and freeze for up to 2 months. To thaw and reheat: Use frozen or let thaw in the bag at room temperature. Remove from the bag, place on a heatproof plate, and microwave for 15 to 30 seconds if thawed, or up to 1 minute 30 seconds if frozen; or, bake in a preheated 350°F oven for 5 to 7 minutes if thawed, or up to 15 minutes if frozen. Serve immediately.

Glaze, ice, or dust the cake or rolls with powdered sugar after the bread has been thawed and heated, just before serving.

Biscuits, Quick Breads, Muffins, and Waffles

To freeze quick bread loaves, biscuits, scones, muffins, pancakes, crêpes, and waffles, bake according to the recipe and cool to room temperature. For loaves, wrap in plastic, then foil, or store in a double layer of plastic freezer bags. Slices of quick breads can be warmed in a microwave oven for 30 seconds, but loaves are best reheated, wrapped in foil, in a 325°F oven for about 20 minutes, depending on the size of the loaf.

Place biscuits, scones, and muffins directly in plastic freezer bags or an airtight plastic container. Or, you can place them on a baking sheet, freeze until firm to prevent clumping, and then transfer to an appropriate container. To thaw and reheat: Use frozen or let thaw in the bag at room temperature. Remove the roll from the bag, place on a heatproof plate, and microwave for 15 to 30 seconds if thawed, or up to 60 seconds if frozen, or bake at 350°F for 5 to 10 minutes in a preheated oven. Serve immediately.

Pancakes should be frozen in a single layer on a baking sheet, then stacked in freezer bags. Reheat pancakes directly from the freezer in a microwave oven for 1 to 2 minutes, covered with a paper towel, depending on how many you are reheating at one time. Separate stacked, cooled waffles with plastic wrap, waxed paper, or parchment, then place in plastic freezer bags or an airtight plastic container. Waffles are best reheated in a toaster directly from the freezer. Freeze crêpes by stacking them right on top of each other and storing in a plastic freezer bag; crêpes are ready to be filled after thawing in the bag in the refrigerator. The maximum storage time for frozen quick breads is about 2 months.

I never freeze popovers, as they should be served straight from the oven and are prone to collapsing.

Always serve reheated breads immediately, because they harden quickly as they cool.

THE ELEMENTS OF A LOAF:
Ingredients

Ingredients as simple as flour, salt, water, and yeast are at the core of the baker's art. Each recipe calls for these items in different proportions. Understanding these ingredients is an important component in building the intuitive and scientific knowledge needed to become an experienced baker. No matter if you have much or little experience, the feel of the dough is the ultimate guide to making good bread.

YEAST

Yeast raises dough and gives it the characteristic flavor we associate with bread. To be activated and multiply, yeast needs moisture, warmth, air, and something to feed on. Yeast is killed by too much heat; around 140°F is its limit. Below 50°F, it goes into a state of suspended animation, which allows dough to be refrigerated or frozen for periods of time. Maximum fermentation occurs between 80° and 90°F.

Yeast eats the sugars and complex carbohydrates in flour and reproduces at a rapid rate. The by-products of this activity are alcohol—the beerlike smell in a raw dough—and carbon dioxide, which becomes trapped within the stretchy meshlike gluten structure of the dough during the process of rising. The heat of the oven kills the yeast, burns off the alcohol, and sets the porous texture of bread.

When using yeast, consider the type of dough you are making as a guide to what type of yeast to use. Use bread machine yeast for bread machine loaves, and quick-rise yeast if you like to use the one-step method in an electric mixer. Instant yeast is excellent for bread machines and is best combined with the dry ingredients utilizing the rapid-mix method or for overnight retarded refrigerator doughs. Use instant, active dry, or fresh yeast interchangeably in sugar and fat-rich sweet doughs or lean French-style breads and dinner rolls. More yeast is needed if the doughs are rich and sweet than if they are lean. Sugar and fat tend to retard the yeast's action, as do embellishments such as nuts and dried fruits. If your dough is lean, it can take a very small percentage of yeast; just count on the fact that the fermentation period will be much longer. Of course, more yeast may be used if you wish to speed up the process, but the flavor will be slightly stronger.

Yeast is sold in five different forms: active dry yeast, compressed fresh cake yeast, quick-rise yeast, instant dried yeast, and bread machine yeast. Domestic dried yeasts are marketed by Fleishmann's and Red Star. Nutritional yeasts, such as brewer's and torula, are not leavening agents because the yeast cells are dead.

Active Dry Yeast

Active dry yeast is sold in dated 0.25-ounce packets (three in a strip), 4-ounce jars, and in bulk at natural foods stores and supermarkets. One scant tablespoon of dry yeast is equal to a 0.25-ounce premeasured package or a 0.06-ounce cube of fresh cake yeast. Weight for weight, dry yeast is about twice as potent as compressed fresh. Dry yeast is not activated until it is dissolved in warm (105° to 115°F) liquid. Use an instant-read yeast thermometer to be certain of your liquid temperature until you can tell the correct warmth by feel. Keep dry yeast in the refrigerator in a tightly covered container. If properly stored, dry yeast can remain active for up to one year. To be certain, always proof your yeast, especially if there are long lapses between baking sprees, and do not use packages that have exceeded their expiration date. Approximately 1 to 2 tablespoons of yeast are sufficient for a dough made with 8 cups of flour. Resist the temptation to add more yeast than called for in a recipe; too much dry yeast makes for a strong, sour flavor.

Compressed Fresh Cake Yeast

Fresh cake yeast is sold in 0.06-ounce cubes, 2-ounce cakes in natural food stores (in the refrigerated section), and 1-pound blocks, which are sometimes available from local bakeries. The 1-pound professional size is absolutely the best fresh yeast for a dedicated baker and I highly recommend it if you can find it; use a small kitchen scale to weigh out amounts. The smaller cakes sold in the supermarket are stabilized with starch to prolong shelf life, which tends to slightly decrease their overall potency. When it is fresh, cake yeast is tan-gray with no discoloration and it breaks with a clean edge. Fresh yeast is highly perishable; it must be refrigerated at around 30°F, and will keep for about 2 weeks wrapped in plastic before molding. Compressed yeast should be dissolved in tepid liquids (about 80° to 95°F) before being added to the dry ingredients. The difference between fresh and dry yeast lies in the moisture content only, not their rising powers. Compressed yeast may be successfully frozen for several months, but its potency decreases.

Quick-Rise Yeast

Quick-rise is a strain of low-moisture active dry yeast that is fed with larger amounts of phosphorus and ammonia to increase the enzyme activity. It contains conditioners in the form of emulsifiers and antioxidants that increase the dough activity 50 percent faster than regular active dry yeast. The finer particles work best when added directly to the dry ingredients without prior rehydration, and with the liquid temperature about 120° to 125°F. Follow the manufacturer's instructions, since dough temperature and rising times are different with quick-rise yeast. I find there is a small loss of flavor and storage quality in the finished loaves because of the yeast's fast fermentation. I avoid using it when other yeast is available, but it is totally interchangeable with other dry yeasts if necessary. Use a bit less quick-rise yeast in a recipe where a slower, more normal rising time is desired. Quick-rise yeast is available in 0.25-ounce packages (three-package per strip), and 4-ounce jars.

Instant Yeast

Instant yeast is a European strain dried in small batches until it has a very low percentage of moisture. Its rod-shaped, free-flowing granules were developed with the goal of easy measuring. Instant yeast is coated with ascorbic acid and a form of sugar that enables the yeast to activate immediately on contact with warm liquid, so it doesn't need to be proofed (in comparison to domestic active dry yeast, which needs some sugar or starch to activate it). Instant yeast enables a dough to be baked without any initial rising time. With three times as many yeast cells as active dry yeast, you can use up to 25 percent less instant yeast in a recipe than active dry yeast, and one-third the amount of fresh cake yeast. Use only a bit less in converting a recipe using quick-rise yeast. It works very well in bread doughs made in a food processor or bread machine.

Regular Instant is an all-purpose brand of instant yeast that cannot tolerate a lot of sugar or long, slow proofing temperatures because it is constantly rising. Another brand, Special Instant, is sugar-tolerant for use in sweet doughs and for use in long-rise yeast-fortified sponges and slow-rise doughs. Sold in one-pound vacuum-packed bags, instant yeast is highly perishable, because the dried fresh yeast cells are highly sensitive to oxidation. Store instant yeast in an airtight container in the freezer.

Bread Machine Yeast
Bread machine yeast, the latest member of the yeast family, is marketed to meet the increased demand of electronically-oriented home bakers. It is finely granulated and coated with ascorbic acid and a flour buffer so that it is stable enough to be mixed directly with the flour and other dry ingredients before the liquid is added. It is not as sensitive to temperature changes as active dry yeast. With care, it may be used interchangeably with active dry yeast and quick-rise yeast.

FLOUR
Flour is the major ingredient and the foundation for all baking, and the type of flour used in a dough or batter will determine the nature of the loaf. Wheat comes in hard and soft varieties: spelt (known as the bread wheats), Kamut, and durum (known as the pasta wheats). Wheat flour is composed of proteins, which form gluten, starch granules, fat from the wheat germ, enzymes, which convert into simple sugars that are food for the yeast and facilitate browning, mineral ash, and moisture. All yeast breads require some wheat flour for proper structure.

Measure flour with the "dip and sweep" method: Dip the measuring cup into the flour and fill to overflowing. With a knife or spatula, sweep off the excess to level the top. One cup of unsifted all-purpose flour weighs about 4½ ounces. One cup of unsifted bread flour or whole-wheat flour weighs about 5 ounces.

In addition to wheat flour, rye, corn, oat, and buckwheat are easily mixed in small proportions with wheat flour for nutritious, flavorful loaves. They are discussed in the chapter on whole-grain breads, page 79.

Bread Flour

This cream-colored unbleached flour (also called high-gluten flour or bread flour), made from hard, red spring wheat that is aged without chemicals or preservatives, gives the best results. It has a protein content of 12 to 14 percent. High-gluten wheats absorb more liquid than other flours, creating a more elastic dough and light-textured bread. Flours milled from organic wheats will have a more pronounced taste, aroma, and texture than supermarket varieties.

All-Purpose Flour

Unbleached all-purpose flour is perfectly good for bread, being blended from a variety of wheats to an approximate combination of 80 percent hard wheat and 20 percent soft. Brands of unbleached all-purpose flour vary in different regions, for example, unbleached flour in the southern states has a higher percentage of soft wheat, whereas the northern, midwestern, and western states contain a higher percentage of hard wheat. Unbleached all-purpose flour is aged naturally to oxidize the proteins and bleach out the natural yellow pigment present in freshly milled flour (also known as green flour). Bleached all-purpose flour is aged quickly with chlorine dioxide gas and has a lower protein content than unbleached all-purpose flour. Store white flours in a cool, dry, dark place (I use a gallon plastic container with airtight lid), for 6 months to a year.

Bran and Wheat Germ

Unprocessed bran and wheat germ are by-products of milling white flours that can be used to add color, nutrition, and fiber to breads.

Cake, Pastry, or "Instant" Flour

Do not use white cake, pastry, or "instant" flour (like Wondra) for baking breads (the exception is whole-wheat pastry flour, which makes wonderful bread), as they only contain about 8 percent protein and are milled very fine. Save them to make biscuits, muffins, cakes, and pastries.

Self-Rising Flour
Never use self-rising flour unless specifically directed (follow the package label), because it contains leavening in the form of bicarbonate of soda and salt. Self-rising flour is a favorite in baking Southern-style biscuits. It cannot be substituted for cake flour.

Gluten Flour
Gluten flour is made by washing the starch from the wheat's endosperm. It is exceptionally high in protein and low in starch; it is used in special diet breads and in breads made in the bread machine, and as a protein booster in low- and non-gluten whole-grain flour doughs. It is also marketed as vital wheat gluten, which is even further concentrated—only 1½ teaspoons per cup of flour is necessary. For more on vital wheat gluten, refer to the chapter on bread machine breads, page 420.

Whole-Wheat and Graham Flours
Whole-wheat and graham flours are ground from the whole wheat berry, including the oil-rich bran and germ, creating intensely nutty flavors and a variety of fine to coarse textures that bake up into chewy crusted breads. They contain less gluten than white flours, which makes each work differently in recipes from the way white flour works. White whole-wheat flour is a strain of light-hulled winter wheat grown in Kansas and Montana that is especially sweet and light colored.

Spelt Wheat
Spelt wheat (an ancient wheat known as *farro* in Italy) has less protein than regular whole wheats, but it has its own unique flavor and is easier to digest than regular whole-wheat flour. White whole wheat and spelt may be substituted for regular whole-wheat flours. Store whole-wheat flours in the refrigerator or freezer 6 months to 1 year.

Semolina Flour
Cream-colored semolina flour is the finely ground endosperm of durum wheat and is used extensively in pasta making. It makes a delicious, high-protein addition to Italian-style breads and

can be used interchangeably with Kamut, a Montana wheat with a sweet aroma. Semolina flour is not the same as semolina meal, which is a coarse ground wheat cereal like farina (ground from the endosperm only) or Wheatina (which is the ground whole-grain wheat) and used in a manner similar to coarse cornmeal.

Cracked Wheat
Cracked wheat is a fine, medium, or coarse cut of the wheat kernel and is different from bulgur wheat, which is parboiled and dried cracked wheat.

Mixed Grain Cereals
Mixed grain cereals are very popular in breads, adding texture, flavor, and fiber: Roman Meal, Cream of Rye, Wheatina, Quaker Multi-Grain Cereal, Cream of Wheat (farina), Museli, and multi-grain blends which can include wheat, rye, barley, triticale, corn, oats, flax, millet, brown rice, wheat germ, wheat bran, and soy grits in varying proportions.

LIQUIDS
Yeast needs a warm liquid in which to be dissolved and activated. Flour needs to absorb liquid in order for its gluten to be activated during the kneading process. Liquids should be about 105° to 115°F, or feel comfortably warm on the back of your hand or inside your wrist.

A loaf made with water has a heavy, crisp crust and a chewy texture, as in French breads. Use spring or bottled water rather than tap as some minerals interfere with the action of the yeast. Fresh milk, very popular for breads, gives a light, even texture and a thin brown crust; the added fat helps to keep bread fresh longer. Nonfat dry milk powder is also excellent, especially for bread machine breads. Milk no longer needs to be scalded and cooled for making bread, unless it is raw; pasteurization and homogenization eliminate any enzymes that would slacken the gluten. Cultured milk products, such as buttermilk, either fresh or dried, sour cream, and yogurt make fine-textured breads with a sour tang. Yeast thrives on the starch of potato water, which makes a moist, dense loaf. Other liquids for making breads include beer, wine, and fruit and vegetable juices.

SWEETENERS

Granulated sugar, brown sugar, honey, maple sugar and syrup, molasses, and barley malt feed yeast, give color to crusts, and sweeten doughs. Even though they are used in small amounts, different sweeteners can change the flavor of a loaf. To substitute honey or other liquid sweeteners for granulated sugar, substitute ¾ cup honey for 1 cup sugar and reduce the total liquid used in the recipe by ¼ cup. For recipes in which no liquid is required, add an extra ¼ cup flour.

FAT

Butter, vegetable shortening, vegetable oil, and lard give a moist, rich-tasting, soft-textured quality to a loaf and act as a natural preservative. Lean doughs with no fat, such as French bread, will begin to stale within a few hours of baking. For good flavor and cholesterol-free diets, substitute such cold-pressed vegetable oils as canola, soy, sunflower seed, and corn oil. Grease pans with cooking sprays, butter, or liquid lecithin, rather than oil, which tends to be absorbed into the dough and can make bread stick to the pan.

SALT

Salt is a flavor enhancer and plays a role in controlling the activity of yeast. Strictly speaking, salt is optional in bread, but a lack is very noticeable in the finished flavor. Too much salt, on the other hand, leaves a bitter taste and can inhibit yeast activity. Too little salt leaves a flat taste and can cause the dough to feel slightly slack during kneading. Either iodized salt or fine sea salt can be used. Coarse salt must be ground before being used in dough.

BACK TO BASICS:
White Bread

It is a mystery to me how the art and craft of baking a fine sandwich-type white pan loaf disintegrated into a bland commercial product such as Wonder Bread. Before you wince at the thought of a basic white bread, consider that a homemade loaf made with milk, butter, and honey bears little resemblance to the packaged sliced breads commonly available. A spongy-textured bread with no flavor, this is what many people think of when they are offered white bread. This type of bread has unfortunately given white bread a bad name and reputation it does not deserve. Time to set the record straight.

Bread made with the finest white wheat flour has historically been among the most coveted of foods. Until the high-powered grain mills of the nineteenth century were able to separate the bran from the ground starchy endosperm, refined white coarsely ground whole grains were the norm. Modern bakers are able to choose from a large selection of finely ground white wheat flours, both all-purpose flour and bread flour, with which to make homemade loaves of premium quality and flavor.

Today's superior white flours yield a beautiful and nutritious loaf with a characteristic soft crust. Many pan bread formulas incorporate milk, eggs, sugar, and some fat to make an excellent-tasting loaf. Since flour is the predominant ingredient, its quality dramatically affects how the loaf looks and tastes. Consider buying a stone-ground flour from a small mill; the flavor and texture will have you craving more. Since most flours are enriched with vitamins and minerals, homemade white breads are almost as nutritious as whole-wheat breads, just minus the fiber.

Other ingredients can be added to plain white bread to vary its flavor: maple syrup, honey, or sugar; grated citrus zest, herbs, or spices; seeds and nuts; cheese and eggs. The breads can be glazed or frosted with a powdered sugar icing or shaped into twists and braids. They can be formed into great dinner rolls. Plain white bread is the loaf that made toast famous. It is new territory for the beginner to explore and the experienced bakers' domain—beautiful, rich white bread with a faint trace of sweetness and a moist even texture.

White Mountain Bread

Makes two 9-by-5-inch loaves

¾ cup warm water (105° to 115°F)

1 tablespoon (1 package) active dry yeast

Pinch of sugar

1½ cups milk (105° to 115°F)

3 tablespoons unsalted butter, melted, or vegetable oil

3 tablespoons honey

1 tablespoon salt

6 to 6¼ cups unbleached all-purpose flour or bread flour

This is a perfect loaf of homemade bread with an appealing, slightly fermented aroma, especially good for buttered toast and sandwiches. The secret is in the flour. Use a good brand of unbleached all-purpose flour or bread flour for the best results. Brands vary, so make several batches, each with a different brand of flour, especially if you are using organic or stone-ground flour from small mills, until you find the one you like the best. The combination of water and milk in this recipe makes for an exceptional crumb.

Although this dough may be made in a heavy-duty standing electric mixer, I recommend you make it by hand the first time, if possible, to feel how a dough is formed during all stages of mixing.

1. Pour ¼ cup of the warm water into a small bowl or 1-cup liquid measuring cup. Sprinkle the yeast and sugar over the surface of the water. Stir gently a few times with the handle of a small spoon or mini whisk to moisten evenly. (Leave the spoon or whisk submerged in the mixture if a lot of yeast has stuck to it.) This mixture is sometimes referred to as a slurry. Let rest at room temperature (75° to 80°F) for about 10 minutes. Within a few minutes the yeast will begin to bubble into a thick foam and double to triple in volume. If you wish to slow this stage of proofing, use a lower temperature water, about 80° to 100°F. While the yeast is proofing, assemble the rest of the ingredients and equipment on your work surface. Place the flour at the side of the work surface for easy access during the kneading.

2. In a large bowl using a whisk or in the bowl of a heavy-duty electric mixer fitted with the paddle attachment, combine the remaining water, milk, butter, honey, salt, and 1 cup of the flour. Beat hard until creamy, about 3 minutes by hand or 1 minute in the mixer. Stir in the yeast mixture. By hand or on low speed in the electric mixer, add the remaining flour, ½ cup at a time, until a soft dough that just clears the sides of the bowl is formed. Switch to a wooden spoon when necessary if making by hand. The dough will be slightly stiff and sticky.

continues next page

3. If kneading by hand, turn the dough out onto a lightly floured work surface. Using a plastic scraper to begin the first knead, if desired, begin by folding the top edges in halfway toward you. Push away with the heels of the hands and then give the dough a quarter turn to keep the area to be worked directly facing you. As you pull back, use your fingers or the scraper to lift the farthest edge of the dough and fold it back toward you to lay it over itself, and push again, allowing the dough to slide across the work surface where it will absorb the flour it needs. Repeat the pushing, turning, and folding sequence, developing a comfortable pace and rhythm and observing the dough as well as feeling it firm up under your hands. Dust with flour as needed. Knead until smooth and springy, a total of 1 to 3 minutes for a machine-mixed dough, since the mixer has begun the kneading process with vigorous mechanical action, and 4 to 7 minutes for a hand-mixed dough.

If kneading by machine, switch from the paddle to the dough hook and knead for 5 to 6 minutes, or until the dough is smooth and springy and springs back when pressed. If desired, transfer the dough to a floured surface and knead briefly by hand. Each batch of dough is unique and presents minor variables in time.

4. Place the dough in a lightly greased deep container (I favor a plastic container with straight sides that encourage the dough to rise up instead of out). Turn the dough once to coat the top so that the plastic wrap does not stick and the surface does not form a crust. Cover completely with a piece of plastic wrap, laying it over loosely rather than tight around the sides to leave room for expansion. Note the level of dough on the container. Let rise at room temperature until doubled in bulk, about 1½ to 2 hours. Press a fingertip into the top of the dough to see if the indentation remains. If it needs to rise more, the indentation will fill back in quickly. Do not worry or rush if the dough takes longer. The dough may be refrigerated at this point, covered tightly with a double layer of plastic wrap, for up to 18 hours, if desired. See page 26 for handling and baking of refrigerated dough.

5. Turn the dough out onto a lightly floured work surface to deflate. Lightly grease the bottom and sides of two 9-by-5-inch loaf pans. Without working the dough further, divide it into 2 equal portions with a metal scraper or a knife. Pat each portion of dough into a long rectangle; it does not need to be exact. Fold the dough into thirds, overlapping the 2 opposite ends in the middle. Beginning at the short edge, tightly roll up the dough jelly-roll fashion into a log that is about the same length as your pan. Pinch the ends and the long seam to seal. While placing the loaf in the pan, tuck the ends under to make a neat, snug fit. The log should be of an even thickness and fill the pans about two-thirds full. Cover loosely with plastic wrap and let rise again at room temperature until the dough is fully doubled in bulk and about 2 inches over the rims of the pans, about 45 minutes.

6. Twenty minutes before baking, preheat the oven to 375°F. Remove the plastic wrap and, using a serrated knife, with a quick motion of your wrist make a long slash lengthwise down the center of the loaf, no more than ¼ inch deep, to create a long groove that will spring open, giving the dough room for expansion. Immediately place on the center rack of the oven and bake 40 to 45 minutes, or until the loaves are golden brown in color and the sides slightly contract from the pan. Lift one end of the loaf out of the pan to peek underneath to check for an even browning on the bottom and tap on the top and bottom with your finger; the loaf should sound hollow. If the bottom crust is too pale, remove the loaf from the pan and place it directly on the rack for 5 more minutes and check again. Transfer the loaves from the pans immediately. Gently set each loaf on its side on a wire or wood cooling rack. For proper cooling, air must circulate all around the loaf, so leave plenty of room between the loaves and at least 1 inch of space under rack to keep the crust from getting soggy. Be sure to let the loaves rest for at least 15 minutes, to allow excess moisture to evaporate so the center will not be doughy and to finish the baking process. Loaves are best slightly warm or at room temperature.

VARIATION: *White Mountain Bread may also be made into 2 round loaves.*

French Bread

Pain Ordinaire

**Makes 3 long baguettes
or round boules**

2 cups warm water
(105° to 115°F)

1½ tablespoons
(1½ packages)
active dry yeast

1 tablespoon sugar

3 cups bread flour

1 tablespoon salt

About 3 cups unbleached
all-purpose flour

Cornmeal,
for sprinkling

1 large egg beaten
with 2 teaspoons
water, for glazing

Originally published in my first book, *Bread,* this is an important recipe to master, because it lends itself to a great variety of shapes and can be the basis for both hard rolls such as the Onion Rolls (page 47), flatbreads (see pages 48–49), and breads with fillings. The depth of character of *Pain Ordinaire* is based on the purity of its ingredients and on the long rising time, which develops the dough's flavor.

1. In a large bowl using a whisk or in the bowl of a heavy-duty mixer fitted with the paddle attachment: pour in the warm water and sprinkle the yeast and sugar over the surface of the water. Stir until combined. Let stand at room temperature until dissolved and foamy, about 10 minutes.

2. Add 2 cups of the bread flour and the salt. Beat hard until smooth, about 3 minutes. Add the remaining 1 cup bread flour and most of the all-purpose flour, ½ cup at a time, until a shaggy dough that clears the sides of the bowl is formed.

3. If kneading by hand, turn the dough out onto a lightly floured work surface and knead until soft, silky, and resilient, 5 to 8 minutes, dusting with flour only 1 tablespoon at a time as needed to prevent sticking. The dough should not be sticky. If kneading by machine, switch to the dough hook and knead for 1 to 3 minutes, or until dough is smooth and springy.

4. Place the dough in a lightly greased deep bowl. Turn once to coat the top and cover with plastic wrap. Let rise in a cool area until tripled in bulk, 1½ to 2 hours. If you have time, punch down the dough and allow it to rise again for about 1 hour. The dough may also rise in the refrigerator overnight.

5. Gently deflate the dough. Turn it out onto a lightly floured work surface. Grease or parchment-line a baking sheet and sprinkle with cornmeal. Divide the dough into 3 equal portions. Knead in more flour now if the dough seems sticky. Shape the portions into tight round balls for boules. Or flatten each portion into a rectangle for baguettes. Roll each rectangle up tightly with your thumbs to form a long sausage shape; roll back and forth with your palms to adjust the length. Place the loaves 4 inches apart on the baking sheet.

6. Quick method: Directly after forming the loaves, slash the tops diagonally no deeper than ¼ inch and brush the entire surface with the glaze. Place in a cold oven on the middle or lower rack. Turn the oven thermostat to 400°F and bake for 35 to 40 minutes, or until crusty and the loaves sound hollow when tapped with your finger. Eat immediately or transfer the loaves to a cooling rack.

7. Standard method: Preheat a baking stone at 450°F for at least 20 minutes, if using; otherwise, preheat the oven to 400°F. Cover the loaves loosely with plastic wrap and let rise until puffy and doubled, about 30 to 40 minutes. Slash the tops of the loaves diagonally no more than ¼ inch deep and brush the entire surface with the glaze. Spray a mist of water into the oven, or throw a few ice cubes onto a gas oven floor to crisp the crust, if desired. Turn the oven thermostat to 400°F if using a stone and bake for 35 to 40 minutes, or until crusty and the loaves sound hollow when tapped with your finger. Eat immediately or transfer the loaves to cooling rack.

ONION ROLLS

Makes 16 medium rolls

1 recipe French Bread dough (page 46)

2 large yellow onions, chopped

4 tablespoons (½ stick) unsalted butter

¼ cup heavy cream

Cornmeal, for sprinkling

1. Prepare the French Bread dough. While it is rising, prepare the onions. Melt the butter in a large, heavy skillet over medium heat. Cook the onions until soft, stirring frequently, about 15 minutes. Add the cream, raise the heat to high, and cook the mixture until reduced by half. The mixture will be very thick. Cool to room temperature.

2. Gently deflate the dough and divide into 16 equal portions. Grease or parchment-line 2 baking sheets and sprinkle with cornmeal. Shape each portion into a ball. Place the balls about 2 inches apart on the baking sheets. Using kitchen shears or a sharp knife, snip an **X** into the center of each roll ½ inch deep. Using your fingers, press a deep depression in the center of each **X**. Place 1 to 2 tablespoons of onions in the center of the depression.

3. Twenty minutes before baking, preheat the oven to 425°F. Place 1 pan immediately on the lowest rack and bake for 15 to 18 minutes, or until golden brown and crusty. Repeat with the second pan. Serve immediately, if possible, or cool and freeze for later.

GRILLED HERB AND CHEESE FLATBREAD

Serves 8

1 recipe French Bread dough (page 46)

½ cup chopped fresh basil, marjoram, thyme, and/or parsley

1 cup olive oil, plus additional for drizzling

Sprigs of rosemary, thyme, or lavender, for grilling

¾ cup grated Asiago or Parmesan cheese

1. Prepare the French Bread dough and let it rise until doubled in bulk. Gently deflate the dough. Turn the dough out onto a lightly floured work surface and divide it into 8 equal portions. Roll each out to an 8-inch free-form round with a rolling pin. Sprinkle each with ½ tablespoon herbs and use a rolling pin to press the herbs into the dough surface. Drizzle each with 1 tablespoon olive oil and flip over onto a sheet of aluminum foil or parchment paper. Sprinkle again with herbs and oil. Stack the flatbreads on their foil. Wrap in plastic and refrigerate for up to 2 hours if not grilling immediately.

2. Prepare an outdoor charcoal or wood chip fire in one half of the barbecue grill. When the coals are covered with gray ash, throw a few herb sprigs on top of the coals for extra aroma while grilling. For a gas grill with 2 burners, preheat 1 burner on high, leaving the other off. For a single burner, preheat on high then lower the flame while baking the second side. Spray a clean grill with olive oil cooking spray and place it 4 inches above the fire. Flip the flatbread onto the hot side of the grill. Remove the foil or parchment immediately. Grill as many breads as will fit at once, usually 2 to 3.

3. Cook 1 to 2 minutes, until firm and puffed, then turn once with metal tongs to grill the other side, moving it to the area of the grill with indirect heat, for a total of 7 to 8 minutes. Sprinkle with cheese. Remove from the grill with a large metal spatula or insulated mitts. Serve warm in a basket with extra olive oil.

VARIATION: *Olive pieces or strips of sun-dried tomatoes may be also spread on the dough rounds if desired.*

GARDEN FLATBREADS

Makes twelve 6-inch flatbreads

1 recipe French Bread dough (page 46)

Cornmeal, for sprinkling

½ cup olive oil

½ cup herb mixture (see Variations)

1. Prepare the French Bread dough and let rise until doubled in bulk. Gently deflate the dough. Turn it out onto a lightly floured work surface. Grease or parchment-line 2 or 3 baking sheets and sprinkle with cornmeal. Divide the dough into 12 equal portions. Roll or pat out each portion into an irregular round shape, about ½ inch thick.

2. Place the dough on the baking sheets. Brush the tops of the dough with plenty of olive oil (the dough will soak it up). Sprinkle each with an herb mixture and press the mixture in. The breads may be slashed decoratively to make a ladder shape, if desired.

3. Twenty minutes before baking, preheat the oven to 450°F. Place one pan at a time on the lowest shelf (or on the floor of a gas oven) and bake for 12 to 15 minutes, or until the bottoms are nicely browned. Transfer the loaves immediately to a cooling rack. Eat hot or at room temperature.

VARIATIONS

- *Chopped Italian flat-leaf parsley, chopped fresh thyme, and julienned red bell pepper*
- *Chopped fresh rosemary or sage and coarse salt with chunks of fresh garlic*
- *Fresh oregano leaves, chopped fresh chives, and thinly sliced shallots*
- *Sliced tomatoes, chunks of sun-dried tomato, chopped Italian flat-leaf parsley, and slivers of garlic*
- *Chopped yellow onions sautéed in butter, walnut halves, and chopped fresh flat-leaf parsley*
- *Fresh leaves of basil, chunks of sun-dried tomato, and slivers of garlic*
- *Slices of sautéed Japanese eggplant and freshly grated Parmesan*
- *Prosciutto, slivers of black olives, and chopped yellow bell peppers*
- *Chopped Italian flat-leaf parsley and drained capers*

Tuscan Peasant Bread

Makes 1 large loaf

2 cups warm water (105° to 115°F)

2½ teaspoons (1 scant envelope) active dry yeast

3¼ to 3½ cups unbleached all-purpose flour

½ cup coarse-grind whole-wheat flour

Pinch of salt

Pinch of sugar

For centuries, Tuscan cooks have been making their saltless peasant loaf. Traditionally baked once a week in wood-fired ovens, *pane toscano*, also called *pane sciocco*, or tasteless bread, is a crisp-crusted, practical staple for a cuisine high in such salty foods as prosciutto. Vigorous kneading is important for developing the gluten and keeping the dough moist in order to produce the light, moist interior that is characteristic of this bread. It has a spongelike interior and does not mold (since there is no salt to hold excess moisture), but it dries out quickly.

Break or slice off pieces of the chewy loaf for eating throughout the meal. For the freshest texture and flavor, eat the bread within 12 hours; leftovers can be stored in plastic wrap at room temperature up to 2 days for use as toast or in recipes.

To make in the bread machine, see page 449.

1. In a large bowl using a whisk or in the work bowl of a heavy-duty electric mixer fitted with the whisk attachment, pour in the warm water. Sprinkle the yeast over the surface of the water. Stir to dissolve. The mixture will look milky. Add 1 cup of the unbleached flour and all of the whole-wheat flour. Beat hard until combined, about 1 minute. Cover with plastic wrap or a clean cotton towel and let stand at room temperature until foamy, about 1 hour.

2. Using a wooden spoon or switching to the flat paddle attachment of the mixer, beat in the salt, sugar, and 1 cup more of the flour until smooth, about 1 minute. Add the remaining flour, ½ cup at a time, beating vigorously between additions until a soft dough that just clears the sides of the bowl is formed.

3. Gently deflate the dough. Turn the dough out onto a lightly floured work surface and knead vigorously until soft, smooth, yet quite pliable, at least 5 to 8 minutes, dusting with the flour only 1 tablespoon at a time as needed to prevent sticking.

If kneading by machine, switch from the paddle to the dough hook and knead for 4 to 5 minutes, or until the dough is smooth and springy and springs back when pressed. If desired, transfer the dough to a floured surface and knead briefly by hand.

4. Place the dough on a floured work surface, dust the top with flour, and cover it with plastic wrap or a clean cotton towel. Let rise at room temperature until doubled in bulk, 1 to 1½ hours.

5. Parchment-line and lightly flour a baking sheet or pizza pan. Gently flatten the dough and form into 1 tight round or into an oblong loaf. Place the loaf on the baking sheet or pizza pan. Dust the top of the loaf with additional flour. Let rest 20 minutes. Meanwhile line the lowest and highest racks of the oven with baking stones or unglazed terra-cotta tiles.

6. Twenty minutes before baking, preheat the oven to 425°F. Using a serrated knife, slash a tic-tac-toe pattern on top of the round loaf or slash 3 diagonal slits on the oblong loaf no more than ¼ inch deep. Place the pan on the lowest rack of the oven and bake 55 to 60 minutes, or until very crusty and deep brown and the loaf sounds hollow when tapped with your finger. The loaf will look done at around 45 minutes, but needs the extra few minutes to bake the interior thoroughly. Transfer the loaf immediately to a cooling rack. Cool completely, about 2 hours, before serving.

TUSCAN PEASANT BREAD WITH OLIVES: *Add 1½ teaspoons salt and ⅓ cup each finely chopped, pitted green and black olives to the dough during the mixing in step 2, after you have added all the flour. Proceed as directed.*

Homestyle White Bread with Poppy Seeds

Makes two 9-by-5 inch loaves or two round loaves

¾ cup warm water
(105° to 115°F)

1 tablespoon
(1 package)
active dry yeast

Pinch of sugar

1½ cups warm milk
(105° to 115°F)

8 tablespoons (1 stick)
unsalted butter,
at room tempera-
ture, cut into pieces

2½ teaspoons salt

5 to 5½ cups unbleached
all-purpose flour or
bread flour

Rich Egg Glaze

1 large egg yolk or
1 large egg, at room
temperature

1 tablespoon milk or
cream

2 tablespoons poppy
seeds

This is a quintessential American country bread made with unbleached flour. It can be made in a loaf pan or free-form. It can also be made in pullman pans for a rectangular shape good for croutons and sandwiches such as a *Croque Monsieur*. Pullman pans have lids that slide over the top, sealing the pan and keeping the bread in a perfectly rectangular shape. Serve spread with fruit preserves, or layered with slices of prosciutto, fresh mozzarella, and a dab of olive paste.

1. Pour the warm water in a small bowl. Sprinkle the yeast and sugar over the surface of the water. Stir to dissolve and let stand at room temperature until foamy, about 10 minutes.

2. In a large bowl using a whisk or in the work bowl of a heavy-duty electric mixer fitted with the paddle attachment combine the milk, butter, salt, 2 cups of the flour, and yeast mixture. Beat hard to combine. Add the remaining flour, ½ cup at a time, beating with a wooden spoon after each addition, until a shaggy dough that clears the sides of the bowl is formed.

3. Turn the dough out onto a lightly floured work surface and knead for 3 to 5 minutes, or until the dough is smooth and satiny, adding the flour only 1 tablespoon at a time as needed to prevent sticking.

If kneading by machine, switch from the paddle to the dough hook and knead for 3 to 4 minutes, or until the dough is smooth and springy and springs back when pressed. If desired, transfer the dough to a floured surface and knead briefly by hand.

4. Place the dough in a greased deep container. Turn once to coat the top and cover with plastic wrap. Let rise at room temperature until doubled in bulk, 1 to 1½ hours.

5. Gently deflate the dough. Turn it out onto a floured work surface. Grease two 9-by-5-inch clay or metal loaf pans, or grease or parchment-line a baking sheet. Divide the dough into 2 equal portions. Form the portions into round or standard loaves. Place the dough in the loaf pans or on the baking sheet. Cover lightly with plastic wrap and let rise in a warm place until doubled in bulk, 30 to 45 minutes.

6. Twenty minutes before baking, preheat the oven to 375°F. In a small bowl, beat the egg and milk with a small whisk or fork. Brush the glaze gently over the top of the loaves. Immediately sprinkle each loaf evenly with 1 tablespoon of the poppy seeds. Place the pans on the center rack of the oven and bake 40 to 45 minutes (10 minutes longer for clay pans), or until the loaves are brown, pull away from the pans and sound hollow when tapped with your finger. Transfer the loaves immediately to a cooling rack before slicing.

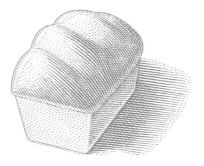

Buttermilk Honey Bread

Makes two 9-by-5-inch loaves or two round loaves

³/₄ cup warm water
(105° to 115°F)

1 tablespoon
(1 package)
active dry yeast

1 teaspoon sugar

1¹/₂ cups buttermilk,
warmed just to take
off the chill

2 tablespoons unsalted
butter, melted

3 tablespoons honey

1 tablespoon salt

6 to 6¹/₄ cups unbleached
all-purpose flour or
bread flour

Rich Egg Glaze
(page 52)

This is the breadmaker's "little black dress," a beautiful bread to grace any table, to toast to your heart's content, and to give as a gift. You may also use this dough to make swirled breads with a sweet filling (see page 424). To make in the bread machine, see page 430.

1. Pour the warm water in a small bowl. Sprinkle the yeast and sugar over the surface of the water. Stir to combine and let stand at room temperature until foamy, about 10 minutes.

2. In a large bowl using a whisk, or in the work bowl of a heavy-duty electric mixer fitted with the paddle attachment, combine buttermilk, butter, honey, and yeast mixture. Add the salt and 2 cups flour. Beat hard to combine. Add the remaining flour, ¹/₂ cup at a time, beating with a wooden spoon after each addition, until a shaggy dough is formed.

3. Turn the dough out onto a lightly floured work surface and knead about 5 minutes, until the dough is smooth and satiny, dusting with flour only 1 tablespoon at a time as needed to prevent sticking.

If kneading by machine, switch from the paddle to the dough hook and knead for 3 to 4 minutes, or until the dough is smooth and springy and springs back when pressed. If desired, transfer the dough to a floured surface and knead briefly by hand.

4. Place the dough in a greased bowl. Turn the dough once to grease the top and cover with plastic wrap. Let rise at room temperature until doubled in bulk, 1 to 1¹/₄ hours.

5. Gently deflate the dough. Turn the dough out on a lightly floured work surface. Grease two 9-by-5-inch loaf pans or grease or parch-ment-line a baking sheet. Divide the dough into 2 equal portions. Form the portions into standard or round loaves. Place the dough in the pans or on the baking sheet. Cover lightly with plastic wrap and let rise until fully doubled in bulk, 30 to 45 minutes.

6. Twenty minutes before baking, preheat the oven to 375°F. Brush the top of the loaves with the egg glaze. Put the pans on the center rack of the oven and bake about 45 minutes, or until loaves are nicely brown, pull away from the sides, and sound hollow when tapped with your finger. Remove the loaves immediately to a cooling rack. Cool completely before slicing.

Buttermilk

Buttermilk is a creamy, tangy, cultured milk product, no longer the byproduct of butter making. Many of the recipes in this book use buttermilk as the primary liquid. You can use full fat, low fat, and nonfat interchangeably. It acts as a tenderizer in quick breads and is an excellent ingredient in biscuits and pancakes due to its addition of a delicate sharp flavor. As a substitute for buttermilk, with every 2 cups of lowfat milk add 2 tablespoons of lemon juice or vinegar and allow the mixture to stand and thicken for 5 minutes. Dehydrated buttermilk is a powder that is perfect for baking use; mix the powder with the dry ingredients. After opening, refrigerate buttermilk powder up to a year. Fresh buttermilk tends to separate when heated, so take care to warm gently and remove from the heat immediately; never boil buttermilk or it will form curds.

Farm-Style White Bread with Cardamom

Makes four 9-by-5-inch loaves

4 cups boiling water

1²/₃ cups instant nonfat dried milk

4 tablespoons (½ stick) unsalted butter

1 tablespoon salt

1 cup sugar

½ cup warm water (105° to 115°F)

2 tablespoons (2 packages) active dry yeast

Pinch of sugar

10 cardamom pods

About 12 cups unbleached all-purpose flour or bread flour

Rich Egg Glaze (page 52)

Known for years around the house as Judy Larsen's Mother's White Bread from Sweden, this was the first bread I mastered over 20 years ago. This recipe makes 4 big loaves of country white bread: one to eat immediately, one for the next day's sandwiches and toast, one to give away, and one for the freezer. It may also be made into 2 or 3 large braids.

1. In a very large bowl using a whisk or in the work bowl of a heavy-duty electric mixer fitted with the paddle attachment, combine the boiling water, dried milk, butter, salt, and sugar. Stir until the butter melts and let stand at room temperature until lukewarm, about 20 minutes.

2. Pour the warm water into a small bowl. Sprinkle the yeast and pinch of sugar over the surface of the water. Stir to dissolve and let stand at room temperature until foamy, about 10 minutes. Remove the seeds from the cardamom pods and crush with a rolling pin on a piece of wax paper. Set aside.

3. Add 4 cups of the flour, the cardamom seeds, and yeast mixture to the milk and butter mixture. Beat hard until smooth and creamy, 2 minutes. Switch to a wooden spoon and add the remaining flour, ½ cup at a time, until a soft, shaggy dough that clears the sides of the bowl is formed.

4. Turn the dough out onto a lightly floured work surface and knead until the dough is smooth and resilient to the touch but not dry, 5 to 8 minutes, dusting with the flour only 1 tablespoon at a time as needed to prevent sticking.

If kneading by machine, switch from the paddle to the dough hook and knead for 3 to 5 minutes, or until the dough is smooth and springy and springs back when pressed. If desired, transfer the dough to a floured surface and knead briefly by hand.

5. Place the dough in a greased deep container. Turn once to coat the top and cover with plastic wrap. Let rise at room temperature until doubled in bulk, about 1½ hours.

6. Gently deflate the dough. Turn the dough out onto a floured work surface. Grease four 9-by-5-inch loaf pans. Divide the dough into 4 equal portions. Shape the portions into rectangular loaves and place in pans. Cover loosely with plastic wrap and let rise until 1 inch above the rim of the pans, about 40 minutes.

7. Twenty minutes before baking, preheat the oven to 350°F. With a serrated knife, slash the tops decoratively no more than ¼ inch deep. Brush the tops with the glaze. Place the loaf pans on the center rack of the oven and bake about 40 to 45 minutes, or until the loaves are brown and sound hollow when tapped with your finger. Transfer the loaves immediately to a cooling rack.

Honey and Seed Bread

Makes two 9-by-5-inch loaves

3/4 cup warm water
(105° to 115°F)

1 1/2 tablespoons
(1 1/2 packages)
active dry yeast

1 teaspoon sugar

1 1/2 cups warm milk
(105° to 115°F)

2 tablespoons unsalted
butter, melted

2 tablespoons honey

5 1/2 to 6 cups unbleached all-
purpose flour or
bread flour

1 tablespoon salt

2 tablespoons raw
whole millet

1 tablespoon poppy
seeds

1 tablespoon raw
sesame seeds

Rich Egg Glaze
(page 52; optional)

This is a glorious golden loaf with a lot of crunch for lovers of seeds. The combination of seeds can vary with your mood and what's available. This bread makes excellent toast, and it's good as a base for an open-faced grilled cheese sandwich.

1. Pour the warm water in a small bowl. Sprinkle the yeast and sugar over the surface of the water. Stir to dissolve and let stand at room temperature until foamy, about 10 minutes.

2. In a large bowl using a whisk or in the work bowl of a heavy-duty electric mixer fitted with the paddle attachment, combine the milk, butter, honey, and yeast mixture. Add 2 cups flour, salt, millet, poppy seeds, and sesame seeds. Beat hard until smooth, about 3 minutes. Add the remaining flour, 1/2 cup at time, until a shaggy dough is formed.

3. Turn the dough out onto a lightly floured work surface and knead until smooth and silky, 4 to 5 minutes, dusting with the flour only 1 tablespoon at a time as needed to prevent sticking.

If kneading by machine, switch from the paddle to the dough hook and knead for 3 to 4 minutes, or until the dough is smooth and springy and springs back when pressed. If desired, transfer the dough to a floured surface and knead briefly by hand.

4. Place the dough in a greased deep bowl. Turn once to grease the top and cover with plastic wrap. Let the dough rise at room temperature until doubled in bulk, 1 to 1 1/2 hours.

5. Gently deflate the dough. Turn the dough out onto a lightly floured work surface. Grease two 9-by-5-inch loaf pans. Divide the dough into 2 equal portions. Form each portion into a loaf and place it seam side down into the loaf pan. Cover loosely with plastic wrap and let rise to 1 inch above the rims of the pans, about 45 minutes. Brush with egg glaze, if desired, for a dark and glossy crust.

6. Twenty minutes before baking, preheat the oven to 375°F. Put the loaf pans on the center rack of the oven and bake 40 to 45 minutes, or until golden brown, and the loaves sound hollow when tapped with your finger. Transfer the loaves immediately to a cooling rack. Cool before slicing.

Homemade Bread Crumbs, Croutons, and Crostini

A practical and delicious use of day-old bread is to make fresh bread crumbs, toasted croutons, or twice-baked bread. Melba toasts, rusks, crostini, and croutons are all variations of the same process. Any size and type of sliced bread can be dried slowly in an oven, sautéed in a skillet, toasted under a broiler, or grilled over an open fire. Do not underestimate these humble toasts as a companion for dips, meat or vegetable pâtés, or as a crisp complement to soups and salads.

The toasts are very tasty and can be piled in a basket as a crisp appetizer or floated atop a bowl of soup. Croutons may be topped with cheese, herbs, garlic, or spreads. They can be in the form of large or small slices or cut with a biscuit or cookie cutter into squares, rectangles, diamonds, or hearts; leave the crusts on or slice them off.

Bread Crumbs

For dry bread crumbs, cut day-old bread into pieces, leaving the crusts on. Place on a foil- or parchment-lined baking sheet. Bake in a preheated 300°F oven until dry and golden, but not brown, 10 to 15 minutes; cool. Grind in small batches in a food processor to the desired degree of fineness. Make sure your storage container is completely dry. Dry bread crumbs will keep for 2 months in an airtight container. They should not be refrigerated, but they can be frozen in an airtight container for up to 2 months.

For Italian-style seasoned dry bread crumbs, add 2 tablespoons finely grated Parmesan cheese and ½ teaspoon each dried savory, basil, and tarragon to every cup of fine dry bread crumbs. Use immediately or store in the refrigerator for up to 1 week.

For fresh bread crumbs, cut thick slices of bread and remove crusts, if desired. Cut into cubes and place in a food processor and process until coarse, uniform crumbs are formed, about 1 minute. Three ounces of fresh bread (1 to 2 thick slices), will make about 1 cup of fresh crumbs. Use within 2 days, or place in an airtight container and freeze for up to 2 months.

Note that dry and fresh bread crumbs are not interchangeable in recipes, as the dry crumbs absorb more liquid than the fresh. Check recipes carefully to avoid using the wrong type.

Small Croutons

Any good homemade bread, such as egg, pumpernickel, or whole wheat, makes good salad croutons. Cut day-old bread, with the crusts, into 1-inch cubes.

Sauté lightly in a combination of olive oil and pressed garlic until just golden, stirring constantly.

To make in the oven, place the cubed bread on a foil- or parchment-lined baking sheet. Drizzle the bread with melted butter or olive oil and bake in a preheated 375°F oven until dry and golden, stirring about every 5 minutes to keep them from burning. Remove from the oven when just golden and drizzle with more melted butter or oil, then sprinkle with pressed fresh garlic, a few tablespoons of grated Parmesan, and chopped fresh parsley. Toss to combine. Use the same day they are made.

Large Croutons

Cut day-old bread into slices ½ to ¾ inch thick, or split day-old rolls in half horizontally. In a skillet, sauté over medium heat in butter, olive oil, or an equal combination of the two. Turn as necessary, until crisp and golden brown. Remove with tongs and drain on paper towels. Serve immediately.

Garlic Croutons

Melt ½ cup olive oil and ½ cup butter together in a small saucepan. Place a small whole head of garlic, center root and outside excess paper removed and cloves broken apart but unpeeled, in a blender or food processor with 3 tablespoons water; process until puréed. Pour the garlic mixture into the warm butter and stir until combined. Cut 1 to 2 French baguettes into ½-inch-thick slices. Using a pastry brush, brush the garlic butter on one side of the bread slices. Place on an ungreased or parchment-lined baking sheet. Place the pan on the center rack of a preheated 450°F oven and bake for 5 to 7 minutes, or until crisp. Serve immediately, or when cool.

Brie Croutons

Cut 1 large round loaf day-old French or Italian bread into ½-inch-thick horizontal slices. Place on a foil-lined baking sheet. Toast one side under the broiler until golden, 1 to 2 minutes. Spread the other side with ½ cup Dijon mustard. Cut 1 pound of Brie into slices and lay on top. Sprinkle with ¼ cup chopped fresh parsley, if desired. Place under a preheated broiler until melted and bubbly. Serve immediately.

Melba Toast

Cut 1 loaf of firm day-old or frozen bread into slices ¼ to ½ inch thick. Bake on an ungreased baking sheet on the center rack of a preheated 300°F oven for 30 to 45 minutes, or until crisp and evenly golden, depending on the size of the slice. Melba toasts can be made ahead and stored in an airtight container at room temperature up to 2 weeks. They are perfect for accompanying pâtés or to spread with sweet butter and caviar.

Crostini

Cut ten ½-inch-thick slices Italian or French bread. Using a pastry brush, brush both sides of each slice with olive oil. Place on a foil- or parchment-lined baking sheet. Bake in a preheated 350°F oven for 5 to 8 minutes, until dry and lightly golden. Turn and bake 3 to 5 minutes longer, until lightly toasted. Plain crostini will keep in an airtight container for 2 days.

Bruschetta

In a small saucepan, heat ¾ cup olive oil until just warm and add 6 medium garlic cloves, squeezed through a press. Remove from the heat and set aside to let cool. (The oil may sit for up to 2 days.) Twelve 2-inch-thick slices country-style, French, sourdough, or whole-wheat Italian bread. Place the bread slices in a toaster, under a preheated broiler, or on an oiled rack about 4 inches above glowing coals or a gas grill. Toast both sides until golden brown. Generously brush one side of each slice with the garlic oil and serve hot with extra olive oil for drizzling.

Dessert Rusks

Similar to biscotti, dessert rusks are good with tea or as an accompaniment to sorbets and fresh fruits. Slice day-old egg bread, brioche, sweet bread with fruits and nuts, or savarin into 1-inch-thick slices; cut into thick finger-sized rectangles. Sprinkle with sugar and a spice, such as nutmeg, cinnamon, or cardamom. Place in a single layer on an ungreased or parchment-lined baking sheet. Bake in a preheated 300°F oven until golden, crisp, and dry, 30 to 45 minutes, depending on the size. Transfer from the baking sheet to a cooling rack. Store in an airtight container up to 5 days.

THE BAKER'S APEX:
Egg Breads and Brioche

Breads enriched with eggs bake up into the most tender, cakelike textured yeast breads ever. Many amateur bakers may never attempt any bread beyond a challah or a holiday sweet bread, but they can boast that these are the best they have ever made. I think that egg bread lovers are as much elitists as country bread and sourdough aficionados; they are a group who prefers this type of homemade bread. A mandatory Jewish festival loaf steeped in tradition, challah is related to the perfect food, the daily manna of the Promised Land sent to each family by God Himself. Celebratory meals are just not complete without an egg-bread centerpiece.

Egg doughs mix up soft and supple with an almost translucent quality. They are easy to knead and very forgiving at baking time, because egg breads grow a lot in the heat of the oven and irregularities disappear. They bake up soft with a thin, deep-brown crust. They can be formed in beautiful shapes such as long, fat braids of two to six strands, crown-like wreaths, domed spirals, plump triangles, myriad roll shapes, sandwich buns, flat onion and poppy seed pretzels, or small sections to be easily pulled apart in loaves like the brioche, nanterre, and parisienne.

Obviously there is a tremendous difference between a white flour and a whole-wheat flour egg bread, as the whole-grain flour has the bran and germ still intact, making a heartier textured and tasting loaf. Homestyle white pan breads use milk or water, or a combination of the two as their liquid components, and brioche, the richest egg bread, depends solely on eggs as its moistener, but egg breads use both. Doughs can have 1 to 8 eggs for 6 to 8 cups of flour, making doughs of varying richness. They end up with the classic flavor and moist character that make egg breads so popular.

Jewish Egg Braid
Challah

Makes four 9-by-5-inch loaves or four medium freestanding braids

About 7½ cups unbleached all-purpose flour

2½ cups warm water (105° to 115°F)

2 tablespoons (2½ packages) active dry yeast

⅓ cup plus 1 tablespoon sugar

3 large eggs, at room temperature

½ cup vegetable oil

2 teaspoons salt

Rich Egg Glaze (page 52)

2 tablespoons sesame or poppy seeds (optional)

Time to master a classic. Jewish Egg Braid, known familiarly as Challah, is a rich white flour loaf leavened with eggs paired with yeast. This recipe comes from my friend Ilana Sharaun's Russian great-grandmother; it was translated for me from cursive Hebrew. There is a short prefermentation period followed by three rises to develop the subtle flavor. The dough is mixed by hand using the old-fashioned well method, but using a bowl rather than working directly on the work surface. It is said that when this traditional bread is made on Friday for the Sabbath meal, an atmosphere, not just food is created. A must also for any holiday dinner or celebration, the egg bread can be sculpted and baked into a variety of intricate shapes, including a turban, a triangle or tricorne, an oversized braid, a braided wreath, an oval loaf topped with a string of five balls, or stacked tiers of different-size braids. It makes excellent morning toast, a fine French toast, and is good for grilled sandwiches. To make Jewish Egg Bread in a bread machine, see page 428.

1. In a large bowl or in the work bowl of a heavy-duty electric mixer fitted with a paddle attachment, place 6 cups of the flour. Make a well in the center with your hand and pour ½ cup of the water into the well. Sprinkle the yeast and 1 tablespoon of the sugar over the water. Stir gently to dissolve (a bit of flour will also be incorporated) and let stand 15 minutes. Add the remaining sugar, remaining water, eggs, oil, and salt to the well and beat until a shaggy mass of dough is formed. This dough comes together quickly, so long mixing is unnecessary.

2. Turn the dough out onto a lightly floured work surface and knead until soft and springy, 5 to 8 minutes, dusting with flour only 1 tablespoon at a time, just enough as needed to prevent sticking. The dough will be smooth and springy but not dry.

If kneading by machine, switch from the paddle to the dough hook and knead for 4 to 5 minutes, or until the dough is smooth and springy and springs back when pressed. If desired, transfer the dough to a floured surface and knead briefly by hand.

continues next page

3. Place the dough in a lightly greased deep container. Turn the dough once to coat the top and cover with plastic wrap. Let rise at room temperature until doubled in bulk, about 2 to 2¼ hours. Do not allow the dough to rise over double, as it has a tendency to tear and the baked loaf will not be as full-volumed as it can be. Gently deflate the dough with your fist, re-cover, and let rise again until doubled in bulk, about 1 to 1¼ hours.

4. Gently deflate the dough. Turn the dough out onto a lightly floured work surface. Lightly grease the bottom and sides of the 9-by-5-inch loaf pans or parchment-line baking sheets. Without working the dough further, divide the dough into 4 equal portions. Further divide each portion into 3 equal portions. Roll each section under your palms into a rope that is tapered at each end. Gently dust the work surface with flour to lightly coat each rope (this keeps the shape more distinct during rising). Be sure the ropes are of equal size and shape. Place the 3 ropes parallel to each other. Begin braiding, starting in the center rather than at the ends for a more even shape. Take one of the outside ropes and fold it over the center rope, then repeat the movement from the opposite side. When completed, turn the dough around and repeat the procedure from the middle out to the other end. Adjust or press the braid to fix any irregularities. Tuck the ends under and set into a loaf pan or pinch the ends into tapered points and place the loaf on the baking sheet. Brush the top with some of the egg glaze, taking care not to let the egg glaze drip down onto the sides of the pan, or the bread will stick. Cover loosely with plastic wrap. Repeat with the remaining portions of dough. Let rise until the dough is almost doubled in bulk and about 1 inch over the rims of the pans, about 40 minutes. This bread needs only a three-quarter proof before baking; if longer, it can collapse during baking.

5. Twenty minutes before baking, preheat the oven to 350°F. Brush the surface of the loaves a second time with the egg glaze and sprinkle with seeds or leave plain. Place the pans on a rack in the center of the oven and bake 40 to 45 minutes, or until the loaves are deep golden brown, the sides slightly contract from the pan, and the loaves sound hollow when tapped with your finger. Transfer the loaves immediately to a cooling rack. Loaves are best slightly warm or at room temperature.

VARIATIONS

* Shape the dough into plain rectangular loaves, 1 or 2 large free-form braids (check the size of your oven first) for celebrations, 3 spiral turbans, or 2 large braided wreaths.

* Dress up the basic recipe with 1 to 2 cups chopped dried fruit and/or nuts, candied peels, grated cheese, or ¼ cup chopped fresh herbs.

* Make a cinnamon egg braid by rolling and coating the ropes in ground cinnamon before shaping the braid.

Freeze Now / Bake Later Challah

Prepare the dough, let it rise, and shape it into four 3-strand braids. Place the number of loaves you wish to freeze on a parchment-lined baking sheet; let the other loaves rise and bake. Cover tightly with 2 layers of plastic wrap and immediately place in the freezer to set overnight until solid. Remove the frozen dough twists from the baking sheet and place each in a plastic freezer bag. Label the type of bread and date. Store in the freezer up to 1 month.

To bake, remove the twist from the freezer, unwrap, and place on a parchment-lined baking sheet. Cover lightly with plastic wrap and let thaw and rise at room temperature 6 to 7 hours, until puffy and doubled in bulk.

Preheat the oven to 350°F 20 minutes before baking. Combine the ingredients for the egg glaze and brush the surfaces. Sprinkle with poppy seeds or sesame seeds. Bake 35 to 40 minutes, or until deep golden brown and the bottom sounds hollow when tapped with your finger. Transfer the bread to a rack and cool before slicing.

Sweet Vanilla Challah

Makes 2 turban loaves

 1 tablespoon
   (1 package) active
   dry yeast

 ½ cup sugar

 1 tablespoon salt

6½ to 7 cups unbleached
   all-purpose flour or
   bread flour

 1¾ cups hot water
   (120°F)

 4 large eggs, at room
   temperature, lightly
   beaten

 ½ cup vegetable oil

1½ tablespoons pure
   vanilla extract

Vanilla Egg Glaze

 1 large egg yolk

 1 teaspoon pure
   vanilla extract

 ½ teaspoon sugar

I have transformed my classic challah recipe into a tantalizing sweet bread. A traditional blend served for Rosh Hashanah, these can be made in different sizes and degrees of richness. The turban swirl bakes up a fascinating plump loaf.

1. In a large bowl with a whisk or in the work bowl of a heavy-duty electric mixer fitted with the paddle attachment, combine the yeast, sugar, salt, and 2 cups of the flour. Add the hot water, eggs, oil, and vanilla. Beat hard until smooth, about 3 minutes. Scrape down the sides of the bowl occasionally. Add the remaining flour, ½ cup at a time, switching to a wooden spoon when necessary if making by hand. Continue beating until the dough is too stiff to stir.

2. Turn the dough out onto a lightly floured work surface with the plastic pastry scraper and knead until soft and springy and a layer of blisters shows under the skin, about 4 minutes. Dust with flour only 1 tablespoon at a time as needed to prevent sticking. The dough needs to be slightly firm for free-form loaves.

If kneading by machine, switch from the paddle to the dough hook and knead for 3 to 4 minutes, or until the dough is smooth and springy and springs back when pressed. If desired, transfer the dough to a floured surface and knead briefly by hand.

3. Place the dough in a greased deep container. Turn the dough once to coat the top and cover with plastic wrap. Let rise at room temperature until doubled in bulk, 1½ to 2 hours.

4. Grease or parchment-line 1 or 2 baking sheets or the springform pans. Gently deflate the dough. Turn the dough out onto a lightly floured work surface. Divide the dough into 2 equal portions. Roll each portion out into a smooth, thick strip about 30 inches long, with 1 end 2 to 3 inches wider than the other. Roll to lengthen and taper the thinner end. With the wide end on the work surface, lift the tapered end and wind the rest of the dough around the corner section 2 or 3 times, forming a compact coil. Pinch the end and tuck it under. Place the coils, with the swirl pattern facing up, on the baking sheets or in the springform pans. Cover loosely with plastic wrap and let rise until almost doubled in bulk, 30 to 40 minutes. Because of the eggs, this loaf does not need to double completely; it will rise enough in the oven.

5. Twenty minutes before baking, preheat the oven to 350°F. To make the vanilla egg glaze, in a small bowl, whisk together the egg yolk, vanilla, and sugar. Beat until well blended. Gently brush the dough surfaces with a thick layer of the glaze. Place the baking sheet or pans on a rack in the center of the oven and bake 40 to 45 minutes, or until a deep golden brown and the loaves sound hollow when tapped with your finger. Carefully lift the turbans off the baking sheets with a spatula and transfer to cooling racks. If using springform pans, release the sides and then carefully remove the turbans from the pan bases. Cool completely before slicing.

BAKER'S WISDOM
Eggs

Eggs add a wonderful, golden color, rich flavor, and a tender cakelike texture to breads. Recipes in this book were tested with A or AA grade large eggs. All eggs should be at room temperature when added to quick breads. Store eggs in the refrigerator in their carton no longer than 4 weeks. Egg whites can be frozen in ice cube trays for up to 6 months and defrosted to room temperature before using. The yolks cannot be frozen, because they are predominantly fat. Use duck or quail eggs, if you happen to have them, to vary color and flavor. Measure out an amount equivalent to the amount of chicken eggs called for in the recipe.

SUBSTITUTIONS: *One whole large egg may be substituted for two large egg yolks and vice versa. Three whole small eggs may be substituted for two whole large eggs. Use the following equivalents as a guide when making substitutions.*

1 large egg	=	¼ cup liquid measure (2 ounces)
1 large egg yolk	=	1½ tablespoons liquid measure (about 1 ounce)
1 large egg white	=	2½ tablespoons liquid measure (about 1 ounce)
2 large egg whites	=	¼ cup liquid measure (2 ounces)
8 large egg whites	=	1 cup liquid measure (8 ounces)

Lemon Whole-Wheat Egg Bread with Nasturtium Butter

Makes two 9-by-5-inch loaves

Sponge

1 tablespoon (1 package) active dry yeast

2 cups warm water (105° to 115°F)

¾ cup instant nonfat dried milk

½ cup honey

3 cups whole-wheat flour, finely ground if possible

Dough

Zest of 2 medium lemons

About 3 cups whole-wheat pastry flour

6 tablespoons (¾ stick) unsalted butter, melted and cooled

1 tablespoon salt

4 large eggs, at room temperature

½ cup rolled oats, for sprinkling

Nasturtium Butter (recipe follows)

Lemon adds a refreshing, zesty counterpoint to sweet whole grains and honey in baking when added in small amounts. The spicy watercress–like flavor of nasturtiums turns plain butter into something special. It will take on the summer perfume of the flowers and taste very rich.

1. To prepare the sponge: In a large bowl or deep plastic container using a whisk or in the work bowl of a heavy-duty electric mixer fitted with the paddle attachment, beat together the yeast, warm water, dried milk, honey, and whole-wheat flour. Beat hard until smooth and creamy, about I minute. Scrape down the sides with a spatula and cover with plastic wrap. Let stand at room temperature until foamy, about 2 hours. Gently stir down.

2. Remove the zest of the lemons with a sharp knife, a fine grater, or a zester in strips, taking care to avoid the white part. Place in a food processor or blender with ½ cup of the whole-wheat pastry flour and process until the zest is incorporated into the flour.

3. Sprinkle the lemon flour, butter, and salt over the sponge and beat hard. Use a wooden spoon if mixing by hand. Add the eggs, one at a time, then ½ cup of the pastry flour. Beat hard again to make a smooth batter. Add the remaining flour, ½ cup at a time, until a soft, shaggy dough that clears the sides of the bowl is formed.

4. Turn the dough out onto a lightly floured work surface and knead until soft, slightly sticky, yet springy, about 5 minutes, dusting with the pastry flour only I tablespoon at a time, as needed to prevent sticking.

If kneading by machine, switch from the paddle to the dough hook and knead for 3 to 4 minutes, or until the dough is smooth and springy and springs back when pressed. If desired, transfer the dough to a floured surface and knead briefly by hand. The dough will also have a mildly abrasive quality from the whole grains. The dough must remain soft, or the baked loaf will be dry. The dough should just be able to hold its own shape.

5. Place the dough in a greased deep container. Turn once to coat the top and cover with plastic wrap. Let rise at room temperature until doubled in bulk, 1½ to 2 hours.

6. Gently deflate the dough. Turn the dough out onto the work surface. Sprinkle the bottom and sides of each pan with half the rolled oats. Divide the dough into 4 equal portions. With the palms of your hands, roll the dough into 4 oblong pieces, about 10 inches long. Place the 2 oblongs side by side. Starting in the center, wrap each around the other to create a fat twist effect. Place one twist in one of the loaf pans. Repeat the procedure to make the second loaf. Let rise at room temperature, uncovered, for about 30 minutes, or until level with the sides of the pans. The loaves should not completely double in bulk.

7. Twenty minutes before baking, preheat the oven to 375°F. Place the pans on a rack in the center of the oven and bake for 35 to 40 minutes (10 minutes longer for clay pans), or until deep brown and the loaves sound hollow when tapped with your finger. Cover with a piece of aluminum foil if the loaves seem to be browning too fast. Transfer the loaves immediately to a cooling rack. Cool completely before slicing. Serve with Nasturtium Butter.

NASTURTIUM BUTTER

Makes 1 cup

1 cup (2 sticks) unsalted butter, at room temperature

5 fresh-picked unsprayed nasturtium flowers, rinsed and patted dry

1. Cream the butter with a wooden spoon, an electric mixer, or a food processor until fluffy. Place 1 nasturtium flower, face up, on the bottom of a glass serving bowl that will comfortably hold 1 cup creamed butter.

2. Pack in one third of the butter. Evenly space 3 blossoms facing out and evenly spaced around the sides of the bowl, using butter to hold them in place. Fill with the remaining butter, pressing carefully to press and cover the flowers in place.

3. Smooth the top and press the remaining blossom, face up, on top. Cover and refrigerate for 24 hours before serving.

Brioche

Makes 16 to 18 petites brioches à tête

4½ cups unbleached all-purpose flour

1 tablespoon (1 package) active dry yeast

¼ cup sugar

2 teaspoons salt

½ cup hot water (120°F)

6 large eggs, at room temperature

1 cup (2 sticks) unsalted butter, at room temperature, cut into small pieces and softened

Rich Egg Glaze (page 52)

Originally a homemade egg- and butter-rich loaf designed to bake free-form in the diminishing heat of wood-fired ovens, brioche has evolved over the centuries to the rich bread we now know. Its texture is a cross between cake and bread, with an even crumb and a dairy-sweet flavor. The best loaves are baked in tin or metal molds, rather than earthenware or tempered glass, to create the desired hairline-thin crust. The classic shape, with a fluted base and a topknot, is called *brioche à tête*.

Once made arduously by hand (see page 73), brioche is easily made by even beginning bakers with a heavy-duty electric mixer. The dough must stay cold at all stages of mixing, rising, and forming in order to keep the butter from melting. The rises are slow, but the loaf will rise dramatically in the oven because of the eggs. This brioche can be made to be used as a showcase for delicately flavored sweet and savory fillings.

1. In the bowl of a heavy-duty electric mixer fitted with a paddle attachment, combine 1 cup of the flour, and the yeast, sugar, and salt. Add the hot water and beat at medium speed for 2 minutes, or until smooth.

2. Add the eggs, one at a time, beating well after each addition. Gradually add 2 more cups of the flour. When well blended, add the butter a few pieces at a time. Beat just until completely incorporated, about 30 seconds. Gradually add the remaining 1½ cups flour at low speed. Beat until thoroughly blended and creamy in consistency, about 30 seconds. The dough will be very soft and have a batter-like consistency.

3. Using a spatula, scrape the dough into a greased bowl. Cover tightly with plastic wrap and let rise at a cool room temperature until doubled in bulk, about 3 hours.

4. Gently deflate the dough with a spatula, cover tightly with plastic wrap, and refrigerate 12 hours or overnight. (*The dough may be frozen at this point for up to 2 weeks. When ready to use, put in the refrigerator to thaw for 1 day.*)

5. Turn the chilled dough out onto a lightly floured work surface (it will deflate) and divide it into four portions. Roll each portion into a 12-by-1-inch rope. Divide each rope into four 2-inch pieces and four 1-inch pieces. Round the pieces with your fingers to make 16 large balls and 16 small ones. Do not worry if the rolls vary slightly in size. If you must shape the brioche in 2 batches, divide the dough in half and refrigerate one half to shape and bake later.

6. Grease sixteen 3½-inch fluted molds or 18 standard muffin cups. Put the larger balls in the molds and snip an **X** on the tops of each with scissors. Push your finger through the middle of the dough to the bottom. Place a small ball in each center. Place the individual molds on a baking sheet for easier handling. Let rise at a cool room temperature until doubled in bulk, about 45 minutes. (The butter will separate from the dough if it is risen in the warm place called for in most bread recipes.)

7. Twenty minutes before baking, preheat the oven to 400°F. Brush each brioche gently with the egg glaze. Place the baking sheet on the center rack of the oven and bake for 10 to 15 minutes, or until golden brown and the loaves sound hollow when tapped with your finger. Remove from the molds to cool completely on a rack before eating. Brioche is best reheated. (Brioche keeps up to 4 days at room temperature, although it is best the day it is baked, and freezes perfectly.)

CROUSTADE: *A croustade is an edible serving vessel made from a large loaf of bread. Croustades can be made from day-old round or rectangular brioche loaves as well as pullman loaves, large round rustic loaves, or rolls, which are nice for individual servings. Remove the top crust of the brioche and cut out the inside crumb, leaving a shell at least 1 inch thick all around. Brush the insides with melted butter or flavorful oil. Dry in a preheated 350°F oven until crisp. Croustades are especially good filled with creamed wild mushrooms, devilled seafood, or chicken.*

GROSSE BRIOCHE À TÊTE: *Divide the dough in half and divide each piece into 2 unequal pieces and shape them into balls. Place the large balls in 2 greased 8-inch fluted molds, charlotte pans, or round baking dishes, snip and insert the small balls. Let rise at cool room temperature until doubled in bulk, about 1½ hours. Brush gently with the glaze. Bake in a preheated 375°F oven for 35 to 40 minutes, or until golden brown and a cake tester inserted into the center of the brioche comes out clean. Remove from the pans and cool completely on racks. Slice in wedges to serve. Makes two 8-inch grosses brioches.*

PAIN BRIOCHE: *To make a large braided loaf, or two 9-by-5-inch standard or pull-apart brioche nanterre or brioche parisienne loaves, follow these shaping directions.*

- To form a large braided loaf, divide the brioche dough into 3 equal portions. Roll each portion into a smooth rope about 14 inches long, tapering towards the ends. Lay the ropes side by side on a greased or parchment-lined baking sheet, and beginning at the middle, braid together. Turn the dough around and braid the other side from the middle. Holding the 2 ends, pinch together and tuck any excess under.

- To form a rectangular loaf, divide the dough in half. Pat each section of dough into a flat rectangle and roll up tightly to form a fat log the length of the loaf pan. Pinch the seams to seal and place each, seam side down, in a lightly greased loaf pan. Flatten to fill the pans.

- To form brioche nanterre, divide the dough in half and divide each half into 6 or 8 equal pieces. Shape each piece into a smooth ball 2 to 3 inches in diameter, pulling the surface taut to the underside. Pinch the bottoms. Place 6 balls, seam side down, in a lightly greased loaf pan to form 2 even rows of 3 to 4 balls or place in a zigzag pattern to fill the pan. Flatten to fill the pans.

- To form brioche parisienne, divide the dough in half and divide each half into 5 equal pieces. Flatten each into a small rectangle and roll up from the short edge to form fat cylinders of dough about 5 inches long to fit the width of the pans. Lay cylinders tightly side by side in a parallel pattern to fill the pans.

Cover the loaves lightly with buttered plastic wrap. Let the loaves rise until doubled in bulk, about 1½ to 2 hours. Twenty minutes before baking, preheat the oven to 375°F. Just before baking, glaze the surface of the loaves gently. Bake in the center of the oven for 35 to 40 minutes, or until golden brown and a cake tester inserted into the center of a loaf comes out clean. Remove from the pans and cool completely on a rack.

Yields and Baking Times for One Recipe of Brioche

TYPE	TEMPERATURE	TIME
16 to 18 petites brioches à tête (3½-inch mold)	400°F	10 to 15 minutes
8 petites brioches (4½-inch mold)	375°F	20 to 25 minutes
2 grosses brioches à tête (8-inch mold)	375°F	35 to 40 minutes
Two 9-by-5-inch loaves	375°F	35 to 40 minutes
1 large braid	375°F	50 to 60 minutes
2 mousselines	350°F	35 to 40 minutes
(1-pound coffee cans or tall cylinder molds)		
1 couronne (crown)	375°F	35 to 40 minutes

Making Brioche Dough by Hand

Traditional brioches are quickly and easily made with a heavy-duty electric mixer, but this unique dough may be made by hand by the traditional French method. Either way, a cool day is best for making brioche.

Put all but ½ cup of the flour in a pile on a clean work surface, preferably a marble surface. Make a well in the center. Place the yeast, I tablespoon of sugar, and warm water (105° to 115°F) in the well. Stir to dissolve. Let stand at room temperature until foamy, about 10 minutes. Sprinkle the rim of the well with the remaining sugar and salt. Add all the eggs into the yeast mixture and blend thoroughly with your fingers. Using your fingertips, gradually bring the dry ingredients into the center of the well. The dough will be very sticky, yet elastic. Alternately, lift the dough with your fingers and slap it onto the work surface to develop the dough. Knead vigorously in this manner for 8 to 10 minutes, gradually adding the last ½ cup flour as needed to prevent the dough from sticking. The dough will be smooth and satiny, and can be lifted easily in one mass.

To incorporate the butter in small amounts, divide the softened butter into 4 equal portions. Position each portion at each corner of the dough. Hold the 4 fingers of your working hand stiffly and slap the butter until malleable. Quickly smear the butter into the mass of dough alternately from each corner. The goal is to incorporate the butter quickly and evenly into the dough with a slapping action without allowing it to melt from the friction of your hand. The total working time should be no more than about 5 minutes. Knead the dough gently a few times by hand to finish incorporating the butter, but do not crash or slap the dough anymore at this point. Form the dough into a ball and let rise, form, and bake as for Brioche (page 70).

Marzipan Brioche with Apricot Brandy Glaze

Makes one 10-inch coffee cake

1 recipe Brioche dough (page 70), risen overnight in the refrigerator

Almond Crème

½ cup currants or dried apricots, snipped into small pieces

3 tablespoons brandy

8 tablespoons (1 stick) unsalted butter at room temperature

½ cup sugar

1 large egg

1 cup whole almonds, ground

1 teaspoon almond extract

Apricot Brandy Glaze

¾ cup good-quality apricot jam, puréed in a blender or food processor until smooth

3 tablespoons brandy, Cognac, Grand Marnier, or apricot-flavored brandy

This rich cake-bread is swirled with marzipan. The marzipan in this recipe is a creamy almond filling rather than the firm marzipan used for molding. This bread freezes well, but wait until ready to serve before gilding it with the apricot-hued glaze.

1. To prepare the almond crème: In a small bowl, combine the dried fruit and brandy. Let stand at room temperature for 1 hour to macerate.

2. Cream the butter and sugar until fluffy with a wooden spoon, an electric mixer, or a food processor. Add the egg and beat until smooth. Stir in the macerated fruit, almonds, and almond extract until just combined. Set aside at room temperature. (The crème may be made 1 day ahead and refrigerated. Bring to room temperature before using.)

3. Gently deflate the chilled Brioche dough. Place the dough on a lightly floured work surface and divide it in half. Roll out half of the dough into a circle 14 inches around, like a pie crust. Place the circle in an ungreased 10-inch springform pan, preferably nonstick. Press the dough into the bottom and all the way up the sides. Trim any overhang until it is even with the pan rim.

4. Roll out the other half of the dough into an 18-by-12-inch rectangle. Spread it evenly with almond crème, leaving a ½-inch border around the edges. Starting at the long end, roll the dough up jelly-roll fashion. Using a serrated knife, cut it into 8 equal portions. Lay the rolls, cut side up, in the dough-lined pan, placing 7 around the edges and 1 in the middle, all barely touching. Cover loosely with plastic wrap and let rise at a cool room temperature until doubled in bulk and puffy, about 1½ hours.

5. Twenty minutes before baking, preheat the oven to 350°F. Place the pan on the center rack and bake 65 to 75 minutes, or until golden and a cake tester inserted in the center comes out clean.

6. Just before taking the cake out of the oven combine the jam and liquor in a small saucepan; heat to boiling. Remove from the heat and keep warm.

7. Remove the cake from the oven and immediately pour the glaze over the hot cake in the pan. Let stand for 15 minutes before removing the sides of the pan. Place on a rack to cool completely. Cut into wedges to serve.

BAKER'S WISDOM
Butter

Butter tenderizes dough and quick bread batters. Unsalted butter is recommended for the best results in baking. It has no added color or salt, but it does have a delicate flavor, a sweet aroma, and a lower percentage of moisture than salted butter. Whipped butter contains 40 percent air, so it is not recommended for baking unless you measure by weight instead of volume. French butter is known as an excellent flavorful addition to baked goods; it differs from American butter in that it is made with matured rather than sweet cream and has a slightly higher moisture content. Look for a brand like Plugra, a favorite of professional bakers available from delicatessens or specialty food stores. These butters can be used interchangeably in recipes. Butter freezes well for storage up to 6 months.

Cornmeal Brioche

Makes two 8½-by-4½-inch loaves or twelve sandwich buns

3½ cups unbleached all-purpose flour

1 cup medium-grind yellow cornmeal, preferably stone ground

1 tablespoon (1 package) active dry yeast

2 tablespoons granulated sugar

2 teaspoons salt

½ cup hot water (120°F)

5 eggs, at room temperature

1 cup (2 sticks) unsalted butter at room temperature, cut into small chunks

Slices of brioche make the ultimate sandwich, especially when the bread is made with crunchy, flavorful cornmeal. Made with a heavy-duty electric mixer, this loaf is one of the easiest yeast breads to make, baking into an unbelievably soft, rich, and uniformly textured bread. Cornmeal brioche makes impeccable BLTs and is good spread with flavored cream cheese and topped with shredded arugula for canapés or served toasted alongside panfried trout for breakfast. Fluffy brioche sandwich buns are very special with the addition of capers or bits of sun-dried tomato.

1. In a large bowl using a whisk or in the work bowl of a heavy-duty electric mixer fitted with the paddle attachment, combine ½ cup of the flour, the cornmeal, yeast, sugar, and salt. Add the hot water and beat at medium speed for 2 minutes, or until smooth. Add the eggs, one at a time, beating well after each addition. Gradually add 1½ cups more flour.

2. When well blended, add the butter a few pieces at a time. Beat until just incorporated. Gradually add the remaining 1½ cups flour at low speed. Beat until thoroughly blended and creamy, about 1 minute. The dough will have a soft, batter-like consistency.

3. With a spatula, scrape the dough into a greased deep container. Cover lightly with plastic wrap and let rise at a cool room temperature until doubled in bulk, about 3 hours.

4. Gently deflate the dough with a spatula. Cover it tightly with plastic wrap and refrigerate for 12 hours or overnight, to chill the dough for easier handling.

5. Turn the chilled dough out onto a very lightly floured work surface. Grease two 8½-by-4½-inch loaf pans or parchment-line 2 baking sheets if making rolls. Divide the dough into 2 equal portions and form into standard loaves. Place in the loaf pans; the dough will fill them no more than half full. To make buns, divide into 12 equal portions and form into rounds. Place on the baking sheets, 6 to each sheet, at least 2 inches apart. Press with your palm to flatten. Let rise at a cool room temperature until doubled in bulk, about 1½ hours for the loaves (or until the dough is level with the tops of the loaf pans), or 1 hour for the rolls (until puffy). Note: Cool room temperature is preferred for rising, because the butter will separate from the dough if it is risen in the traditional "warm place" called for in most bread recipes.

6. Twenty minutes before baking, preheat the oven to 375°F. Bake the loaves on the center rack of the oven for 35 to 40 minutes, and the rolls for 20 to 25 minutes, or until golden brown and a cake tester comes out clean when inserted into the center. Transfer immediately from the pans to cool completely on racks before serving. Serve at room temperature or reheat to serve warm.

CORNMEAL BRIOCHE WITH SUN-DRIED TOMATOES: *Add ½ cup oil-packed sun-dried tomatoes, drained and coarsely chopped, to the dough after incorporating the eggs in Step 1.*

CORNMEAL BRIOCHE WITH CAPERS: *Add ¼ cup small (nonpareil) capers or chopped large capers, rinsed and drained, to the dough after incorporating the eggs in Step 1.*

Brie in Brioche

Makes 1 round loaf

1 recipe Brioche dough (page 70)

One 8-inch wheel or three 4-inch wheels 60 percent fat Brie cheese, rind on

1 large egg, beaten with a pinch of salt

Brie cheese baked in brioche is an elegant presentation on a buffet or hors d'oeuvre table. Besides plain brie, consider herbed, pepper, or mushroom brie. Brie in Brioche can be assembled and refrigerated overnight before baking. Or wrap it in aluminum foil and freeze, then let stand at room temperature for 3 hours before baking. It can be baked several hours before serving and kept at room temperature. An 8-inch wheel will serve about 30 people with a selection of other hors d'oeuvres. For smaller parties, use a 4-inch wheel. Half a recipe of brioche dough will be enough to wrap three 4-inch wheels of brie. Serve with thin-sliced French bread or crackers and fresh fruit such as apples, pears, figs, grapes, or berries.

1. Prepare the Brioche dough and refrigerate overnight. Divide the chilled dough into 2 equal portions, reserving 1 portion for another use. On a lightly floured work surface, roll out the dough to 16 inches in diameter and no less than ¼ inch thick. Place the wheel of Brie in the exact center and fold the edges of the dough up around the cheese. Enclose the Brie by trimming away the excess dough (save the scraps for decorations) and press the edges together to seal.

2. Grease or parchment-line a large baking sheet. Turn the cheese over and put it on the baking sheet. Brush with the beaten egg. Cut a small hole in the top of the dough to allow steam to escape. Brush the top and sides of the dough with the egg. Decorate the top with dough forms, if desired, fastening them with the beaten egg. A grape and tendril pattern works well.

3. Twenty minutes before baking, preheat the oven to 375°F. Let the loaf stand at room temperature for 15 minutes, if refrigerated. Place the baking sheet on a rack in the center of the oven and bake in the center about 40 minutes, or until golden brown and puffy. Cool on a rack. Serve warm or at room temperature.

ABUNDANT GRAIN:
Whole-Grain Breads

The imaginative addition of other flours or whole grains to wheat loaves creates bread with a fascinating variety of new flavors, aromas, and textures. But if you tried to create a yeasted loaf from all or a large percentage of non-white flour, you would produce a dense, flat loaf. It's necessary to use only a small amount of low-starch and low-gluten grains and flours in order to create a light-textured, yet hearty loaf.

Most people have become well acquainted with the virtues of whole grains through the highly publicized need for more fiber in today's diet. Insoluble fiber is the rough part of a plant that provides bulk as an aid to a healthy gastrointestinal tract. Grains such as wheat bran, whole-wheat flour, corn, rye, millet, oats, and barley, as well as nuts and seeds are in this category. Soluble fiber, which helps regulate blood sugar, fat, and cholesterol levels, is found in foods like oatmeal or apples that thicken after being cooked. The best sources of soluble fiber are oats, wheat, corn, rice brans, and legumes. Unbleached flour contains about 75 percent of the fiber contained in whole-wheat flour.

Grains, which are high in valuable water-soluble fiber and a major source of complex carbohydrates, vitamins, and minerals make us feel satisfied and well fed. They provide an even flow of energy and stamina as well as balancing body chemistry. Cholesterol free and low in fat, grains have the lowest percentage of chemical and inorganic residues found in foods today.

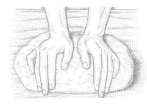

Baking with Whole Grains

For traditional high-domed loaves of bread when baking with whole grains or whole-grain flour, keep the ratio of specialty grains and flours, which have little or no gluten, small in proportion to wheat flour, which is high in gluten. A good rule of thumb is about 1 cup whole grains or whole-grain flour per 5 cups unbleached all-purpose flour or bread flour. For whole-wheat flour keep the proportion to 50 to 75 percent.

When mixing and kneading, keep whole-grain dough more moist than dough using all white flour. Whole grains and whole-grain flours tend to soak up lots of moisture as they rest and rise. Look for a "tacky" and "springy" feel, rather than a "smooth" and "stiff" quality. Always keep a reserve of ¼ to ½ cup of the required amount of flour. During kneading, add the remaining flour 1 tablespoon at a time as needed to prevent sticking and knead until it is completely absorbed. This ensures a moist loaf rather than a dry, crumbly one. Whole-grain doughs benefit from the use of a prefermented sponge and from being mixed in a heavy-duty electric mixer to develop a light texture.

Allow dough to rise only until just doubled in bulk for the best-formed baked loaves and the richest grain flavor. Overrising creates a sour, yeasty flavor.

Whole-grain breads are best when they are cooled completely after baking. This gives excess moisture a chance to evaporate, and sets the crumb; otherwise, the bread will easily collapse when cut.

Some uncooked grains, such as millet and quinoa, may be added to raw dough. Others must be soaked or cooked before adding, such as bulgur. Each recipe has specific instructions. Leftover cooked grains, such as rice, are perfect additions to bread dough.

Rinsing whole grains to remove dust and debris is optional. Use a strainer under running water. Cracked, rolled, and processed grains do not need rinsing.

Store whole grains and whole-grain flours in tightly covered containers in a cool, dry place for a maximum of about a month. For longer storage, keep grains and flours in the refrigerator or freezer.

Whole-Wheat Flour

Whole-wheat flour is ground from the fiber-rich whole grain that includes the endosperm, bran, and germ. Each commercial brand is a different grind, and each gives a slightly different texture to baked goods. Stone-ground flours are milled with slow-moving millstones rather than huge steel rollers that generate a lot of heat and reduce nutrients and flavor. With fine grinds, all the parts of the grain are equally ground. Medium and coarse grinds have varying amounts of bran dispersed through the flour, giving a slightly more crumbly texture to baked goods than fine-ground flour. Whole-wheat flour is denser than white flour and contains more fiber than white flours. It has a complex, nutty-sweet flavor and is more nutritious. Whole-grain flours contain a high percentage of oil and should be stored in the refrigerator to protect them from rancidity.

WHITE WHOLE-WHEAT FLOUR: A strain of wheat with bran coating that is white rather than the familiar rust color. It is lighter in taste than other whole-wheat flours and may be substituted exactly for darker whole-wheat flours.

GRAHAM FLOUR: A special grind of whole wheat that leaves the bran very coarse. It is easily substituted for whole-wheat flour and has a particularly rich, unique flavor not to be missed.

WHOLE-WHEAT PASTRY FLOUR: Flour from soft wheat. It is excellent in pastry and quick breads where regular whole-wheat flour would be too heavy.

KAMUT AND SPELT: Hardy ancient varieties of wheat cultivated for centuries in Europe. Now grown domestically, when ground into flours, they can be used as a one-for-one substitute for whole-wheat flours in baking recipes, although their flavors will vary.

Sesame Whole-Wheat Bread

Makes 3 oval loaves

1½ cups warm water (105° to 115°F)

1 tablespoon (1 package) active dry yeast

Pinch of light brown sugar

¼ cup (packed) light brown sugar

¼ cup light molasses

2¼ cups whole-wheat flour

¼ cup vegetable or sesame oil

¼ cup sesame seeds

¼ cup medium-grind yellow cornmeal

2½ teaspoons salt

3 large eggs, at room temperature

5 to 5½ cups unbleached all-purpose flour or bread flour

Cornmeal and sesame seeds, for sprinkling

High in fiber and nutrients, this loaf is a favorite bread with the health conscious. It tastes good, is easy to make, and has a great moist texture because of the addition of eggs. You may glaze the crust with beaten egg, but I prefer the matte finish with the sesame seeds peeking out. In the early days of my restaurant baking, we often made this popular old-fashioned recipe that filled the bakery with a grain-sweet aroma. The free-form loaves should be quickly shaped and compact for the best results. Substitute graham flour for the whole-wheat flour, if you wish, or add ¼ cup barley flour for more sweetness.

1. In a large bowl using a whisk or in the work bowl of a heavy-duty electric mixer fitted with the paddle attachment, pour in the water. Sprinkle the yeast and the pinch of sugar over the surface of the water. Stir to dissolve and let stand at room temperature until foamy, about 10 minutes.

2. Add the ¼ cup sugar, molasses, and whole-wheat flour. Beat until smooth. Cover with plastic wrap and set aside at room temperature until foamy, about 1 hour.

3. Add the oil, sesame seeds, cornmeal, salt, eggs, and 1 cup of the flour to the whole-wheat batter. Beat until smooth, about 2 minutes. Add the remaining unbleached flour, ½ cup at a time, until a soft dough that just clears the sides of the bowl is formed, switch to a wooden spoon when needed if making by hand.

4. Turn the dough out onto a lightly floured work surface and knead gently until the dough is no longer sticky, smooth on the surface and soft, about 4 minutes, dusting with flour only 1 tablespoon at a time as needed to prevent sticking.

If kneading by machine, switch from the paddle to the dough hook and knead for 3 to 4 minutes, or until the dough is smooth and springy and springs back when pressed. If desired, transfer the dough to a floured surface and knead briefly by hand. It is important that this dough remain soft and pliable, or the bread will be too dry. If it is kneaded too long, the dough will continue to absorb flour and make a much firmer loaf, so stop even if is slightly sticky.

5. Place the dough in a greased deep container. Turn once to coat the top and cover with plastic wrap. Let rise at room temperature until doubled in bulk, 1½ to 2 hours.

6. Turn the dough out onto a floured work surface. Grease or parchment-line a baking sheet and dust with cornmeal. Without working the dough further, divide it into 3 portions. Form each portion into a fat rectangular loaf. Place the loaf, seam side down, on the baking sheet. Cover loosely with plastic wrap and let rise until almost doubled in bulk, about 1 hour.

7. Twenty minutes before baking, preheat the oven to 350°F. Using a serrated knife, slash 3 parallel lines no more than ¼ inch deep down the sides of each loaf to form a herringbone effect. Place the baking sheet on the center rack of the oven and bake 35 to 40 minutes, or until evenly golden brown and the loaves sound hollow when tapped with your finger. Do not overbake. Remove the loaves by pulling them apart and place on a cooling rack. Cool completely before slicing.

Old-fashioned 100 Percent Whole-Wheat Bread

Makes 3 medium round loaves

Sponge

- 3 cups warm water (105° to 115°F)
- 1 cup dried buttermilk
- 2 tablespoons (2 packages) active dry yeast
- 3/4 cup honey
- 3 cups fine to medium grind whole-wheat flour, preferably stone ground

Dough

- 1/2 cup vegetable oil
- 1 1/4 tablespoons salt
- 5 to 5 1/2 cups fine to medium grind whole-wheat flour, preferably stone ground
- Rolled oats, for sprinkling

The flavor of this whole-wheat loaf is sweet and nutty. The secrets to a moist, fine-textured loaf are a technique known as the "sponge method" and using a whole-wheat flour that has been as finely ground as possible. The sponge method evenly moistens and slightly ferments whole-grain batter before it is mixed and kneaded. It is important to retain the moisture in the dough by using plastic wrap during all risings; this prevents the formation of a skin, which would dry out the top of the loaf and prevent it from attaining a full, rounded dome during baking. Mastering this loaf is satisfying indeed. To make this bread in the bread machine, see page 434.

1. To prepare the sponge: In a large bowl, whisk together the water, dried buttermilk, yeast, honey, and the 3 cups whole-wheat flour and beat until smooth. Scrape down the sides with a spatula. Cover with plastic wrap and let stand in a warm place until foamy and doubled in bulk, about 1 hour. Gently stir it down with a wooden spoon.

2. In a large bowl using a whisk or in the bowl of a heavy-duty electric mixer fitted with the paddle attachment, add the oil, salt, 2 cups of the flour, and the sponge. Beat hard until smooth, about 1 minute. Add the remaining flour, 1/2 cup at a time, using a wooden spoon if making by hand, until a soft dough that just clears the sides of the bowl is formed.

3. Turn the dough out onto a lightly floured work surface and knead until smooth and springy, yet slightly tacky, about 5 minutes, dusting with the flour only 1 tablespoon at a time as needed to keep the dough from sticking.

If kneading by machine, switch from the paddle to the dough hook and knead for 4 to 5 minutes, or until the dough is smooth and springy and springs back when pressed. If desired, transfer the dough to a floured surface and knead briefly by hand. Do not add too much flour, as the dough must retain a definite sticky quality, which will smooth out during the rising process. The dough will also have a slightly abrasive quality from the whole grains.

4. Place the dough in a greased deep container. Turn once to coat the top and cover with plastic wrap. Let rise at room temperature until puffy and almost doubled in bulk, 1½ to 2 hours.

5. Turn the dough out onto a floured work surface. Grease or parchment-line a baking sheet and sprinkle it with rolled oats. Divide it into 3 equal portions. Form each portion into 3 round balls and place them at least 4 inches apart on the baking sheet. Cover loosely with plastic wrap and let rise until not quite doubled in bulk, about 45 minutes.

6. Twenty minutes before baking, preheat the oven to 375°F. Place the baking sheet in the center of the oven and bake 40 to 45 minutes, or until deep brown and the loaves sound hollow when tapped with your finger. Place a piece of aluminum foil over the tops to slow browning, if needed. Transfer the loaves immediately to a cooling rack. Cool completely before slicing.

Italian Walnut-Raisin Whole-Wheat Bread

Makes 3 round loaves or 2 thick baguettes

2½ cups warm water (105° to 115°F)

2 tablespoons (2 packages) active dry yeast

Pinch of light brown sugar or 1 teaspoon honey

½ cup extra-virgin olive oil

¼ cup honey

1 tablespoon salt

4 cups fine-grind whole-wheat flour, preferably stone ground

1½ to 1¾ cups unbleached all-purpose flour

2 cups (10 ounces) dark raisins, plumped in hot water 1 hour and drained on paper towels

3 cups (12 ounces) broken or chopped walnuts

2 tablespoons whole-wheat flour, for sprinkling

2 tablespoons unprocessed wheat bran, for sprinkling

I think this bread, known as *pane alle noci e uva*, is one of the best breads in the Western world. It is distinctly stamped with the fragrance of raisins and walnuts. Use a fruity Italian extra-virgin olive oil for the bread; the special quality the oil gives it is very desirable.

1. In a small bowl pour in ½ cup of the warm water. Sprinkle the yeast and sugar over the surface of the water. Stir to dissolve and let stand at room temperature until foamy, about 10 minutes.

2. In a large mixing bowl with a whisk or the work bowl of a heavy-duty electric mixer fitted with the paddle attachment, combine the remaining 2 cups warm water, the olive oil, honey, salt, and 2 cups of the whole-wheat flour. Add the yeast mixture. Beat vigorously until smooth, about 1 minute. Add the remaining whole-wheat flour, ½ cup at a time. Add the unbleached flour, ¼ cup at a time, until a soft dough that just clears the sides of the bowl is formed. Switch to a wooden spoon when necessary if making by hand.

3. Turn the dough out onto a very lightly floured work surface and knead until soft and springy yet resilient to the touch, dusting with flour only 1 tablespoon at a time as needed to prevent sticking, about 6 minutes.

If kneading by machine, switch from the paddle to the dough hook and knead for 5 to 6 minutes, or until the dough is smooth and springy and springs back when pressed. If desired, transfer the dough to a floured surface and knead briefly by hand. The dough should retain a smooth, soft quality, with some tackiness under the surface, yet still hold its shape. Do not add too much flour, or the loaf will be too dry and hard to work.

4. Place the dough in a greased deep container. Turn once to coat the top and cover with plastic wrap. Let rise at room temperature until doubled in bulk, 2 to 2½ hours.

5. Grease or parchment-line a baking sheet. In a small bowl, combine the whole-wheat flour and wheat bran and sprinkle on the baking sheet. Turn the dough out onto a lightly floured work surface without punching it down. Pat it into a large oval and sprinkle evenly with half the drained raisins and half the walnuts. Press the nuts and fruit into the dough and roll it up. Pat the dough into an oval once again and sprinkle it evenly with the remaining raisins and walnuts. Press the addition in and roll the dough up again. Divide the dough into 2 or 3 equal portions. Shape the portions into 3 tight round loaves or 2 baguettes each about 14 inches long. Gently pull the surface taut from the bottom on both. Place the loaves on the prepared pans. Cover loosely with plastic wrap and let rise at room temperature until doubled in bulk, 45 minutes to 1 hour.

6. Twenty minutes before baking, preheat the oven at 400°F, with a baking stone, if desired. Using a serrated knife, slash the round or baguette loaves quickly with 2 parallel lines and one intersecting line no more than ¼ inch deep. Place the baking sheet directly on the stone or on an oven rack and bake until the loaves are brown, crusty, and sound hollow when tapped with your finger, 35 to 40 minutes for the round loaves and 25 to 30 minutes for the baguettes. Transfer the loaves immediately to a cooling rack. Cool completely before slicing.

Cracked Wheat Bread

Makes 3 medium round loaves

Cracked wheat gives a special nutty texture and added nutrition to this homey loaf. Bulgur can be used interchangeably with cracked wheat in this recipe. To make this bread in a bread machine see page 436.

³/₄ cup cracked wheat or bulgur

1½ cups boiling water

1½ tablespoons (1½ packages) active dry yeast

Pinch of sugar

¼ cup warm water (105° to 115°F)

1 cup warm buttermilk (105° to 115°F)

¼ cup molasses

1 tablespoon honey

4 tablespoons (1 stick) unsalted butter, cut into pieces

1 tablespoon salt

¼ cup raw sesame seeds

2 cups whole-wheat flour

2½ to 3 cups unbleached all-purpose flour or bread flour

2 tablespoons butter, melted, for brushing loaves

1. In a small bowl, put in the cracked wheat and pour the boiling water over it. Let stand 1 hour to soften.

2. Pour the warm water in a small bowl. Sprinkle the yeast and sugar in over the surface of the warm water. Stir to dissolve and let stand at room temperature until foamy, about 10 minutes.

3. In a small bowl, combine the buttermilk, molasses, honey, and butter. In a large bowl, using a whisk or in the work bowl of a heavy-duty electric mixer fitted with the paddle attachment, combine the salt, sesame seeds, and whole-wheat flour. Stir in the milk and yeast mixtures and beat until smooth, about 3 minutes. Strain the cracked wheat and stir it into the flour mixture. Add the unbleached flour, ½ cup at a time, until a soft dough forms, using a wooden spoon.

4. Turn the dough out onto a floured work surface and knead until soft and springy to the touch, about 5 minutes, dusting with flour only 1 tablespoon at a time as needed to prevent sticking.

If kneading by machine, switch from the paddle to the dough hook and knead for 4 to 5 minutes, or until the dough is smooth and springy and springs back when pressed. If desired, transfer the dough to a floured surface and knead briefly by hand. The dough will remain quite tacky.

5. Place the dough in a greased deep container. Turn to coat the top and cover with plastic wrap. Let rise at room temperature until doubled in bulk, about 1½ hours.

6. Gently deflate the dough. Turn the dough out onto a lightly floured work surface. Grease or parchment-line a baking sheet. Divide the dough into 3 equal portions and shape the portions into rounds or oblong loaves. Place the loaves on the baking sheet. Brush the top of the loaves with melted butter and cover loosely with plastic wrap. Let rise at room temperature until doubled in bulk, about 30 minutes. Brush the top of the loaves again with melted butter.

7. Twenty minutes before baking, preheat the oven to 350°F. Place the baking sheet on the center rack of the oven and bake 35 to 45 minutes, or until brown and the loaves sound hollow when tapped with your finger. Transfer the loaves immediately to a cooling rack.

Graham Bread

Makes four 9-by-5-inch loaves

4½ cups warm water (105° to 115°F)

2 tablespoons (2 packages) active dry yeast

1 cup brown sugar

1²/₃ cups instant nonfat dried milk

8 tablespoons (1 stick) unsalted butter, melted, or vegetable oil

³/₄ cup molasses

1 tablespoon plus 1 teaspoon salt

4 large eggs, at room temperature, lightly beaten

3 cups graham flour

9 to 10 cups unbleached all-purpose flour or bread flour

Rich Egg Glaze (page 52)

This Swedish bread was brought to my home for a potluck dinner years ago by my friend, Judy Larsen. In those first years of serious breadmaking, Judy and I had a lot of conversations about bread. The recipes she shared with me from her mother in Minnesota gave me a standard by which I could judge all others. She was also helpful with the myriad questions I always seemed to have as a beginning breadmaker. Scandinavians are notoriously good bakers, gifted in working with the temperamental whole grains. Graham flour is technically whole-wheat flour, but has a much richer flavor. This loaf is the essence of a comforting, wholesome winter bread. Note that this is a large recipe, yielding four standard loaves.

1. Pour ½ cup of the warm water in a small bowl. Sprinkle the yeast and the pinch of brown sugar over the surface of the water. Stir to dissolve and let stand at room temperature until foamy, about 10 minutes.

2. In a large bowl using a whisk or in the work bowl of a heavy-duty electric mixer fitted with the paddle attachment, combine the remaining 4 cups water, dried milk, the remaining brown sugar, butter, molasses, and salt. Add the yeast mixture and eggs to the liquid ingredients. Beat to combine. Add the graham flour. Beat hard until smooth, about 3 minutes. Add the flour 1 cup at a time, with a wooden spoon until a shaggy dough that just clears the side of the bowl is formed.

3. Turn the dough out onto a well-floured work surface and knead until dough is smooth and very springy, for a full 10 minutes, dusting with flour only 1 tablespoon at a time, as needed to prevent sticking.

If kneading by machine, switch from the paddle to the dough hook and knead for 8 to 9 minutes, or until the dough is smooth and springy and springs back when pressed. If desired, transfer the dough to a floured surface and knead briefly by hand. Do not add too much flour or the dough will become very stiff and hard to work.

4. Place the dough in a greased deep container. Turn once to coat the top and cover with plastic wrap. Let rise in a warm area until doubled in bulk, about 1½ hours. Gently deflate the dough and, if possible, let it rise again for 45 minutes. This extra rise helps the flavor and texture develop.

5. Gently deflate the dough. Turn the dough out onto a lightly floured work surface. Grease four 9-by-5 loaf pans. Divide the dough into 4 equal portions. Form each portion into a loaf and place in the loaf pans. Cover loosely with plastic wrap and let rise until doubled in bulk, or no more than 1 inch above the rim of the pan, 30 to 40 minutes. This also makes lovely round free-form loaves, if desired.

6. Twenty minutes before baking, preheat the oven to 350°F. Brush the top of the loaves with egg glaze. Place the pans on the center rack of the oven and bake 40 to 45 minutes or until golden. Cool the loaves for 5 minutes in the pans and transfer the loaves immediately to a cooling rack, laying each loaf on its side. Cool completely before slicing.

Bran-Molasses-Sunflower Bread

Makes two round or two 9-by-5-inch loaves

3/4 cup warm water (105° to 115°F)

1 tablespoon (1 package) active dry yeast

2 tablespoons sugar

1½ cups warm milk (105° to 115°F)

4 tablespoons (1 stick) unsalted butter, melted

1/3 cup molasses

1½ cups wheat bran

1 tablespoon salt

1/2 cup raw sunflower seeds

About 5 cups unbleached all-purpose flour or bread flour

This is the bread that started my baking career. The customers in the restaurant where I worked demanded brown bread, so I took a white bread recipe and added bran. A few years later, I received a large bag of sunflower seeds by accident, and they appeared in the bread. In the presence of heat, sunflower seeds exude their flavorful and nutritious oil into bread. The whole-grain flavor and aroma are intoxicating. If you find the bread a bit too heavy, cut back on the bran until you get your perfect loaf. To make this bread in a bread machine, see page 437.

1. Pour the warm water in a small bowl. Sprinkle the yeast and the sugar over the surface of the water. Stir to dissolve and let stand at room temperature until foamy, about 10 minutes.

2. In a large bowl using a whisk or in the work bowl of a heavy-duty electric mixer fitted with a paddle attachment, combine the milk, butter, molasses, bran, salt, and seeds. Beat hard. Add 2 cups flour and the yeast mixture. Beat hard until smooth and creamy, about 2 minutes. Add the flour ½ cup at a time, using a wooden spoon, and beat until the dough is stiff.

3. Turn the dough out onto a lightly floured work surface and knead until smooth, about 5 minutes, dusting with flour only 1 tablespoon at a time as needed to prevent sticking.

If kneading by machine, switch from the paddle to the dough hook and knead for 4 to 5 minutes, or until the dough is smooth and springy and springs back when pressed. If desired, transfer the dough to a floured surface and knead briefly by hand.

4. Place the dough in a greased bowl. Turn once to coat the top and cover with plastic wrap. Let rise at room temperature until doubled in bulk, 1 to 1½ hours.

5. Punch the dough down gently and turn out onto a lightly floured work surface. Grease or parchment-line baking sheet or baking pans. Divide the dough into 2 equal portions. Form each portion into a round or 9-by-5-inch loaf. Place the loaves, seam side down, on the baking sheet or in the pans. Cover loosely with plastic wrap and let rise until doubled in bulk, about 45 minutes.

6. Twenty minutes before baking, preheat the oven to 375°F. Place the sheet or pans on a rack in the center of the oven and bake about 45 minutes, or until nicely browned and the loaves sound hollow when tapped with your fingers. Transfer the loaves immediately to a cooling rack.

Brans

The protective outer layer covering the whole-grain kernel before milling, bran is acknowledged for its contribution to nutrition. It provides roughage in the form of soluble fiber and is a plentiful source of several minerals. It is a by-product of refined flours during the bolting process that separates the bran and wheat germ from the starchy center after milling. Because brans are rather tasteless, they are used with flours to boost the nutrition and fiber content, rather than being used exclusively. Brans are high in natural oils, so refrigeration is recommended for freshness. Wheat brans are sometimes marketed as miller's bran or unprocessed wheat bran and are a favorite ingredient in quick breads and muffins. Other brans include: oat bran, the outer coating of a hulled oat groat; rice bran, the outer counting on brown rice; and corn bran, whole-grain corn.

Oatmeal-Potato Bread

Makes two 9-by-5-inch or two round loaves

> 1 russet potato (about 6 ounces), scrubbed and cut into large chunks
>
> 2 tablespoons unsalted butter, at room temperature
>
> 1 tablespoon (1 package) active dry yeast
>
> 1 tablespoon sugar
>
> 1½ cups warm milk (105° to 115°F)
>
> 1 tablespoon salt
>
> 1½ cups regular rolled oats
>
> 5½ to 6 cups unbleached all-purpose flour or bread flour
>
> Rolled oats, for coating the bottoms of the loaves

A noble loaf, this crusty, deep-colored bread has a nubby, moist texture and sweet taste. It is an easy bread to master and one of the first highly successful breads I ever made. I have baked it often as a gift for a friend, as well as for myself. For an excellent flavor, use imported Irish oatmeal, available in a bright green box in the cereal section of your supermarket. For those who dare go Highland style, substitute a jigger or two of single-malt scotch in place of an equal amount of milk.

1. In a medium saucepan, put in the potato chunks and cover with water. Bring to a boil, reduce the heat to low, and cook until tender, about 20 minutes. Drain, reserving ½ cup of the liquid. Let the potato water cool to 105° to 115°F. Meanwhile, peel the potato and pass it and the butter through a food mill placed over a bowl or purée it in a food processor fitted with the metal blade just until smooth. You will have ¾ to 1 cup purée.

2. Pour the potato water in a small bowl. Sprinkle the yeast and a pinch of the sugar over the surface of the water. Stir to dissolve and let stand at room temperature until foamy, about 10 minutes.

3. In a large mixing bowl with a whisk or in the work bowl of a heavy-duty electric mixer fitted with the paddle attachment, combine the puréed potato, yeast mixture, the remaining sugar, the warm milk, salt, rolled oats, and 2 cups of the flour. Beat hard to combine, about 1 minute. Add the remaining flour, ½ cup at a time, beating until a shaggy dough that just clears the sides of the bowl is formed.

4. Turn the dough out onto a lightly floured work surface. Knead until just smooth and springy, about 4 minutes, dusting with flour only 1 tablespoon at a time as needed to prevent sticking.

    If kneading by machine, switch from the paddle to the dough hook and knead for 3 to 4 minutes, or until the dough is smooth and springy and springs back when pressed. If desired, transfer the dough to a floured surface and knead briefly by hand. Take care not to add too much flour, because the oats will absorb extra moisture during rising and the dough will become too dry.

5. Place the dough in a greased deep container. Turn once to coat the top and cover with plastic wrap. Let rise at room temperature until doubled in bulk, about 1½ hours.

6. Gently deflate the dough. Turn the dough out onto a lightly floured work surface. Grease the 9-by-5-inch clay or metal loaf pan, or grease or parchment-line a baking sheet. Divide it into 2 equal portions. Form the dough into rectangular or round loaves. Roll the bottom surfaces of each loaf in rolled oats to coat. Put the dough into the loaf pans or on the baking sheet. Cover lightly with plastic wrap and let rise at room temperature until doubled in bulk, about 40 minutes.

7. Twenty minutes before baking, preheat the oven to 425°F, with a baking stone, if desired. Place the loaf pans or baking sheet on a rack in the center of the oven and bake for 10 minutes. Reduce the oven thermostat to 350°F and continue baking 35 to 40 minutes (10 minutes longer for clay pans), or until the loaves are browned and sound hollow when tapped with your finger. Remove the loaves immediately to cooling racks. Cool completely before slicing.

Oats

Rolled oats are the most familiar cereal on the market and a favorite ingredient in both yeast and quick breads. Whole groats are hulled, steamed, and flattened into old-fashioned flakes. When rerolled they become quick-cooking oats. Quick and old-fashioned oats can be used interchangeably in breadmaking, with the old-fashioned variety retaining its shape more distinctly. Rolled oats can be ground in a food processor into an earthy oat flour or a coarse meal suitable for bread making. The mild, nutty flavor and moist, nubby texture of oats are favorites in breads.

Oatmeal-Bulgur Bread

*Makes three round or three
8-by-4-inch loaves*

Sponge

1 tablespoon
   (1 package) active
   dry yeast

2 tablespoons light
   brown sugar

²/₃ cup bulgur wheat,
   fine or medium grind

2¼ cups warm water
   (105° to 115°F)

2 cups unbleached
   all-purpose flour or
   bread flour

Dough

1¼ cups regular rolled
   oats

¼ cup wheat bran

¼ cup light brown
   sugar

3 tablespoons
   vegetable oil

1 tablespoon salt

3 to 3½ cups unbleached
   all-purpose flour or
   bread flour

Bulgur consists of wheat kernels that have been steamed, dried, and crushed. Bulgur is entirely different from plain cracked wheat, which has not been precooked. The crunchy quality bulgur gives to bread is most satisfying when combined with sweet, mild oats to make a great-tasting, old-fashioned, homemade bread.

1. To make the sponge: In a large bowl or the work bowl of a heavy-duty electric mixer fitted with the paddle attachment, pour in the water. Sprinkle the yeast, 2 tablespoons brown sugar, and bulgur wheat over the surface of the water and let stand for 5 minutes. Add 2 cups of the flour and beat hard until well moistened and creamy, about 2 minutes. Cover with plastic wrap and let stand at room temperature until foamy, about 1 hour.

2. To make the dough: To the bowl with the sponge, add the rolled oats, bran, brown sugar, oil, and salt. Beat hard for about 1 minute. Add more flour, ½ cup at a time, and beat for another 1 minute, or until stretchy and well-moistened. Add more flour, ½ cup at a time, until the dough pulls away from the sides of the bowl. Switch to a wooden spoon when needed if mixing by hand.

3. Turn the dough out onto a lightly floured work surface and knead until smooth and elastic, about 4 minutes, dusting with the flour 1 tablespoon at a time as needed to prevent sticking.

If kneading by machine, switch from the paddle to the dough hook and knead for 3 to 4 minutes, or until the dough is smooth and springy and springs back when pressed. If desired, transfer the dough to a floured surface and knead briefly by hand.

4. Place the dough in a greased deep container. Turn once to coat the top and cover with plastic wrap. Let rise at room temperature until doubled in bulk, 1½ to 2 hours.

5. Gently deflate the dough. Turn the dough out onto a floured work surface. Grease or parchment-line a baking sheet or grease three 8-by-4-inch loaf pans. Divide the dough into 3 equal portions. Form each portion into a round or rectangular loaf and put on the baking sheet or in the loaf pans. Cover loosely with plastic wrap and let rise until doubled in bulk, about 45 minutes.

6. Twenty minutes before baking, preheat the oven to 375°F. Using a serrated knife, gently slash the top of the loaves no more than ¼ inch deep. Place the baking sheet or pans on a rack in the center of the oven and bake 35 to 40 minutes, or until the loaves are browned and sound hollow when tapped with your finger. Let the loaves cool in the pans for 5 minutes, then turn the loaves out immediately onto a cooling rack. Cool completely before slicing.

Rain and Sun

Makes 2 braids

Buckwheat Dough

1/2 cup warm water
(105° to 115°F)

1 tablespoon
(1 package) active
dry yeast

3 tablespoons brown
sugar

1 cup warm buttermilk
(105° to 115°F)

3 tablespoons unsalted
butter, melted

1 large egg, at room
temperature, lightly
beaten

Grated zest of
1/2 orange

2 teaspoons salt

1/2 cup buckwheat flour

1 cup whole-wheat
flour

2 to 2 1/4 cups unbleached
all-purpose flour or
bread flour

Cornmeal Dough

1/2 cup warm water
(105° to 115°F)

1 tablespoon
(1 package) active
dry yeast

Pinch of sugar

2/3 cup half-and-half or
light cream

1/4 cup maple syrup

4 tablespoons
(1/2 stick) unsalted
butter, melted

Rain and Sun refers to this light-and-dark braided loaf of buckwheat and cornmeal doughs. It's delicious with a garden salad, a pyramid chèvre, and black grapes.

1. To make the buckwheat dough: Pour the warm water in a small bowl. Sprinkle the yeast and a pinch of brown sugar over the surface of the water. Stir to dissolve and let stand at room temperature until foamy, about 10 minutes.

2. In a large bowl using a whisk or in the work bowl of a heavy-duty electric mixer fitted with the paddle attachment, combine the buttermilk, the remaining brown sugar, butter, and egg. Add the orange zest, salt, and buckwheat and whole-wheat flours. Beat hard with the whisk until smooth about 3 minutes. Add the yeast mixture and beat well. With a wooden spoon, beat in the unbleached flour, 1/2 cup at a time, to make a soft dough.

3. Turn the dough out onto a lightly floured work surface and knead rather soft and sticky but is elastic and holds it shape, about 4 minutes, dusting with the flour 1 tablespoon at a time as needed to prevent sticking.

If kneading by machine, switch from the paddle to the dough hook and knead for 3 to 4 minutes, or until the dough is smooth and springy and springs back when pressed. If desired, transfer the dough to a floured surface and knead briefly by hand.

4. Put in a greased deep bowl. Turn the dough once to coat the top and cover with plastic wrap. Let rise at room temperature until doubled in bulk, 1 to 1 1/2 hours.

5. To make the cornmeal dough: Pour the warm water in a small bowl. Sprinkle the yeast and sugar over the surface of the water. Stir to dissolve and let stand at room temperature until foamy, about 10 minutes.

6. In a large bowl, using a whisk or in the work bowl of a heavy-duty electric mixer fitted with the paddle attachment, combine the half-and-half, maple syrup, butter, eggs, salt, and cornmeal. Beat hard until smooth, about 2 minutes. Add the yeast mixture and beat well. Add the unbleached flour 1/2 cup at a time, until a soft dough that clears the sides of the bowl is formed.

2 large eggs, at room temperature, lightly beaten

1½ teaspoons salt

⅔ cup fine or medium-grind yellow cornmeal, preferably stone ground

3 to 3½ cups unbleached all-purpose flour or bread flour

Rich Egg Glaze (page 52)

7. Turn the dough out onto a lightly floured work surface and knead until smooth and springy, about 4 minutes. The dough will be grainy in texture and slightly sticky.

If kneading by machine, switch from the paddle to the dough hook and knead for 3 to 4 minutes, or until the dough is smooth and springy and springs back when pressed. If desired, transfer the dough to a floured surface and knead briefly by hand.

8. Place the dough in a greased deep bowl. Turn once to coat the top and cover with plastic wrap. Let at room temperature until doubled in bulk, 1 to 1¼ hours.

9. Gently deflate the doughs. Turn the doughs onto a lightly floured work surface. Grease or parchment-line a baking sheet. Divide each dough into 3 equal portions. Roll each third out into a 16-inch-long rope. On the baking sheet, lay 2 strands of cornmeal dough with 1 strand of buckwheat dough parallel in the middle. Braid the strands and tuck under at the ends. Repeat with the other 3 strands, placing the single cornmeal strand in the middle. Cover each loaf loosely with plastic wrap and let rise at room temperature until doubled in bulk, about 30 minutes. Brush the top of the loaves with the egg glaze.

10. Twenty minutes before baking, preheat the oven to 375°F. Put the baking pan on the center rack of the oven and bake 40 to 45 minutes, or until brown and crusty and the loaves sound hollow when tapped with your finger. Transfer the loaves from the pan immediately to a cooling rack.

Buckwheat

A very hardy plant native to Siberia, buckwheat grows rapidly even in poor, rocky soil and extreme climates. Though not a grain but the seed of a red-stemmed plant related to rhubarb, buckwheat contains all eight essential amino acids, including lysine, and is a good source of calcium. It is particularly rich in both vitamin E and the B-complex vitamins. Buckwheat flour, which may be light, medium, or dark, is low in protein, which makes for a tender baked product with an assertive, slightly bitter flavor. The buckwheat grown in Europe has a rather mild taste, distinctly different from the buckwheat grown in the United States, which can be quite strong. Small amounts of buckwheat flour combined with wheat flour make delicious bread.

Swedish Rye Bread

Makes 2 oval loaves

1¾ cups warm water
(105° to 115°F)

1 tablespoon
(1 package)
active dry yeast

Pinch of light brown
sugar

¼ cup light or dark
unsulfured molasses

¼ cup (packed) light or
dark brown sugar

2 tablespoons
unsalted butter,
melted,
or vegetable oil

1 tablespoon salt

2 teaspoons caraway
or fennel seeds

Grated zest of 1 large
orange or lemon

2½ cups medium rye
flour

2¼ to 2½ cups unbleached
all-purpose flour or
bread flour

Melted butter,
for brushing
(optional)

This rye bread looks as if it will be dense and hard to work. On the contrary. Although the gluten in rye is different from the gluten in wheat—an all-rye loaf would be very dense—the even combination of the two flours makes for a soft, workable dough that rises high and is elastic to work with. This is a sweet rye bread in the Scandinavian tradition, with the traditional flavoring of molasses, orange, and spicy seeds.

1. In a small bowl or 1-cup liquid measuring cup, pour in ¾ cup of the warm water. Sprinkle the yeast and the sugar or honey over the surface of the water. Stir to dissolve and let stand at room temperature until foamy, about 10 minutes.

2. In a large bowl using a whisk or in the bowl of a heavy-duty electric mixer fitted with the paddle attachment, combine the remaining water, molasses, brown sugar, melted butter or oil, salt, seeds, zest, and rye flour. Beat hard until creamy, about 1 minute. Stir in the yeast mixture. Add the unbleached flour, ½ cup at a time, until a soft, shaggy dough that just clears the sides of the bowl is formed. Switch to a wooden spoon when necessary if making by hand.

3. Turn the dough out onto a lightly floured work surface and knead until soft and springy, 1 to 3 minutes for a machine-mixed dough and 4 to 7 minutes for a hand-mixed dough, dusting with flour only 1 tablespoon at a time, just enough as needed to prevent sticking.

If kneading by machine, switch from the paddle to the dough hook and knead for 3 to 4 minutes, or until the dough is smooth and springy and springs back when pressed. If desired, transfer the dough to a floured surface and knead briefly by hand. The dough will be smooth and springy with a definite tacky quality. It is very important that this dough not be too dry.

4. Place the dough in a lightly greased deep container. Turn the dough once to coat the top and cover with plastic wrap. Let rise at room temperature until doubled in bulk, about 2 to 2½ hours. Do not let rise more than double or the dough will overferment.

5. Turn the dough out onto a lightly floured work surface to deflate. Grease or parchment-line a baking sheet. Without working the dough further, divide the dough into 2 equal portions. Form into 2 oval balls. Lift up the loaf and pull the bottom center together for extra tautness. This makes for a high, well-rounded loaf. If the loaf is flat, repeat the process. Place the loaves, seam side down, on the baking sheet. Brush the tops with the melted butter or dust with flour, as desired. Cover loosely with plastic wrap and let rise at room temperature until the dough is fully double in bulk, about 2 hours.

6. Twenty minutes before baking, preheat the oven to 375°F. Using a serrated knife, slash the loaves decoratively with 3 diagonal cuts, no more than ¼ inch deep. Place the pan on the center rack of the oven and bake 25 to 30 minutes, or until the loaves are golden brown and sound hollow when tapped with your finger. Transfer the loaves immediately to a cooling rack. Loaves are best slightly warm or at room temperature.

Black Russian Rye Bread

Makes 2 medium round loaves

½ cup warm water (105° to 115°F)

2 tablespoons (2 packages) active dry yeast

Pinch of sugar

½ cup molasses

¼ cup apple cider vinegar

4 tablespoons (½ stick) unsalted butter

1 ounce unsweetened chocolate

½ cup whole-wheat flour

3 cups medium rye flour

3 cups unbleached all-purpose flour or bread flour

1 cup wheat bran

2 tablespoons caraway seeds

½ teaspoon fennel seeds

1 tablespoon salt

1 tablespoon instant espresso powder

1 tablespoon minced shallot

¼ cup medium-grind yellow cornmeal

1 tablespoon unbleached all-purpose flour

1 teaspoon caraway seeds

All bakers should have a dark rye in their repertoire. There is immense satisfaction in making a good pumpernickel-style loaf. The bread stays fresh at room temperature for several days. You can alter the density of this bread by varying the proportion of the flours: For a lighter bread, replace some of the whole-grain flours with white flour. Be sure to cool the bread completely before slicing. Bake it in mini loaf pans for cocktail-size slices.

1. Pour the warm water in a small bowl. Sprinkle the yeast and sugar over the surface of the water. Stir to dissolve and let stand at room temperature until foamy, about 10 minutes.

2. In a small saucepan, heat 2 cups water, molasses, vinegar, butter, and chocolate to 105° to 115°F. The butter and chocolate will melt. Set aside. In a large bowl, combine the whole-wheat, rye, and white flours. Set aside.

3. In a large bowl using a wooden spoon or in the work bowl of a heavy-duty mixer fitted with a paddle attachment, combine 2 cups mixed flours, bran, seeds, salt, espresso, and shallot. Add the yeast and chocolate mixtures. Beat vigorously until smooth, about 3 minutes. Add the remaining mixed flours, ½ cup at a time, until the dough clears the sides of the bowl. The dough will be very sticky, but firm.

4. Turn the dough out onto a lightly floured work surface. Knead in more of the flour mixture to make a springy yet dense dough, about 3 minutes. Not all of the flour may be necessary. Form the dough into a ball.

If kneading by machine, switch from the paddle to the dough hook and knead for 2 to 3 minutes, or until the dough is smooth, shiny and soft, and springs back when pressed. If desired, transfer the dough to a floured surface and knead briefly by hand. Form the dough into a ball.

5. Place the dough in a greased deep container. Turn once to coat the top and cover with plastic wrap. Let rise at room temperature until doubled in bulk, 1½ to 2 hours.

6. In a small bowl, combine the cornmeal, flour, and caraway and set aside. Gently deflate the dough. Turn it out onto a clean work surface.

1 tablespoon corn-
starch mixed with
1/2 cup water, for
glazing (optional)

Grease or parchment-line a baking sheet and sprinkle with the cornmeal-caraway mixture. Divide the dough into 2 equal portions and shape each into a tight round loaf. Place the loaves, seam side down, on the baking sheet. Cover loosely with plastic wrap and let rise until puffy and almost doubled in bulk, 45 minutes to 1 hour.

7. Twenty minutes before baking, preheat the oven to 350°F. Prepare the Cornstarch Glaze if a shiny crust is desired. Place the cornstarch and water in a small saucepan. Using a wire whisk, stir constantly and bring the mixture to a boil. Reduce the heat to medium and cook until thick and translucent. Use immediately, while hot.

8. Using a serrated knife, slash the top of the loaves with an **X** no more than 1/4 inch deep. Brush the loaves with the glaze. Place the baking sheet on the center rack of the oven and bake for 30 minutes. Rewarm the glaze and brush the loaves with more glaze. Bake for an additional 15 to 20 minutes, or until the loaves are crusty and sound hollow when tapped with your finger (it is difficult to see the loaves browning because they are so dark colored). Transfer the loaves to a cooling rack. Cool completely before slicing.

VARIATION: *To make mini loaves, grease eight 4-by-2½-inch loaf pans. In Step 6, divide the dough into 8 equal portions. Pat each portion into a rectangle and roll up to form mini standard loaves. Arrange each loaf in a pan, filling each slightly higher than the rim. Cover loosely with plastic wrap and let rise until puffy and an inch over the rim of the pans, about 30 minutes. Brush the loaves with the glaze, if desired, and bake in the center of the preheated oven 20 to 25 minutes until crusty and the loaves sound hollow when tapped with your finger. Transfer the loaves to a cooling rack. Cool completely before slicing.*

Potato and Rye Vienna Twist

Makes 2 long twists

Rye Dough

½ cup warm water
(105° to 115°F)

2 teaspoons active
dry yeast

1 cup flat beer,
warmed slightly to
burn off some of the
alcohol

1 tablespoon barley
malt syrup

1 large egg, at room
temperature

1½ teaspoons salt

1 tablespoon ground
coriander

1 cup medium rye
flour

3 cups unbleached
all-purpose flour or
bread flour

Potato Dough

1 unpeeled 6-ounce
russet potato,
scrubbed and cut
into large chunks

1½ teaspoons active
dry yeast

⅞ cup warm milk
(105° to 115°F)

4 tablespoons
(½ stick) unsalted
butter, at room
temperature

1 tablespoon sugar

1 large egg, at room
temperature

This is a humble name for a spectacular bread from Austria. *Verheiratesbrot,* literally marriage bread, is made of two distinctly different doughs, one a creamy potato flavored with anise, and the other a beer rye flavored with coriander, twisted together. This recipe is adapted from one developed by master baker Diane Dexter of San Francisco East Bay's Metropolis Bakery.

1. To make the rye dough: In a large bowl using a whisk or in the work bowl of a heavy-duty electric mixer fitted with the paddle attachment, pour in the warm water. Sprinkle the yeast over the surface of the water and stir until smooth. Add the warm beer, malt, egg, salt, spice, and rye flour. Beat until smooth, about 1 minute. Add the unbleached flour all at once and beat to make a smooth dough that clears the sides of the bowl, about 3 minutes.

2. Turn the dough out onto a lightly floured work surface and knead until smooth and springy, about 10 kneads. Add no more flour; this dough should be soft.

If kneading by machine, switch from the paddle to the dough hook and knead for 1 to 2 minutes, or until the dough is smooth and springy and springs back when pressed. If desired, transfer the dough to a floured surface and knead briefly by hand.

3. Place the rye dough in a greased deep container. Turn once to coat the top and cover with plastic wrap. Let rise at room temperature until doubled in bulk, about 1½ hours.

4. To make the potato dough: In a medium saucepan, cover the potato chunks with water. Bring to a boil, reduce the heat to low, and cook the potatoes until tender, about 20 minutes. Drain the potatoes, reserving ¼ cup of the potato water. Let the water cool to warm, 105° to 115°F. Meanwhile, peel the potato and purée with a food mill or electric mixer to make ⅔ cup of purée.

5. In a large bowl using a whisk or in the work bowl of a heavy-duty electric mixer fitted with the paddle attachment, pour in the potato water. Sprinkle the yeast over the potato water and stir until smooth. Add the potato purée, milk, butter, sugar, egg, aniseed, salt, and 1 cup of the

1½ teaspoons whole
    aniseed

1½ teaspoons salt

3½ to 3¾ cups unbleached
    all-purpose flour or
    bread flour

flour. Beat until smooth, about 1 minute. Add 2½ cups more
unbleached flour and beat with a wooden spoon until a smooth dough
that clears the sides of the bowl is formed, about 3 minutes.

6. Turn the dough out onto a lightly floured work surface and knead
until smooth and springy, about 10 kneads, dusting with flour only 1
tablespoon at a time as needed to prevent sticking.

    If kneading by machine, switch from the paddle to the dough hook
and knead for 1 to 2 minutes, or until the dough is smooth and springy
and springs back when pressed. If desired, transfer the dough to a
floured surface and knead briefly by hand.

7. Place the potato dough in a greased deep container. Turn once to
coat the top and cover with plastic wrap. Let rise at room temperature
until doubled in bulk, about 1 hour.

8. Gently deflate the doughs. Turn the doughs out onto a lightly floured
work surface. Grease or parchment-line a baking sheet. Divide each
dough into 2 equal portions. Roll each piece into a log about 14 inches
long. Lay 1 log of the rye and one of the potato dough side by side and
pinch the ends together. Twist the logs around each other with 4 or 5
turns. Pinch the ends and tuck them under. Place the loaf on the baking
sheet, arranging the loaf so that it is neat and even. Repeat the procedure
to form a second loaf. Cover loosely with plastic wrap and let rise until
almost doubled in bulk, about 40 minutes.

9. Twenty minutes before baking, preheat the oven to 450°F, if using a
baking stone, or 400°F without a stone. Mist the loaves with water and
sieve them all over with 1 to 2 tablespoons of unbleached flour. Reduce
the oven thermostat to 400°F if using a baking stone. Place the baking
sheet on the center rack of the oven and bake 35 to 40 minutes, or until
golden brown and crusty and the loaves sound hollow when tapped with
your finger. Transfer loaves immediately to a cooling rack. Cool completely before slicing.

Squaw Bread

Makes 4 medium round or oval loaves

2¼ cups warm water (105° to 115°F)

⅓ cup vegetable oil

¼ cup honey

¼ cup (packed) brown sugar

¼ cup dark raisins

1½ tablespoons (1½ packages) active dry yeast

Pinch of brown sugar

3 to 3¼ cups unbleached all-purpose flour or bread flour

½ cups whole-wheat flour

1½ cups medium rye flour

½ cup instant nonfat dry milk

2½ teaspoons salt

Cornmeal, for sprinkling

2 tablespoons unsalted butter, melted, for brushing

The unique flavor of Squaw Bread comes from "raisin water," which adds a very special sweetening to the grains. To make this bread in a machine, see page 446.

1. In a blender or food processor, combine ½ cup of the warm water, the oil, honey, brown sugar, and raisins. Let stand for 5 minutes to soften the raisins, then purée. Add 1½ cups water and process just to combine. Set the raisin water aside.

2. Pour ¼ cup of the warm water in a small bowl. Sprinkle the yeast and pinch of sugar over the surface of the water. Stir to dissolve and let stand at room temperature until foamy, about 10 minutes.

3. In a large bowl using a whisk or in the work bowl of a heavy-duty electric mixer fitted with the paddle attachment, combine 1 cup of the unbleached flour, all the whole-wheat and rye flours, dried milk, and salt. Add the raisin water and yeast mixture. Beat hard for 1 minute. Gradually add the remaining unbleached flour ½ cup at a time, until a soft dough that just clears the sides of the bowl is formed. Switch to a wooden spoon when needed if making by hand.

4. Turn the dough out onto a lightly floured work surface and knead until smooth and springy, about 3 minutes, dusting with the flour only 1 tablespoon at a time as needed to prevent sticking. The dough will have a tacky quality.

If kneading by machine, switch from the paddle to the dough hook and knead for 3 to 4 minutes, or until the dough is smooth and springy and springs back when pressed. If desired, transfer the dough to a floured surface and knead briefly by hand.

5. Place the dough in a greased deep container. Turn once to coat the top and cover with plastic wrap. Let rise at room temperature until doubled in bulk, about 1½ hours.

6. Gently deflate the dough. Turn the dough out onto a floured work surface. Grease or parchment-line 2 baking sheets and sprinkle with coarse cornmeal. Divide the dough into 4 equal portions. Form the portions into tight round loaves. Place the loaves seam side down on the baking sheets. Cover loosely with plastic wrap and let rise again at room temperature until doubled in bulk, about 45 minutes.

7. Twenty minutes before baking, preheat the oven to 425°F with a baking stone, if desired, or to 375°F without a baking stone. Using a serrated knife, slash the loaves decoratively with a cross, no more than ¼ inch deep. Brush the tops with melted butter. Reduce the oven heat to 375°F if using a baking stone. Put the sheets in the oven and bake for 35 to 40 minutes, or until crusty, browned, and the loaves sound hollow when tapped with your finger. Transfer the loaves immediately to a cooling rack. Cool before serving.

Anadama Bread with Tillamook Cheddar Cheese

Makes two 9-by-5-inch loaves

½ cup fine or medium-grind yellow cornmeal, preferably stone ground

2 cups (8 ounces) shredded Tillamook mild Cheddar cheese

½ cup mild honey

2 tablespoons unsalted butter, at room temperature

⅔ cup warm water (105° to 115°F)

1 tablespoon (1 package) active dry yeast

6 to 6½ cups unbleached all-purpose flour or bread flour

2 teaspoons salt

2 teaspoons ground paprika

4 tablespoons unsalted butter, melted, for brushing

Cornmeal, for sprinkling

Cornmeal may be either stone ground from whole dried corn or degerminated by a process that removes part of the bran and the germ to allow for longer storage. Seek out the best stone-ground cornmeal you can find for this traditional Early American bread. Cornmeal mush is combined with robust, Cheddar cheese and thick honey and made into a super-delicious bread with a hairline-thin swirl of sweet paprika. Serve with roasted meat or with soup for a winter dinner.

1. In a medium saucepan, combine the cornmeal and 1½ cups water. Cook over medium heat, stirring constantly with a whisk, until bubbly and thickened, about 3 minutes. Remove from the heat. Stir in the cheese, honey, and 2 tablespoons of the butter. Stir until the butter is melted. Set aside and let cool to warm.

2. In a large bowl using a whisk or in the work bowl of a heavy-duty electric mixer fitted with the paddle attachment, pour in the warm water. Sprinkle the yeast over the surface of the water. Stir to dissolve and let stand at room temperature until foamy, about 10 minutes.

3. Slowly mix in the cornmeal-cheese mixture, 2 cups of the flour, and salt. Beat for 2 minutes. Add the remaining flour, ½ cup at a time, until a soft dough that just clears the sides of the bowl is formed. Switch to a wooden spoon when necessary if making by hand.

4. Turn the dough out onto a lightly floured work surface and knead until a soft, smooth dough with a grainy texture is formed, about 3 minutes, dusting with flour only 1 tablespoon at a time as needed to prevent sticking.

If kneading by machine, switch from the paddle to the dough hook and knead for 3 to 4 minutes, or until the dough is smooth and springy and springs back when pressed. If desired, transfer the dough to a floured surface and knead briefly by hand.

5. Place the dough in a greased deep container. Turn once to coat the top and cover with plastic wrap. Let rise at room temperature until doubled in bulk, about 1½ hours.

6. Gently deflate the dough. Turn the dough out onto the work surface. Grease the 9-by-5-inch loaf pans and sprinkle with cornmeal. Divide the dough into 2 equal portions. Pat or roll each portion into a 9-by-5-inch rectangle of even thickness. Spread each rectangle evenly with 1 tablespoon of the remaining soft butter. Sprinkle each lightly with 1 teaspoon ground paprika. Beginning with the short end, roll up the dough jelly-roll fashion. Pinch the ends and long seams to seal. Place the loaves seam-side down, in the loaf pans. Brush the tops of each loaf with some melted butter and sprinkle lightly with cornmeal. Cover loosely with plastic wrap and let rise at room temperature until doubled in bulk or 1 inch above the rims of the pans, about 45 minutes.

7. Twenty minutes before baking, preheat the oven to 350°F. Place the pans on a rack in the center of the oven and bake 45 to 50 minutes, or until browned and the loaves sound hollow when tapped with your finger. Transfer the loaves immediately to a cooling rack. Cool completely before slicing.

Brown Rice Bread with Dutch Crunch Topping

Makes two 9-by-5-inch loaves

- 1 cup warm water (105° to 115°F)
- 2 tablespoons (2 packages) active dry yeast
- 1 teaspoon sugar or honey
- 1 cup warm buttermilk (105° to 115°F)
- ½ cup honey
- ¼ cup vegetable oil
- 1 tablespoon salt
- 2 cups cooked and cooled short-grain brown rice
- 5½ to 6 cups unbleached all-purpose flour or bread flour

Dutch Crunch Topping

- 2 tablespoons (2 packages) active dry yeast
- 1 cup warm water (105° to 115°F)
- 2 tablespoons sugar
- 2 tablespoons vegetable oil
- ½ teaspoon salt
- 1½ cups rice flour

I've always loved the classic Dutch Crunch Topping made with rice flour, but the breads underneath seemed terribly plain. Not any more. Here is a delicious toasting bread with a nubby texture. Use white or brown rice flour, available at natural foods stores. Do not use sweet rice flour used for Oriental baking.

1. Pour the warm water in a small bowl. Sprinkle the yeast and sugar over the surface of the warm water. Stir to dissolve and let stand at room temperature until foamy, about 10 minutes.

2. In a large bowl using a whisk or in the work bowl of a heavy-duty mixer fitted with the paddle attachment, combine the buttermilk, honey, oil, and salt. Add the rice and beat until smooth. Add the yeast mixture and 2 cups flour. Beat hard until smooth for 3 minutes. Add the flour, ½ cup at a time, until a soft, bulky dough that just clears the side of the bowl is formed.

3. Turn the dough out onto a lightly floured work surface and knead until smooth and springy, about 5 minutes, dusting with flour 1 tablespoon at a time as needed to prevent sticking. This dough will be slightly sticky.

If kneading by machine, switch from the paddle to the dough hook and knead for 4 to 5 minutes, or until the dough is smooth and springy and springs back when pressed. If desired, transfer the dough to a floured surface and knead briefly by hand.

4. Place the dough in a greased deep bowl. Turn the dough once to coat the top and cover with plastic wrap. Let rise at room temperature until doubled in bulk, 1½ to 2 hours.

5. Gently deflate the dough. Turn the dough out onto a lightly floured work surface. Grease two 9-by-5-inch loaf pans. Divide the dough into 2 equal portions. Form the portions into loaves. Let rest 15 minutes.

6. To prepare the topping: Combine all ingredients in a large bowl and beat with a whisk; beat hard to combine. Let stand 15 minutes. Coat the top of each loaf with a thick layer of topping. Let stand, uncovered, 20 minutes, until dough rises level with the tops of the pans.

7. Twenty minutes before baking, preheat the oven at 375°F. Place the pans on a rack in the center of the oven and bake 45 to 50 minutes or until brown and the loaves sound hollow when tapped with your finger. Transfer the loaves to a cooling rack. Cool completely before slicing.

Wild Rice–Molasses Bread

Makes 2 round loaves

1¼ cups warm water (105° to 115°F)

2 tablespoons (2 packages) active dry yeast

Pinch of brown sugar

1 cup warm milk (105° to 115°F)

½ cup walnut oil or melted butter

½ cup unsulfured light molasses

1½ cups cooked wild rice (see Note)

2½ teaspoons salt

2½ cups whole-wheat flour

About 4½ cups unbleached all-purpose flour or bread flour

This whole-grain loaf is light, yet chewy and as soul-satisfying as good bread gets. Add the flour judiciously to keep the dough very soft. For best results, use an unsulfured light molasses, which is light and sweet, rather than the strong blackstrap variety. Enjoy this bread with dinner, for sandwiches the next day, or toasted with soft cheese. To make this bread in a bread machine, see page 452.

1. Pour the warm water in a small bowl. Sprinkle the yeast and sugar over the surface of the water. Stir to dissolve and let stand at room temperature until foamy, about 10 minutes.

2. In a large bowl using a whisk or in the work bowl of a heavy-duty electric mixer fitted with the paddle attachment, combine the milk, oil or butter, molasses, wild rice, salt, and whole-wheat flour. Add the yeast mixture. Beat hard for 3 minutes, or until smooth. Add the unbleached flour, ½ cup at a time, until a soft dough that just clears the sides of the bowl is formed. Switch to a wooden spoon when necessary if mixing by hand.

3. Turn the dough out onto a well-floured work surface and knead until firm, yet quite soft and still springy, about 5 minutes, dusting with the flour 1 tablespoon at a time as needed to prevent sticking. The dough will retain a tacky quality because of the whole-grain flour. Do not add too much flour, or the dough will be hard and the bread will be dry.

If kneading by machine, switch from the paddle to the dough hook and knead for 4 to 5 minutes, or until the dough is smooth and springy and springs back when pressed. If desired, transfer the dough to a floured surface and knead briefly by hand.

4. Place the dough in a greased deep container. Turn once to coat the top and cover with plastic wrap. Let rise at room temperature until doubled in bulk, 1½ to 2 hours. Do not worry if rising takes a bit longer.

5. Gently deflate the dough. Turn the dough out onto a lightly floured work surface. Grease or parchment-line a baking sheet. Divide the dough into 2 equal portions. Form the dough into tight round loaves and place on the baking sheet. Cover loosely with plastic wrap and let rise until doubled in bulk, 40 to 50 minutes.

6. Twenty minutes before baking, preheat the oven to 375°F. Using a serrated knife, gently slash the top of the loaves with 3 parallel cuts no deeper than ¼ inch. Put the baking sheet on the center rack and bake 40 to 45 minutes, until the loaves are brown and sound hollow when tapped with your finger. Transfer from the pans immediately to cooling racks.

NOTE: *To cook wild rice, bring 1½ cups water to a rolling boil in a medium saucepan over high heat. Add ¾ cup wild rice. Bring back to a rolling boil. Cover tightly and reduce the heat to the lowest setting. Cook 55 minutes for paddy-cultivated rice, 30 minutes for hand-harvested rice, or until the rice is tender and all liquid has been absorbed. Set aside to cool or refrigerate up to 3 days. Makes about 1½ to 2 cups cooked rice.*

Wild Rice

Sometimes called the "gourmet grain," wild rice is not really a rice but the seed of an aquatic grass native to the Great Lakes region. Delicious on its own or in combination with other rices, wild rice is chewy with a strong woodsy flavor. It is an excellent addition to breads and quick breads, scones, muffins, and pancakes. Each brand of wild rice has its own particular taste, so if you had a brand that was a bit too strong for your palate, experiment with others. For a milder taste use hand-harvested wild rice, so labeled on the package. Some wild rice is still grown and harvested by hand in lakes by Native Americans in the traditional manner. The harvesting of wild rice takes place in Minnesota in late August and early September, for example. Local Chippewa tribes process the rice using traditional techniques, such as parching the grains over an open fire. This grain has very large uneven kernels with a rich, sweet flavor and soft texture. Hand-harvested wild rice is never black; this distinguishes it from cultivated paddy rice, which turns black when it is left out in the sun to cure. Most wild rice, however, is cultivated in paddies, with California the biggest producer. Clear Lake and Sutter County produce good hybrids that can be recognized by their dark, shiny kernels. They are readily available in supermarkets. Other varieties are available by mail order (see page 471).

Seven-Grain Honey Bread

Makes three medium round or two 9-by-5-inch loaves

1½ cups boiling water

1 cup seven-grain cereal

¼ cup warm water (105° to 115°F)

1½ tablespoons (1½ packages) active dry yeast

Pinch of sugar

¼ cup warm buttermilk (105° to 115°F)

⅓ cup honey, preferably local

3 tablespoons corn or other vegetable oil

2 tablespoons unsalted butter, melted

3 large eggs, at room temperature

1 tablespoon salt

4½ to 5 cups unbleached all-purpose flour or bread flour

The commercial seven-grain cereal blend of cracked wheat, rye, oats, barley, millet, flax, and corn makes a delicious bread. If possible, use a local honey. This is a light, even-textured bread that is excellent for sandwich making.

1. In a small bowl, pour the boiling water over the seven-grain cereal. Let stand for 1 hour to soften and allow the mixture to cool to room temperature.

2. Pour the warm water in a small bowl. Sprinkle the yeast and sugar over the surface of the water. Stir to dissolve and let stand at room temperature until foamy, about 10 minutes.

3. In a large bowl using a whisk, or in the work bowl of a heavy-duty electric mixer fitted with the paddle attachment, combine the buttermilk, honey, oil, butter, eggs, salt, and 1 cup of the flour. Beat hard until smooth, about 1 minute. Add the cereal, yeast mixture and the remaining flour, ½ cup at a time, until a soft, sticky dough that just clears the sides of the bowl is formed. Switch to a wooden spoon when necessary if mixing by hand. This dough may also be mixed in a heavy-duty electric mixer, if desired.

4. Turn the dough out onto a lightly floured work surface and knead until soft and springy, about 4 minutes, adding the flour 1 tablespoon at a time as needed to prevent sticking. The dough will be nubby and slightly tacky.

If kneading by machine, switch from the paddle to the dough hook and knead for 3 to 4 minutes, or until the dough is smooth and springy and springs back when pressed. If desired, transfer the dough to a floured surface and knead briefly by hand.

5. Place the dough in a greased deep container. Turn the dough once to coat the top and cover with plastic wrap. Let rise at room temperature until doubled in bulk, 1 to 1¼ hours.

6. Gently deflate the dough. Turn the dough out onto a floured work surface. Grease or parchment-line a baking sheet or grease two 9-by-5-inch clay or metal loaf pans. Divide the dough into 3 equal portions and

add walnuts

form into round loaves. Or divide into 2 equal portions and form into 9-by-5-inch loaves. Put the round loaves on the baking sheet; put the standard loaves in the loaf pans. Cover loosely with plastic wrap and let rise at room temperature until doubled in bulk, 30 to 40 minutes.

7. Twenty minutes before baking, preheat the oven to 375°F. Place the pans on a rack in the center of the oven and bake for 35 to 40 minutes or until golden brown and hollow sounding when tapped. Transfer the loaves immediately to cooling racks. Cool completely before slicing.

TRADITIONAL ROOTS:
Country Hearth Breads

Country breads are a combination of the simplest ingredients: flour, water, salt, and leavening. For these breads, the longer the rise, the better the flavor and texture of the baked loaf. This slow rise is achieved by letting the bread rise at a cool room temperature rather than in a warm place.

Many of these breads utilize a starter or sponge, which is simply flour, water, and sometimes a small amount of yeast combined and allowed to ferment to leaven the dough. Starters give strength to weak flours and produce a wonderful aroma and crumb under a characteristically thick crust. A starter can produce a loaf with a tang ranging from a slightly sour taste to the sharp bite of true San Francisco sourdough, depending on the length of time it ferments.

The secret to producing crusty hearth bread in a home oven is to bake on a ceramic baking stone. Some bakers also place a second stone on the topmost shelf to further simulate a brick oven. Breads may be baked directly on the stone or on baking sheets or on pans placed on the stone. Avoid placing doughs that drip butter or sugar on the stone's porous surface, as drips burn quickly and will produce a bitter-smelling smoke-filled oven and stains that cannot be cleaned.

Baking Country Bread in a Dutch Oven

Country bread baked in a Dutch oven is a real taste treat. The crust is exceptionally thin and crisp and the crumb sweetly fragrant. This bread is reminiscent of that baked outdoors by early American mountain sheepherders. Whether you are rafting the Colorado, camping in the Sierra or the Alleghenies, or picnicking in the backyard, the combination of hot cast-iron radiant heat from all sides, glowing coals, and fresh air contributes to a loaf similar in consistency to one baked in an enclosed outdoor oven.

Butter the inside of a 12-inch (6-quart) seasoned cast-iron Dutch oven cooking pot. Line the bottom with parchment, if desired. Add a ball of dough at any point in its rising cycle. Cover the pot with the lid and let the dough rise at room temperature until doubled in bulk, about 1½ hours. Make a wood and/or charcoal fire, setting aside some larger hot coals. Place the Dutch oven on a grill or balance it on three stones ½ inch above a ring of 6 to 8 evenly spaced hot coals. Set 12 to 16 large coals directly on the pot lid around the edges and in the middle. This allows even heat distribution from the top and the bottom of the oven. Fan coals periodically. Check the bread after 35 minutes. Take care: the handle will be very hot. Use a pair of pliers to lift off the lid and wear heatproof mitts to avoid burns. Bake for a total of 45 to 50 minutes, or until the bread is golden brown, crisp, and sounds hollow when tapped with your finger. Remove the loaf carefully from the oven using the oven mitts. Cool before serving.

Farmstead Sourdough Bread

Makes two 9-by-5-inch loaves

1½ cups warm water
(105° to 115°F)

1 tablespoon (1 pack-
age) active dry yeast

1 tablespoon sugar

1 cup Classic
Sourdough Starter
(see page 120)

8 tablespoons
(1 stick) unsalted
butter, melted

1 tablespoon salt

5½ to 6 cups unbleached all-
purpose flour or
bread flour

¼ cup fine yellow or
white cornmeal, for
sprinkling

Before the invention of commercial yeast, bakers used starters to make breads rise. American settlers and pioneers kept naturally fermenting sourdough starters on hand to make pancakes and biscuits as well as bread. While most sourdough breads are free-form, this recipe is designed to be baked in two large loaf pans. To make a similar bread in a bread machine, see page 453.

1. Pour ½ cup of the warm water in a small bowl. Sprinkle the yeast and a pinch of the sugar over the surface of the water. Stir to dissolve and let stand at room temperature until foamy, about 10 minutes.

2. In a large bowl using a whisk or in the bowl of a heavy-duty electric mixer fitted with the paddle attachment, combine the sourdough starter, the remaining water, sugar, melted butter, salt, and 3 cups of the flour. Beat until smooth, about 1 minute. Add the yeast mixture and beat for 1 minute more. Add the remaining flour, ½ cup at a time, until a soft shaggy dough that just clears the sides of the bowl is formed. Switch to a wooden spoon when necessary if making by hand.

3. Turn the dough out onto a lightly floured work surface and knead until smooth and elastic, 1 to 2 minutes for a machine-mixed dough and 3 to 4 minutes for a hand-mixed dough, dusting with flour only 1 tablespoon at a time, just enough as needed to prevent sticking.

If kneading by machine, switch from the paddle to the dough hook and knead for 3 to 4 minutes, or until the dough is smooth and springy and springs back when pressed. If desired, transfer the dough to a floured surface and knead briefly by hand.

4. Place the dough in a greased deep container. Turn once to coat the top and cover with plastic wrap. Let rise at room temperature until doubled in bulk, 1 to 1½ hours.

5. Gently deflate the dough. Lightly grease the loaf pans (use clay loaf pans if you have them), and sprinkle with the cornmeal. Turn the dough out onto a lightly floured work surface. Divide the dough into 2 equal portions. Shape the portions into rectangular loaves and place in the pans. Cover loosely with plastic wrap and let rise until doubled in bulk, and the dough rises about 1 inch above the rim of the pans, about 1 hour.

6. Twenty minutes before baking, preheat the oven to 350°F. Place the pans on a rack in the center of the oven and bake 35 to 40 minutes (10 minutes longer in clay pans), or until the tops are golden brown, the sides slightly contracted from the pan, and the loaves sound hollow when tapped with your finger. Transfer the loaves immediately to a cooling rack. Cool completely before slicing.

VARIATIONS: *Add 1 to 2 cups raisins or dried blueberries, or 1 cup granola to the dough in Step 2.*

CLASSIC SOURDOUGH STARTER

Makes 3 cups

2 cups lukewarm water (90°F to 100°F)

1 teaspoon active dry yeast, or ½ teaspoon instant yeast, or ⅓ of a .06 ounce cake of fresh yeast

1 tablespoon sugar or honey

¼ cup nonfat dry milk, dry goat milk, or buttermilk powder

⅓ cup plain yogurt

2 cups bread flour

1. Pour the warm water into a medium bowl. Sprinkle the yeast, sugar, and milk powder over the surface of the warm water. Stir with a large whisk to dissolve. Stir in the yogurt, then add the flour and beat until well blended. Transfer to a glass jar, ceramic crock, or plastic container; cover loosely with plastic wrap or a double thickness of cheesecloth and let stand at warm room temperature for at least 48 hours, whisking the mixture 2 times each day, or up to 4 days depending on how sour you wish the starter. It will be bubbly and begin to ferment. A clear liquid will form on the top; stir it back in. On the fourth day, feed with ¼ cup water and ⅓ cup flour, let stand overnight, then store in the refrigerator, loosely covered. Feed the starter every 2 weeks.

2. Bring to room temperature before using. Remove the amount of starter needed for the sourdough bread. Add 1 cup flour and ½ cup nonfat milk to the remaining starter, stirring to incorporate. Let stand at room temperature for 1 day to begin fermenting again, then refrigerate. The starter improves with age. If a pinkish color or strong aroma develops, indicating undesirable airborne pathogens, discard immediately and start anew.

SOURDOUGH STARTER FROM A COMMERCIAL SOURDOUGH STRAIN

Makes 1¼ cups

1 package (½ ounce) commercial dry sourdough starter

1 cup bread flour

1 tablespoon nonfat dry milk, dry goat milk, or buttermilk powder

¾ cup warm water (90° to 100°F)

In a medium bowl, combine the packaged starter with the flour and dry milk. Whisk in the warm water until smooth. Transfer to a glass jar or crock; cover loosely with plastic wrap, and let stand at room temperature 48 hours, stirring the mixture 2 to 3 times each day. It will be bubbly and begin to ferment. Follow the instructions from the Classic Sourdough Starter recipe for storing and feeding. Store in the refrigerator, loosely covered.

Using a Baking Stone

The best way to bake crusty bread in a home oven is to use an unglazed clay baking stone on the lowest rack in an electric oven or on the oven floor in a gas range. Bread may be baked directly on the stone or on baking sheets placed on the stone. Some bakers also place a second stone on the topmost shelf to further imitate a baker's brick oven. (Doughs that would drip butter or sugar, however, should not be placed directly on the stone; the drips burn quickly and produce a bitter smoke-filled oven and stains that cannot be scrubbed clean.) Baking stones need to be preheated for 20 minutes, usually at 425° to 450°F.

Use commercial pizza stones sold in gourmet shops, kiln shelves from a pottery supply store, or unglazed 6-inch-square quarry tiles. Pizza stones are available in two round sizes, 12 inches and 16 inches, and as a 12-by-14-inch rectangle. They are usually preheated for 20 to 30 minutes at a very high temperature, 450° to 500°F. You may also use the base of La Cloche (see page 133) baked with or without the top, as a stone. Always leave two inches of air space between the stone and the oven walls for heat to circulate. The stone will produce a steady, moderately radiating heat that encourages oven spring and good crust formation.

Italian Olive Oil Bread

Makes 2 medium round loaves

Sponge

1 cup lukewarm water
(about 100°F)

1 cup lukewarm milk
(about 100°F)

1½ teaspoons active
dry yeast

3 cups fine whole-
wheat flour,
preferably stone
ground

Dough

1 teaspoon active dry
yeast

1 tablespoon salt

¼ cup olive oil

¼ cup wheat bran,
raw wheat germ,
or Roman Meal
Cream of Rye cereal

2¼ to 2½ cups unbleached
all-purpose flour or
bread flour

Unbleached all-
purpose flour or
bread flour,
for dusting

Coarse-grind
yellow cornmeal
or semolina,
for sprinkling

This is my *pane casalingo*, a good whole-wheat loaf in the Italian tradition. In Italy, daily loaves made with a sponge starter come in many rustic guises, from the simple round *pagnotta* or *ruota*, *treccia* (braid), *quattrocorna* (four horns), and *corona* (crown). To make this bread in a bread machine, see page 447.

1. To prepare the sponge: In a large bowl, pour in the lukewarm water and milk. Sprinkle the yeast over the surface of the water and milk. Stir to dissolve. Add the flour and beat with a whisk until smooth. The starter will be thick and sticky. Cover loosely with a few layers of cheese-cloth and let stand at cool room temperature 8 to 12 hours. It will be bubbly and pleasantly fermented. (This sponge can be stored up to 1 week in the refrigerator before using, if necessary.)

2. In a large bowl using a whisk or in the bowl of a heavy-duty electric mixer fitted with the paddle attachment, combine the yeast, salt, oil, bran, wheat germ or rye flakes, and ½ cup of the unbleached flour with the sponge. Beat hard with a wooden spoon for 2 minutes, or for 1 minute with the paddle attachment. Add the remaining flour, ½ cup at a time, until a sticky dough that clears the sides of the bowl is formed. Switch to a wooden spoon when necessary if making by hand.

3. Turn the dough out onto a lightly floured work surface and knead vigorously until very elastic, yet still moist and tacky, about 3 minutes. This is important for a good, light texture. Slam the dough hard against the work surface to develop the gluten. Set aside, uncovered, 5 to 10 minutes to relax. Knead again for 2 to 3 minutes, and the sticky dough will smooth out without any extra flour.

If kneading by machine, switch from the paddle to the dough hook and knead for 5 to 6 minutes, letting the dough relax halfway through kneading, or until the dough is smooth and springy and springs back when pressed. If desired, transfer the dough to a floured surface and knead briefly by hand.

4. Place the dough in a greased deep container. Cover with plastic wrap and let rise at room temperature until tripled in bulk, for 3 hours to overnight.

5. Gently deflate the dough. Turn the dough out onto a lightly floured work surface. Grease or parchment-line a baking sheet and sprinkle with cornmeal or semolina. Divide the dough into 2 equal portions. Knead each portion lightly into rounds and flatten slightly. Dust lightly all over with flour. Place, the dough smooth side up, on the baking sheet. Let rise, uncovered, until soft and springy, about 1 hour.

6. Twenty minutes before baking, preheat the oven to 425°F, with a baking stone, if desired. Using a serrated knife, slash the loaves with 4 strokes to form a diamond design no more than ¼ inch deep. Place the baking sheet in the oven, directly on the baking stone, if desired, and bake 15 minutes. Reduce the oven thermostat to 375°F and continue to bake 25 to 30 minutes more, or until golden brown and crusty and the loaves sound hollow when tapped with your finger. Transfer the loaves immediately to a cooling rack. Cool completely before slicing.

Semolina Sesame Seed Twist

Makes 2 large twists

Sponge

- 1 tablespoon (1 package) active dry yeast
- 3 cups lukewarm water (100°F)
- 2 cups fine semolina flour
- 2 cups unbleached all-purpose flour or bread flour

Dough

- 1 tablespoon salt
- 3 tablespoons olive oil
- 1 cup fine semolina flour
- 2½ to 3 cups unbleached all-purpose flour or bread flour

- Fine semolina flour, for sprinkling
- 1 large egg beaten with 1 teaspoon water, for glaze
- ¼ cup sesame seeds, for sprinkling
- 3 tablespoons olive oil, for drizzling

When I was a child, supermarkets were closed on Sundays, so after church, my mother and I would stop by the neighborhood Jewish delicatessen. One of my favorite loaves was a thick, oblong Italian bread coated with sesame seeds. This bread is shaped into many traditional forms, such as a twist, a crown, or an **S**. Use the cream-colored semolina flour milled for making pasta for this loaf. If you find this grind too coarse, whirl it in the food processor until silky. Do not use the coarse semolina meal or farina; save that for sprinkling like cornmeal. Or substitute canary-yellow durum flour, which contains the bran and germ. The bread is best eaten the day it is made; it should be frozen if kept beyond that point. This bread is also excellent made in the bread machine (page 435).

1. To prepare the sponge: In a large bowl or plastic bucket, whisk together the yeast, lukewarm water, and flours. Beat hard until smooth, about 30 seconds. Cover loosely with plastic wrap and let the sponge rise at room temperature until foamy and at least doubled in bulk, about 3 hours.

2. To prepare the dough: In a large bowl with a whisk or in the work bowl of a heavy-duty electric mixer fitted with the paddle attachment, combine the salt, olive oil, semolina flour, ½ cup of the unbleached flour, and the sponge. Beat until smooth, 1 minute. Add the remaining flour, ½ cup at a time, until a soft dough that just clears the sides of the bowl is formed. Switch to a wooden spoon when necessary if making by hand.

3. Turn the dough out onto a lightly floured work surface and knead vigorously until soft and springy, about 5 minutes, dusting with flour only 1 tablespoon at a time as needed to prevent sticking.

If kneading by machine, switch from the paddle to the dough hook and knead for 5 to 6 minutes, or until the dough is smooth and springy and springs back when pressed. If desired, transfer the dough to a floured surface and knead briefly by hand. It is important that this dough be quite soft and springy, yet not sticky, and able to hold its own shape.

4. Place the dough in a deep container brushed lightly with olive oil. Turn once to coat and cover with plastic wrap. Let rise at room temperature until tripled in bulk, 2 to 3 hours. Gently deflate the dough and let rise again until doubled in bulk, about 1 hour.

5. Gently deflate the dough. Turn the dough out onto a lightly floured work surface. Grease or parchment-line a baking sheet and sprinkle with semolina flour. Divide into 2 equal portions. With your palms, roll 1 portion out into a log about 1 yard long. Twist the entire log and leave on the work surface as the base. Twist the second portion and attach the 2 twisted logs at one end. Loop one log around the other 4 or 5 times to form a fat, twisted loaf. Pinch the ends to seal. Transfer the loaf to the baking sheet, tucking the ends under to make a high, tightly twisted loaf. Repeat with the remaining portions to form the second loaf. Cover loosely with plastic wrap and let rise at room temperature until almost doubled in bulk, about 1 hour.

6. Twenty minutes before baking, preheat the oven to 425°F, with a baking stone, if desired. Gently brush the surfaces with the egg glaze and sprinkle the loaves heavily with the sesame seeds. Using a serrated knife, slash decoratively each loaf several places along its length about ½ inch deep. Drizzle each slash with olive oil. Place the baking sheet on the center rack and bake for 15 minutes. Reduce the oven thermostat to 375°F and bake 25 to 30 minutes longer, or until golden brown and crusty and the loaves sound hollow when tapped with your finger. Transfer the loaves immediately to a cooling rack. Cool completely before slicing.

Semolina

The finest white flours are ground exclusively from the endosperm of whole-grain wheat. Cream-colored semolina flour, also known as durure flour, is the finely ground endosperm of durum wheat. It makes a delicious, high-protein addition to Italian-style breads. Semolina flour is not the same as semolina meal, which is a coarse-ground cereal like farina (which is the ground endosperm of spring or winter wheat) or Wheatina (which is ground whole-grain wheat) and is used in a manner similar to coarse cornmeal.

Vienna Bread

Makes 3 oval loaves

Sponge

1 cup warm water
  (105° to 115°F)

1½ tablespoons
  (1½ packages)
  active dry yeast

1 tablespoon sugar

1 cup warm milk
  (105° to 115°F)

2 cups unbleached
  all-purpose flour or
  bread flour

Dough

1 tablespoon salt

3 tablespoons unsalted
  butter, melted and
  cooled

3½ to 4 cups unbleached
  all-purpose flour or
  bread flour

Rich Egg Glaze
  (page 52)

3 tablespoons sesame
  seeds

Vienna Bread is a crusty French-style loaf with the flavorful qualities of milk and a bit of butter added. It is a versatile daily bread, good for sandwiches, French toast, or soaking up meat juices. It stays fresh for two to three days at room temperature.

1. To make the sponge: In a large bowl using a whisk or in the work bowl of a heavy-duty electric mixer fitted with the paddle attachment, pour in the warm water. Combine the yeast, sugar, milk, and flour. Beat hard until smooth and creamy, 1 minute. Cover loosely with plastic wrap and let the sponge rise at room temperature until foamy or doubled in bulk, about 1 hour.

2. To make the dough: Add the salt, butter, and 1 cup of the flour to the sponge. Beat for 1 minute. Add the remaining flour, ½ cup at a time, until a soft dough that just clears the sides of the bowl is formed.

3. Turn the dough out onto a lightly floured work surface and knead until smooth and springy, about 4 minutes, dusting with flour only 1 tablespoon at a time as needed to prevent sticking.

If kneading by machine, switch from the paddle to the dough hook and knead for 3 to 4 minutes, or until the dough is smooth and springy and springs back when pressed. If desired, transfer the dough to a floured surface and knead briefly by hand. The dough should be firm enough to hold its own shape.

4. Place the dough in a greased deep container. Turn once to coat the top and cover with plastic wrap. Let rise at room temperature until the dough is doubled or tripled in bulk, about 2 hours.

5. Turn the dough out onto a lightly floured work surface. Grease or parchment-line a baking sheet. Divide the dough into 3 equal portions. Shape each portion into a fat oval loaf. Taper the ends by pinching them firmly. Place the loaves seam side down on the baking sheet. Cover loosely with plastic wrap and let rise until almost doubled in bulk, about 1 hour.

6. Twenty minutes before baking, preheat the oven to 425°F, with a baking stone, if desired. Using a serrated knife, slash decoratively the top of the loaves with 3 parallel gashes no more than ¼ inch deep. Pinch the ends gently to redefine the tapering. Brush the dough gently with the egg glaze and sprinkle with the sesame seeds. Place the baking sheet on a rack in the center of the oven and bake for 10 minutes. Reduce the thermostat to 375°F and bake another 25 to 30 minutes, or until brown and crusty and the loaves sound hollow when tapped with your fingers. Transfer the loaves immediately to a cooling rack. Remove the loaves immediately to a cooling rack. Cool before serving.

BAKER'S WISDOM
The Sponge Method

A sponge, or starter, allows for an initial period of fermentation that begins to develop the gluten and gives the bread a fine texture and distinctive flavor similar to a mellow sourdough. Yeast, a pinch of sugar, a portion of the total liquid, and some flour are beaten with a whisk until creamy and batterlike, covered loosely, and allowed to rise at room temperature until bubbly, usually 1 hour to overnight, depending on the kind of bread. Any salt or fat required by the recipe are added with the remaining ingredients in the later stages when the dough is formed. The dough is mixed, risen, formed, and baked as in any other bread recipe.

Pain de Campagne

Makes 1 large or 2 medium round loaves

Starter

- 1 tablespoon (1 package) active dry yeast
- ½ cup whole-wheat flour
- ½ cup lukewarm water (90° to 100°F)

Sponge

- 2 cups lukewarm water (90° to 100°F)
- 1½ cups unbleached all-purpose flour or bread flour
- 1½ cups whole-wheat flour

Dough

- 3½ to 4 cups unbleached all-purpose flour or bread flour
- 4 teaspoons salt
- 1 large egg beaten with 2 teaspoons water, for glazing

This whole-wheat country loaf is the home-style version of *boule de Poîlane.* The Boulangerie de Poîlane at 8, rue du Cherche-Midi is perhaps the most famous bakery in Paris, on the site of Présmontrés, a twelfth-century convent. Steep winding stairs descend to the vaulted cellar where the bread is mixed, rises, and is baked around the clock in brick ovens. This big round loaf has been made in Paris since the Middle Ages. It is the flavor of France, utilizing the age-old baking wisdom of *la technique,* which brings out the best flavors in bread. The whole-grain bread is traditionally decorated with a bunch of grapes made of dough. A healthful bread with no fat, it is baked to a deep brown on the third day after it is first mixed. It has a chewy texture and complements both elegant and casual meals. Because it uses a starter, this loaf will stay moist for two to three days at room temperature. To make this bread in a bread machine, see page 454.

1. Day One: To make the starter, place the yeast and whole-wheat flour in a deep bowl or a plastic 4-quart bucket with a lid. Add the water and whisk hard until a smooth batter is formed. Cover and let stand at room temperature until foamy and it begins to ferment, about 24 hours.

2. Day Two: To make the sponge, add 2 cups warm water to the starter. Whisk to combine. Add the unbleached and the whole-wheat flours alternately, 1 cup at a time, changing to a wooden spoon when necessary, until a smooth batter is formed. The sponge will be very wet. Scrape down the sides of the bowl, cover with plastic wrap, and let rise again at room temperature for about 24 hours.

3. Day Three: To make the bread dough, stir down the sponge with a wooden spoon. Add 1 cup of the unbleached flour and the salt. Gradually add most of the remaining flour, ½ cup at a time, to make a firm and resilient dough.

4. Turn the dough out onto a lightly floured work surface and knead until smooth, slightly tacky, and springy, about 5 to 7 minutes, dusting with flour only 1 tablespoon at a time as needed to prevent sticking. The dough will form little blisters under the surface when ready to rise.

If kneading by machine, switch from the paddle to the dough hook and knead for 6 to 7 minutes, or until the dough is smooth and springy and springs back when pressed. If desired, transfer the dough to a floured surface and knead briefly by hand.

5. Place the dough in a greased deep container. Turn to coat the top of the dough once. Cover tightly with plastic wrap. Let rise at room temperature until fully doubled in bulk, 1½ to 2 hours.

6. Gently deflate the dough. Turn the dough out onto a lightly floured work surface. Grease or parchment-line a baking sheet. Reserve a small amount of the dough to use as decoration, if desired. Shape the remaining dough into a tight round and place it on the baking sheet. (Or shape to fit a long or round cloth-lined basket lightly dusted with flour; cover lightly with plastic wrap. Let rise about 1 hour before turning the dough out onto a prepared baking sheet or onto a hot baking stone.) Cover the dough loosely with plastic wrap and let rise about 1 hour at room temperature.

7. Twenty minutes before baking, preheat the oven to 425°F, with a baking stone placed on the center rack, if desired. Using a serrated knife, slash the loaf decoratively. Brush the entire surface of the loaf with the glaze. If you have reserved dough for decoration, form into a bunch of grapes, a leaf or two and a few tendrils. It is important that any decoration made from reserved dough be applied after the loaf has had its final rise and glazing. Glaze the decoration after applying.

8. Place the baking sheet on a rack in the center of the oven and bake for 40 to 45 minutes, or until the loaves are browned, crisp, and sound hollow when tapped with your finger. Transfer the loaves immediately to a cooling rack. Cool completely before slicing.

Pain de Campagnard

Makes 2 oblong loaves

Starter

2 teaspoons active dry yeast

1 cup stone-ground whole-wheat flour

1 cup lukewarm water (90° to 100°F)

Sponge

1½ cups lukewarm water (90° to 100°F)

2 cups unbleached all-purpose flour or bread flour

Dough

¼ cup wheat berries

Boiling water, to cover

1 teaspoon active dry yeast

⅓ cup medium or pumpernickel rye flour

2 to 2¼ cups unbleached all-purpose flour or bread flour

1 tablespoon salt

Glaze

1 teaspoon cornstarch

⅓ cup water

Here is a superb bread similar to the earthy wheat-rye loaves once made at harvest time in the French countryside. It takes three days from start to finish, but the amount of hands-on work totals about half an hour and the rest is devoted to allowing the natural fermentation to work its magic. Organic flours and pure spring water will give the best results. Note that the starter must begin fermenting two days before mixing the dough and baking.

1. Day One: To prepare the starter, place the yeast and whole-wheat flour in a deep bowl or a plastic 2-quart bucket with a lid. Add the lukewarm water and whisk hard until a smooth batter is formed. Cover and let stand at room temperature for about 24 hours. The starter will foam and begin to ferment.

2. Day Two: To prepare the sponge, alternately add the lukewarm water and the unbleached flour to the starter in 3 additions. Whisk to combine, changing to a wooden spoon if necessary, beating until a smooth batter is formed. The sponge will be very sticky. Scrape down the sides of the bowl. Cover with plastic wrap and let stand again at room temperature until doubled in bulk, 12 to 24 hours. The sponge will be thick and have a pleasant sour aroma.

3. Day Three: To prepare the dough, in a small bowl, cover the wheat berries with boiling water. Cover with plastic wrap and let soak 4 hours at room temperature. When the wheat berries are ready, stir down the sponge with a wooden spoon. Sprinkle it with the yeast mixture. Drain the wheat berries and add the berries, rye flour, 1 cup unbleached flour, and salt to the sponge. Beat hard until well combined, about 1 minute. Add the remaining unbleached flour, ½ cup at a time, until a firm, resilient dough is formed.

4. Turn the dough out onto a lightly floured work surface and knead until smooth, slightly tacky, and springy, 4 to 6 minutes, dusting with flour only 1 tablespoon at a time as needed to prevent sticking.

If kneading by machine, switch from the paddle to the dough hook and knead for 4 to 6 minutes, or until the dough is smooth and springy and springs back when pressed. If desired, transfer the dough to a floured surface and knead briefly by hand. Keep the dough moist, because too much flour make the baked bread too dry.

5. Place the dough in a greased deep container. Turn once to coat the top and cover with plastic wrap. Let rise at room temperature until doubled in bulk, 2 to 2½ hours.

6. Gently deflate the dough. Turn the dough out onto a lightly floured work surface. Grease or parchment-line a baking sheet. Divide the dough into 2 equal portions. Pat each into a fat, uneven rectangle. Roll up each rectangle, starting at a short end, into a tight cylinder. Pinch together the seams, tuck them under, and taper the ends to form an oblong shape that is fatter in the middle than at the ends. Place the loaves on the baking sheet. Cover the dough loosely with floured plastic wrap and let rise at room temperature until doubled in bulk, 1 to 1½ hours.

7. Twenty minutes before baking, preheat the oven to 425°F, with a baking stone placed on the lowest rack, if desired. (To produce a crisp crust, about 15 minutes before putting the loaves into the oven, pour hot water into a broiler pan and place the pan on the bottom rack to create steam in the oven for the initial baking period.) Using a serrated knife, slash decoratively with 3 diagonals no more than ¼ inch deep. To prepare the glaze, in a small bowl, whisk together the cornstarch and water and brush the entire surface of each loaf. Place the baking sheet on the center rack of the oven and bake 30 to 35 minutes, or until the loaves are browned, crisp, and sound hollow when tapped with your finger. Halfway through the baking time, the surface of the loaves may be brushed once more with the glaze. Transfer the loaves immediately to a cooling rack. Cool completely before slicing.

Pain de Seigle

Makes 2 round loaves

Starter

1 tablespoon
(1 package) active
dry yeast

1 cup unbleached
all-purpose flour or
bread flour

1 cup lukewarm water
(90° to 100°F)

Sponge

2 cups warm water
(105° to 115°F)

2 tablespoons
molasses

1½ cups medium rye
flour

1½ cups unbleached
all-purpose flour or
bread flour

Dough

1½ teaspoons
(½ package) active
dry yeast

3 tablespoons
vegetable oil

2 tablespoons
molasses

4 teaspoons salt

4 teaspoons caraway
seed

½ cup medium rye
flour

3 to 3½ cups unbleached
all-purpose flour or
bread flour

This French-style sour rye bread is baked after the dough is fermented in stages for three days. The flavor boasts a good tang for sourdough lovers. Because of the starter, this loaf of rye will stay moist at room temperature for about three days. To keep the bread any longer, freeze it.

1. Day One: To prepare the starter, place the yeast and flour in a deep bowl or 4-quart plastic bucket with a lid. Add the water and whisk hard until a smooth batter is formed. Cover the dough with plastic wrap and let stand at room temperature until foamy and it ferments, about 24 hours.

2. Day Two: To prepare the sponge, add the water and molasses to the starter. Whisk to combine. Add the flours 1 cup at a time and beat to form a smooth batter. The sponge will be very wet. Scrape down the sides of bowl. Cover with plastic wrap and let rise again at room temperature about 24 hours.

3. Day Three: To prepare the dough, stir down the sponge with a wooden spoon. Add the yeast, oil, molasses, salt, caraway seed, and rye flour to the sponge and beat hard with a whisk to combine. Add unbleached flour, ½ cup at a time, with a wooden spoon until a soft dough is formed.

4. Turn the dough out onto a lightly floured work surface and knead vigorously for 7 to 10 minutes, dusting with flour only 1 tablespoon at a time as needed to prevent sticking. Knead the dough until soft, springy and does not stick to work surface.

If kneading by machine, switch from the paddle to the dough hook and knead for 5 to 7 minutes, or until the dough is smooth and springy and springs back when pressed. If desired, transfer the dough to a floured surface and knead briefly by hand. The dough should be smooth, yet retain a bit of stickiness.

5. Place the dough in a greased bowl. Turn the dough once to grease the top and cover with plastic wrap. Let rise at room temperature until doubled in bulk, about 1 hour.

Rye flakes or coarse
cornmeal,
for sprinkling

Rich Egg Glaze
(page 52)

6. Gently deflate the dough. Turn the dough out onto a lightly floured work surface. Grease or parchment line a baking sheet and sprinkle liberally with rolled rye or coarse cornmeal. Divide the dough into 2 equal portions. Shape into round or oval loaves. Place the loaves on the baking sheet and turn the dough to coat the bottom and sides. Cover loosely with plastic wrap and let rise at room temperature until puffy and almost doubled in bulk, 45 minutes to 1 hour.

7. Twenty minutes before baking, preheat the oven to 450°F, using a baking stone if desired. Slash the loaves decoratively on the diagonal no more than ½ inch deep. Brush the entire surface of the loaves with the egg glaze. Place the baking sheet on a rack in the center of the oven, reduce the thermostat to 375°F, and bake 40 to 45 minutes, or until brown and crusty and the loaves sound hollow when tapped with your finger. Transfer the loaves immediately to a cooling rack. Cool completely before slicing.

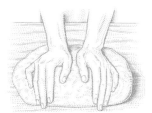

BAKER'S WISDOM
La Cloche

La Cloche is an unglazed clay baking dish with 2-inch sloping sides and a domed cover. It is useful for baking a large crackly-crusted country loaf. To use La Cloche, place the bottom on the lowest oven rack and preheat for 20 minutes at 450°F just as you would a baking stone. While the bottom is heating, soak the top in cold water. Sprinkle the dish with flour, cornmeal, or semolina, and place the dough ball in the center of the dish. Using a serrated knife, slash the top surface decoratively, no more than ¼ inch deep. Cover with the domed cover. Bake as directed in the recipe. About 15 minutes before the bread is done, remove the cover with heavy oven mitts to allow the loaf to brown thoroughly. Continue baking until the bread is golden brown, crisp, and sound hollow when tapped with your finger. Carefully remove the dish from the oven and transfer the loaf to a cooling rack. To clean La Cloche dish, tap out the excess flour and scrub off any stuck-on bits with a brush and water only. Do not use soap, which can impart a taste to the next baked loaf.

Sour Poppy Seed Rye

Makes 2 oblong loaves

Sour Starter

¼ teaspoon active dry yeast

1 cup medium or light rye flour

1 cup lukewarm whole milk, goat milk, or buttermilk (90° to 100°F)

Sponge

1 cup lukewarm water (90° to 100°F)

½ teaspoon active dry yeast

1 cup medium or light rye flour

Dough

1½ teaspoons active dry yeast

Pinch of sugar

¼ cup light molasses

2 tablespoons unsalted butter, melted, or vegetable oil

1 large egg, at room temperature

1 tablespoon salt

1 teaspoon ground coriander

1 heaping tablespoon caraway seeds

1 heaping tablespoon poppy seeds

½ cup rye flakes

3¼ to 3½ cups unbleached all-purpose flour or bread flour

This bread is exceptional. If you love the flavor of sourdough breads, make this immediately. I prepare the sour starter in the morning, the sponge late in the evening, and mix the dough the following morning. I use Roman Meal's Cream of Rye flakes (available in natural-food stores) for extra texture.

1. Day One: To prepare the sourdough starter, put the yeast and flour in a deep bowl or 4-quart plastic bucket with a lid. Add the milk and whisk hard until a smooth batter is formed. Cover the dough with plastic wrap and let stand at room temperature until it is foamy and it ferments, 8 to 12 hours.

2. Day Two: To prepare the sponge, add the lukewarm water and the yeast to the starter. Whisk to combine. Add the flour and beat to form a smooth batter. The sponge will be very wet. Scrape down the sides of the bowl. Cover with plastic wrap and let rest at room temperature 8 to 12 hours.

3. Day Three: To prepare the dough, stir down the sponge with a wooden spoon. Place the sponge in a large bowl using a whisk or in the work bowl of a heavy-duty electric mixer fitted with the paddle attachment. Add the yeast, sugar, molasses, butter or oil, egg, salt, coriander, caraway and poppy seeds, and rye flakes to the sponge and beat hard to combine about, about 1 minute. Add the yeast mixture and 1 cup of the unbleached flour. Beat hard until combined, about 2 minutes more. Add the unbleached flour, ½ cup at a time, until a soft dough that just clears the sides of the bowl is formed.

4. Turn the dough out onto a lightly floured work surface and knead vigorously until it is soft and springy and no longer sticks to the work surface, about 5 minutes, dusting with flour only 1 tablespoon at a time as needed to prevent sticking.

If kneading by machine, switch from the paddle to the dough hook and knead for 4 to 5 minutes, or until the dough is smooth and springy and springs back when pressed. If desired, transfer the dough to a floured surface and knead briefly by hand. The dough will be smooth, yet feel rather dense and remain a little sticky.

Rye flakes or
coarse-grind yellow
cornmeal,
for sprinkling

1 large egg white
beaten with
1 tablespoon water,
for glaze

2 to 3 tablespoons sesame
seeds

5. Place the dough in a greased deep container, turn once to coat the top and cover with plastic wrap. Let rise at cool room temperature until doubled in bulk, about 2 hours.

6. Gently deflate the dough. Turn the dough out onto a lightly floured work surface. Grease or parchment-line a baking sheet and sprinkle liberally with rye flakes or cornmeal. Divide the dough into 2 equal portions. Shape each portion into oblong loaves. Place the dough on the baking sheet. Turn the loaves to coat the bottom and part of the sides. Cover loosely with plastic wrap and let rise at room temperature until puffy and almost doubled in bulk, 45 minutes to 1 hour.

7. Twenty minutes before baking, preheat the oven to 425°F, with a baking stone placed on the center rack. Using a serrated knife, slash 5 diagonals down the center of the loaf no more than ½ inch deep. Brush the entire surface of each loaf with the egg glaze and sprinkle with the sesame seeds. Place the baking sheet on the center or lowest rack of the oven, and immediately reduce the oven thermostat to 375°F. Bake 35 to 40 minutes until brown and crusty and the loaves sound hollow when tapped with your finger. Transfer the loaves immediately to a cooling rack. Cool completely before slicing.

SOUR FOUR-SEED RYE: *Add ½ cup each raw pumpkin seeds and sunflower seeds in Step 3. Proceed as directed.*

NATURE'S BOUNTY:
Vegetable, Herb, Cheese, and Nut Breads

Using fresh produce in bread baking is a great way to celebrate the seasons. Besides vegetables and herbs to accent the hearty and complex grain foundation flavors, cheese, nuts, and seeds can also be included. The result is a family of fragrant, unusual, and enticingly flavored country-style breads that pair well with soups, salads, and sandwich fixings.

Use fresh herbs as soon as possible after buying or cutting in your garden, as their flavor languishes with time. Fresh herb breads have a colorful tone and are evenly flecked throughout each slice. Dried herbs also have their place as an accent to other ingredients and fillings.

Cheese can be incorporated into the dough or made into a savory filling, either a single cheese or a combination. Remember, though, that cheese makes bread much moister so adjust the liquid for this. Nuts make breads ever so tasty. The rich oils are released in the heat of the oven, allowing the loaf to take on a character all its own. Firm cured olives bring their warm, salty Mediterranean flavor to doughs. All these ingredients make interesting and exceptionally flavorful breads.

Seeded Dill Rye

Makes two 9-by-5-inch loaves

2 cups warm water (105° to 115°F)

1½ tablespoons (1½ packages) active dry yeast

3 tablespoons light brown sugar

1½ cups rye flour

½ cup instant nonfat dried milk

1 tablespoon dill weed

1 tablespoon dill seed

1 teaspoon caraway seeds

2½ teaspoons salt

3 tablespoons unsalted butter, melted

3½ to 4 cups unbleached all-purpose flour or bread flour

Rich Egg Glaze (page 52; optional)

The umbrella-shaped dill plant is known for the characteristic strong, aromatic flavor it adds to pickled cucumbers and potato salad. It adds an exciting, warm quality to this savory rye bread. Dill is also known as one of the best digestive herbs. I always bake this bread in standard loaves; it is one of the greatest sandwich breads from the home baker.

1. Pour ½ cup of the warm water in a small bowl. Sprinkle the yeast and a pinch of brown sugar over the surface of the water. Stir to dissolve and let stand at room temperature until foamy, about 10 minutes.

2. In a large bowl using a whisk, combine the rye flour, dried milk, remaining brown sugar, dill weed, dill seeds, caraway seeds, and salt. Add the remaining water, butter, and yeast mixture. Beat hard until smooth, about 3 minutes. Add the flour, ½ cup at a time, with a wooden spoon until a shaggy dough is formed.

3. Turn the dough out onto a lightly floured work surface and knead until smooth and silky, about 5 minutes, dusting with flour only 1 tablespoon at a time as needed to prevent sticking.

If kneading by machine, switch from the paddle to the dough hook and knead for 3 to 4 minutes, or until the dough is smooth and springy and springs back when pressed. If desired, transfer the dough to a floured surface and knead briefly by hand.

4. Place the dough in a greased bowl. Turn once to grease the top and cover with plastic wrap. Let rise at room temperature until doubled in bulk, 1 to 1½ hours.

5. Gently deflate dough. Turn the dough out onto a lightly floured work surface. Grease two 9-by-5-inch loaf pans. Divide the dough into 2 equal portions. Shape each portion into loaves and put in the pans. Cover loosely with plastic wrap and let rise to 1 inch above the rim of pans, about 40 minutes. Brush with the egg glaze, if desired, for a dark and glossy crust.

6. Twenty minutes before baking, preheat the oven to 375°F. Place the pans on a rack in the center of the oven and bake for 40 to 45 minutes, or until golden brown and the loaves sound hollow when tapped with your finger. Transfer the loaves to a cooling rack. Cool before slicing.

Buttermilk Potato Bread

Makes two 9-by-5-inch loaves, one large round loaf, or two dozen rolls

1 large russet potato (about ¾ pound)

2 tablespoons (2 packages) active dry yeast

2 tablespoons sugar

1 cup cold buttermilk

2 tablespoons unsalted butter

1 tablespoon salt

6 to 7 cups unbleached all-purpose flour or bread flour

Flour, for dusting or Rich Egg Glaze (page 52) and poppy seeds

The humble potato ranks as one of the world's most important foods. It has sustained humankind during famines, revolutions, and mass migrations. Surprisingly enough, the potato was discovered and brought to Europe only in the 1500s. It was a staple food for the Andean Indians living above eleven thousand feet, where corn would not grow. Yeast thrives on potato starch, and the bread it produces has a characteristically fluffy texture and rather sweet flavor. As with other vegetables, a recently harvested homegrown potato has no rival. The dough may be shaped into one very large round loaf and baked on a stone or in two standard loaves. The dough may also be formed into dinner rolls. To make this in a bread machine, see page 450.

1. Peel the potato and cut it into large pieces. Place the pieces in a saucepan, cover with water, bring to a boil, and cook until soft. Drain, reserving the liquid, and add water as necessary to make 1 cup. Mash the potato and set aside.

2. Warm or cool the potato water to 105° to 115°F. Pour the warm water in a small bowl. Sprinkle the yeast and a pinch of sugar over the surface of the potato water. Stir to combine and let stand at room temperature until foamy, about 10 minutes.

3. In a saucepan, warm buttermilk and butter until the butter melts. Stir in the remaining sugar, salt, and mashed potato. If the potatoes are lumpy, beat until smooth, otherwise there will be lumps in the bread.

4. In a large bowl using a whisk or in the work bowl of a heavy-duty electric mixer combine the yeast and potato mixture with 2 cups flour. Beat hard until smooth, about 3 minutes. Add the flour, ½ cup at a time, with a wooden spoon until a soft dough is formed.

5. Turn the dough out onto a lightly floured work surface and knead about 5 minutes, dusting with flour only 1 tablespoon at a time as needed to produce a smooth and springy dough. Do not let the dough get too dry by adding too much flour.

If kneading by machine, switch from the paddle to the dough hook and knead for 3 to 5 minutes, or until the dough is smooth and springy

and springs back when pressed. If desired, transfer the dough to a floured surface and knead briefly by hand.

6. Place the dough in a greased deep bowl and turn once to grease the top and cover with plastic wrap. Let rise at room temperature until doubled in bulk, about 1 hour. Do not worry if it takes up to 2 hours.

7. Turn the dough out onto a lightly floured work surface. Grease two 9-by-5-inch pans. Divide the dough into 2 equal portions. Shape each portion into a rectangle and roll up into loaves. Place each loaf seam side down into the loaf pans. Cover loosely with plastic wrap and let rise about 30 minutes. Dust with flour or brush with the egg glaze and sprinkle with poppy seeds.

8. Twenty minutes before baking, preheat the oven to 375°F. Place the pan on a rack in the center of the oven and bake for 45 minutes or until loaves are deep brown, have a crisp crust, and the loaves sound hollow when tapped with your finger. Transfer the loaves immediately to a cooling rack. Cool completely before slicing.

BUTTERMILK POTATO ROLLS: *Preheat the oven to 375°F. After turning out the risen dough in Step 7, pat the dough into a rectangle ¾ to 1 inch thick on a lightly floured work surface. Dust the top of the dough lightly with flour. Using a sharp knife, cut the dough into pieces about 2 inches square. Place the squares 1 inch apart on a greased or parchment-lined baking sheet. Cover loosely with plastic wrap and let rise in a warm place for 20 minutes. The rolls will be puffy. Bake in for 25 to 30 minutes, or until golden brown.*

Whole-Wheat Basil Bread

Makes two 9-by-5-inch loaves

½ cup warm water
(105° to 115°F)

1 tablespoon
(1 package)
active dry yeast

Pinch of sugar

1 cup warm buttermilk
(105° to 115°F)

1 cup warm water
(105° to 115°F)

¼ cup honey

4 tablespoons unsalted
butter, melted

5 to 5½ cups whole-wheat
flour

½ cup minced fresh
basil

½ cup pine nuts,
chopped

2½ teaspoons salt

Oil Wash

1 tablespoon butter

1 tablespoon olive oil

1 garlic clove, crushed

Pinch of cayenne

Parmesan cheese,
for sprinkling
(optional)

The air around a garden patch of basil is very sweet indeed; it is a strongly aromatic herb. In this wonderful bread, only fresh basil will give the proper pungent flavor, which is paired with a natural mate, the extravagant pine nut. Serve with any food using fresh or cooked tomato to form a natural trinity.

1. Pour the warm water in a small bowl. Sprinkle the yeast and sugar over the surface of the water. Stir to dissolve and let stand at room temperature until foamy, about 10 minutes.

2. In a large bowl using a whisk or in the work bowl of a heavy-duty electric mixer fitted with a paddle attachment, combine the buttermilk and water. Stir in the honey and melted butter. Place 2 cups flour, the basil, nuts, and salt in a large bowl. Add the milk and the yeast mixtures and beat until smooth, about 3 minutes. Add the flour, ½ cup at a time, with a wooden spoon until a soft dough that just clears the sides of the bowl is formed.

3. Turn the dough out onto a lightly floured work surface and knead until soft, slightly sticky, and very pliable, about 5 minutes, dusting with the flour only 1 tablespoon at a time as needed.

If kneading by machine, switch from the paddle to the dough hook and knead for 3 to 4 minutes, or until the dough is smooth and springy and springs back when pressed. If desired, transfer the dough to a floured surface and knead briefly by hand. Keep the dough on the soft side, because the bread will be lighter this way.

4. Put the dough in a greased deep bowl. Turn the dough once to grease the top and cover with plastic wrap. Let rise at room temperature until doubled in bulk, 1 to 1½ hours. Don't let this dough rise more than double in volume. Gently deflate the dough and let it rise again, if you have time. It will take only half the time to rise the second time.

5. Gently deflate the dough. Turn the dough out onto a lightly floured work surface. Grease two 9-by-5-inch loaf pans. Divide the dough into 2 equal portions. Shape each portion into a loaf and put in the pans. Cover loosely with plastic wrap and let rise again until doubled in bulk, about 30 minutes.

6. Meanwhile, prepare the oil wash: In a small pan, melt the butter and olive oil. Stir in garlic and cayenne. Brush the loaves with the oil wash and sprinkle them with Parmesan cheese, if desired.

7. Twenty minutes before baking preheat the oven to 350°F. Place the pans on the rack in the center of the oven and bake 50 to 60 minutes, or until the loaves are brown and sound hollow when tapped with your finger. Transfer the loaves immediately to a cooling rack. Cool completely before slicing.

Cheddar Cheese Bread with Toasted Sesame Seeds

Makes two 9-by-5-inch or six 5 1/2-by-3-inch loaves

- 1/3 cup sesame seeds
- 2 cups warm water (105° to 115°F)
- 1 tablespoon (1 package) active dry yeast
- Pinch of sugar
- 2 tablespoons vegetable oil
- 2 teaspoons salt
- 2 large eggs, at room temperature
- 5 1/2 to 6 cups unbleached all-purpose flour or bread flour
- 3 cups shredded sharp Cheddar cheese (12 ounces)

The combination of toasted sesame seeds and a nutty-tasting sharp Cheddar cheese is a gustatory delight. The cheese sets into a marbled pattern that is quite beautiful when sliced. This is a recipe adapted from Betsy Oppenneer, a talented baker who reminded me of how dramatic cheese-enhanced country breads are.

1. To toast the sesame seeds: Place them in a small skillet over medium heat. Shaking the pan often, cook until golden brown, about 2 minutes. Immediately remove the seeds from the skillet to a small bowl to cool completely.

2. Pour 1/2 cup of the warm water in a small bowl. Sprinkle the yeast and sugar over the surface of the water. Stir to dissolve and let stand at room temperature until foamy, about 10 minutes.

3. In a large bowl using a whisk or in the work bowl of a heavy-duty electric mixer fitted with the paddle attachment, combine the remaining 1 1/2 cups warm water, oil, salt, eggs, sesame seeds, 2 cups of the flour, and the yeast mixture. Beat hard until smooth, about 1 minute. Add half of the shredded cheese and the remaining flour, 1/2 cup at a time, until a shaggy dough is formed. Switch to a wooden spoon when necessary if making by hand.

4. Turn the dough out onto a lightly floured work surface and knead until smooth and silky, about 4 minutes, dusting with flour only 1 tablespoon at a time as needed to prevent sticking.

If kneading by machine, switch from the paddle to the dough hook and knead for 3 to 4 minutes, or until the dough is smooth and springy and springs back when pressed. If desired, transfer the dough to a floured surface and knead briefly by hand.

5. Place the dough in a greased deep container. Turn once to coat the top and cover with plastic wrap. Let rise at room temperature until doubled in bulk, 1 1/2 to 2 hours.

6. Gently deflate the dough. Turn the dough out onto a lightly floured work surface. Grease two 9-by-5-inch or six 5 1/2-by-3-inch loaf pans.

Pat the dough into a thick, 12-inch-long rectangle. Sprinkle with the remaining cheese, fold the dough around the cheese, and knead gently a few times to distribute the cheese throughout the dough. This will produce the marble effect. Cover the dough with a tea towel or plastic wrap to prevent drying and let rest 5 to 10 minutes on the work surface to relax the dough. Divide the dough into 2 equal portions and shape each portion into a rectangular loaf. Place each loaf seam side down into the loaf pans. Alternatively, divide the dough into 6 equal portions and shape each into a loaf. Place each loaf seam side down into the miniloaf pans. Cover loosely with plastic wrap and let rise until doubled in bulk or 1 inch above the rims of the pans, about 45 minutes.

7. Twenty minutes before baking, preheat the oven to 375°F. Using kitchen shears, gently snip each loaf 5 or 6 times at a 45-degree angle 2 inches deep and down the length of the loaf, to create a pronounced off-center jagged pattern. Place the pans on a rack in the center of the oven and bake 40 to 45 minutes for the standard loaves or 25 to 30 minutes for the miniloaves, or until the loaves are golden brown and sound hollow when tapped with your finger. Transfer the loaves immediately to a cooling rack. Cool completely before slicing.

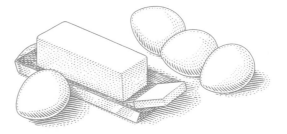

Gruyère Pullman Loaf

Makes one large or two small pullman loaves or two 9-by-5-inch loaves

- ⅓ cup warm water (105° to 115°F)
- 2 tablespoons (2 packages) active dry yeast
- 1 teaspoon sugar
- 1¾ cups warm milk (105° to 115°F)
- 4 tablespoons (½ stick) unsalted butter, melted
- 1 tablespoon salt
- 5 to 5½ cups unbleached all-purpose flour or bread flour
- 1¼ cups grated Gruyère cheese, mixed with 2 tablespoons flour to prevent clumping

The rectangular loaf known as a pullman or as *pain de mie* in French is characterized by its even slices and absence of crust. The pullman pan for home baking comes in a traditional 9-by-5-inch size and a larger 13-by-4-inch size. Both have a fitted lid that slides into place and helps shape the loaf by containing its rising, producing bread with a dense crumb suited to thin slicing for toast, melba toast, and fancy English tea sandwiches. The cheese makes the flavor of this bread exceptional. The dough may also be formed into bread sticks.

1. Pour the warm water in a small bowl. Sprinkle the yeast and sugar over the surface of the water. Stir to dissolve and let stand at room temperature until foamy, about 10 minutes.

2. In a large bowl using a whisk, or in the work bowl of a heavy-duty electric mixer fitted with the paddle attachment, combine the milk and butter. Add the yeast mixture, salt, and 2 cups of flour. Beat until smooth. Continue to add the flour, using a wooden spoon, until stiff. Add the cheese.

3. Turn the dough out onto a lightly floured work surface and knead until smooth, about 5 minutes, dusting with the flour 1 tablespoon at a time as needed to prevent sticking.

If kneading by machine, switch from the paddle to the dough hook and knead for 3 to 4 minutes, or until the dough is smooth and springy and springs back when pressed. If desired, transfer the dough to a floured surface and knead briefly by hand.

4. Place the dough in a greased bowl. Turn once to grease the top and cover with plastic wrap. Let rise at room temperature until doubled in bulk, 1 to 1½ hours.

5. Gently deflate the dough. Turn the dough out onto a lightly floured work surface. Grease 1 large or 2 small pullman pans, or two 9-by-5-inch loaf pans. Roll the dough out to form a 10-by-15-inch rectangle. Roll the dough up tightly in jelly-roll fashion, pinch the seam, and place the loaf seam side down in loaf pan or pans. The dough will fill the pans from one-third to one-half full. Cover the dough with plastic wrap and let rise to fill the pans four-fifths full, about 30 minutes. Grease the covers of the pullman pans and put the covers in place. For standard loaves, grease one side of a baking sheet to cover the pans. Weigh down the baking sheet with a brick.

6. Twenty minutes before baking, preheat the oven to 400°F. Place the pans on a rack in the center of the oven and bake for 25 minutes. Remove the lids and bake another 15 minutes, or until the loaves are brown, solid to the touch and sound hollow when tapped with your finger. Transfer the loaves immediately to a cooling rack. Cool the loaves completely before slicing.

CHEESE BREAD STICKS: *Preheat the oven to 375°F. Divide the dough into 4 equal portions. Divide each portion into 10 to 12 portions. Roll each portion with your palms into a stick about 1 inch thick. Let the dough rest for 5 minutes, then roll to ½ inch thick. Place the sticks on a greased or parchment-lined baking sheet and bake for 25 to 30 minutes, or until golden brown.*

Olive Bread

Makes two round or two 9-by-5-inch loaves

3/4 cup warm water (105° to 115°F)

1 tablespoon (1 package) active dry yeast

Pinch of sugar

1 1/2 cups warm milk (105° to 115°F)

1/3 cup good olive oil

1 1/2 teaspoons salt

5 to 5 1/2 cups unbleached all-purpose flour or bread flour

1 cup Spanish-style pimiento-stuffed green olives, drained, patted dry, and halved

2 cups pitted black olives, drained, patted dry, and halved

Olive trees abound throughout the Mediterranean, where the fruit is a dietary staple. This colorful country loaf is studded with sharp green and mellow black olives. Although traditional European loaves are often baked with the whole olive, I prefer to remove the pits. Serve with egg dishes or as a base for hors d'oeuvre toppings.

1. In a small bowl pour in the warm water. Sprinkle the yeast and sugar over the surface of the water. Stir to dissolve and let stand at room temperature until foamy, about 10 minutes.

2. In a large bowl using a whisk or in the work bowl of a heavy-duty electric mixer fitted with the paddle attachment, combine the milk, olive oil, yeast mixture, salt, and 2 cups of the flour. Beat hard until creamy and smooth, about 1 minute. Add the remaining flour, 1/2 cup at a time, until a soft, shaggy dough that clears the sides of the bowl is formed. Switch to a wooden spoon when necessary if mixing by hand.

3. Turn the dough out onto a lightly floured work surface and knead for 4 minutes, dusting with flour only 1 tablespoon at a time as needed to prevent sticking. The dough should be smooth and springy, but not dry.

If kneading by machine, switch from the paddle to the dough hook and knead for 3 to 4 minutes, or until the dough is smooth and springy and springs back when pressed. If desired, transfer the dough to a floured surface and knead briefly by hand.

4. Place the dough in a greased deep container. Turn the dough once to coat the top and cover with plastic wrap. Let rise at room temperature until doubled in bulk, about 1 1/2 hours.

5. Gently deflate the dough. Turn the dough out onto a lightly floured work surface. Grease or parchment-line a baking sheet or grease two 9-by-5-inch loaf pans. Divide the dough into 2 equal portions. Pat the dough into flat ovals. Scatter a mixture of both kinds of olives evenly over the surface of the dough and press them in lightly. Using a rolling pin, roll the dough to encase the olives. Shape the dough into tight rounds or standard rectangular loaves. Place the dough on the baking sheet or in the loaf pans (clay pans are nice). Cover lightly with plastic wrap and let rise, about 45 minutes.

6. Twenty minutes before baking, preheat the oven to 375°F. Place the sheet or pans on a rack on the center of the oven and bake for 40 to 45 minutes, or until the bread is browned and pulls away from the sides of the pan, and the loaves sound hollow when tapped with your finger. Transfer the loaves immediately to cooling racks. Cool completely before slicing.

OLIVE TOASTS FOR HORS D'OEUVRES: *Preheat the oven to 325°F. Cut day-old or frozen loaves into thin slices or fat fingers. Place on an ungreased baking sheet. Bake on the center rack for 25 minutes, or until just crisp and golden around the edges. Serve warm. (The toasts may be made a day ahead and stored in an airtight container at room temperature.)*

French Nut Bread

Makes 2 round loaves

2½ cups hazelnuts, lightly toasted and skinned (see page 375)

2½ cups whole-wheat flour

1¼ cups warm water (105° to 115°F)

2 tablespoons (2 packages) active dry yeast

¼ cup (packed) brown sugar

1 cup warm milk (105° to 115°F)

½ cup walnut oil

2½ teaspoons salt

About 3 cups unbleached all-purpose flour or bread flour

This dense, moist brown bread is one of the great breads of Europe. It can also be made with walnuts, almonds, or a mixture of nuts as well as hazelnuts. You could also use the all-American pecan.

1. Combine 1¼ cups of the hazelnuts and 1 cup of the whole-wheat flour and grind to the consistency of fine meal in a blender or food processor. Set aside.

2. Pour ¼ cup of the warm water in a small bowl. Sprinkle the yeast and a pinch of brown sugar over the surface of the water. Stir until dissolved and let stand at room temperature until foamy, about 10 minutes.

3. In a large bowl with a whisk or in the work bowl of a heavy-duty electric mixer using the paddle attachment, combine the remaining 1 cup water, the milk, oil, sugar, and salt. Add the yeast and nut mixtures. Add the remaining whole-wheat flour 1 cup at a time, mixing with a wooden spoon. Add the unbleached flour, ½ cup at a time, until a soft dough that just clears the sides of the bowl is formed.

4. Turn the dough out onto a well-floured work surface and knead until firm yet still springy, 5 to 7 minutes, dusting with flour only 1 tablespoon at a time as needed to prevent sticking. Because of the whole-grain flour, the dough will retain a tacky quality. Do not add more flour than required, because the dough will get hard and be very dry.

If kneading by machine, switch from the paddle to the dough hook and knead for 5 to 7 minutes, or until the dough is smooth and springy and springs back when pressed. If desired, transfer the dough to a floured surface and knead briefly by hand.

5. Place the dough in a greased bowl. Turn once to grease the top and cover with plastic wrap. Let rise in a warm place until doubled in bulk, 1 to 1½ hours or longer.

6. Gently deflate the dough. Turn the dough out onto a lightly floured work surface. Grease or parchment-line a baking sheet. Knead the nut pieces into the dough. They will tend to keep falling out, but just push them back in. Divide the dough into 2 equal portions. Shape the dough into round loaves. Place the loaves on the baking sheet and cover loosely with plastic wrap. Let rise about 40 to 50 minutes, or until doubled in bulk.

7. Twenty minutes before baking, preheat the oven to 375°F. Using a serrated knife, slash the loaves decoratively with 3 or 4 parallel gashes, no more than ¼ inch deep. Place the pan on a rack in the center of the oven and bake for 45 to 50 minutes, or until brown and the loaves sound hollow when tapped with your finger. Transfer the loaves immediately to a cooling rack. Cool completely before slicing.

California Walnut Bread

Walnut bread has its origin in the baking traditions of France, where it is immensely popular. Walnut oil comes in both cold-pressed, which is clear and light-flavored, or made from toasted nuts, which is a dark amber in color and assertively flavored. Choose as your palate dictates to control the character of this bread.

Makes two 8-by-4-inch loaves, three round loaves, or twenty dinner rolls

Sponge

2 tablespoons (2 packages) active dry yeast

¼ cup warm water (105° to 115°F)

2 cups unbleached all-purpose flour or bread flour

3 tablespoons honey or sugar

2 cups whole milk at room temperature

Dough

1½ cups shelled walnuts

½ cup walnut oil

1 tablespoon salt

About 3 cups unbleached all-purpose flour or bread flour

1. To prepare the sponge: In a large bowl using a whisk or in the work bowl of a heavy-duty electric mixer fitted with the paddle attachment, combine the yeast, water, 2 cups of the flour, honey or sugar, and milk. Beat hard until smooth and creamy about 1 minute. Cover loosely with plastic wrap and let rest at room temperature until bubbly, about 1 hour.

2. Meanwhile, preheat the oven to 350°F. Chop the walnuts and spread them evenly on a baking sheet. Bake until lightly toasted, about 3 minutes. Remove from the oven and let cool.

3. Add the oil, salt, and 1 cup of the flour to the sponge and stir with a wooden spoon to combine. Add the walnuts and the remaining flour, ½ cup flour at a time, until a soft, shaggy dough that clears the sides of the bowl is formed.

4. Turn the dough out onto a lightly floured work surface and gently knead until smooth and springy, about 4 minutes, dusting with flour only 1 tablespoon at a time as needed to prevent sticking. Push any walnuts that fall out during kneading back into the dough. This dough should be moist and soft, yet hold its own shape. Take care not to add too much flour, or the loaf will be dry.

If kneading by machine, switch from the paddle to the dough hook and knead for 3 to 4 minutes, or until the dough is smooth and springy. It should hold a finger imprint. If desired, transfer the dough to a floured surface and knead briefly by hand.

5. Place the dough in a greased deep container. Turn once to coat the top and cover with plastic wrap. Let rise at room temperature until doubled in bulk, 1½ to 2 hours.

6. Gently deflate the dough. Turn the dough out onto a lightly floured work surface. Grease or parchment line a baking sheet or grease two 8-by-4-inch loaf pans. Divide the dough into 2 or 3 equal portions. Shape into 2 standard or 3 round loaves. Place the loaves on the baking sheet or loaf pans. Cover loosely with plastic wrap and let stand to rise until doubled in bulk, about 45 minutes.

7. Twenty minutes before baking, preheat the oven to 375°F. Place the baking sheet or loaf pans on a rack in the center of the oven and bake for 35 to 40 minutes, or until brown and the loaves sound hollow when tapped with your finger. Transfer the loaves immediately to a cooling rack. Cool completely before slicing.

WALNUT ROLLS: *After deflating the dough in Step 6, divide the dough into 4 equal portions. Cut each portion into 5 portions and roll each into a ball. Place the balls 1 inch apart on a greased or parchment-lined baking sheet. Flatten each ball with your palm. With clean kitchen scissors dipped in flour, make 4 evenly spaced cuts around the edge of each roll almost to the center. Cover loosely with plastic wrap and let rise at room temperature until almost doubled, about 30 minutes. Bake as directed, for about 15 to 18 minutes. Serve warm.*

Pain Hawaiian

Makes 3 round loaves

Sponge

2 cups warm water
(105° to 115°F)

1 tablespoon
(1 package) active
dry yeast

Pinch of sugar

1½ cups unbleached
all-purpose flour or
bread flour

Dough

4 to 4½ cups unbleached all-
purpose flour or
bread flour

3 tablespoons nut oil,
such as almond or
walnut

½ teaspoon salt

1½ cups coarsely
chopped salted
macadamia nuts

There is magic in the transformation of a simple dough with the addition of the gloriously flavored macadamia nut. This is not a sweet bread, but is rich and crunchy with nuts. Constructed in the French style, this bread makes wonderful toast and freezes well.

1. To prepare the sponge: In a large bowl with a whisk or in the work bowl of a heavy-duty electric mixer fitted with the paddle attachment, pour in the warm water. Sprinkle the yeast, sugar, and flour over the surface of the water. Beat hard until smooth and creamy, about 1 minute. Cover loosely with plastic wrap and let stand at room temperature until bubbly, 30 minutes to 1 hour.

2. To prepare the dough: Add ½ cup of the flour, the oil, salt, and nuts to the sponge, and beat until smooth, about 1 minute. Add the remaining flour, ½ cup at a time, until a soft, sticky dough that just clears the side of the bowl is formed. Switch to a wooden spoon when necessary if making by hand.

3. Turn the dough out onto a lightly floured work surface and knead vigorously until smooth and springy, about 5 minutes, dusting with flour only 1 tablespoon at a time as needed to prevent sticking. The dough will be soft and smooth. Push back any nuts that fall out during the kneading.

If kneading by machine, switch from the paddle to the dough hook and knead for 4 to 5 minutes, or until the dough is smooth and springy and springs back when pressed. If desired, transfer the dough to a floured surface and knead briefly by hand.

4. Place the dough in a greased deep container. Turn once to coat the top and cover with plastic wrap. Let rise at room temperature until doubled in bulk, 1½ to 2 hours.

5. Gently deflate the dough. Turn the dough out onto a lightly floured work surface. Grease or parchment-line a baking sheet. Divide the dough into 3 equal portions. Shape each portion into a tight round loaf, dusting the entire round of dough with a bit of flour. Place each loaf seam side down at least 4 inches apart on the baking sheet. Dust the tops with flour. Cover loosely with plastic wrap and let rise until puffy, about 45 minutes.

6. Twenty minutes before baking, preheat the oven to 450°F with a baking stone on the bottom rack if desired. If not using a stone, preheat the oven to 400°F. Using kitchen shears, gently cut 3 **V**s at a 45-degree angle down the center or at the four corners no more than ¼ inch deep. Place the baking sheet on a rack in the center of the oven. Reduce the oven thermostat to 400°F if using a baking stone, and bake 30 to 35 minutes, or until crusty, brown, and the loaves sound hollow when tapped with your finger. Transfer the loaves immediately to a cooling rack. Cool completely before slicing.

Roasted Chestnut Bread

Makes 2 round loaves

15 fresh chestnuts (see Note)

1 tablespoon (1 package) active dry yeast

¼ teaspoon freshly grated nutmeg

2 teaspoons salt

½ cup chestnut flour

4½ to 5 cups unbleached all-purpose flour or bread flour

¾ cup milk

¾ cup water

¾ cup mild honey

8 tablespoons (1 stick) unsalted butter, at room temperature

3 large eggs, at room temperature

Powdered sugar or Vanilla Powdered Sugar (page 303), for dusting (optional)

Chestnuts are sweet and starchy yet low in fat. They have a tough outer shell and must be cooked before using in recipes. Chestnut flour, ground from dried chestnuts, is nutty in flavor, and silky in texture; it must be stored in the refrigerator for freshness to keep it from turning rancid. High-quality imported chestnut flour is available by mail order (see page 471).

1. Preheat the oven to 400°F. To prepare the chestnuts for baking, using a short-bladed or chestnut knife, carve an **X** onto the flat side of each nut to prevent it from bursting. Place in a single layer on a baking sheet and roast for 15 to 20 minutes. Or cook the nuts in the microwave for about 5 minutes on high. The nuts should be mealy in the center when pierced with the tip of a knife. Remove the nuts immediately from the baking sheet to a thick, clean cloth. When barely cool enough to handle, crack the nuts with your hands and then use the same knife to peel off the outer shell and the thin inner skin. *(At this point the nuts may be covered tightly and refrigerated until needed.)* Coarsely chop the nuts and set aside.

2. In a large mixing bowl with a whisk or in the work bowl of a heavy-duty electric mixer fitted with the paddle attachment, combine the yeast, nutmeg, salt, chestnut flour, and 2 cups of the unbleached flour. In a small saucepan, combine the milk, water, honey, and butter and heat until just hot. Stir to melt the butter. Let cool to 120°F.

3. Add the hot milk mixture to the dry ingredients and beat hard until creamy, about 1 minute. Beat in the eggs and chopped chestnuts. Add the remaining unbleached flour, ½ cup at a time, until a soft dough that just clears the sides of the bowl is formed. Switch to a wooden spoon when necessary if making by hand.

4. Turn the dough out onto a lightly floured work surface and knead until smooth, springy, and soft, about 4 minutes, dusting with flour only 1 tablespoon at a time as needed to prevent sticking. Push back any nuts that fall out during kneading.

If kneading by machine, switch from the paddle to the dough hook and knead for 3 to 4 minutes, or until the dough is smooth and springy

and springs back when pressed. If desired, transfer the dough to a floured surface and knead briefly by hand.

5. Place the dough in a greased deep container. Turn once to coat the top and cover with plastic wrap. Let rise at room temperature until doubled in bulk, 1½ to 2 hours.

6. Gently deflate the dough. Turn the dough out onto a floured work surface. Grease or parchment-line a baking sheet. Divide the dough into 2 equal portions. Shape each portion into a tight round ball and place at least 3 inches apart on the baking sheet. Using a serrated knife, slash a decorative **X** on the top of each loaf no more than ½ inch deep. Cover loosely with plastic wrap and let rise again at room temperature until doubled in bulk, about 45 minutes.

7. Twenty minutes before baking, preheat the oven to 350°F. Place the baking sheet on a rack in the center of the oven and bake 40 to 45 minutes, or until browned and the loaves sound hollow when tapped with your finger. Transfer the loaves immediately to cooling racks. Cool completely before slicing. Dust the loaves with powdered sugar before serving, if desired.

NOTE: *Commercial fresh-frozen steam-peeled chestnuts may be substituted for the cooked raw chestnuts.*

Celeste's Sunflower-Oatmeal Bread

Makes 3 small round loaves

1¼ cups warm water
(105° to 115°F)

1 tablespoon
(1 package)
active dry yeast

Pinch of sugar

1¼ cups warm
buttermilk
(105° to 115°F)

¼ cup honey

2 tablespoons
molasses

2 tablespoons unsalted
butter

1 cup whole-wheat
flour

1 cup rolled oats

¾ cups raw sunflower
seeds

1 tablespoon salt

1 large egg, at room
temperature, lightly
beaten

4 to 5 cups unbleached
all-purpose flour or
bread flour

Rich Egg Glaze
(page 52)

Rolled oats, for
sprinkling

Celeste was my baking assistant for years. She is a sculptor and has the temperament of a true artist, and makes outstanding bread. She was inspired to make this bread one day. I loved the subtle blend of grains and wrote the ingredients down.

1. Combine the warm water, yeast, and sugar in a small bowl. Stir to dissolve and let stand at room temperature until foamy, about 10 minutes.

2. In a small bowl, combine the buttermilk, honey, molasses, and butter.

3. In a large bowl using a whisk or in the work bowl of a heavy-duty electric mixer fitted with the paddle attachment, combine whole-wheat flour, oats, sunflower seeds, and salt. Add the buttermilk mixture, yeast, and egg. Beat hard for about 3 minutes. Add the flour, ½ cup at a time, until a soft dough that just clears the sides of the bowl is formed.

4. Turn the dough out onto a lightly floured work surface and knead for about 5 minutes, dusting with flour only 1 tablespoon at a time as needed to prevent sticking. The dough will be smooth and springy.

If kneading by machine, switch from the paddle to the dough hook and knead for 3 to 4 minutes, or until the dough is smooth and springy and springs back when pressed. If desired, transfer the dough to a floured surface and knead briefly by hand.

5. Place the dough in a greased bowl. Turn once to grease the top and cover with plastic wrap. Let rise at room temperature until doubled in bulk, about 1½ hours.

6. Gently deflate the dough. Turn the dough out onto a lightly floured surface. Grease or parchment-line a baking sheet and sprinkle with oats. Divide the dough into 3 equal portions. Shape the portions into round loaves. Place on the baking sheet. Cover loosely with plastic wrap and let rise until doubled in bulk, for about 30 minutes. Brush with the Rich Egg Glaze and sprinkle with oats.

7. Twenty minutes before baking, preheat the oven to 375°F. Place the baking sheet on a rack in the center of the oven and bake for 40 minutes or until brown and loaves sound hollow when tapped with your finger. Transfer the loaves immediately to a cooling rack. Cool completely before slicing.

THE ROLL BASKET:
Dinner Rolls, Sandwich Buns, Bread Sticks, and Bagels

Classic dinner rolls are fine-textured, soft and chewy, golden and fragrant. Whether a few bites or a miniature pull-apart loaf, they are meant to accent a meal with a mellow wheat flavor, rather than to be eaten alone. Fresh from the oven, dinner rolls slathered with butter are a traditional accompaniment to the American meal. Because they are best eaten very fresh and hot, the convenience of refrigerating or freezing the shaped dough makes homemade rolls adaptable to the busiest schedule. Making doughs ahead allows home baking to be relaxing and gratifying.

Expect hand-formed rolls and buns to vary slightly in size and shape. For easiest handling, the dough should be left a bit softer than for regular loaves, but it must be able to hold its own shape. If the dough becomes overly springy or resists being shaped while working, cover it with a clean cloth and let it rest on the work surface for about ten minutes. The dough may rise a bit, but it will relax enough for you to continue shaping. Be certain to allow for the full rising time required in each recipe, as this helps create a light texture.

Commercial breadsticks are usually uniformly thin and very crisp, but handmade ones tend to be charmingly irregular. Any lean bread dough made with high-protein bread flour can be used to make excellent Italian-style breadsticks. Breadsticks can be fat or thin, very crisp or quite soft, and flavored with anything from herbs to seeds to cheese. Breadsticks are never given a final proof unless you want them soft. To make, shape the dough, place on a baking sheet, and pop into a hot (425°F) oven. For more uniform sizes, cut the rolled-out dough with a pizza cutter or old-fashioned noodle cutter. They are perfect for snacks and make an impressive appetizer.

Another low-fat bread, bagels are very popular. Identified by their center hole, they sport a chewy texture and come in a myriad of flavors from pumpernickel to raisin. I associate bagels with weekend breakfast, but they have become an everyday favorite in place of toast. Although hand-rolling bagels takes a little time, the results are worth it. Bagels are first boiled, then baked to end up with their unique chewy texture. Bagels freeze perfectly, so make a large batch.

My Favorite Buttermilk Dinner Rolls

Makes 16 dinner rolls

- 1 tablespoon (1 package) active dry yeast
- Pinch of sugar
- 1/4 cup warm water (105° to 115°F)
- 1 cup warm buttermilk (105° to 115°F)
- 2 tablespoons sugar or honey
- Grated zest of 1 lemon
- 4 tablespoons (1/2 stick) unsalted butter, melted, or olive oil
- 1 large egg, at room temperature
- 2 teaspoons salt
- 4 to 4 1/2 cups unbleached all-purpose flour
- Rich Egg Glaze (page 52)
- 3 tablespoons sesame, poppy, or fennel seeds

Dinner rolls are made from a rich soft roll dough which is easy to sculpt into a variety of shapes. It contains more sugar and fat than for lean hard rolls, like French *petits pains* or Kaiser rolls. Dinner rolls are well suited to freezing at several steps during the formation of the dough and they hold up nicely for up to twenty-four hours of retarded rising in the refrigerator before baking. Buttermilk creates an exceptionally tender product.

1. Combine the yeast, sugar, and warm water in a small bowl and stir to dissolve. Let stand at room temperature until foamy, about 10 minutes.

2. In a large bowl using a whisk or in the bowl of a heavy-duty electric mixer fitted with the paddle attachment, combine the buttermilk, sugar, zest, melted butter, egg, and salt. Stir in 1 1/2 cups of the flour and the yeast mixture and beat hard for 2 minutes, or until the mixture is smooth and creamy. Add the flour, 1/2 cup at a time, with a wooden spoon until a soft dough that just clears the sides of the bowl is formed. Switch to a wooden spoon when necessary if making by hand.

3. Turn the dough out onto a lightly floured work surface and knead until soft, smooth, and elastic, 1 to 3 minutes for a machine-mixed dough and 4 to 7 minutes for a hand-mixed dough, dusting with flour only 1 tablespoon at a time, just enough as needed to prevent sticking.

If kneading by machine, switch from the paddle to the dough hook and knead for 3 to 4 minutes, or until the dough is smooth and springy and springs back when pressed. If desired, transfer the dough to a floured surface and knead briefly by hand.

4. Place the dough in a greased bowl. Turn once to grease the top and cover with plastic wrap. Let rise at room temperature until doubled in bulk, about 1 to 1 1/2 hours.

5. Gently deflate the dough. Turn the dough out onto a lightly floured work surface. Grease or parchment-line 2 baking sheets. Divide the dough in half, then roll each half into a 2- to 3-inch cylinder. With the metal dough scraper or chef's knife, cut the cylinder into 8 equal portions. Repeat with the second cylinder, making a total of 16 portions. Shape each piece of dough into a small oval. Cover loosely with plastic wrap and let rise at room temperature until doubled in bulk, about 30 minutes. Soft rolls are given a full proof.

6. Twenty minutes before baking, preheat the oven to 375°F. Gently brush each roll with egg glaze and sprinkle with seeds, if desired, or leave plain. Using a serrated knife or kitchen shears, gently cut 2 or 3 diagonal slashes no more than ¼ inch deep on the top surface of each roll. Place in the center of the oven and bake for 15 to 18 minutes, or until golden brown. If using 2 baking sheets, place on the upper and lower racks, and switch positions halfway through baking. Transfer the rolls immediately to a cooling rack. Serve warm, or cool to room temperature and reheat. Unless otherwise specified, this baking method applies to all the shapes below.

BOW KNOTS AND ROSETTES: *After deflating the dough in Step 5, cut it in half and then divide each portion into 8 equal portions. Roll each piece into a 10-inch rope ½ inch in diameter. To make a bow knot, tie loosely in a knot, leaving 2 long ends. For a rosette, tuck one end over and under the roll; bring the other end up and over to tuck into the roll center. Place the rolls about 2 inches apart on the prepared baking sheet.*

BRAIDED ROLLS: *Divide the dough into 3 equal portions. Roll each portion into a rope about 24 inches long. Place the ropes side by side and braid them loosely. Cut the braid into 16 equal portions and pinch the ends to taper them.*

BUTTERFLY ROLLS: *Roll the dough into a 10-by-20-inch rectangle. Brush the surface with melted butter. Roll up, from the long edge, jelly-roll fashion. Place seam side down and, with the metal bench scraper or chef's knife, cut the log into 18 equal portions. Press each portion in the center with the handle of a wooden spoon laid across the top to create a fan effect out of the sides.*

CLOVERLEAF ROLLS: *Divide the dough in half, then each half into 8 equal portions. Pinch off 3 equal pieces of the dough from each portion (a total of 48 pieces) and shape each into 1-inch smooth balls. Place 3 balls touching each other in each of 16 greased standard muffin cups.*

CRESCENT ROLLS: *Cut the dough in half. On a lightly floured work surface, roll each half into an 8-inch circle. Brush with corn oil. With a knife or pastry wheel, cut each circle into 8 equal wedges. Beginning at the wide end, firmly roll each wedge up toward the point. Place, point side down, on the prepared baking sheets and curve the ends inward.*

DOUBLE CRESCENT ROLLS: *Cut the dough in half. Roll each piece into a 10-by-6-inch rectangle about ¼ to ½ inch thick. Cut each into 3 long strips. Roll each strip*

continues next page

into a 10-inch rope. Divide each rope into 3 equal pieces. Roll each piece and taper the ends. Shape into a half-circle. Lay 2 crescents back to back on the prepared baking sheets. The crescents should be just touching. Lay a small strip of dough over the center and tuck it underneath on each side.

PARKER HOUSE ROLLS: Turn the dough out onto the lightly floured work surface and roll out into a 12-inch square about 1/2 to 3/4 inch thick. Using a sharp knife or pastry wheel, cut the dough into 4 equal sections across and 4 lengthwise to form sixteen 3-inch squares. Stretch each one slightly to elongate it and, using the handle of a wooden spoon to mark the fold, mark the roll lengthwise a little off center. Fold the small half over the larger half. Press the folded edge gently to adhere. Place 1 inch apart on baking sheets.

SNAILS: Cut the dough in half and divide it into 8 equal portions. Roll each portion into an 8-inch-long rope 1/2 inch in diameter. Starting at one end, wind the strip of dough around itself to form a spiral. Tuck the edge firmly underneath.

REFRIGERATOR ROLLS:

Method One: After kneading the dough in Step 3, place it in a greased deep container, bowl, or gallon-size plastic food storage bag. Brush the surface of the dough with melted butter or oil. Cover tightly with plastic wrap or seal the bag, leaving room for the dough to expand. Refrigerate for up to 4 days, deflating the dough as necessary.

To form refrigerator rolls, remove the amount of dough desired about 3 hours before serving. Shape as desired. Place on greased or parchment-lined baking sheets, cover loosely with plastic wrap, and let rise at room temperature until almost doubled, about 1 1/2 to 2 hours. Bake as directed in Step 6.

Method Two: After the dough has risen in Step 4, gently deflate it and shape the rolls. Place on parchment-lined baking sheets and brush the tops with melted butter. Cover loosely with oiled wax paper or parchment, then with plastic wrap, taking care to cover all edges tightly. Immediately refrigerate for 2 to 24 hours.

When ready to bake, remove the pans from the refrigerator, uncover, and let stand at room temperature for 20 to 30 minutes while preheating the oven. Bake as directed in Step 6.

FREEZER ROLLS: Mix, rise, and shape the rolls as directed in Steps 2 through 5. Place on a nonstick, disposable, or parchment-lined baking sheet that will fit into your freezer. Cover tightly with plastic wrap. Freeze until firm, about 2 to 3 hours. Remove the rolls from the baking sheet and transfer to a plastic freezer bag. Freeze the rolls for up to 2 weeks but no longer, as the leavening power of the yeast will begin to decrease.

To defrost and serve freezer rolls, unwrap the frozen rolls and place on a greased or parchment-lined baking sheet. Cover loosely with plastic wrap and let stand at warm room temperature to rise until doubled in bulk, 4 to 6 hours. The dough may also be thawed overnight in the refrigerator. Bake as directed in Step 6.

HOMEMADE BROWN-AND-SERVE ROLLS: Mix, rise, and shape the rolls as directed in Steps 1 through 5. Place on greased or parchment-lined baking sheets, or ungreased disposable aluminum baking pans. Cover loosely with plastic wrap, and let rise at room temperature until doubled in bulk, 1½ to 2 hours. Bake in the center of a preheated 300°F oven until the rolls are fully baked, but not browned, 15 to 20 minutes. Remove from the pan and cool on a rack. Place the rolls in a heavy-duty plastic bag and refrigerate up to 3 days or freeze for up to 3 weeks. To serve, let the frozen rolls thaw at room temperature in the bag. Place in a single layer on an ungreased or parchment-lined baking sheet. Bake in a preheated 375°F oven until golden brown, 15 minutes.

French-Style Mexican Hard Rolls
Bolillos

Makes 20 rolls

Sponge

1½ tablespoons (1½ packages) active dry yeast

¼ cup sugar

3 cups warm water (105° to 115°F)

4 cups unbleached all-purpose flour

Dough

1 tablespoon salt

6 tablespoons (¾ stick) butter or vegetable shortening, at room temperature

3 to 3½ cups unbleached all-purpose flour

1 large egg white, beaten with 1 tablespoon water, for glazing

In the 1860s during French rule in Mexico, the Emperor Maximilian brought his own bakers over from Europe. One of the living artifacts of that period is the *bolillo* roll, similar in shape to a weaving spindle. A bit sweeter and softer than its French *petit pain* counterpart, this roll is now an integral part of daily Southwest and Mexican baking. Although the roll may be made from any lean French- or Italian-style plain dough, this version calls for a short sponge starter for a great-tasting roll.

1. To prepare the sponge: In a 3- or 4-quart bowl or plastic container, sprinkle the yeast and sugar over the water and stir until dissolved. Let stand at room temperature until foamy, about 10 minutes. Add the 4 cups of unbleached flour. With a whisk, beat hard until smooth and thick. Scrape the sides with a spatula. Cover loosely with plastic wrap and let stand at room temperature, until bubbly, about 1 hour.

2. To prepare the dough: Add the salt, butter, and ½ cup of the flour to the sponge. Beat hard with a whisk for 5 minutes, or 2 minutes on medium speed in the bowl of a heavy-duty electric mixer fitted with the paddle attachment. Add the remaining flour, ½ cup at a time, mixing on low speed until a soft dough that just clears the sides of the bowl is formed. Switch to a wooden spoon when necessary if making by hand.

3. Turn the dough out onto a lightly floured work surface and knead vigorously to create a soft, moist, and elastic dough that will still feel sticky, 5 to 8 minutes, dusting with flour only 1 tablespoon at a time as needed. Use a dough scraper to clean off the film of dough that accumulates on the work surface as you go along. Take care not to add too much flour; this dough should just hold its shape, yet retain a slightly moist quality.

If kneading by machine, switch from the paddle to the dough hook and knead for 4 to 5 minutes, or until the dough is smooth and springy and springs back when pressed. If desired, transfer the dough to a floured surface and knead briefly by hand.

4. Place the dough in a deep greased container. Turn once to coat the top and cover with plastic wrap. Let rise at room temperature until doubled in bulk, 1 to 1½ hours.

5. Gently deflate the dough. Turn the dough out onto a lightly floured work surface. Grease or parchment-line 1 or 2 baking sheets. Divide the dough into 2 equal portions. Divide each portion into 10 equal portions. Pat each one into a 3-by-2-inch rectangle and roll up to form into a tight oval. Pinch the seams to seal and arrange about 2 inches apart on the pans. Pinch the ends, pulling slightly to form a spindle shape. Cover loosely with plastic wrap and let rise at room temperature until doubled in bulk, about 30 minutes.

6. About 20 minutes before baking, preheat the oven to 400°F with a baking stone or tiles on the lowest rack, as desired. Using a sharp knife, gently slash the rolls with a lengthwise cut down the middle, no deeper than ¼ inch. Brush the top of each roll with the glaze. Place the baking sheet directly on the hot stone and bake for 10 minutes. Brush the rolls again with the wash. Reduce the oven thermostat to 375°F and bake for 15 to 18 minutes more, or until the tops are golden brown and the rolls sound hollow when tapped with your finger. Transfer the rolls immediately to a cooling rack. They are best slightly warm or at room temperature. (Bolillos *may be frozen for up to 1 month.*)

MEXICAN FLAT ROLLS (TELERAS): *After deflating the dough in Step 5, divide it into 20 portions. Flatten the ball of dough into an oval with the heel of your hand or a rolling pin. Press twice into the top of the roll with the side of your hand to make 2 indentations. Let rise and press again to re-form the indentations. Bake and cool as directed.*

Squash Cloverleafs

Makes about 20 cloverleaf rolls

¼ cup warm water
(105° to 115°F)

1 tablespoon
(1 package)
active dry yeast

Pinch of brown
sugar

¾ cup warm milk
(105° to 115°F)

¼ cup orange liqueur,
such as Grand
Marnier

1 cup winter squash
or pumpkin purée
(see Note), or one
12-ounce package
frozen cooked winter
squash, defrosted

3 tablespoons brown
sugar

Grated zest of
1 orange

2 teaspoons salt

6 tablespoons
(¾ stick) unsalted
butter, melted

4 to 4½ cups unbleached
all-purpose flour or
bread flour

Melted butter for
brushing (optional)

During the fall I enjoy cooking with different kinds of winter squash. You can make these subtly orange-tinged dinner rolls from a purée of globular green acorn, tapered tan butternut, ribbed Golden Nugget sugar pumpkin, smooth calabazas, striped turban, or the dense oval Blue Hubbard with equal success.

1. Pour the warm water in a small bowl. Sprinkle the yeast and pinch of brown sugar over the surface of the water. Stir to dissolve and let stand at room temperature until foamy, about 10 minutes.

2. In a large bowl using a whisk or in the work bowl of a heavy-duty electric mixer fitted with the paddle attachment, combine the milk, liqueur, squash, brown sugar, orange zest, salt, and butter. Add the yeast mixture and 2 cups of the flour. Beat until smooth and creamy, about 2 minutes. Gradually add the remaining flour, ½ cup at a time, until a soft dough that just clears the sides of the bowl is formed. Switch to a wooden spoon when necessary if mixing by hand.

3. Turn the dough out onto a lightly floured work surface and knead until satiny and elastic, about 4 minutes, dusting with flour only 1 tablespoon at a time as needed to prevent sticking. This should be a very smooth dough.

If kneading by machine, switch from the paddle to the dough hook and knead for 3 to 4 minutes, or until the dough is smooth and springy and springs back when pressed. If desired, transfer the dough to a floured surface and knead briefly by hand.

4. Place the dough in a greased deep container. Turn once to coat the top and cover with plastic wrap. Let rise at room temperature until doubled in bulk, about 1 hour.

5. Gently deflate the dough. Turn the dough out onto the lightly floured work surface. Lightly grease twenty 1⅝-inch round muffin cups. Divide the dough into 4 equal portions. Divide each of these portions into 3 equal portions, and shape these into small balls about the size of a walnut (about 1 inch in diameter). Arrange 3 balls of dough in each of the muffin cups. Cover loosely with plastic wrap and let rise until doubled in bulk, about 20 minutes.

6. Twenty minutes before baking, preheat the oven to 400°F. Place the muffin tins on a rack in the center of the oven and bake for 12 to 15 minutes, or until golden brown and the rolls sound hollow when tapped with your finger. Remove the rolls immediately from the muffin tins and transfer to cooling racks. Serve them warm.

REFRIGERATOR SQUASH CLOVERLEAFS: *Brush the tops of the rolls with melted butter and cover loosely with 2 layers of plastic wrap with some room for expansion, taking care to tightly wrap all the edges. Immediately refrigerate for 2 to 24 hours. When ready to bake, preheat the oven to 400°F. Uncover the rolls and let stand at room temperature no more than 20 minutes. Bake as directed.*

NOTE: *To make pumpkin or squash purée, wash a medium sugar, pumpkin, or other winter squash and cut off the top. Cut the pumpkin in half and then into large cubes, leaving the skin intact. Scoop out the seeds and fibers. Place the pumpkin, flesh side down, in a baking dish filled with about 1 inch of water. Cover and bake at 350°F for 1 to 1½ hours, or until tender. Let the pumpkin cool. Peel off and discard the skin. Purée the pulp until smooth in a food mill, blender, or food processor. (The purée may be refrigerated, covered, for up to 5 days or frozen for up to 9 months.) One pound of raw pumpkin will yield about 1 cup purée.*

Petits Pains au Lait

Makes 20 small rolls

4½ to 5 cups unbleached all-purpose flour or bread flour

½ cup nonfat dry milk powder

1 tablespoon (1 envelope) active dry yeast

2 tablespoons sugar

2 teaspoons salt

1½ cups hot water (120°F)

1 large egg, at room temperature

5 tablespoons unsalted butter, at room temperature, cut into pieces

½ cup coarse-grind white cornmeal or farina, for dusting

The round shape of this milk roll is a familiar sight in European bakeries. The rolls have a crisp crust and delicate flavor, making them perfect for accompanying any meal or for making little sandwiches. Note that the rising time for this dough is a full four to five hours. The results are worth the time.

1. In a large bowl with a whisk or in the work bowl of a heavy-duty electric mixer fitted with the paddle attachment, combine 2 cups of the flour, the milk powder, yeast, sugar, and salt. Add the hot water and egg. Beat hard for 2 minutes. Beat in the butter pieces. Add the remaining flour, ½ cup at a time, until a soft dough that just clears the sides of the bowl is formed. Switch to a wooden spoon when necessary if making by hand.

2. Turn the dough out onto a lightly floured work surface and knead until smooth and springy, about 4 minutes, dusting with flour only 1 tablespoon at a time as needed to prevent sticking.

If kneading by machine, switch from the paddle to the dough hook and knead for 3 to 4 minutes, or until the dough is smooth and springy and springs back when pressed. If desired, transfer the dough to a floured surface and knead briefly by hand.

3. Place the dough in a greased deep container. Turn once to coat the top and cover with plastic wrap. Let rise at cool room temperature until fully doubled in bulk, 4 to 5 hours, or in the refrigerator overnight. Gently deflate the dough, re-cover, and let rise until almost doubled in bulk (or tripled, if the dough was chilled), about 1½ hours.

4. Gently deflate the dough. Turn the dough out onto a very lightly floured work surface. Grease or parchment-line 2 baking sheets and sprinkle with cornmeal or farina. Divide the dough into 4 equal portions. Further divide each quarter into 5 equal portions to form 20 small portions. Shape each portion into a tight round roll. Dust the rolls lightly all over with the flour. Place the rolls on 1 or 2 greased or parchment-lined baking sheets dusted with cornmeal or farina. The rolls should be just touching one another in rows of four, with about 2 inches between the rows. Cover loosely with plastic wrap and let rest at room temperature for about 30 minutes.

5. Twenty minutes before baking, preheat the oven to 450°F with a baking stone on the lowest rack, or to 400°F without a stone. Using a serrated knife, slash each roll quickly down the middle no more than ¼ inch deep. Place 1 baking sheet directly on the baking stone, if using, or directly on the oven rack. If the oven is set at 450°F, immediately reduce the thermostat to 400°F and bake the rolls 12 to 15 minutes, or until golden brown. Remove the sheet from the oven and place the second sheet in the oven to bake. Immediately pile the baked rolls into a basket to serve, or transfer to a cooling rack.

Black Bread Rolls

Makes 12 sandwich rolls

2¼ cups warm water (105° to 115°F)

2 tablespoons (2 packages) active dry yeast

Pinch of sugar

6 tablespoons (¾ stick) unsalted butter, melted

3 tablespoons molasses

1 tablespoon instant coffee powder

1 tablespoon salt

1 tablespoon caraway seeds

1 teaspoon fennel seeds

⅓ cup wheat bran

¼ cup unsweetened cocoa powder

3 cups medium rye flour

3 to 3½ cups unbleached all-purpose flour

Cornmeal, for sprinkling (optional)

Black breads are usually made with whole-grain flours, such as rye, and darkened with coffee, cocoa, carob, molasses, toasted crumbs, or caramel. This recipe calls for instant coffee powder and cocoa.

1. Pour ½ cup of the warm water in a small bowl. Sprinkle the yeast and sugar over the surface of the water. Stir to dissolve and let stand at room temperature until foamy, about 10 minutes.

2. In a large bowl using a whisk or in the work bowl of a heavy-duty electric mixer fitted with the paddle attachment, combine the butter, molasses, instant coffee powder, salt, caraway seeds, fennel seeds, bran, cocoa powder, and rye flour. Whisk until smooth and add yeast mixture. Beat for about 3 minutes. Add the unbleached flour, ½ cup at a time, and continue beating with a wooden spoon until too stiff to stir.

3. Turn the dough out onto a lightly floured work surface and knead until smooth, elastic, and no longer sticky, about 5 minutes, dusting with flour only 1 tablespoon at a time as needed to prevent sticking.

  If kneading by machine, switch from the paddle to the dough hook and knead for 4 to 5 minutes, or until the dough is smooth and springy and springs back when pressed. If desired, transfer the dough to a floured surface and knead briefly by hand.

4. Place the dough in a greased bowl. Turn once to grease the top and cover with plastic wrap. Let rise at room temperature until doubled in bulk, 1 to 1½ hours.

5. Gently deflate the dough. Turn the dough out onto a lightly floured work surface. Grease or parchment-line 2 baking sheets and sprinkle with cornmeal, if desired. Divide the dough into 12 equal portions. Shape each dough portion into a round ball and place it seam side down on the baking sheet. Flatten each ball with your palm. Cover loosely with plastic wrap and let rise until doubled in bulk and puffy, about 25 minutes.

6. Twenty minutes before baking, preheat the oven to 375°F. Place the baking sheets on the center to lower rack in the oven and bake for 40 minutes, or until slightly browned and firm to the touch. Transfer to a rack to cool.

Water Rolls

*Makes about 12 sandwich buns
or 24 dinner rolls*

1¾ cups warm water
(105° to 115°F)

1 tablespoon
(1 package)
active dry yeast

Pinch of sugar

2 tablespoons
vegetable oil

2 teaspoons salt

2 egg whites,
lightly beaten

About 5 cups unbleached
all-purpose flour or
bread flour

⅓ cup rice flour
or sifted unbleached
flour, for dusting

These round rolls are crusty just out of the oven; as they cool, they soften and are suitable for sandwiches. A liberal dusting of rice flour gives the rolls a finished look. This flour is available at natural foods stores.

1. In a large bowl, pour in ¼ cup warm water. Sprinkle the yeast and sugar over the surface of the water. Stir to dissolve and let stand at room temperature until foamy, about 10 minutes.

2. Combine the remaining water, oil, salt, and egg whites into the yeast mixture with a whisk. Beat in the flour, 1 cup at a time, with a wooden spoon until a soft dough that just clears the sides of the bowl is formed.

3. Turn the dough out onto a lightly floured work surface and knead until smooth and elastic, about 5 minutes, dusting with flour only 1 tablespoon at a time as needed to prevent sticking.

If kneading by machine, switch from the paddle to the dough hook and knead for 3 to 4 minutes, or until the dough is smooth and springy and springs back when pressed. If desired, transfer the dough to a floured surface and knead briefly by hand.

4. Place the dough in a greased container. Turn once to grease the top and cover with plastic wrap. Let rise at room temperature until doubled in bulk, about 1 hour.

5. Gently deflate the dough. Turn the dough out onto a lightly floured work surface. Grease or parchment-line 2 baking sheets. For sandwich buns, divide the dough into 12 equal portions. Shape the portions into balls, place them about 1 to 2 inches apart the baking sheets, and flatten each with the palm of your hand. Dust them with rice flour. Cover loosely with plastic wrap and let rise until doubled in bulk, about 25 minutes. Using the back of a knife, slash a cross or spoke pattern on the top of the roll no more than ½ inch deep. Let rest 15 minutes only.

6. Twenty minutes before baking, preheat the oven to 400°F. Place the pans on a rack in the center of the oven and bake for 20 minutes, or until brown. Transfer the rolls immediately to a cooling rack.

Sesame Burger Buns

Makes 12 rolls

1¾ cups warm water
(105° to 115°F)

1 tablespoon
(1 package) active
dry yeast

2 tablespoons plus
½ teaspoon sugar

⅓ cup nonfat dry milk
powder

2½ teaspoons salt

3 tablespoons unsalted
butter, melted

4½ to 5 cups unbleached
all-purpose flour or
bread flour

1 large egg beaten
with 2 teaspoons
water, for glazing

½ cup sesame seeds

Although any good yeast bread recipe may be divided into small portions and formed into a roll for sandwiches, this is the quintessential burger bun. It is fine-textured, moist, and not too chewy, so that the filling can be showcased.

1. In a small bowl pour in ½ cup of the warm water. Sprinkle the yeast and ½ teaspoon sugar over the water. Stir to dissolve and let stand at room temperature until foamy, about 10 minutes.

2. In a large bowl using a whisk or in the work bowl of a heavy-duty electric mixer fitted with the paddle attachment, combine the remaining 1¼ cups water, dried milk, the remaining sugar, salt, and butter. Add 2 cups of the flour. Beat hard until creamy, about 1 minute. Add the remaining flour, ½ cup at a time, until a soft, shaggy dough that just clears the sides of the bowl is formed. Switch to a wooden spoon when necessary if mixing by hand.

3. Turn the dough out onto a lightly floured work surface and knead for about 4 minutes, dusting with flour only 1 tablespoon at a time as needed to make a smooth and soft dough.

If kneading by machine, switch from the paddle to the dough hook and knead for 3 to 4 minutes, or until the dough is smooth and springy and springs back when pressed. If desired, transfer the dough to a floured surface and knead briefly by hand.

4. Place the dough in a greased deep container. Turn once to coat the top and cover with plastic wrap. Let rise at room temperature until doubled in bulk, 1 to 1¼ hours.

5. Gently deflate the dough. Turn the dough out onto a lightly floured work surface. Grease or parchment-line a baking sheet. Divide the dough into 12 equal portions. Shape each into a tight round ball and place each ball seam side down and at least 2 inches apart on the baking sheet. Use a second baking sheet rather than crowd the rolls. Flatten each ball with your palm. Cover loosely with plastic wrap and let rise until puffy, about 20 minutes.

6. Twenty minutes before baking, preheat the oven to 350°F. Brush each roll with the egg glaze and sprinkle the tops with sesame seeds. Place the baking sheet on a rack in the center of the oven and bake 20 to 25 minutes, or until slightly brown and firm to the touch. Transfer the rolls immediately to a cooling rack. Cool completely before splitting.

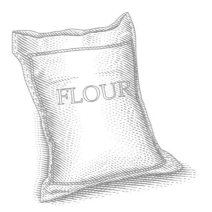

Sesame Whole-Wheat Long Rolls

Makes 16 rolls

1½ cups warm water (105° to 115°F)

1½ tablespoons (1½ packages) active dry yeast

2 tablespoons brown sugar

¾ cup warm milk (105° to 115°F)

4 tablespoons (½ stick) butter, melted

1 tablespoon salt

2 tablespoons raw sesame seeds

1½ cups whole-wheat flour

4 to 4½ cups unbleached all-purpose flour or bread flour

Rich Egg Glaze (page 52; optional)

Homemade soft, thick rolls are a very special treat. Whether used for blanketing hot meats at barbecue time or as a cold sandwich roll, there is nothing ordinary about them.

1. Pour the warm water in a small bowl. Sprinkle the yeast and a pinch of brown sugar over the surface of the water. Stir to combine and let stand at room temperature until foamy, about 10 minutes.

2. In a large bowl using a whisk, or in the work bowl of a heavy-duty electric mixer fitted with the paddle attachment, combine the milk, butter, remaining brown sugar, salt, sesame seeds, and whole-wheat flour. Beat hard until smooth, about 3 minutes. Add the yeast mixture and the unbleached flour, ½ cup at a time, until a dough that just clears the sides of the bowl is formed. Switch to a wooden spoon when necessary if making by hand.

3. Turn the dough out onto a lightly floured work surface. Knead for about 5 minutes, dusting with flour only 1 tablespoon at a time as needed to make a smooth, soft, slightly sticky dough.

If kneading by machine, switch from the paddle to the dough hook and knead for 3 to 4 minutes, or until the dough is smooth and springy and springs back when pressed. If desired, transfer the dough to a floured surface and knead briefly by hand.

4. Place the dough in a greased deep bowl. Turn once to grease the top and cover with plastic wrap. Let rise at room temperature until doubled in bulk, 45 minutes to 1 hour.

5. Gently deflate the dough. Turn the dough out onto a lightly floured work surface. Grease or parchment-line 2 baking sheets. Divide the dough into 16 equal portions. Shape each portion into an oblong oval. Roll each oval up from the long end tightly and pinch the seam closed, like a mini French loaf. Place the rolls 2 inches apart on the baking sheets. Cover loosely with plastic wrap and let rest until puffy and almost doubled, about 30 minutes. Brush with the Rich Egg Glaze, if desired.

6. Twenty minutes before baking, preheat the oven to 375°F. Place the baking sheets on a rack in the center of the oven and bake for 20 to 25 minutes, or until lightly browned. Transfer the rolls immediately to a cooling rack.

California Olive Rolls

Makes 12 rolls

1¼ cups warm water
(105° to 115°F)

1 tablespoon
(1 package)
active dry yeast

Pinch of sugar

½ cup rye flour

3 to 3¼ cups unbleached
all-purpose flour or
bread flour

⅓ cup olive oil,
preferably a fruity
domestic brand

1 tablespoon unsalted
butter, at room
temperature

1 teaspoon salt

¾ to 1 cup canned domestic
black olives, pitted
and coarsely
chopped

Use a flavorful California olive oil for this crusty, yet elegant dinner roll.

1. In a large bowl using a whisk or in the work bowl of a heavy-duty electric mixer fitted with the paddle attachment, pour in the warm water. Sprinkle the yeast, sugar, rye and ½ cup of the unbleached flour over the surface of water. Beat well until smooth and creamy. Cover loosely with plastic wrap and let rise at room temperature until foamy, 30 minutes to 1 hour.

2. Add ½ cup more of the flour, the oil, butter, salt, and olives, and beat until smooth, about 1 minute. Add the remaining flour, ½ cup at a time, until a soft dough that just clears the sides of the bowl is formed. Switch to a wooden spoon when necessary if mixing by hand.

3. Turn the dough out onto a lightly floured work surface and knead until smooth and springy, about 4 minutes, dusting with flour only 1 tablespoon at a time as needed to prevent sticking.

If kneading by machine, switch from the paddle to the dough hook and knead for 3 to 4 minutes, or until the dough is smooth and springy and springs back when pressed. If desired, transfer the dough to a floured surface and knead briefly by hand.

4. Place the dough in a greased deep container. Turn once to coat the top and cover with plastic wrap. Let rise at room temperature until puffy, 1 hour.

5. Gently deflate the dough. Turn the dough out onto a lightly floured work surface. Grease or parchment-line a baking sheet. Divide the dough into 12 equal portions. Shape each portion into an oval and place at least 2 inches apart on the baking sheet. Cover loosely with plastic wrap and let rise at room temperature for 20 minutes.

6. Twenty minutes before baking, preheat the oven to 450°F with a baking stone or to 425°F without a stone. Using kitchen shears, snip the top of each roll 3 times at a 45-degree angle down the center. Reduce the oven thermostat to 425°F if using a baking stone. Place the baking sheet on a rack in the center of the oven and bake for 25 to 30 minutes, or until crusty and brown. Serve immediately, or transfer to cooling racks and reheat later.

Italian Bread Sticks

Grissini

Makes 24 grissini

2	tablespoons active dry yeast
1½	cups warm water (105° to 115°F)
¼	cup olive oil, plus about ½ cup additional olive oil, for dipping
1	teaspoon salt
1	cup semolina flour
1	cup whole-wheat flour
1½ to 1¾	cups unbleached all-purpose flour
About 1¼	cups semolina flour, for sprinkling and rolling

Authentic *grissini* are hand shaped by rolling the dough out to a desired length and then baked at a high temperature in a stone-lined oven. They look very different from machine extruded breadsticks, which are all exactly alike; *grissini* are charmingly nubby and irregular. They have to bake until crisp, otherwise they will bend and break when you serve them.

1. In the work bowl of a heavy-duty electric mixer fitted with the paddle attachment, combine the yeast, water, olive oil, salt, semolina flour, and whole-wheat flour. Beat hard until creamy, about 1 minute. Add the unbleached flour, ½ cup at a time, until a soft, shaggy dough that just clears the sides of the bowl is formed. Switch to a wooden spoon when necessary if making by hand.

2. Turn the dough out onto a lightly floured work surface and knead until soft and springy, 1 to 3 minutes, dusting with flour only 1 tablespoon at a time as needed to prevent sticking. Leave the dough moist and soft, yet at the same time smooth and springy.

If kneading by machine, switch from the paddle to the dough hook and knead for 1 to 2 minutes, or until the dough is smooth and springy and springs back when pressed. Leave the dough moist and soft. If desired, transfer the dough to a floured surface and knead briefly by hand.

3. Dust the work surface with semolina flour and pat the dough into a thick 12-by-6-inch rectangle. You can leave the dough to rise on the work surface (especially if it is a marble slab), or transfer it to an 11-by-17-inch baking sheet. Brush the top with olive oil. Cover with plastic wrap and let rise at room temperature until doubled in bulk, about 1 hour.

4. Preheat the oven to 425°F, placing a baking stone on the center rack. Grease 2 heavy 11-by-17-inch baking sheets. Place the additional olive oil and semolina flour in two shallow bowls. Press the dough all over to gently deflate and turn out of the pan onto a floured work surface. Using a pastry or pizza wheel, cut the dough into four equal sections lengthwise; the dough will deflate a bit more. Cut each section into 6 thick strips lengthwise. Pick up the end of each strip and stretch to the desired shape, or roll out each strip between your palms, stretching from the center out to the ends, to a size that will fit your baking sheet. Dip each strip in the olive oil and then roll in semolina flour. Place the strips evenly spaced apart on the baking sheets. Each sheet will hold 12 *grissini*. Place each sheet in the center of the oven and bake for 15 to 20 minutes, or until the *grissini* are lightly browned and crisp. Transfer from the pan to cool on racks. Cool completely before serving. *Grissini* keep indefinitely stored in an airtight container at room temperature, but are best eaten within a few days of baking.

Wild Rice Bread Sticks

Makes 2 dozen bread sticks

1½ cups warm water
(105° to 115°F)

1 tablespoon
(1 package)
active dry yeast

Pinch of brown
sugar

¼ cup olive oil

2 teaspoons salt

1 cup cooked wild rice
(see page 113)

½ cup whole-wheat
flour

3½ to 4 cups unbleached
all-purpose flour or
bread flour

Egg Glaze (page
276)

Coarse salt

Olive oil, for
brushing

Serve these crunchy bread sticks for dinner, for snacking, with antipasto. They may be plainly shaped or snipped to form stalks, which look very special on a buffet table. For more on wild rice, see page 113.

1. In a large bowl using a whisk or the work bowl of a heavy-duty electric mixer fitted with the paddle attachment, pour in the warm water. Sprinkle the yeast and brown sugar over the surface of the water. Stir to dissolve and let stand at room temperature until foamy, about 10 minutes.

2. Beat in the oil, salt, wild rice, and whole-wheat flour until smooth, about 1 minute. Add the unbleached flour, ½ cup at a time, until a soft dough that just clears the sides of the bowl is formed. Switch to a wooden spoon when necessary if mixing by hand.

3. Turn the dough out onto a lightly floured work surface and knead until smooth, about 4 minutes, dusting with flour only 1 tablespoon at a time as needed to prevent sticking. The dough will be nubby from the rice and not stiff.

If kneading by machine, switch from the paddle to the dough hook and knead for 3 to 4 minutes, or until the dough is smooth. If desired, transfer the dough to a floured surface and knead briefly by hand.

4. Place the dough in a greased deep container. Turn once to coat the top and cover with plastic wrap. Let rise at room temperature until doubled in bulk, about 1 hour.

5. Gently deflate the dough. Turn the dough out onto the work surface. Grease or parchment-line a baking sheet. Divide into 4 equal portions. Cut each portion into 6 equal pieces. Using your palms, roll each piece into a long rope, preferably the size of your baking sheet. Place the sticks parallel and no less than 1 inch apart on the baking sheet. Brush the surfaces with olive oil. Let stand at room temperature until puffy, about 20 minutes.

6. Twenty minutes before baking, preheat the oven to 375°F. Gently brush the glaze on the surface of the sticks and sprinkle with coarse salt, if desired. Place the baking sheet on a rack in the center of the oven and bake 20 to 25 minutes, or until crisp and golden brown. These sticks will be a bit dry, not soft like a roll. Transfer the sticks from the baking sheet to a cooling rack. Store in them in an airtight container at room temperature.

Egg Bagels

Makes about thirty bagels or three 9-by-5-inch loaves

1 or 2 large russet potato (about ¾ pound total)

2½ cups water

2 tablespoons (2 packages) active dry yeast

1½ tablespoons sugar, plus more as needed

1½ tablespoons salt, plus more as needed

7 to 7½ cups unbleached all-purpose flour or bread flour

¼ cup corn oil

4 large eggs

Egg Glaze (page 276)

Sesame seeds or poppy seeds, for garnishing

Bagels are immersed in boiling water before baking; this gives them their characteristic hairline crust and firm, chewy interior. Despite this initial boiling process, bagels are faster to make than many yeast breads. Homemade bagels will never be as evenly shaped as commercial ones, so don't despair at uneven rounds. Bagel bread, formed and baked in a traditional yeast loaf shape, is also delicious.

1. Peel the potato and cut into large chunks. Place the pieces in a small saucepan and cover with 2½ cups water. Bring to a boil, reduce the heat, and simmer uncovered until the pieces are soft. Drain the potato, reserving 2 cups of the potato water. Let cool to 120°F. (Use the potato for other purposes.)

2. In a large bowl using a whisk or in the work bowl of a heavy-duty electric mixer fitted with the paddle attachment, combine the yeast, 1½ table-spoons sugar, 1½ tablespoons salt, and 2 cups of the flour. Add the potato water and oil. Beat on medium speed for 2 minutes. Add 1 cup of the flour and the eggs and beat again for 2 minutes. Add the remaining flour, ½ cup at a time, until a soft dough that just clears the sides of the bowl is formed. Switch to a wooden spoon when necessary if mixing by hand.

3. Turn the dough out onto a lightly floured work surface and knead until smooth and springy, about 5 minutes, dusting with flour only 1 tablespoon at a time as needed to prevent sticking. If kneading by machine, switch from the paddle to the dough hook and knead for 4 to 5 minutes, or until the dough is smooth and springy and springs back when pressed. If desired, transfer the dough to a floured surface and knead briefly by hand.

4. Place the dough in a greased deep container. Turn once to coat the top and cover with plastic wrap. Let rise at room temperature until doubled in bulk, 1 to 1½ hours.

5. To form bagels: Gently deflate the dough. Turn the dough out onto a lightly floured work surface. Divide it into quarters. Divide each quarter into 6 to 8 equal portions. Shape each ball of dough into a smooth round, tucking the excess dough underneath. Flatten each ball with your palm. Poke a floured finger through the middle of the ball. Stretch the hole with your finger to make it about 1 inch in diameter. Spin the dough around your finger. The hole will be quite large as you spin, but will shrink slightly when you stop. Set aside on a lightly floured work surface while forming the other bagels. The bagels will need no further rising at this point.

6. Twenty minutes before baking, preheat the oven to 425°F. Grease or parchment-line 2 baking sheets. Meanwhile, in a large pot, bring 3 to 4 quarts of water to a boil. Add 2 tablespoons of salt or sugar to the boiling water, depending on the flavor you want the crust to have. Reduce the heat to maintain a gentle low boil.

7. With a slotted spatula, lower 3 to 4 bagels at a time into the gently boiling water. They will drop to the bottom and then rise to the surface. As they come to the surface, turn each bagel and boil it 3 minutes on the other side. This goes very quickly; if you are making the entire batch of bagels, use a second pot of boiling water.

8. Remove the bagels from the boiling water with a slotted spoon and place each 1 inch apart on the baking sheets. When all the bagels have been boiled, brush with the glaze and sprinkle with the seeds, if desired. Place the baking sheet in the oven, and bake for 25 to 30 minutes, or until deep golden. Transfer the bagels immediately to a cooling rack.

9. To form and bake a bagel loaf: In Step 5, turn the dough out onto a lightly floured work surface and divide it into 3 equal portions. Form into rectangular loaves and place in 3 greased 9-by-5-inch loaf pans. Cover loosely with plastic wrap and let rise at room temperature until just level with the tops of the pans (these loaves will rise a lot in the oven), about 40 minutes. Twenty minutes before baking, preheat the oven to 375°F.

Brush the tops gently with the Egg Glaze, and, using kitchen shears, carefully snip the top of the dough about ½ inch deep at 2-inch intervals down the center of the loaf. Bake in the center of the preheated oven until crusty, golden brown, and the top sounds hollow when tapped with your finger, 40 to 45 minutes. Transfer the loaves to a cooling rack. Cool completely before slicing.

continues next page

WHOLE-WHEAT BAGELS: Substitute 3 cups whole-wheat flour for an equal portion of the unbleached flour.

ORANGE-OATMEAL BAGELS: Substitute 1½ cups oatmeal for an equal portion of the unbleached flour. Add 1 tablespoon grated orange zest and 2 tablespoons honey.

CINNAMON-RAISIN BAGELS: Increase the sugar to ¼ cup. Add 1 tablespoon ground cinnamon, 1 teaspoon ground mace or nutmeg, and ½ teaspoon ground cardamom with the flour in the initial mixing. Add 1½ cups golden or dark raisins during mixing. This dough may be formed into a loaf, glazed, and topped with sesame seeds.

PUMPERNICKEL BAGELS: Substitute 2 cups medium or dark rye flour for an equal portion of unbleached flour. Add ¼ cup molasses, 1 tablespoon unsweetened cocoa, and 1 tablespoon powdered instant coffee. Glaze the tops and sprinkle with caraway seeds.

ONION BAGELS: Sauté 1 finely chopped medium onion, in 4 tablespoons unsalted butter until limp. Set aside. Halfway through baking, glaze the bagel tops and spread 2 teaspoons of onion mixture over each bagel. Finish baking.

THE GOLDEN CRUST:
Biscuits, Shortcakes, Scones, and Soda Breads

The techniques for making biscuits, scones, soda breads, and shortcakes are very simple. Some type of ice-cold vegetable shortening, butter, or lard is cut into a mixture of flour, baking powder, and salt. Generally, 2 to 3 tablespoons of fat per 1 cup of flour is the ratio to look for. Always use all-purpose or cake flour; they have smaller amounts of gluten than bread flour, which would make these breads too tough. The swift motion of fingers, a pastry blender, fork, or two knives should be used to break up the fat to form coarse crumbs. (An electric mixer or food processor makes good biscuits, but it is important not to overmix.) Cutting the fat and keeping the dough moist is what gives biscuits, scones, and soda breads their unique flaky texture. The moisture that evaporates from the cold fat where it comes in contact with the hot temperature of the oven creates a fine-grained layering effect similar to puff pastry.

Cold liquid, usually heavy cream, buttermilk, or milk, is added to the flour-fat mixture all at once and stirred to create a soft ball that just holds together. Any other wet ingredients, such as eggs (which are optional), are added at this time. Always reserve about 2 tablespoons of the liquid to add after mixing in case the dough is too dry. The dough should be quite soft and barely worked, just enough to keep the mixture together.

Handling the dough gently and using just enough flour to make it manageable are the secrets to delicate batter breads. Use a light touch to knead the very soft dough a few times with the heel of the hand and distribute the moisture gently by a soft folding and rolling action. Too much kneading makes biscuits and their relatives tough.

Classic Buttermilk Biscuits

Makes about twelve 2-inch dinner biscuits or twenty-four 1¼-inch cocktail biscuits

2 tablespoons flour, for sprinkling

2 tablespoons cornmeal, for sprinkling

2 cups unbleached all-purpose flour

2 teaspoons baking powder

¼ teaspoon baking soda

¼ teaspoon salt

6 tablespoons (¾ stick) cold unsalted butter, or solid vegetable shortening, cut into pieces

1 large egg

¾ cup cold buttermilk

This classic biscuit has a proportion of three parts dry ingredients to one part liquid to create a dough that will bake high and crisp-crusted. The biscuits sit as easily fresh and hot at a regal dinner as they do rewarmed and slightly chewy, spread with jam the next morning. Consider this recipe a springboard to infinite flavor possibilities.

1. Preheat the oven to 425°F. Grease or parchment-line a baking sheet and sprinkle with cornmeal and flour. In a large bowl using a whisk or an electric mixer, combine the flour, baking powder, baking soda, and salt.

2. Using a pastry blender or 2 knives, cut the butter into the dry ingredients. The mixture will resemble coarse crumbs, with no large chunks of butter. If the butter gets very soft at this point, refrigerate the mixture for 20 minutes to rechill. Add the egg and buttermilk, stirring just to moisten all the ingredients. The dough will be moist, then stiffen while stirring. It should be slightly shaggy, but not sticky.

3. Turn the dough out onto a lightly floured work surface and knead gently about 6 times, or just until the dough holds together. Roll or pat out the dough into a rectangle to no more than ¾ inch thick. Take care not to add too much flour at this point or the biscuits will be tough. Cut with a floured 2½-inch biscuit cutter, pushing straight down without twisting. Cut as close together as possible for a minimum of scraps. Pack together and reroll the scraps to cut out additional biscuits.

4. Place the biscuits ½ inch apart on the baking sheet. Place the baking sheet on a rack in the center of the oven and bake 15 to 18 minutes, or until golden brown. Let rest a few minutes and serve hot.

PECAN BISCUITS: *Add ⅓ cup coarsely chopped toasted or raw pecans to the dry ingredients in Step 1. Proceed to mix, form, and bake as directed. For tea biscuits, add 3 tablespoons sugar with the nuts.*

WILD RICE BISCUITS: *Add ⅔ cup cooled cooked wild rice (see page 113) to the dry ingredients in Step 1. Proceed to mix, form, and bake as directed.*

JALAPEÑO BISCUITS: *Add ¼ cup coarsely chopped fresh or canned jalapeños with the liquid ingredients in Step 2. Proceed to mix, form, and bake as directed.*

BLUEBERRY BISCUITS: *Add ¼ cup sugar to the dry ingredients in Step 1. Add ½ cup fresh or frozen blueberries (unthawed) and the grated zest of 1 orange with the liquid ingredients in Step 2. Proceed to mix, form, and bake as directed.*

WHOLE-WHEAT BISCUITS: *Substitute ¾ cup whole-wheat flour or 2 cups whole-wheat pastry flour for an equal amount of unbleached flour and add to the dry ingredients in Step 1. Proceed to mix, form, and bake as directed.*

BAKER'S WISDOM
Making Biscuits and Shortcakes in a Food Processor

Place the dry ingredients in the work bowl fitted with the steel blade. Process a few seconds just to aerate and mix. Place the butter in pieces on top of the flour mixture and replace the top. Process by pulsing just until the butter is the size of small peas. Do not completely incorporate butter with the flour or the biscuits will be tough. Add the cold liquid through the feed tube and pulse just until a wet mass is formed. Remove the dough from the work bowl and continue to form and bake as directed.

Sweet Potato Biscuits

Makes about 12 biscuits

1 large sweet potato
(about 10 ounces),
baked and peeled

1 2/3 cup unbleached
all-purpose flour

1 tablespoon light
brown sugar

2 1/2 teaspoons baking
powder

1/2 teaspoon salt

6 tablespoons
(3/4 stick) cold
unsalted butter,
cut into pieces

1/4 cup cold whole milk
or heavy cream

I have been making these biscuits every fall for years and I never tire of them. The sweet potato makes them dense, sweet, and moist, They are as excellent served with roasted and grilled meats as they are with butter and honey. These biscuits are a must for winter holiday tables. They also make a filling hors d'oeuvre, sandwiching slices of smoked turkey.

1. Mash or purée the sweet potato pulp by hand, in a blender, or in a food processor until smooth for a total of ¾ cup.

2. Preheat the oven to 425°F. Grease or parchment-line a baking sheet. In a bowl using a whisk or an electric mixer, combine the flour, sugar, baking powder, and salt.

3. Using a pastry blender or two knives, cut the butter into the dry ingredients. The mixture will resemble coarse crumbs, with no large chunks of butter. If the butter gets very soft at this point, refrigerate the mixture to chill the butter. Add the sweet potato pulp and milk or cream, stirring just to moisten all the ingredients. The dough will be moist, then stiffen while stirring. It should be slightly shaggy, but not sticky.

4. Turn the dough out onto a lightly floured work surface and knead gently about 6 times, or just until the dough holds together. Roll or pat out the dough into a rectangle no more than ¾ inch thick. Take care not to add too much flour at this point or the biscuits will be tough. Cut with a floured 2-inch biscuit cutter, pushing straight down without twisting. Reroll the scraps to cut out additional biscuits.

5. Place the biscuits ½ inch apart on the baking sheet. Place the baking sheet on a rack in the center of the oven and bake 15 to 18 minutes, or until golden brown. Let rest a few minutes and serve hot.

Cornmeal-Orange Biscuits

Makes 16 square biscuits

- 2 tablespoons flour, for sprinkling
- 2 tablespoons cornmeal, for sprinkling
- 3 cups unbleached all-purpose flour
- 1 cup fine-grind yellow cornmeal, preferably stone ground
- 2 tablespoons baking powder
- 2 tablespoons sugar
- 1 teaspoon cream of tartar
- ½ teaspoon salt
- Grated zest of 1 large orange
- ¾ cup (1½ sticks) cold unsalted butter, cut into pieces
- 1 cup cold buttermilk
- ½ cup orange juice

The nubby texture of cornmeal mingling with the orange undertones makes a mouth-watering dinner or brunch biscuit.

1. Preheat the oven to 425°F. Grease or parchment-line a baking sheet and sprinkle with flour and cornmeal. In a bowl using a whisk or electric mixer, combine the flour, cornmeal, baking powder, sugar, cream of tartar, salt, and zest.

2. Using a pastry blender or two knives, cut the butter into the dry ingredients. The mixture will resemble coarse crumbs, with no large chunks of butter. If the butter gets very soft at this point, refrigerate the mixture to chill the butter. Add the buttermilk and orange juice, stirring just to moisten all the ingredients. The dough will be moist, then stiffen while stirring. It should be slightly shaggy, but not sticky.

3. Turn the dough out onto a lightly floured work surface and knead gently about 6 times, or just until the dough holds together. Roll or pat out the dough into a rectangle no more than ¾ inch thick. Take care not to add too much flour at this point or the biscuits will be tough. Cut with a sharp knife or pastry wheel to form 16 small squares, pushing straight down without twisting.

4. Place the biscuits ½ inch apart on the baking sheet. Place the baking sheet on a rack in the center of the oven and bake for 15 to 18 minutes, or until golden brown. Let rest a few minutes and serve hot.

Old-fashioned Shortcake Biscuits

Makes 8 shortcakes

2 cups unbleached all-purpose flour

2 tablespoons sugar

1 tablespoon baking powder

½ teaspoon salt

8 tablespoons (1 stick) cold unsalted butter, cut into pieces

1 large egg

½ cup cold whole milk, cultured buttermilk, or heavy cream

Grand Marnier Strawberries and Crème Chantilly (recipe follows)

Genuine fruit shortcakes are an American summer passion. It is the balance of sweet, juicy fruit, fluffy whipped creams, and crumbly, rich biscuits that make them irresistible. This version serves them up with liqueur-spiked Strawberries and Whipped Cream, the brainchild of my baker friend, Janet Gentes. Start with ripe berries, then whip the cream with just a dash of sugar and a splash of liqueur for a hint of flavoring. If whipped cream is not part of your diet, substitute plain yogurt, or frozen yogurt. The biscuit must be impeccably fresh, crisp on the outside and soft on the inside.

1. Preheat the oven to 400°F. Parchment-line a baking sheet, if desired. In a large bowl using a whisk or electric mixer, combine the flour, sugar, baking powder, and salt.

2. Using a pastry blender or two knives, cut the butter into the dry ingredients. The mixture will resemble coarse cornmeal laced with small chunks of butter. Combine the egg and milk, buttermilk, or cream in a measuring cup. Add to the dry ingredients, stirring just until moistened. Add more milk, buttermilk, or cream, 1 tablespoon at a time, if the mixture seems too dry.

3. Turn the dough out onto a clean work surface and knead about 6 times, or just until the dough comes together. The dough will not be totally smooth. Roll out the dough into a rectangle about 1 inch thick. Cut the dough into 4-inch circles, squares, or hearts. Individual short-cakes can be made as small as 1½ inches (the dough can also be formed into 1 large biscuit that can be filled and cut into wedges to serve).

4. Place the individual shortcakes about 1 inch apart on the baking sheet. Place the baking sheet on a rack in the center of the oven and bake for 15 to 18 minutes, or until the tops are brown and firm to the touch. Cool on racks.

5. Using a serrated knife, cut the warm or room temperature biscuits in half crosswise. Place the lower portion of each biscuit on an individual serving plate and top with the Grand Marnier Strawberries and Crème Chantilly. Cover with the biscuit tops. Serve immediately.

GRAND MARNIER STRAWBERRIES AND CRÈME CHANTILLY

Serves 8

3 to 4 pint baskets ripe strawberries, washed, dried, and hulled

2 to 3 tablespoons orange liqueur, such as Grand Marnier

5 tablespoons superfine sugar, or to taste

2 cups cold heavy cream

1. In a large bowl, crush 1 pint of the strawberries. Mix in 1 tablespoon of the orange liqueur and 3 tablespoons of the sugar. Slice or halve the remaining berries and add to the crushed berries. Set aside.

2. In a chilled bowl with an electric mixer, whip the heavy cream with the remaining 2 tablespoons sugar and 1 to 2 tablespoons of the orange liqueur until soft peaks form. Cover and chill until serving.

Lemon Cream Scones

Makes 8 scones

2 cups unbleached all-purpose flour

2 tablespoons sugar

1 tablespoon baking powder

Grated zest of 2 lemons

1/4 teaspoon salt

4 tablespoons (1/2 stick) cold unsalted butter, cut into pieces

2 large eggs

1/2 cup cold heavy cream

1/2 teaspoon ground cinnamon mixed with 2 tablespoons sugar, for sprinkling (optional)

One bite of this warm, homemade scone and you'll fall in love with these exquisitely simple tea breads. The thin, slightly crunchy crust hides a dense, yet moist and fluffy interior. Cream is better for producing the crumb, but you may substitute milk if you must.

1. Preheat the oven to 400°F. Grease or parchment-line a baking sheet. In a medium bowl using a whisk or electric mixer, combine the flour, sugar, baking powder, lemon zest, and salt. Using a fork or electric mixer, cut in the butter. The mixture will resemble coarse crumbs. In a small bowl or 1-cup measure, whisk together the eggs and cream. Add to the dry ingredients, stirring just until a shaggy, sticky dough is formed.

2. Turn the shaggy dough out onto a lightly floured work surface and knead gently, about 6 times, just until the dough holds together. Divide into 3 equal portions and pat each into a 1-inch-thick round about 6 inches in diameter. Using a knife or straight edge, cut each round into quarters, making 4 wedges. The scones can also be formed by cutting out with a 3-inch biscuit cutter to make 10 to 12 smaller scones.

3. Place the scones about 1 inch apart on the baking sheet. Sprinkle the tops with the cinnamon sugar, if desired. Place the baking sheet on a rack in the center of the oven and bake 15 to 20 minutes, or until crusty and golden brown. Serve immediately.

Fig-Walnut Scones

Makes 12 scones

3 cups unbleached all-purpose flour

1/3 cup sugar

1 tablespoon baking powder

1/2 teaspoon baking soda

1/2 teaspoon salt

Grated zest of 1 orange

3/4 cup (1 1/2 sticks) cold unsalted butter, cut into small pieces

3/4 cup coarsely chopped dried figs

1/2 cup chopped walnuts

1 cup cold buttermilk

2 tablespoons sugar mixed with 1/4 teaspoon each ground cinnamon, allspice, and mace, for sprinkling

California is the home of beautiful black, amber, and violet figs: Mission, Kadota, and Calimyrna. A lover of temperate weather, the fig is a prolific and succulent summer fruit. Dried, it is intensely sweet. The combination of nuts and figs in these scones will give you a good reason to make them more often.

1. Preheat the oven to 400°F. Grease or parchment-line a baking sheet. In a medium bowl using a whisk or electric mixer, combine the flour, sugar, baking powder, baking soda, salt, and zest. Using a fork or electric mixer, cut in the butter. The mixture will resemble coarse crumbs. Stir in the figs and walnuts. Add the buttermilk to the dry mixture, stirring just until a shaggy sticky dough is formed.

2. Turn the shaggy dough out onto a lightly floured work surface and knead gently about 6 times, just until the dough holds together. Divide into 3 equal portions and pat each into a 1-inch-thick round about 6 inches in diameter. Using a knife or straight edge, cut each round into quarters, making 4 wedges. The scones can also be formed by cutting out with a 2-inch-biscuit cutter to make 12 to 14 small scones.

3. Sprinkle the tops lightly with the spiced-sugar mixture. Place the scones about 1 inch apart on the baking sheet. Place the baking sheet on a rack in the center of the oven and bake 15 to 20 minutes, or until crusty and golden brown. Serve immediately.

Graham Scones with Pine Nuts and Raisins

Makes 12 scones

2¼ cups graham or fine whole-wheat flour

3 tablespoons light brown sugar

2 teaspoons baking powder

½ teaspoon baking soda

¼ teaspoon salt

8 tablespoons (1 stick) cold unsalted butter, cut into pieces

½ cup pine nuts

½ cup golden raisins

2 large eggs

⅔ cup cold buttermilk

These days we all know the virtues of whole-grain flour: the fiber, the carbohydrates, the vitamins, the minerals—good nutrition in every bite. But beyond these virtues is the gloriously nutty flavor that is unique to graham flour, a special grind of whole wheat. Although fine whole-wheat flour is perfectly acceptable, do search out coarse-textured graham flour for these scones, and savor the taste.

1. Preheat the oven to 400°F. Grease or parchment-line a baking sheet. In a medium bowl using a whisk or electric mixer, combine the flour, brown sugar, baking powder, baking soda, and salt. Using a fork or an electric mixer, cut the butter into the dry ingredients. The mixture will resemble coarse crumbs. Add the pine nuts and raisins and toss to combine. In a small bowl or 1-cup measure, whisk together the eggs and buttermilk. Add the mixture to the dry mixture, stirring until a shaggy sticky dough is formed.

2. Turn the shaggy dough out onto a lightly floured work surface and knead gently about 6 times, just until the dough holds together. Divide into 3 equal portions and pat each into a 1-inch-thick round about 6 inches in diameter. Using a knife or straight edge, cut each round into quarters, making 4 wedges. The scones can also be formed by cutting out with a 2-inch biscuit cutter to make 13 or 14 smaller scones.

3. Place the scones about 1 inch apart on the baking sheet. Place the baking sheet on a rack in the center of the oven and bake 15 to 20 minutes, or until crusty and golden brown. Serve immediately.

Irish Soda Bread with Caraway and Drambuie

Makes 2 medium round loaves

- 1½ cups golden raisins
- 6 tablespoons Drambuie
- 2 cups unbleached all-purpose flour
- 2 cups whole-wheat flour, preferably stone ground
- ¼ cup (packed) light brown sugar
- 2 teaspoons baking powder
- 1 teaspoon baking soda
- 1 teaspoon salt
- 1 tablespoon caraway seeds
- 1½ cups cold buttermilk
- 2 large eggs
- 2 tablespoons unsalted butter, melted

Soda breads are Celtic country hearth breads made throughout the British Isles and originally baked in wood-fired clay ovens built into home chimneys. It is a bread easily mixed and baked, ready to serve in less than an hour. Drambuie is a liqueur made of good Scotch whisky, heather honey, and a secret collection of herbs. Soda breads beg to be eaten crusty and warm.

1. In a small bowl, combine the raisins and liqueur. Let stand at room temperature to macerate 30 minutes.

2. Preheat oven to 375°F. Grease or parchment-line a baking sheet or two 8-inch cake pans. In a large bowl using a whisk or electric mixer, combine the flours, sugar, baking powder, baking soda, salt, and caraway seeds. In another bowl, combine the buttermilk, eggs, and butter and beat slightly with a whisk. Add the macerated raisins.

3. Make a well in the dry ingredients and pour in the buttermilk mixture. Stir with a wooden spoon just to moisten. The dough will not be as stiff as yeast bread dough. Turn the dough out onto a lightly floured work surface and knead gently about 6 times, or until the dough comes together. Form into 2 round loaves by hand and place on the baking sheet or into the pans. Using a serrated knife, slash the tops with an **X** no more than ¼ inch deep on each top to allow for expansion and even baking.

4. Place the baking sheet or bread pan on a rack in the center of the oven and bake 40 to 50 minutes, or until the loaves sound hollow when tapped with your finger and are brown and crusty. Transfer the loaves to a cooling rack. Serve warm or at room temperature the same day.

Whole-Wheat Irish Herb Bread

Makes 2 medium round loaves

2 cups unbleached all-purpose flour

2 cups whole-wheat flour

1/3 cup packed light brown sugar

1 tablespoon baking powder

1 teaspoon baking soda

1 teaspoon salt

1 teaspoon dried basil

1/2 teaspoon dried thyme

1/2 teaspoon dried marjoram or oregano

1/2 cup raw sunflower seeds

1 cup dried currants

1 1/2 cups cold buttermilk

2 large eggs

2 tablespoons unsalted butter, melted

Irish soda bread is often truly underestimated, except by the few who crave this homestyle bread. This is a basic recipe lends itself to substitutions.

1. Preheat the oven to 375°F. Grease or parchment-line a baking sheet or two 8-inch cake pans. In a large bowl using a whisk or electric mixer, combine flours, brown sugar, baking powder, baking soda, salt, herbs, seeds, and currants. In another bowl using a whisk or electric mixer, combine buttermilk, eggs, and butter. Beat slightly. Add the wet ingredients to the dry and stir with a wooden spoon just to moisten.

2. Turn the dough out onto a lightly floured work surface and knead gently about 6 times until the dough comes together. Divide into 2 equal portions. Place the dough on the baking sheet or in the cake pans. Using a sharp knife, slash tops with an **X** about 1/2 inch deep. Place the baking sheet or cake pans on a rack in the center of the oven and bake for 30 to 40 minutes, or until brown and crusty. Serve warm or at room temperature.

NOTE: *Substitute up to 1 cup oat flour (available in health-food stores) for an equal amount of whole-wheat flour.*

Whole-Wheat Bran Bread with Dates

Makes two 8-by-4-inch loaves

2¼ cups whole-wheat flour

1¾ cups wheat bran

¼ cup (packed) light brown sugar

1½ teaspoons baking soda

½ teaspoon baking powder

½ teaspoon salt

1¾ cups buttermilk

1 large egg

⅓ cup molasses

⅔ cup chopped pitted dates

This unusual bread is a coarse-textured, mildly sweet loaf made with no butter or oil. Considering how economical the ingredients, the resulting flavor of this loaf is distinctive.

1. Preheat the oven to 350°F. Grease and flour the loaf pans. In a large bowl using a whisk, combine the flour, bran, brown sugar, baking soda, baking powder, and salt.

2. In a small bowl using a whisk or electric mixer, combine the buttermilk, egg, and molasses. Beat until frothy. Add the dates and stir to combine. Pour over the dry ingredients, stirring just until moistened.

3. Spoon the batter into the loaf pans. Place the pans on a rack in the center of the oven and bake 60 to 70 minutes, or until a cake tester inserted into the center comes out clean and the top is crusty. Let the loaves rest in the pan 15 minutes. Remove the loaves to a cooling rack and cool completely. Wrap tightly in plastic wrap and let stand at room temperature overnight before serving.

SAVORY SPECIAL OCCASIONS:
Picnic Breads

An old-fashioned picnic creates a world of its own, and people who love picnicking are dedicated to its simple, spontaneous pleasures. It is a celebration of the earth. Whether miles from home in the wine country, viewing the sunset from a neighboring mountain, under a park's big shade oak, or at a table spread in your own backyard, a picnic is a shared adventure, a free-spirited style of eating.

Picnic fare demands abundance, contrasting textures, and strong flavors to satisfy robust appetites. The natural beauty of the food itself sets the table, and bread is an essential part of any picnic. Think beyond the traditional sandwich to make-ahead main-dish breads that are easy to pack and good to eat. Meat or fish, cheese, and vegetables baked into bread, incorporate all elements into one dish. The emphasis should always be on substantial and nourishing seasonally fresh ingredients.

Sausage Bread

Makes 1 large loaf

1 recipe Basic Pizza Dough (page 213)

2 pounds sweet turkey Italian sausage with black pepper and fennel seeds

1 large yellow onion, chopped

Freshly ground black pepper, to taste

Olive oil, for brushing

One bread that all my Italian friends remember from their childhoods is sausage bread. It uses any pizza dough recipe and is a great picnic food, late-night snack, or brunch accompaniment to scrambled eggs.

1. Prepare the pizza dough and let it rise. Meanwhile, place a heavy skillet over medium heat. Remove the sausage from its casings, crumble into the skillet, and sauté until the fat is rendered, 5 minutes. Blot or spoon off most of the fat and add the onion. Sauté until the meat is cooked through and the onion is limp. Remove from the heat, season with pepper, and cool to room temperature.

2. Parchment-line a large baking sheet. Turn the dough out onto a lightly floured work surface. With a rolling pin, roll out the dough to a 14-by-10-inch rectangle. Spread the sausage filling evenly over the dough, leaving a 1-inch border all around. Beginning at the long edge, roll up jelly-roll fashion to form a long, tight loaf. Pinch the edges and bottom seam tightly to seal. Place on the parchment-lined baking sheet, with one end positioned in the center of the pan. Keeping this end in place, coil the roll into a spiral, tucking the outside end under. Brush the top with olive oil and cover loosely with plastic wrap. Let rise at room temperature until doubled in bulk, about 1 hour. Twenty minutes before baking, preheat the oven to 375°F, with a baking stone set on the center rack, if desired.

3. Brush the top again with olive oil and bake in the center of the oven until brown and firm to the touch, 45 to 55 minutes. Remove from the baking sheet to cool on a wire rack before slicing. Serve warm or at room temperature, spread with mustard if desired. Store, wrapped in plastic in the refrigerator, for up to 2 days.

Shallot and Poppy Seed Braid

Makes 1 large or 2 small braids

Dough

1 tablespoon
(1 package)
active dry yeast

3 tablespoons sugar

2 teaspoons salt

4 to 4½ cups unbleached
all-purpose flour or
bread flour

1 cup hot milk (120°F)

½ cup hot water
(120°F)

1 large egg

8 tablespoons (1 stick)
unsalted butter, at
room temperature,
cut into small pieces

**Shallot–Poppy Seed
Filling**

4 teaspoons unsalted
butter

2 tablespoons olive oil

⅔ cup chopped shallots
(about 6 medium to
large shallots)

⅔ cup chopped pearl
onions (4 small
onions)

3 tablespoons grated
parmesan cheese

5 tablespoons poppy
seeds

Rich Egg Glaze
(page 52)

1 tablespoon poppy
seeds, for sprinkling

The common shallot is a small bulb about the size of a large nut. Its flavor is more delicate than that of onion and less pungent than that of garlic. Shallots are unsurpassed as an ingredient in this savory stuffed bread.

1. To prepare the dough: In a large bowl using a whisk or in the work bowl of a heavy-duty electric mixer fitted with the paddle attachment, combine the yeast, sugar, salt, and 1½ cups of the flour. Add the milk and water and beat until creamy about 1 minute. Add the egg and butter pieces with ½ cup more flour and beat until the butter is incorporated. Add the remaining flour, ½ cup at a time, until a soft dough that just clears the sides of the bowl is formed. Switch to a wooden spoon when necessary if mixing by hand.

2. Turn the dough out onto a lightly floured work surface and knead gently until a soft, yet springy, dough is formed, dusting with flour only 1 tablespoon at a time as needed to prevent sticking, about 6 minutes.

If kneading by machine, switch from the paddle to the dough hook and knead for 4 to 6 minutes, or until the dough is smooth and springy and springs back when pressed. If desired, transfer the dough to a floured surface and knead briefly by hand.

3. Place the dough in a greased deep container. Turn once to coat the top and cover with plastic wrap. Let rise at room temperature until doubled in bulk, about 1½ hours.

4. To prepare the filling: In a medium skillet or sauté pan, melt the butter and oil. Add the shallots and white onions and cook until just limp and translucent but not browned, or the filling will be bitter. Remove from the heat and stir in the cheese and poppy seeds. Set aside to cool to room temperature.

5. Gently deflate the dough. Turn the dough out onto lightly floured work surface. Grease or parchment-line a baking sheet. Roll the dough out with a rolling pin to an 18-by-12-inch rectangle, moving the dough frequently to prevent sticking. Cut the dough lengthwise into three 4-inch-wide strips. Carefully spread the filling over the center of each strip, leaving a 1-inch margin of dough all the way around. Fold over the edges and pinch them together, encasing the filling. Lift the ropes gently onto the baking sheet and place them 1 inch apart. Beginning in the middle, braid each rope loosely to each end. Pinch the ends and tuck them under securely. Cover loosely with plastic wrap and let rise until doubled in bulk, about 30 minutes.

6. Twenty minutes before baking, preheat the oven to 350°F. Gently brush the dough with Egg Glaze and sprinkle lightly with poppy seeds. Place the baking sheet on a rack in the center of the oven and bake 35 to 40 minutes, or until golden brown and a cake tester inserted in the center of a loaf comes out clean. Transfer immediately from the baking sheet to a cooling rack. Cool completely before serving.

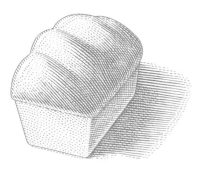

Crescia al Formaggio

Makes 1 large ring loaf

¾ cup warm water (105° to 115°F)

1 tablespoon (1 package) active dry yeast

Pinch of sugar

½ teaspoon salt

¾ cup grated Parmesan cheese

About 3½ cups unbleached all-purpose flour

5 large eggs, at room temperature

8 tablespoons (1 stick) unsalted butter at room temperature, cut into small pieces

3 cups (12 ounces) coarsely shredded Emmenthaler or Gruyère cheese

This savory cheese bread has been traditional Easter fare in Italy for hundreds of years. It is a dramatic and truly beautiful golden loaf of rich egg dough streaked with cheese. The name *crescia* (from the Italian *crescere*, or to grow) describes the puffy doming of the dough above its mold during baking. It is an ideal picnic bread.

1. In a large bowl using a whisk, or in the work bowl of a heavy-duty electric mixer fitted with the paddle attachment, pour in the water. Sprinkle the yeast and sugar over the surface of the water. Stir until dissolved and let stand at room temperature until foamy, about 10 minutes.

2. Add the salt, Parmesan cheese, and 1 cup of the flour to the yeast mixture. Beat with until creamy, about 1 minute. Add 4 of the eggs, one at a time. Add the remaining flour, ½ cup at a time, to form a soft dough that just clears the sides of the bowl is formed. Switch to a wooden spoon when necessary if mixing by hand.

3. Turn the dough out onto a lightly floured work surface and knead gently until springy and satiny, about 5 minutes, dusting with flour only 1 tablespoon at a time as needed to prevent sticking. The dough will have a slightly gritty feel from the cheese.

If kneading by machine, switch from the paddle to the dough hook and knead for 3 to 4 minutes, or until the dough is smooth and springy and springs back when pressed. If desired, transfer the dough to a floured surface and knead briefly by hand.

4. Place the dough in a greased deep container and dot all over with the pieces of butter. Cover with plastic wrap and let rise at room temperature until doubled in bulk, about 1½ hours.

5. Using a wooden spoon or an electric mixer, beat the butter into the dough. Turn the dough out onto a lightly floured work surface and pat into a 10-by-4-inch rectangle. In a small bowl, beat the remaining egg and toss with the shredded cheese. Spread the cheese mixture evenly over the dough surface, leaving a 1-inch border all around the edges. Starting from the long end, roll up jelly-roll fashion and pinch the seams to seal. Place the rope in a greased 12-cup mold with a center funnel; the mold should be no more than half full. Cover with plastic wrap and let rise at room temperature until fully doubled in bulk, about 45 minutes.

6. Twenty minutes before baking, preheat the oven to 375°F. Place the mold onto the lowest rack of the oven and bake 40 to 45 minutes, or domed and golden brown. Loosely place a piece of foil over the top if it is becoming too brown. Remove the mold from the oven and let stand 15 minutes before turning out onto a cooling rack. Cool completely before serving.

NOTE: *The bread may also be baked in 2 coffee cans or two 8-by-4-inch loaf pans.*

Pancetta-Onion Gruyère Ring

Makes 1 large ring loaf

Dough

1½ tablespoons
(1½ packages)
active dry yeast

1 tablespoon sugar

¼ cup wheat bran

4 to 4½ cups unbleached
all-purpose flour or
bread flour

2 teaspoons salt

½ cup hot water
(120°F)

1 cup hot milk (120°F)

2 large eggs, at room
temperature

2 tablespoons Dijon
mustard

8 tablespoons (1 stick)
unsalted butter at
room temperature,
cut into pieces

Filling

10 slices, ¼ inch thick,
pancetta (see Note)

1 medium onion,
chopped

8 ounces cream cheese

2 large eggs, at room
temperature

2 cups (8 ounces)
shredded Gruyère
cheese

¼ cup sesame seeds

Pale straw-colored Gruyère is a prince among French cheeses, as tasty for eating in thin wedges cut from the wheel as for melting in fondue. Here it's paired with pancetta and onion to make a very special ring-shaped bread that is the essence of a perfect picnic loaf.

1. To make the dough: In a large bowl using a whisk or in the work bowl of a heavy-duty mixer fitted with paddle attachment, combine the yeast, sugar, bran, 1 cup of the flour, and salt. Add the water, milk, eggs, and mustard. Beat until evenly moistened, about 1 minute. Add 1 cup more of the flour and the butter in pieces, beating to incorporate it into the dough. Beat in the remaining flour, ½ cup at a time, until a soft dough that just clears the sides of the bowl is formed. Switch to a wooden spoon when necessary if mixing by hand.

2. Turn the dough out onto a lightly floured work surface and knead until smooth and soft dough, about 5 minutes, dusting with flour only 1 tablespoon at a time as needed to prevent sticking.

If kneading by machine, switch from the paddle to the dough hook and knead for 3 to 4 minutes, or until the dough is smooth and springy and springs back when pressed. If desired, transfer the dough to a floured surface and knead briefly by hand.

3. Place the dough in a greased deep container. Turn once to coat the top and cover with plastic wrap. Let rise at room temperature until doubled in bulk, about 1 hour.

4. To make the filling: In a large skillet or sauté pan, cook the pancetta and onion over medium heat until well browned. Drain on a paper towel and cool.

5. Separate 1 of the eggs, reserving the white for glazing. In a medium bowl, beat the cream cheese with the yolk and the remaining egg until smooth. Fold in the pancetta-onion mixture and the shredded cheese.

6. Gently deflate the dough. Grease a 10-inch tube pan or fluted mold. Turn the dough out onto a lightly floured work surface and roll out into an 18-by-8-inch rectangle. Mound the cheese mixture down the center of the rectangle. Fold each short side over the filling, overlapping the dough 2 inches. Using your palm, shape the dough into a long cylinder, twist it into a spiral and place it seam side down in the pan; it will spiral around 12 times in the pan, forming 2 layers. The dough should fill the mold about two thirds full. Cover with plastic wrap and let rest at room temperature for about 30 minutes, or until puffy.

7. Twenty minutes before baking, preheat the oven to 375°F. Beat the reserved egg white with 1 tablespoon water until foamy. Brush the top of the dough with the glaze and sprinkle it with sesame seeds. Place the mold on a rack in the center of the oven and bake 50 minutes to 1 hour, or until golden brown and hollow sounding when tapped with your finger. Remove from the pan immediately right side up to a cooling rack. Let cool for at least 30 minutes before serving.

NOTE: *Pancetta is a round Italian bacon available at specialty food stores.*

Garlic and Mozzarella Stromboli

Serves 4 to 6

2 teaspoons active dry yeast

Pinch of sugar, or 1 teaspoon honey or barley malt syrup

½ cup whole-wheat pastry flour

1 cup warm water (105° to 115°F)

1 large egg, at room temperature

2 tablespoons olive oil

½ teaspoon salt

2 to 2½ cups unbleached all-purpose flour

Garlic-Mozzarella Filling

1 cup (4 ounces) shredded whole-milk mozzarella cheese

½ cup (2 ounces) shredded smoked mozzarella cheese

½ cup grated Parmesan cheese

3 tablespoons minced Italian flat-leaf parsley

1 large garlic clove, minced

1 large egg, at room temperature

Olive oil, for brushing

I don't need a special occasion to pack a homemade stromboli roll, sliced cucumbers and crisp red peppers, fresh fruit, and a chilled bottle of mineral water in my old basket and head up to the local winery to enjoy the day. It is important to allow the cheese roll to rest for at least an hour after baking, for the easiest and neatest slicing. The stromboli is excellent at room temperature, cold, or warm. To serve it warm, reheat the slices on a baking sheet at 350°F for about ten minutes. If not eaten the same day it is made, store wrapped in plastic in the refrigerator.

1. Pour the warm water in a small bowl. Sprinkle the yeast, sugar or other sweetener, and 1 tablespoon of the whole-wheat flour over the surface of water. Stir to dissolve and let stand at room temperature until foamy, about 15 minutes.

2. In a large bowl with a whisk or in the work bowl of a heavy-duty electric mixer fitted with the paddle attachment, combine the egg, oil, salt, the remaining whole-wheat flour, 1 cup of the unbleached flour, and the yeast mixture. Beat hard until smooth, about 1 minute. Add the remaining unbleached flour, ¼ cup at a time, until a soft, sticky dough that just clears the sides of the bowl is formed. Switch to a wooden spoon when necessary if making by hand.

3. Turn the dough out onto a lightly floured work surface and knead vigorously, about 5 minutes, until springy, dusting with flour only 1 tablespoon at a time as needed to prevent sticking. The dough should be quite soft, smooth, and very springy. Shape into a flattened ball.

If kneading by machine, switch from the paddle to the dough hook and knead for 4 to 5 minutes, or until the dough is smooth and springy and springs back when pressed. If desired, transfer the dough to a floured surface and knead briefly by hand.

4. Place the dough in a greased container. Turn the dough once to coat the top with an extra tablespoon of olive oil and cover with plastic wrap. Let rise at room temperature until tripled in bulk, about 1 hour.

5. To make the filling: Place all the filling ingredients in a bowl and mix until evenly combined and coated with the egg. Set aside in the refrigerator until needed.

6. Gently deflate the dough. Turn the dough out onto a very lightly floured work surface. Parchment-line a baking sheet. Roll into a 16-inch-by-12-inch rectangle. Dust with a bit of flour, if necessary, to prevent sticking. Position the dough so that the shorter ends are to either side. Spread the filling in an even layer over the dough, leaving a full 1-inch border around the edges. (Be careful not to poke any holes which would leak filling.) Starting from a long side, roll up jelly-roll fashion. Pinch together the seams; tuck under the ends, pinching them into tapered points. Using 2 spatulas, carefully transfer the loaf seam side down to the baking sheet. Position the roll on the diagonal if necessary to fit. Cover lightly with plastic wrap and let rest 30 minutes. If you wish a thinner, crispier outer crust and a less breadlike interior, bake immediately.

7. Twenty minutes before baking, preheat the oven to 400°F, with a baking stone, if desired. Brush the top of the roll with olive oil and prick all over with a fork to allow steam to escape. Place the baking sheet on a rack in the center of the oven and bake for 15 minutes, then reduce the oven thermostat to 375°F. Bake 20 to 25 minutes more, or until golden brown and crusty and the loaves sound hollow when tapped with your finger. Let rest on the baking sheet 10 minutes, then transfer to a cooling rack. Cool completely before slicing.

Italian-Style Herb Bread

Serves about 6

- 1½ teaspoons freshly ground black pepper
- 2 teaspoons dried basil
- 2 teaspoons dried chervil
- 2 teaspoons dried thyme
- 2 teaspoons dried savory
- ⅓ cup olive oil
- 1½ tablespoons (1½ packages) active dry yeast
- Sugar
- 1 cup warm water (105° to 115°F)
- 1 cup dry white wine
- 1 tablespoon salt
- About 5½ cups unbleached all-purpose flour or bread flour
- 1½ pounds sweet Italian sausages, removed from casing and crumbled
- 1 large onion, chopped
- 2 garlic cloves, minced
- ¼ cup chopped oil-packed sun-dried tomatoes
- 1 tablespoon anise liqueur, such as Pernod
- 8 ounces whole-milk mozzarella, diced

Mozzarella is a fresh cow's milk cheese, soft, malleable with a mild, tangy flavor. It is used widely in cooking because it melts so beautifully. This spicy-sausage-and-cheese-stuffed bread is the epitome of picnic fare. Use whole-milk rather than skim-milk mozzarella, for better flavor and texture.

1. In a small bowl, combine pepper and herbs with the olive oil and let stand at least 1 hour at room temperature.

2. Pour the warm water in a small bowl. Sprinkle the yeast and a pinch of sugar over the water. Stir to dissolve and let stand at room temperature until foamy, about 10 minutes. In a large bowl using a whisk or in the work bowl of a heavy-duty electric mixer fitted with the paddle attachment, combine the wine, yeast mixture, sugar, salt, and herb-oil mixture. Beat until foamy. Add the flour, 1 cup at a time, stirring with a wooden spoon to make a soft dough.

3. Turn the dough out on a lightly floured work surface and knead until springy, smooth, and resilient, about 5 minutes, dusting with flour only 1 tablespoon at a time as needed.

If kneading by machine, switch from the paddle to the dough hook and knead for 3 to 4 minutes, or until the dough is smooth and springy and springs back when pressed. If desired, transfer the dough to a floured surface and knead briefly by hand.

4. Place the dough in a greased bowl. Turn once to grease the top and cover with plastic wrap. Let rise at room temperature until doubled in bulk, about 1 hour.

5. Meanwhile, in a large skillet, combine the sausages, onion, and garlic and cook over medium heat until the sausage is browned and the onions are soft. Stir in the tomatoes and liqueur. Let cool to room temperature.

6. Twenty minutes before baking, preheat the oven to 400°F with a baking stone, if desired. Gently deflate the dough. Turn the dough out onto a lightly floured work surface. Grease or parchment-line a baking sheet. Pat into a 14-by-10-inch rectangle. Spread the sausage mixture

Olive oil, for
brushing (optional)

evenly over the center third of the dough and sprinkle with the cheese.
Fold the dough into a rectangle by bringing the 2 long ends together
and pinch to close. Fold each short end over about 1 inch and pinch to
close. Lay the long seam side down on the baking sheet. Snip or slash
the top with a knife with cuts 1 inch deep and on an angle. Brush the loaf
with olive oil, if desired. Let rest 10 minutes. Place the baking sheet in
the center of the oven and bake 40 to 50 minutes, or until brown and
the loaf sounds hollow when tapped with your finger. Transfer immediately to a cooling rack. Cool completely before slicing.

Torta d'Erbe

Italian Green Tort

Serves 4 to 6

Olive Oil Pastry

- 1 teaspoon active dry yeast
- Pinch of sugar
- 1/3 cup warm water (105° to 115°F)
- 3 tablespoons olive oil
- 1 large egg, at room temperature
- 1/4 teaspoon salt
- 1 1/2 to 1 2/3 cups unbleached all-purpose flour

Savory Green Filling

- 3 tablespoons olive oil
- 2 small shallots, minced
- 1/2 cup diced zucchini or yellow summer squash
- 2 bunches spinach or swiss chard, washed, stemmed, and coarsely chopped
- Pinch of freshly ground black pepper
- Pinch of freshly grated nutmeg
- 1/4 cup chopped basil leaves
- 1/4 cup chopped parsley
- 8 ounces (1 cup) whole-milk ricotta

Torta d'erbe is a rustic savory yeasted pie filled with cheese, greens, fresh herbs, summer squash, and eggs. Based on a medieval tart, it is related to the French quiche. Borage, sorrel, or beet greens may be substituted for the chard.

1. To prepare the pastry: In a large bowl with a whisk or the work bowl of a heavy-duty electric mixer fitted with the paddle attachment, pour in the warm water. Sprinkle the yeast and sugar over the surface of the water. Stir to dissolve and let stand at room temperature until foamy, about 10 minutes. Add the olive oil, egg, and salt. Gradually beat in 1 1/2 cups of the flour to make a soft dough, about 1 minute. Switch to a wooden spoon when necessary if mixing by hand.

2. Turn the dough out onto a lightly floured work surface and knead no more than 10 times to make a soft, springy ball, adding no more than 2 tablespoons or so of flour to prevent sticking.

If kneading by machine, switch from the paddle to the dough hook and knead for 1 to 2 minutes, or until the dough is smooth and springy and springs back when pressed. If desired, transfer the dough to a floured surface and knead briefly by hand.

3. Place the dough in a greased container. Cover with plastic wrap and let rise at room temperature until puffy, about 1 hour.

4. To make the filling: Heat the oil in a medium skillet or sauté pan and cook the shallots and zucchini or squash until soft. Add the spinach or chard and stir until just wilted. Drain any accumulated liquid. Stir in the pepper, nutmeg, basil, and parsley. Set aside and let cool to room temperature. In a separate bowl, combine the ricotta, mozzarella, eggs, cream, and cheese. Add the cooled vegetable mixture and stir until blended.

5. Twenty minutes before baking, preheat the oven to 350°F. Grease and

½ cup coarsely shredded whole-milk mozzarella

3 large eggs, at room temperature

½ cup heavy cream

¼ cup grated Parmesan or Asiago cheese

dust a 10-inch tart pan with cornmeal. Roll the dough out on a lightly floured work surface to a 10-inch round. Line the tart pan with the dough, pressing the dough up the sides slightly. Let the dough rest 10 minutes. Gently scrape the filling into the prepared tart shell. Place the tart pan on a rack in the center of the oven and bake for 35 to 40 minutes, or until the filling is set and the crust is golden. Let cool for 15 minutes in the pan before removing the sides and cutting into wedges to serve.

Eggplant, Pepper, and Artichoke Pie

Serves 6

Torta Dough

2 teaspoons active
dry yeast

Pinch of sugar

⅓ cup warm water
(105° to 115°F)

⅓ cup whole-wheat
flour

½ teaspoon salt

2 large eggs, at room
temperature

1⅔ cups unbleached
all-purpose flour

8 tablespoons (1 stick)
unsalted butter, at
room temperature,
cut into small pieces

Vegetable Filling

¼ cup olive oil

1 medium onion,
chopped

1 red bell pepper,
cored, seeded,
and cut into thin
strips

4 Japanese or baby
eggplants, scrubbed
and cut into cubes

2 garlic cloves,
chopped

2 teaspoons dried
mixed Italian herbs

½ teaspoon salt

½ teaspoon freshly
ground black pepper

A *torta rustica* is an Italian-style savory pie. This one, adapted from an exceptional recipe by San Francisco Bay Area food writer Cynthia Scheer, is quickly assembled, making it easy for beginning bakers despite the long list of ingredients.

1. To make the torta dough: In a medium bowl using a whisk or the work bowl of a heavy-duty electric mixer fitted with the paddle attachment, pour in the warm water. Sprinkle the yeast and sugar over the surface of the water. Stir to dissolve and let stand at room temperature until foamy, about 10 minutes. Add the whole-wheat flour and salt.

2. Beat until creamy, about 30 seconds. Beat in the eggs, one at a time, until incorporated. Add the unbleached flour, ½ cup at a time, until a soft dough that just clears the sides of the bowl is formed. Switch to a wooden spoon when necessary if mixing by hand. Beat in the butter 1 tablespoon at a time, beating well after each addition. The dough will be soft and sticky.

3. Place the dough on a lightly floured work surface and knead about 6 times to form a smooth ball. Use only a few teaspoons more flour if the dough is very sticky; it is important that the dough be moist and resilient.

If kneading by machine, switch from the paddle to the dough hook and knead for 1 to 2 minutes, or until the dough is smooth and springs back when pressed. If desired, transfer the dough to a floured surface and knead briefly by hand.

4. Place the dough in a greased deep container. Cover with plastic wrap and let rise at room temperature until doubled in bulk, about 1 hour.

5. To make the filling: In a large skillet or sauté pan, heat the oil over medium heat. Add the onion, red pepper, and eggplants, stirring until soft and beginning to brown. Add the garlic, herbs, salt, pepper, and artichoke hearts. Stir and add the tomatoes and their liquid. Bring to a boil, reduce the heat to medium, and cook until the vegetables are tender and the liquid is evaporated, about 10 minutes. Remove from the heat and set aside to cool to room temperature.

2 packages
(9 ounces each)
frozen artichokes,
defrosted

1 can (14½ ounces)
plum tomatoes,
drained (liquid
reserved) and
chopped

3 large eggs, at room
temperature

1½ cups (6 ounces)
shredded Swiss or
Gruyère cheese

½ cup grated
Parmesan cheese
plus 1 tablespoon for
sprinkling

6. Twenty minutes before baking, preheat the oven to 375°F. In a large mixing bowl using a whisk, beat the eggs. Add the cooled vegetables and cheeses and stir to blend evenly. Gently deflate the dough. Turn the dough out onto a lightly floured work surface. Grease an 8-inch springform pan. Divide into 1 large and 1 small portion, about two thirds and one third of the dough respectively. Roll out the larger portion to a 12-inch round and place in a greased 8-inch springform pan. Press the dough up and over the sides of the pan, letting the excess hang over the edge. Add the vegetable mixture and fold in the overhanging dough. Turn the dough under and gently crimp. Roll out the remaining portion of dough to an 8-inch square and cut it into 1-inch-wide strips. Space half the strips evenly over the top of the torta and the other half over the top in the opposite direction to form a lattice weave. Tuck the dough edges under and recrimp. Sprinkle the top with 1 tablespoon of the Parmesan cheese.

7. Place the pan on the center rack of the oven and bake for 50 minutes to 1 hour, or until browned and set. Cool in the pan on a rack for 10 minutes before removing the sides of the pan. Let stand for 1 hour before cutting into wedges. Serve warm or at room temperature. Store leftovers in the refrigerator.

Onion Tart

Filling makes one 12-inch onion tart and enough dough for 2 tarts or 1 shallow 11-by-17-inch sheet

Tart Dough

1 tablespoon (1 package) active dry yeast

1 tablespoon sugar

1 cup warm water (105° to 115°F)

2¾ to 3 cups unbleached all-purpose flour or bread flour

1½ tablespoons salt

2 tablespoons corn oil

1 large egg, at room temperature, slightly beaten

Onion Filling

4 large onions, thinly sliced

8 tablespoons (1 stick) unsalted butter

1 cup sour cream or crème fraîche

3 large eggs, at room temperature

Pinch of salt

1 teaspoon freshly ground black pepper

Here is a relative of quiche: an onion custard baked in yeasted bread dough. In Alsace, the onions would be sautéed in goose fat, in Italy olive oil, and in Germany fresh sweet butter. Since the tart can be eaten hot, warm, or at room temperature, it is good picnic fare.

1. To make the tart dough: Put the yeast, a pinch of the sugar, and ½ cup warm water in a small bowl. Stir until dissolved and let stand at room temperature until foamy, about 10 minutes.

2. In a large bowl using a whisk or in the work bowl of a heavy-duty electric mixer fitted with the paddle attachment, combine 1 cup flour, 1 tablespoon sugar, and the salt. Add the remaining water, oil, egg, and yeast mixture. Beat hard until smooth, about 3 minutes. Add the flour, ½ cup at a time, and beat with a wooden spoon until a shaggy dough that just clears the sides of the bowl is formed.

3. Turn the dough out onto a lightly floured work surface and knead until smooth, resilient, and no longer sticky, about 5 minutes, dusting with flour only 1 tablespoon at a time as needed to prevent sticking. Shape into a ball.

If kneading by machine, switch from the paddle to the dough hook and knead for 3 to 4 minutes, or until the dough is smooth and springy and springs back when pressed. If desired, transfer the dough to a floured surface and knead briefly by hand.

4. Place the dough in a greased bowl. Turn once to grease the top and cover with plastic wrap. Let rise at room temperature until tripled in bulk, 1 to 1½ hours.

5. To make the onion filling: In a skillet sauté pan over low heat, cook the sliced onions in butter until golden and soft, about 20 minutes. Let cool to room temperature. Just before shaping dough, combine sour cream, eggs, salt, and pepper in a bowl; add onions.

6. Gently deflate the dough. Turn out the dough onto a lightly floured work surface. Grease a springform pan or tart tin with a removable bottom. Divide dough into 2 equal portions; freeze 1 for later use. Roll out the remaining portion to fit the pan or tart tin. Pat into the bottom and up the sides. Fold any extra dough down. Pour the onion mixture over the dough.

7. Twenty minutes before baking, preheat the oven to 375°F. Place the pan or tin on a rack in the center of the oven and bake for 35 minutes, or until crispy and golden. The onion filling will be delicate brown and puffy. Let stand 10 minutes before removing the sides of the pan to cool before cutting into wedges.

ARTISTIC PALATE:
Pizza, Calzone, and Focaccia

Pizza evolved from northern Etruscan flatbreads that were baked as ashcakes beneath hot hearth stones. Italian home bakers have long made their own daily flatbreads prepared from family recipes. They also bake calzone (turnovers) and *mezza-lune* (half moons), which are made of folded and stuffed pizza dough. Sicilians roll their pizzas, which are called *bonate* and *stromboli*. Stuffed pizzas are known as *pizza rustica* and *torta rustica*.

Making pizza dough utilizes the same techniques as making regular bread dough; the difference comes in the forming and baking. Although it is hard to reproduce a pizzeria-style pizza without an extremely hot brick oven, a home-made pizza is still very good. The crust is flavorful, chewy, and crisp, the toppings savory and delectable. For best results, use 14-inch tin-lined heavy-gauge aluminum thin-crust pans with Swiss cheese–sized holes, metal screens, or black-finished metal pizza pans, all known as "power pans." I use disposable foil pizza pans, available in the supermarket, for freezing pre-made pizzas. Pizza may also be made with excellent results on top of the stove in a cast-iron skillet with a cover (see page 216). (If using power pans for the first time, season them by placing the empty pan in a 325°F oven for 30 minutes for the shallow pan and 1 hour for the deep dish pan, or until the metal darkens. Remove, using insulated mitts, and cool before filling.)

When pizza dough is folded over and the filling placed inside instead of as a topping, the result is a calzone, stuffed bread convenient for eating out of hand.

Focaccia may well be Italy's oldest traditional bread. It can be topped with sugar and fruit for breakfast, or with herbs, vegetables, and salt for an unparalleled picnic bread.

The best technique for getting crisp crusts on your Italian flatbreads is to bake on ceramic tiles or a baking stone. Lining your oven with a baking stone simulates a commercial deck or pizza oven. The pan is placed directly on the hot stone, and bakes the dough much faster, creating crisp crusts. I use one large stone, 14-by-16-inches, so that wayward filling does not drip onto the bottom of the oven. I have a stone just for baking pizza breads, because with much use, they get very stained. Preheat baking stones for 20 to 30 minutes at 425° to 500°F to heat them all the way through.

Basic Pizza Dough

Makes one 16- to 18-inch crust, two 10- to 12-inch, three 8-inch, or ten 4-inch crust pizzettes

1 cup warm water
(105° to 115°F)

2 teaspoons active dry yeast

Pinch of sugar or
¼ teaspoon honey or
barley malt syrup

2½ to 3 cups unbleached
all-purpose flour

2 tablespoons olive oil

½ teaspoon salt

Cornmeal or
semolina,
for sprinkling

Tomato-Basil Sauce
for Pizza
(page 215), for
coating (optional)

Olive oil, for
brushing (optional)

Toppings
(see page 216)

The combination of flour, water, salt, yeast, and oil never tasted so good. The crust beneath pizza toppings is all important. The humble pie becomes the artist's palate with the hand of the inventive baker choosing the combination of toppings. (See page 216.) No matter which way you mix the dough, bake in a very hot oven lined with a baking stone for best results. To make this dough in a bread machine, see page 456.

1. Pour the warm water in a small bowl. Sprinkle the yeast, sweetening, and 1 tablespoon of the flour over the surface of the water. Stir until dissolved and let stand at room temperature until foamy, about 15 minutes.

2. To Mix by Hand: In a large bowl, place the oil, salt, 1 cup of the flour, and the yeast mixture. Whisk hard until smooth, about 3 minutes. Add the remaining flour, ½ cup at a time, stirring with a wooden spoon until a soft, sticky dough that just clears the sides of the bowl is formed.

To Mix with a Food Processor: Place 2½ cups of the flour and salt in the work bowl of a food processor fitted with a metal blade. Add the oil to the yeast mixture and, with the machine running, pour this mixture through the feed tube. Process mixture through the feed tube. Process until a ball is formed, about 30 seconds.

To Mix with an Electric Mixer: In the work bowl of a heavy-duty electric mixer fitted with the paddle attachment, combine the salt and 1 cup flour. Pour in the yeast mixture, and stir on low to combine. Add the olive oil. Beat for 2 minutes, adding the remaining flour, ½ cup at a time, until a dough that just clears the sides of the bowl is formed.

3. To Knead by Hand: Turn the dough out onto a lightly floured work surface and vigorously knead to form a springy ball, dusting with flour only 1 tablespoon at a time as needed to prevent sticking, about 3 minutes. The dough should be quite soft, smooth, and very springy. Form the dough into a flattened ball.

To Knead by Machine: Switch from the paddle to the dough hook and knead for 2 to 3 minutes, or until the dough is smooth and springy. It should hold a finger imprint. If desired, transfer the dough to a floured surface and knead briefly by hand.

continues next page

4. Place the dough in a greased deep container. Turn once to coat the top and cover with plastic wrap. Let rise at room temperature until tripled in bulk, about 1½ hours. *(The dough may be refrigerated overnight at this point. Let stand at room temperature for 45 minutes before proceeding.)* Prepare the toppings at this time and set them aside at room temperature or in the refrigerator, as necessary.

5. At least 20 minutes before baking, preheat the oven to 500°F or its highest setting. Place a baking stone, if using, on the lowest oven rack.

6. To Shape Dough with a Rolling Pin: Flatten the dough into a disk. On a very lightly floured work surface, roll the dough from the center out, rotating it as you go. Lift the dough edges and flap them to relax them as you work. Place the round of dough directly on a cornmeal- or semolina-sprinkled baker's peel or pizza pan.

To Stretch Dough by Hand: Flour your hands and make 2 fists. Fit your fists under the center of the dough, forming a flat place for the dough to rest on. Gradually pull your fists apart, turning them at the same time to stretch the dough. Flour your hands when the dough becomes sticky. As the center becomes thin, move your fists farther apart. Work the dough to the desired diameter. Adjust the edges with your thumb and index finger to ¼ to ½ inch thick. Place the round of dough directly on a cornmeal- or semolina-sprinkled baker's peel or pizza pan.

To Press out Dough: Use the same technique as in rolling, but use your fingers to press and flatten from the center out in the pizza pan, taking care not to tear the dough, until it is evenly distributed.

To Shape Dough by Tossing: Flour your hands lightly. Make 2 fists and cross your wrists under the center of the dough. In a smooth motion, stretch the dough by pulling it outward and uncrossing your wrists with a twisting motion to give the dough a spin and a toss at the same time. Cross your arms farther down to place your fists father apart. The dough will be stretched in 2 to 3 tosses. Practice is the key here.

7. Immediately after shaping, brush with sauce or olive oil and assemble the toppings on the dough. If using a baker's peel, heavily sprinkle it with cornmeal or flour. Slide the pizza onto the pan or directly onto the baking stone. Place pizza pans on the baking stone, if using. Wipe and dry the peel immediately. Bake at the highest preheated temperature until the dough is crisp, the topping is hot, and the cheese is melted. Pizza cooked directly on a baking stone will take 8 to 10 minutes; in a pan it can take 10 to 15 minutes. Check the bottom of the crust to be sure to have a browned, crisp crust. Transfer the pizza to a cutting board and cut into wedges with a pizza wheel or a serrated bread knife.

WHOLE-WHEAT PIZZA DOUGH: *Substitute ½ cup whole-wheat flour and ¼ cup wheat bran for ¾ cup unbleached flour. The more whole-wheat flour, the harder the dough will be to roll out, so be prepared to patch holes.*

CORNMEAL PIZZA DOUGH: *Substitute ½ cup polenta or medium-grind yellow, white, or blue cornmeal for ½ cup unbleached flour.*

SEMOLINA PIZZA DOUGH: *Substitute ½ cup semolina flour for ½ cup unbleached flour.*

HERBED PIZZA DOUGH: *Mix 2 to 6 tablespoons chopped fresh herbs (or 1 to 3 tablespoons dried herbs), such as basil, tarragon, sage, rosemary, chervil, oregano, parsley, or marjoram, into the dough in Step 2.*

GARLIC PIZZA DOUGH: *Mix 2 cloves sautéed finely chopped garlic into the dough in Step 2.*

SAFFRON PIZZA DOUGH: *Steep ¼ teaspoon saffron threads in 1 cup boiling water. Let cool to 105° to 115°F, then substitute for plain warm water.*

TOMATO-BASIL SAUCE FOR PIZZA

This is an excellent all-purpose sauce for pizza. Please note that it is better to push the tomatoes through a sieve or food mill rather than puréeing them, as a slightly chunky texture is desirable.

Makes 3 cups

- 1 can (28 ounces) plum tomatoes packed in purée
- 2 garlic cloves
- ¼ cup olive oil
- 3 tablespoons red wine
- 2 tablespoons chopped fresh basil, or 2 teaspoons dried basil
- 1 tablespoon chopped fresh oregano, or 1 teaspoon dried oregano
- Freshly ground black pepper, to taste

Coarsely chop or crush the tomatoes or push them through a food mill. In a large skillet or sauté pan, sauté the garlic briefly in the oil. Add the tomatoes and wine. Bring to a boil and reduce heat to low, and cook, uncovered, for 15 minutes. Add the herbs and pepper and cook 5 minutes longer. (The sauce will keep in the refrigerator for 2 days and in the freezer for up to 1 month.)

Pizza Toppings

- OILS: Extra-virgin, virgin, or pure olive oil; walnut oil; corn oil

- TOMATOES: Fresh or canned Italian; sun-dried tomatoes

- CHEESE: Shredded low-moisture mozzarella (buffalo milk, cow's milk, smoked); fontina; provolone; soft Jack; Cheddar or Bel Paese; grated Pecorino Romano; Parmesan; ricotta; a dry Jack; crumbled fresh goat cheese; Gorgonzola

- OLIVES: Any kind, pitted and chopped or halved

- PEPPERS: Roasted or sautéed green, yellow, or red bell peppers; dried or fresh chilies

- MEATS: Cooked sweet or hot sausage, pancetta, or bacon; salami, pepperoni, or prosciutto

- ONIONS AND HERBS: Sautéed onions, shallots, or garlic; raw chives or green onions; fresh and dried herbs

- OTHERS: Anchovies and cooked shrimp; capers; cooked vegetables such as spinach, eggplant, artichokes, and wild and cultivated mushrooms

Tips for Great Pizza

- Coat the dough with a layer of sauce or oil before assembling.

- Limit yourself to three to five topping ingredients.

- Include either a meat or a vegetable, an herb, and a cheese to balance the flavors.

- Distribute the topping ingredients evenly, so that every bite will contain all flavors.

- Leave a full 1-inch margin around the edges to form a crust.

Campers' Pizza

To make pizza in a cast-iron skillet or on top of the stove or over an outdoor fire, roll out the risen pizza dough with a rolling pin or bottle about ¼ to ½ inch thick to fit the bottom of the pan. Preheat pan over medium-high heat. Remove from the heat and sprinkle the bottom with cornmeal to prevent sticking. Immediately lay the round of dough in a flat layer in the bottom of the pan and replace over the medium-high heat. Reduce the heat so the bottom does not burn and brush the top of the dough with plenty of olive oil.

Cook until the dough is crusty and black spots appear on the underside, about 3 minutes. Watch the heat: If it is too high, the bottom will blacken too quickly and the center will not be cooked through. Flip over gently with a spatula. Top as for oven pizza, leaving a small border around the edge and cover. Cook until the crust is crisp, the toppings are hot, and the cheese is melted, 3 to 5 minutes. Slide out of the pan onto a cutting board and cut into wedges to serve immediately.

Grill-Top Baked Pizza

This method for baking pizza over an outdoor gas grill was perfected by my friend and barbecue master, Ray Shanrock. He keeps a baking stone just for this purpose because it turns very black.

Prepare the pizza dough and let it rise. When ready to bake, place a clean rack 4 inches above the burners of a gas grill and place a baking stone on it. Turn the burners on high and preheat the stone for 8 minutes.

Turn the dough out onto a work surface lightly brushed with olive oil and divide it into the desired portions. Roll the dough out or press it with your fingertips into free-form rounds. Top each pizza with sauce, cheese, and desired toppings. Drizzle each with 1 tablespoon olive oil.

Turn both burners to low. Transfer the pizza to a cornmeal-sprinkled baker's peel and slide the pizza onto the hot stone. Close the grill lid and bake for 8 to 10 minutes, until the crust is crisp and the cheese is melted. Check the bottom of the crust with a large spatula during the baking time. Remove the pizza from the stone with a large spatula or insulated mitts. Transfer to a cutting board and cut into wedges. Serve immediately.

Deep Dish Pizza with Sausage and Mozzarella

Makes one 12-inch round torta

Dough

2 teaspoons active dry yeast

Pinch of sugar or 1 teaspoon honey or barley malt syrup

2 to 2½ cups unbleached all-purpose flour

1¼ cups warm water (105° to 115°F)

½ cup semolina flour

¼ cup medium rye flour

¼ cup olive oil

½ teaspoon salt

Olive oil, for brushing

Yellow cornmeal, for sprinkling

Ragù

1 pound mild Italian sausage, casing removed

1 small onion, chopped

½ carrot, minced

½ stalk celery, minced

1 garlic clove, minced

8 ounces mushrooms, trimmed and sliced

1 teaspoon dried marjoram or oregano

Here is a classic pizza dough made into a classic *pizza rustica,* or two-crusted stuffed pizza pie. It translates to "from the country," and belongs to the family of rustic tortas and quiches, all which were once made with bread doughs. Deep dish pizza has the advantage of feeding hungry people with a minimal amount of work; all it needs is a nice salad to go with it. The pie bakes in a moderately hot oven and there is no fuss with the dough, which is simply rolled out with a rolling pin.

1. To prepare the dough: Pour the warm water in a small bowl. Sprinkle the yeast, sugar or other sweetener, and 1 tablespoon of the unbleached flour over the surface of the water. Stir until dissolved and let stand at room temperature until foamy, about 10 minutes.

2. In a large bowl using a whisk or in the work bowl of a heavy-duty electric mixer fitted with the paddle attachment, combine the yeast mixture, semolina flour, rye flour, olive oil, salt, and 1 cup of the unbleached flour. Beat hard until smooth, about 3 minutes by hand and 1 minute by machine. Add the remaining flour, ¼ cup at a time, until a soft, sticky dough that just clears the sides of the bowl is formed. Switch to a wooden spoon when necessary if making by hand.

3. Turn the dough out onto a lightly floured work surface and vigorously knead to form a springy ball, 1 to 2 minutes for a machine-mixed dough and 3 to 4 minutes for a hand-mixed dough, dusting with flour only 1 tablespoon at a time, just enough as needed to prevent sticking. The dough should be quite soft, smooth, and very springy, or else it will be hard to roll out properly. Form into a flattened ball.

If kneading by machine, switch from the paddle to the dough hook and knead for 3 to 4 minutes, or until the dough is smooth and springy and springs back when pressed. If desired, transfer the dough to a floured surface and knead briefly by hand.

3 tablespoons dry red wine

3 tablespoons tomato paste

1 can (14½ ounces) whole tomatoes, puréed or mashed with a fork

Cheese Filling

1 pound ricotta cheese

5 ounces fresh mozzarella cheese, sliced into thin slivers

2 large eggs

¼ cup chopped Italian flat-leaf parsley

Topping

5 ounces fresh mozzarella cheese, sliced thin

⅓ cup shredded Asiago cheese or finely grated Parmesan

10 Italian flat-leaf parsley leaves

4. Place the dough in a greased deep container. Turn once to coat the top and cover with plastic wrap. Let rise at room temperature until tripled in bulk, 1 to 1½ hours. *(The dough may be refrigerated overnight at this point; let stand at room temperature for 45 minutes before proceeding.)*

5. To prepare the ragù: In a medium saucepan, brown the sausage meat with the onion, carrot, celery, and garlic, 5 to 8 minutes. Skim, pour off, or blot up any extra fat with a paper towel, if necessary. Add the mushrooms, oregano, wine, tomato paste, and puréed tomatoes. Bring to a boil and reduce the heat to low. Cook gently, uncovered, for 1 hour until the sauce is thick and chunky. Let cool until warm, but not hot.

6. To prepare the cheese filling: Combine the ricotta, mozzarella, eggs, and parsley in a bowl. Mix to coat evenly with the eggs. Refrigerate until needed.

7. Twenty minutes before baking, preheat the oven to 425°F. Brush a 12-inch springform pan with olive oil and sprinkle the bottom with cornmeal. Turn the dough out onto a lightly floured work surface and divide into 2 portions, one slightly larger than the other. Using a rolling pin, roll the larger portion of dough out into a thin round, about 3 inches larger than the diameter of the pan. Drape the dough over the rolling pin and carefully transfer it to the pan. Shape the sides of the dough to fit the pan. Spread evenly with the cheese filling. Roll out the remaining portion of dough to the exact size of the pan. Fit it over the cheese filling and tuck in the sides to neaten. Spread with all of the ragù to completely cover the second layer of dough.

8. Place the pan immediately on the bottom rack of the oven. Place the pan on a piece of foil if the pan is very full to catch spills. Bake for 15 minutes. Cover the surface evenly with the slices of mozzarella and sprinkle with the Asiago cheese. Sprinkle the surface with the whole parsley leaves. Return the pan to the oven and bake for 15 to 20 minutes more, or until golden brown and bubbly. Let stand 5 minutes. Remove the sides of the springform pan and transfer the pie to a cooling rack. Cool to warm or room temperature, at least 30 minutes. Slice with a serrated knife to serve.

Refrigerate any leftovers and reheat them at 400°F for 10 minutes. *(The pie may be baked for 20 minutes, removed from the oven, and cooled on a rack. Wrap it in plastic, then foil, and freeze up to 1 month. To reheat, remove the layers of plastic and rewrap in foil. Do not thaw. Place on an ungreased baking sheet. Bake at 400°F for 30 minutes. Remove the foil and return to the baking sheet. Continue to bake for 20 minutes more, until golden and bubbly.)*

NOTE: The torta may also be baked in a 15-inch deep-dish round pizza pan or 13-by-9-inch baking dish. Shape the dough to fit the pan.

Pizza Pie with Cheese
Pane al Pizza con Formaggio

Makes one 9-inch pie

1 recipe Basic Pizza Dough (page 213)

1 cup (4 ounces) shredded Italian fontina

1 cup (4 ounces) shredded mozzarella

1 cup (4 ounces) shredded smoked provolone

¾ cup (3 ounces) crumbled soft goat cheese

1 cup (4 ounces) grated Parmesan

Cornmeal, for sprinkling

Freshly ground black pepper, to taste

Egg Glaze (page 276)

This layered pizza-and-cheese pie is served in wedges hot from the oven.

1. Prepare the pizza dough and let it rise until doubled in bulk.

2. Twenty minutes before baking, preheat the oven to 425°F with a baking stone on the lowest oven rack, if using, to 375°F if not. Combine the cheeses, reserving ⅓ cup of the Parmesan. Turn the dough out onto a lightly floured work surface. Grease a 9-inch springform pan and sprinkle with cornmeal. Divide the dough into 3 equal portions. Using a rolling pin, roll the dough out to very thin 10-inch rounds. Place 1 round carefully in the springform pan. Sprinkle with half of the combined cheeses and grind black pepper over the top, leaving a 1-inch border around the edge. Brush the edge with glaze. Add a second round of dough and sprinkle evenly with the remaining cheese and pepper. Brush the edge with more glaze. Place the last layer on top. Roll the edges together in sections to form a rope pattern. Brush the top with the remaining glaze and sprinkle with the reserved Parmesan.

3. Place the pan immediately on the baking stone and reduce the heat to 375°F or place it on the oven rack. Bake 25 to 30 minutes, or until thoroughly browned. Remove the pan from the oven and remove the springform sides. Slide the pie onto a cutting board, let stand 15 minutes and cut it while warm with a serrated knife.

Spinach Calzone

Makes 3 main-course calzones

Dough

1²/₃ cups warm water
(105° to 115°F)

2 teaspoons active dry
yeast

³/₄ cup whole-wheat
flour

3 to 3¹/₄ cups unbleached all-
purpose flour

¹/₂ cup semolina flour

1 teaspoon salt

3 tablespoons olive oil

Filling

1 package (10 ounces)
frozen spinach,
defrosted and
squeezed dry

2 garlic cloves, minced

Freshly ground black
pepper, to taste

3 cups (1¹/₂ pounds)
ricotta cheese

2 large eggs, at room
temperature

¹/₃ cup grated
Parmesan cheese

8 ounces whole-milk
mozzarella,
shredded

3 ounces prosciutto,
chopped

¹/₄ cup chopped fresh
basil

Yellow cornmeal,
for sprinkling

Olive oil,
for brushing

Calzone comes from the word for trousers in Italian because their shape was originally elongated like a tube or a trouser leg. Now a half-moon shape, the pie made of a pizza dough, is filled with any combination used for pizza topping, although these should never be filled with raw meat or vegetables. A calzone should be crisp on the outside and creamy on the inside. This recipe can also be used to make ten 4-inch appetizer calzone.

1. Pour the warm water in a medium bowl. Sprinkle the yeast, whole-wheat flour, and 1 cup of the unbleached flour over the surface of the water. Beat to combine. Let stand at room temperature until bubbly, 30 minutes.

2. In a large bowl using the whisk or in the work bowl of a heavy-duty electric mixer fitted with the paddle attachment, combine the semolina flour, ¹/₂ cup unbleached flour, and salt. Add the yeast sponge and olive oil. Beat hard 1 minute. Add the remaining flour, 2 tablespoons at a time, until a soft, sticky dough that just clears the sides of the bowl is formed. Switch to a wooden spoon when necessary if making by hand.

3. Turn the dough out onto a lightly floured work surface and knead vigorously until springy, 1 to 2 minutes for a machine-mixed dough and a hand-mixed dough 3 to 4 minutes, dusting with flour only 1 tablespoon at a time as needed to prevent sticking. The dough should be quite soft, smooth, and very springy, or else it will be hard to roll out properly. Form into a flattened ball.

If kneading by machine, switch from the paddle to the dough hook and knead for 3 to 4 minutes, or until the dough is smooth and springy and springs back when pressed. If desired, transfer the dough to a floured surface and knead briefly by hand.

4. Place the dough in a greased deep container. Turn once to coat the top and cover with plastic wrap. Let rise at room temperature until triple in bulk, 1 to 1¹/₂ hours. (*The dough may be refrigerated overnight at this point; let stand at room temperature for 45 minutes before proceeding.*)

5. In a medium skillet, heat the oil and add the spinach and garlic. Cook until the spinach is warm and the garlic is fragrant, about 2 to 3 minutes. Season with pepper. Let cool to room temperature.

6. Twenty minutes before baking, preheat the oven to 475°F, using a baking stone on the middle rack, if desired. In a medium bowl, combine the ricotta, eggs, Parmesan, mozzarella, prosciutto, and basil. Stir in the spinach mixture. Gently deflate the dough and divide it into 3 equal portions. Sprinkle the work surface with cornmeal and roll out each one to an 8-inch circle. Divide the filling into 3 portions and cover half of each dough circle with the filling, leaving a ½-inch border around the edge. Fold the dough over the filling to form a turnover. Press the edges together with the tines of a fork to seal; it is important that the edges be well sealed or the filling will leak out. Place on a baking sheet or baker's peel sprinkled with cornmeal. Brush the surface of the dough with olive oil.

7. Place the baking sheet on the stone or slide the calzones on the hot stone and bake 18 to 20 minutes, or until puffed, golden brown, and dry to the touch. Transfer to a cooling rack and let stand 15 minutes to set.

Olive Focaccia

*Makes one 17-by-11-inch
rectangular focaccia*

1 tablespoon
(1 package)
active dry yeast

4½ cups unbleached
all-purpose flour
(exact measure)

1¼ teaspoons salt

1 cup hot water
(120°F)

1 cup hot milk (120°F)

¼ cup olive oil

1 cup coarsely
chopped pitted
black olives, brine-
or olive oil–cured

Olive oil, for oiling
bowl

Olive Pesto (recipe
follows)

My friend Gina de Leon, pastry chef extraordinaire who trained under master baker Jim Dodge, makes the best focaccia I have ever eaten. It is especially fast to make since no kneading is necessary. It is about three inches high, light and fluffy, with a rich aftertaste. Although the exact recipe is a trade secret, she did generously share the techniques with me. This bread is also good without the olives, but topped instead with lots of caramelized onions or spread with fresh basil pesto.

1. In a large bowl with a whisk or in the work bowl of a heavy-duty electric mixer fitted with the paddle attachment, combine the yeast, 2 cups of the flour, and the salt. Add the hot water, hot milk, and the olive oil. Beat until well combined, about 2 minutes. Mix in the olives. Add the remaining flour, ½ cup at a time, until a soft dough that just clears the sides of the bowl is formed. Switch to a wooden spoon when necessary if making by hand. The dough will be sticky soft and oily. Scrape down the sides of the bowl, drizzle the sides of the bowl with a bit more olive oil, and cover loosely with plastic wrap. Let rise at room temperature until doubled in bulk, about 1 hour.

2. Oil or parchment-line a 17-by-11-inch baking sheet. Turn the dough out onto the baking sheet. Spread and gently pull the dough, flattening it to fit the entire baking sheet. Smear the top evenly with all of the pesto. Let rest, uncovered, at room temperature 15 minutes.

3. Twenty minutes before baking, preheat the oven to 450°F, with a baking stone on the bottom rack, if desired. Place the sheet or pans directly on the hot stone, if using, or on the lowest oven rack and bake 15 minutes. Reduce the oven thermostat to 350°F and continue to bake until golden and the bread springs back when pressed gently, 20 minutes more. Let cool in the pan 5 minutes. Using a spatula, loosen the sides with a knife and slip the bread out carefully onto a clean dish towel or to a cooling rack. Cool and serve at room temperature.

1 can (6 ounces)
California pitted
black olives

¼ cup grated
Parmesan

¼ bunch flat-leaf
parsley, stemmed

1 tablespoon capers,
rinsed and drained

2 to 4 tablespoons fruity
olive oil

1 tablespoon fresh
lemon juice

Pinch of fresh or
dried thyme leaves

Freshly ground black
pepper to taste

OLIVE PESTO

Place all the ingredients in a blender or food processor fitted with the metal blade; pulse on and off until a rough-textured purée is made. Store in the refrigerator for up to 5 days before using. Olive Pesto may also be made using a mortar and pestle.

Herbed Focaccia

*Makes one 17-by-11-inch
rectangular focaccia*

2 recipes Basic Pizza
Dough (page 213)

Cornmeal,
for sprinkling

⅓ cup olive oil

1 tablespoon crumbled
dried whole
rosemary or sage, or
2 tablespoons finely
chopped fresh, or to
taste

1 tablespoon crumbled
dried oregano or
basil, or 2
tablespoons finely
chopped fresh
oregano or basil, or
to taste

Coarse salt, for
sprinkling (optional)

The difference between pizza and focaccia is in the thickness. Instead of being baked immediately after shaping to form a thin crisp crust, the dough is left to rise a second time before baking. Top with a simple combination of dried or fresh herbs marinated in good olive oil. Focaccia makes a simple, yet satisfying appetizer or sandwich bread, or it can be cut into chunks to be served alongside roasted meats and salads. Serve focaccia the same day it is baked.

The focaccia can be prepared with pizza dough made in a bread machine (page 456), letting the dough rise a second time. The 1-pound recipe will make a 9-inch square focaccia; the 1½-pound recipe will make a 13-by-9-inch rectangular one.

1. Prepare the pizza dough and let it rise until tripled in bulk, 1½ hours.

2. Grease a 17-by-11-inch baking sheet and sprinkle with cornmeal. Place the dough ball on a lightly floured work surface. Use the heel of your hand to press and flatten the dough. Lift and gently pull the dough, stretching it to the baking sheet. Cover loosely with plastic wrap and let rise at room temperature until doubled in bulk, 30 minutes to 1 hour. Meanwhile, combine the oil and herbs in a small bowl. Let sit 30 minutes at room temperature.

3. Twenty minutes before baking, preheat the oven to 450°F and place a baking stone on the lowest rack of a cold oven, if desired. Otherwise preheat the oven to 400°F. Using your fingertips or knuckles, gently poke indentations all over the dough surface no more than ¼-inch deep. Drizzle the herbed oil over the dough, letting it pool in the indentations. Reduce the oven heat to 400°F if using a stone. Bake the pan directly on the hot stone or an oven rack for 20 to 25 minutes for small rounds and 35 to 40 minutes for the large rectangle, or until nicely browned. Remove to a cooling rack an let cool in the pan. Serve warm plain or sprinkled with coarse salt.

FIRST LOAVES:
Tortillas, Flatbreads, and Fry Breads

The oldest breads, flatbreads, have become the new rage in baking. Baked on a hot iron griddle, over an open fire, in a stone-lined oven, or fried or steamed, the world of flatbreads goes way beyond crackers, pizza, and various kinds of pancakes. They are made from all types of grains and can be paper-thin or a few inches thick. In this chapter there are recipes for a few of the easiest-to-prepare flatbreads: Southwest-style tortillas and fry breads, and pita, the daily bread from the Eastern Mediterranean.

Corn tortillas, the staple bread of the pre-Spanish Southwest, were made from a wet mass of freshly ground corn that had been treated with lime, which softened the tough hulls and released niacin. When the Spanish settled in the Southwest, they brought wheat, and the corn tortilla soon had a sibling that was flakier and more pliable because of the gluten in the wheat flour. They called both kinds of flatbreads "tortilla," Spanish for "little cake." This is a bread that really shows if it is made by the human hand or not. A homemade tortilla still reigns supreme.

You can prepare your own corn dough (several recipes follow), or you can buy plain fresh *masa* dough, or *masa preparada para tortillas* (premixed with lard, salt, and water), by the pound at a Mexican market. Thus with a minimal amount of fuss you can press out and bake your own tortillas.

Fry bread is a common sight at pow-wows, rodeos, and state fairs. It is one of those tales of frugal culinary creativity, having been taught to the interned Navajos at Fort Sumner by the U.S. Army wives. The Navajos had never used wheat flour or baking powder to make dough before being issued monthly rations. Now, the bread is standard fare for Navajos and many other Indian nations. I have been advised that KC baking powder (available on the reservations); Bluebird flour from Cortez; Colorado, Army-issue dry milk; and Crisco solid shortening for frying are the ingredients that give the most traditional flavor.

Corn Tortillas

Tortillas de Maíz

Makes eighteen 7-inch tortillas

4 cups yellow or white *masa harina para tortillas,* preferably stone ground (see Note)

½ teaspoon salt

2⅔ cups hot water

The dried cornmeal specifically used for tortillas, *masa harina para tortillas,* has a distinctively limey taste; it is ground to a fine powdery flour. Corn tortillas are traditionally patted into rounds by hand or flattened in a tortilla press. They can be baked on a cast-iron skillet, a heavy griddle or a *comal,* a traditional griddle designed for baking over an open fire.

1. To mix the tortillas: In a medium mixing bowl using your hands or a wooden spoon, or in the bowl of a heavy-duty electric mixer fitted with the paddle attachment, combine the *masa harina para tortillas,* salt, and most of the water. Mix thoroughly until evenly moistened and the mixture forms a firm springy ball, adding 1 teaspoon water at a time if the dough seems too dry, or more *masa harina* if too wet. Cover with a clean damp dish towel or plastic wrap and let rest for 1 hour at room temperature. Keep covered while pressing or rolling out the tortillas. (*The dough may be wrapped in plastic and refrigerated for up to 24 hours.*)

2. To shape the tortillas: Wet your hands, divide the dough into 18 equal portions about the size of an egg and roll each into a ball. Place one of the portions of the dough between 2 pieces of plastic wrap or wax paper. Press in a tortilla press, turning at regular intervals, until the desired thickness. (Never press out a tortilla directly on the surface of the press.) Often the edges will crack; you can leave them like this, or press on the plastic to smooth, or trim with a knife. Leave in the plastic wrap until ready to cook. (*The shaped tortillas may be refrigerated for up to 8 hours before baking.*)

3. To bake the tortillas: Heat an ungreased cast-iron skillet, griddle, or *comal* over medium-high heat until drops of water sprinkled on the surface dance across it. Peel off both layers of the plastic and place each tortilla onto the hot pan, one at a time, or as many that will fit without touching. Bake for 30 seconds on the first side, turn over, and bake for 1 minute. Turn back to the first side and bake for a final 30 seconds. The tortilla will puff up and be speckled with brown spots. (*The tortillas* *can be baked in advance, stacked, wrapped in plastic or placed in a heavy-duty plastic bag, and refrigerated overnight. Reheat as needed right before serving.)*

NOTE: Masa harina para tortillas is available in the flour section of the supermarket or in Hispanic markets.

BAKER'S WISDOM
Reheating Homemade Tortillas

❧ To reheat in the oven, preheat the oven to 400°F. Place individual tortillas directly on the rack and bake 2 to 3 minutes, or until soft and pliable. Or wrap stacks of eight at a time in aluminum foil and heat the whole stack at once. Or place a stack in a terra cotta tortilla warmer and heat at 350°F for about 15 minutes, depending on the size of the stack.

❧ To reheat on a cast-iron skillet, griddle, or *comal,* heat the pan, ungreased, over medium-high heat until hot. Place a tortilla on the surface and leave just until puffy, about 10 seconds. Turn once. Use a tablespoon of oil if a crisp tortilla is desired.

❧ To reheat on a stovetop grill or outdoor grill, heat the grill to medium-high to hot. Place a tortilla on the surface and leave just until puffy. Turn once.

❧ To reheat in a microwave oven, place individual tortillas in a single layer on the microwave turntable and warm just until puffy, about 30 seconds. Or wrap stacks in plastic wrap and microwave at two-minute intervals, or until the stack is warm and pliable.

❧ To reheat in a bamboo steamer, wrap a stack of tortillas in a clean dish towel and place in a vegetable steamer basket over 1 inch of boiling water. Cover and steam 5 to 8 minutes, or until the stack is warm and pliable.

Blue Corn Tortillas

Tortillas de Maíz Azul

Makes twelve 5-inch tortillas

1 cup blue corn
harinilla or *masa
harina para tortillas*
(see Note)

¾ cup yellow or white
*masa harina para
tortillas*

¼ cup unbleached
all-purpose flour or
bread flour

¼ teaspoon salt

1 cup minus
1 tablespoon hot
water

A specialty of northern New Mexico, blue corn tortillas are an earthy color with a strong corn flavor. It's worth searching out *harinilla* for these tortillas. Eat blue corn tortillas the day they are baked; use the day-olds in enchilada casseroles. This recipe was developed by Southwest food writer Jacquie Higuera McMahan. She and I agree that some special breads may require the touch of a Native baker to be executed properly, to have the "taste of a woman's hands," but this nontraditional recipe comes very close to that.

1. In a medium mixing bowl using your hands or a wooden spoon, or in the bowl of a heavy-duty electric mixer fitted with the paddle attachment, combine the *harinilla,* the *masa harina para tortillas,* flour, salt, and most of the water. Mix thoroughly until evenly moistened and the mixture forms a firm springy ball, not sticky. If too dry, add 1 teaspoonful of water at a time. Cover with a clean damp dish towel or plastic wrap and let rest for 1 hour at room temperature. Keep covered while pressing or rolling out the tortillas as the blue corn dough dries out quickly.

2. Divide the dough into 12 portions and shape into 5-inch rounds as in Step 2 of Corn Tortillas (page 228).

3. To bake, heat an ungreased heavy cast-iron skillet, griddle, or *comal* over medium-high heat until drops of water sprinkled on the surface dance across it. Peel off both layers of the plastic wrap and immediately place each tortilla onto the hot pan, one at a time or as many as will fit without touching. Bake for 30 seconds on the first side. It may be necessary to use a thin metal spatula to release the tortilla if it sticks. Turn over, and bake for another 30 seconds. When the tortilla puffs up, press down immediately with a folded towel. It will be speckled with brown spots. Wrap in a clean dish towel until needed. These are best eaten within 1 hour.

NOTE: *Blue corn* harinilla *and blue corn* masa harina para tortillas *are much finer than regular blue cornmeal and used exclusively in making tortillas.*

Indian Fry Bread

Makes 16 to 20 fry breads

4 cups unbleached all-purpose flour

½ cup nonfat dry milk

1½ tablespoons baking powder

1 teaspoon salt

4 tablespoons vegetable shortening or lard

1½ cups very hot water

Flour or cornmeal, for dusting

2 quarts vegetable oil, for deep frying

Fry bread dough is flattened by hand, which takes practice. Novice bakers usually use a rolling pin and cut the dough into squares or rounds. Some bakers poke a small hole in the middle, a practice left over from the days of flipping the bread with a long stick. Make certain the cooking oil is hot enough, or the fry breads will be doughy, undercooked, and oily. And remember to cool the fry breads with the bubble side (the one that cooks first) up, so that "people won't go hungry, but will get full from your fry bread," as the Navajo say.

1. In a mixing bowl or in the bowl of a heavy-duty electric mixer fitted with the paddle attachment, combine the flour, dry milk, baking powder, and salt. Cut in the shortening or lard until crumbly, using a knife or a pastry blender if making by hand.

2. Add the water and mix well, using a fork if mixing by hand, until the dough comes together into a ball. Knead briefly in the bowl, no more than 10 times, until a soft and smooth, but not sticky, ball forms. Cover loosely with plastic wrap. Let rest at room temperature for at least 30 minutes.

3. On a flour- or cornmeal-dusted work surface, pull off small knobs of dough 2 to 3 inches in diameter to make 16 to 20 pieces. Working with 1 piece at a time (leave the other dough pieces covered with a damp towel), overlap the outer edge toward the center ¼ inch, then roll the knob out into a thin circle with a rolling pin. Cover with plastic wrap and repeat with the remaining pieces. Let rest for about 20 minutes.

4. Heat 2 inches of oil in a Dutch oven, wok, heavy kettle, or deep-fat fryer to 380°F. Working in batches, drop the dough, a piece at a time, into the hot oil, tapping and pushing the pieces gently with tongs to keep them immersed until they bubble up and become golden and crisp. Halfway through the cooking of the first side, gently turn the dough over to cook evenly. Cook for about 2 minutes total on each side, piercing the edge with a fork when turning over. Remove with a slotted spoon and drain, one on top of the other, bubble side up, on paper towels or clean brown paper bags. Breads may also be kept warm in a 200°F oven.

HONEY INDIAN FRY BREAD: *Add ¼ cup honey to the hot water in Step 2. Continue as directed.*

Flour Tortillas

Tortillas de Harina

Makes fifteen 8- to 9-inch tortillas

4 cups unbleached all-purpose flour

1½ teaspoons baking powder

1½ teaspoons salt

½ cup solid vegetable shortening, butter, bacon drippings, or lard

1½ cups warm water

Although all traditional recipes for flour tortillas call for a solid fat, you can use oil, freezing part of the flour with the oil to keep the traditional flaky texture. This technique was developed in the test kitchens of *Eating Well* magazine and shared with me by Jacquie McMahan. The trick of forming the dough ball into a mushroom shape comes from native Texan food writer Elaine Corn. You may substitute evaporated milk for half of the water as in some Spanish recipes.

1. To mix the tortillas: In a medium mixing bowl using your hands or a wooden spoon or in the bowl of a heavy-duty electric mixer fitted with the paddle attachment on the lowest setting, combine the flour, baking powder, and salt. Cut in the shortening or other fat until crumbly, using a fork or pastry blender if making by hand. Gradually add the warm water to the flour mixture, stirring just until the dough sticks together, clears the sides of the bowl, and forms a soft ball. Too much water makes a tough tortilla, so proceed slowly. Knead briefly in the bowl, no more than 10 times, until a smooth, but not sticky, ball forms. Shape into a cylinder and wrap the dough in plastic wrap or a clean dish towel to prevent drying out. Let rest at room temperature for at least 30 minutes or up to 2 hours, until slightly puffy and shiny.

2. To shape the tortillas: Divide the dough into 15 equal portions. Shape each into a ball and place on a baking sheet or marble slab. Cover and let the balls rest for 20 to 30 minutes more. Drape each ball around your forefinger, making a depression on the underside. This makes a mushroom shape and creates an air bubble, which helps it roll out into an even round. On a very lightly floured work surface, flatten the ball with your palm. *(The balls can rest on the greased baking sheet, covered tightly, for 30 minutes at this point if necessary.)* Using a thin rolling pin, roll each ball out from the center to the edge but without pressing on the edge, lifting the dough and giving it a quarter turn several times, to form a thin round 8 to 9 inches in diameter, depending on the size of your griddle. Trim the ragged edges and using a dry pastry brush, dust off any extra flour, if necessary. Stack between layers of plastic wrap to prevent drying out while rolling out the remaining dough. *(The rounds may be refrigerated for up to 6 hours before baking, but baking immediately is best.)*

3. To bake the tortillas: Heat an ungreased heavy cast-iron skillet, griddle, or *comal* over medium-high heat until drops of water sprinkled on the surface dance across it. Place the tortillas, one at a time, or as many as will fit without overlapping in the pan, and bake for 30 seconds. Drape a tortilla over your hand and gently lower 1 edge, then roll it off your hand onto the hot griddle to avoid wrinkles and overlapping of the dough. Or slide the tortilla off a plate. The tortilla will form bubbles; press them down gently with a spatula or folded towel and slightly twist. When you see the bubbles, turn over to the other side and bake for 30 seconds, or until the dough looks dry and brown spots are formed and the tortilla is soft, but not crisp. It is easy to overbake, so take care with the timing. Remove each tortilla to a clean towel or stack between layers of plastic wrap. If not serving right away, wrap in plastic or place in a thick plastic bag when cool. Refrigerate no longer than overnight. Rewarm as needed right before eating.

LOW-FAT FLOUR TORTILLAS: *Prepare the flour, baking soda, and salt mixture. Blend ½ cup vegetable or olive oil with ½ cup of the flour mixture and freeze for 2 hours in a tightly covered plastic freezer container. Substitute this mixture for the solid fat in Step 1. Proceed as directed.*

MESQUITE FLOUR TORTILLAS: *Substitute 1 cup mesquite flour for 1 cup of the all-purpose flour.*

BAKER'S WISDOM
Making Tortilla Dough in a Food Processor

Recipes in this chapter give instructions for making tortilla dough by hand or in a heavy-duty electric mixer. To use a food processor, combine the dry ingredients in the work bowl. Add the fat (if called for) and process until just blended and crumbly; do not overprocess. Add the water slowly through the feed tube and process until a soft ball is formed, about 10 seconds. Remove from the bowl and knead a few times to smooth the dough. Continue as directed in the recipe.

Country-Style Whole-Wheat Pita

Makes sixteen 6-inch round flatbreads

2½ cups warm water (105° to 115°F)

1 tablespoon (1 package) active dry yeast

Pinch of sugar

¼ cup olive oil

1 tablespoon salt

3 cups whole-wheat pastry flour

3 to 3½ cups unbleached all-purpose flour

Pita, also known as Middle Eastern pocket bread, is the simplest of all yeast breads to make. A small round of dough puffs dramatically when baked in a hot oven on a baking sheet or on a hot stone. They collapse as they cool, with a pocket inside that is perfect for filling. Pitas are like French bread: they stale quickly but toast nicely. Brush both sides with olive oil, cut each round into 8 equal pie-shaped wedges, and place in a single layer on a baking sheet. Bake in the center of a 300°F oven for 7 minutes, turn once, and cook for another 7 minutes. The baked pitas will crisp as they cool. Use with dips.

1. In a small bowl or 1-cup liquid measuring cup, pour in ½ cup of the water. Sprinkle the yeast and the pinch of sugar over the surface of the water. Stir to dissolve and let stand at room temperature until foamy, about 10 minutes.

2. In a large bowl using a whisk or in the bowl of a heavy-duty electric mixer fitted with the paddle attachment, combine the remaining water, olive oil, salt, and whole-wheat pastry flour. Beat hard until creamy, about 1 minute. Stir in the yeast mixture. Add the unbleached flour, ½ cup at a time, until a soft, shaggy dough that just clears the sides of the bowl is formed. Switch to a wooden spoon when necessary if making by hand.

3. Turn the dough out onto a lightly floured work surface with a plastic pastry scraper and knead until soft and springy, 1 to 2 minutes for a machine-mixed dough and 3 to 5 minutes for a hand-mixed dough, dusting with flour only 1 tablespoon at a time, just enough as needed to prevent sticking. Leave the dough moist and soft yet at the same time smooth and springy.

If kneading by machine, switch from the paddle to the dough hook and knead for 2 to 3 minutes, or until the dough is smooth and springy and springs back when pressed. If desired, transfer the dough to a floured surface and knead briefly by hand.

4. Place the dough in a lightly greased deep container. Turn the dough once to coat the top and cover with plastic wrap. Let rise at room temperature until doubled in bulk, about 1 to 1½ hours.

5. Preheat the oven to 475°F with a baking stone set on the bottom rack. Parchment-line several baking sheets, or, heavily flour a peel. Gently deflate the dough and divide it in half. Cover half with plastic wrap or a clean towel to prevent forming a skin. Divide into 8 equal portions and form each into a ball. Let rest 10 minutes while dividing the second half of the dough. Dust the work surface with whole-wheat pastry flour. Using a rolling pin, roll the balls into 6-inch circles about ¼ inch thick. Loosely cover the circles. Do not stack, as they will stick together. If the dough does not roll out easily, let it rest for 10 minutes to relax the gluten. Move the dough circles by draping them, one at a time, over a flour-dusted rolling pin and place them on a floured dish towel before transferring to the peel or baking sheets. Let rest 15 minutes, or until puffy.

6. Transfer the circles to a peel or baking sheet. With a quick action of the wrist, slide the pita rounds from the peel directly onto the hot stone. Four will fit on it at once. Or place the baking sheets, one at a time, on the bottom rack directly on the hot stone. Do not open the oven door for a full 4 minutes. Bake 8 to 10 minutes, or until fully puffed and light brown. Watch carefully that the pitas do not overbake or burn. The baking sheet pitas will take longer to bake than the stone-baked ones. Remove the puffed hot breads with a wide metal spatula and stack between clean dish towels.

VARIATION: *Substitute 3 cups unbleached all-purpose flour for the whole-wheat pastry flour. (Do not use bread flour; it will make the pita too tough.) Substitute ⅓ cup of a specialty flour, such as soy, barley, chestnut, or brown rice flour for an equal amount of the whole-wheat pastry flour. For sesame pitas, sprinkle sesame seeds on the work surface and roll the dough ball into them, coating all surfaces, before rolling out the pita.*

A FLASH IN THE PAN:
Pancakes, Waffles, Crêpes, and Popovers

Since pancakes are easy to make and there are so many different ways to prepare them, it is a favorite food to cook for a crowd. Somehow they evolved to Sunday morning or overnight-guest breakfast fare, but frugal epicureans are now using the versatile griddlecake for any meal—as a vehicle for vegetables, whole grains, cheeses, or fresh fruits and nuts. Pancakes may be thick, thin, small, large, rolled, or stacked and sauced. Little yeasted pancakes can be topped and paraded around the most stylish cocktail parties. The pancake family also includes waffles, popovers and oven pancakes, and crêpes.

The batters do well when made a few hours in advance and refrigerated until baking. Gently and quickly assemble the batter, paying no attention to a few lumps. All-purpose flour is a standard ingredient, but many bakers also use cake flour for an extra lighter-than-air texture. If the batter is leavened only with baking powder, not baking soda, it can be made the night before and ladled cold onto the greased, hot griddle. If a batter looks and feels too thick, thin it with a tablespoon or two of liquid; if too thin, whisk in an extra tablespoon or so of flour until the consistency looks right to you.

Serve the pancake family immediately or keep warm in a 200°F oven, covered loosely with foil to prevent drying, until all cakes are baked and ready to serve. It is important that pancakes be warmed in a single layer or, if stacked, separated by a tea towel or paper towels to prevent sogginess. Pancakes also can be cooled, wrapped in plastic freezer bags, and frozen for impromptu reheating in a toaster or microwave.

Old-fashioned Buttermilk Pancakes

Makes twelve 4-inch pancakes

2 cups unbleached all-purpose flour

1 teaspoon baking soda

Large pinch of salt

2¼ cups buttermilk

3 large eggs

4 tablespoons (½ stick) unsalted butter, melted, or vegetable oil

Here lies the perfect American pancake, hotcake, flapjack, call it what you will, in all its glory.

1. In a small bowl, combine the flour, baking soda, and salt. In another bowl, whisk together the buttermilk, eggs, and melted butter. Pour the buttermilk mixture into the dry ingredients, stirring just until moistened. Do not overmix; the batter will have small lumps. Gently fold in any additional ingredients at this time.

2. Heat a griddle or heavy skillet over medium heat until a drop of water dances over the surface, and lightly grease it. Using a ¼-cup measure for each pancake, pour the batter onto the griddle. Cook about 2 minutes, or until bubbles form on the surface, the edges are dry, and the bottoms are golden brown. Turn once, cooking the opposite sides about 2 minutes or until golden. The second side will take half the time to cook as the first side. Serve immediately or keep warm in a 200°F oven until ready to serve.

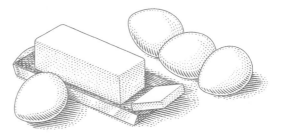

Buttermilk Waffles

Makes 6 to 8 large waffles, depending on iron size

2 cups unbleached all-purpose flour

1 teaspoon baking soda

1/2 teaspoon baking powder

1/4 teaspoon salt

4 eggs, separated

1/4 cup vegetable oil

2 cups buttermilk

Vegetable oil or melted butter, for greasing the grids

Waffles are at home with sweet breakfast toppings as well as savory dinner accompaniments throughout the seasons. These waffles only get better when a handful of toasted pecans or chopped fresh herbs from the garden are added to create an array of sweet or savory crisp honeycombs. If you love waffles, do not miss the variations listed here, each one creating a very different flavor.

1. Preheat a waffle iron to medium-high or follow manufacturer's instructions. In a large bowl, combine the flour, baking soda, baking powder, and salt. In another bowl, using a whisk or electric mixer, beat the egg yolks, oil, and buttermilk until foamy. In a small bowl using an electric mixer, beat the egg whites until soft peaks form. Pour the buttermilk mixture into the dry ingredients, stirring just until moistened. Fold in the whites until no streaks are visible.

2. Brush the waffle iron grids with oil or melted butter. For each waffle, pour about 1 cup of the batter onto the grid. Close the lid and bake until the waffle is crisp and golden brown, about 4 to 5 minutes. Remove from the iron with a fork. Repeat with the remaining batter. Serve immediately. (*Waffles may be cooled, transferred to heavy-duty plastic bags, and frozen for up to 2 months. Reheat in the toaster.*)

SOUR CREAM BUTTERMILK WAFFLES: *Add 2/3 cup sour cream and 2 tablespoons melted unsalted butter when combining the liquid ingredients in Step 1. Continue as directed.*

LEMON BUTTERMILK WAFFLES: *Substitute the zest and juice of 2 large lemons and 2 tablespoons sugar for 1/4 cup of the buttermilk, and 5 tablespoons melted unsalted butter for the oil when combining the liquid ingredients in Step 1. Continue as directed.*

BUTTERMILK WAFFLES WITH RICE: *Add 3/4 cup cold cooked short- or long-grain white or brown rice (try white or brown basmati rice for a real treat) when combining the liquid ingredients in Step 1. Continue as directed.*

SUPER WHOLE-GRAIN BUTTERMILK WAFFLES: *Substitute 3/4 cup whole-wheat flour, 3 tablespoons each oat bran and wheat germ, 2 tablespoons cornmeal or buckwheat flour, and 1 tablespoon brown sugar for 1 cup of the all-purpose flour. Add to the dry ingredients in Step 1. Continue as directed.*

SEVEN-GRAIN BUTTERMILK WAFFLES: *Substitute ½ cup seven-grain cereal for ½ cup of the flour. Combine the cereal and 1 cup of the buttermilk in a bowl, cover, and refrigerate at least 2 hours or overnight to soften the grains. Add the soaked grains and 2 tablespoons maple syrup to the liquid ingredients in Step 1. Continue as directed.*

BAKER'S WISDOM
The Waffle Iron

Electric waffle irons are designed to cook both sides of a waffle fast and evenly. Different models make different shapes: circles, squares, and lobed rounds. Irons are usually made from cast aluminum with plain or nonstick grids in regular and exaggerated Belgian styles. Nonelectric stovetop models with heatproof handles make squares in both waffle styles. The plain grids need to be seasoned before use, but the nonstick, easy-release surfaces do not. It is important to grease the grids before pouring in the batter. On electric models, a built-in thermostat signals when the iron is hot as well as when the waffle is done. Many models have the grids permanently set into their frames, but others snap out for easy washing and reversing to form a flat griddle for grilled sandwiches and pancakes, or they have Italian *pizelle* molds. All models are readily available in hardware, department, and cookware stores.

Seasoning a Waffle Iron or Pancake Griddle: New, uncoated electric and range-top waffle irons or griddles require seasoning to prevent batters from sticking. New equipment usually comes with the manufacturer's instructions for the best result. In case it doesn't, or if you need to reseason, follow these directions: Preheat the iron or griddle to medium-high heat. Brush the entire surface, coating all grids, with vegetable oil. Close the iron and heat just until smoking. Open the iron, remove the griddle from the heat and let stand until completely cool. Wipe the iron or griddle clean with a soft cloth or paper towel. The waffle iron is now ready for use. Discard the first set of waffles baked. If the waffles stick, clean the grids carefully with a damp cloth and reseason.

Sourdough Pancakes and Waffles

Makes 20 pancakes or 8 to 10 waffles

1 cup Classic Sourdough Starter (page 120)

1½ cups whole milk

2 cups unbleached all-purpose flour

2 large eggs

2 tablespoons vegetable oil

1 teaspoon salt

1 teaspoon baking soda

Vegetable oil or melted butter, for greasing

Sourdough creates the most delicate pancakes and waffles. A sponge is made the night before and the pancakes quickly mixed right before baking. If you are making these out camping, substitute water for the milk.

1. The Night Before: In a medium nonreactive mixing bowl, combine the starter, milk, and 1 cup of the flour. Stir, but do not beat too much. Cover and refrigerate.

2. In the Morning: Add the remaining flour, eggs, oil, salt, and baking soda to the sourdough mixture with a whisk, using a few swift strokes. Do not overmix. The batter should be the consistency of heavy cream and bubbly because of the soda.

3. Pancakes: Heat a griddle or heavy skillet over medium heat until a drop of water sprinkled on the surface dances over it. Lightly grease it. Using a ¼-cup measure for each pancake, pour the batter onto the griddle. Cook about 2 minutes, or until bubbles form on the surface, the edges are dry, and the bottoms are golden brown. Turn once, cooking the opposite side about 1 minute, or until golden. Serve immediately or keep warm in a 200°F oven until ready to serve.

Waffles: Heat the waffle iron to medium-high heat or follow manufacturer's instructions. Brush the hot waffle iron grids with oil or melted butter and without stirring down the batter, pour about 1 cup of the batter onto the grid for each waffle. Close the lid and bake until the waffle is golden brown and crisp, 3 to 4 minutes. Remove from the iron with a fork. Repeat with the remaining batter. Keep the waffles warm in a 200°F oven, uncovered, until ready to serve. (*Or cool completely on racks, store in plastic bags and freeze for up to 2 months. Reheat in the toaster.*)

VARIATION: Substitute 1 cup whole-wheat flour for 1 cup of the all-purpose flour.

Blue Cornmeal Pancakes

Makes about fourteen 4-inch pancakes

1½ cups fine-grind blue cornmeal or *harina para atole* (see recipe introduction)

¾ cup unbleached all-purpose flour or whole-wheat pastry flour

1½ teaspoons baking powder

½ teaspoon baking soda

¼ teaspoon salt

2 large eggs

1½ cups buttermilk

¼ cup corn oil

Blue cornmeal pancakes show up on breakfast menus from El Tovar on the rim of the Grand Canyon to Santa Fe, New Mexico. They look very different from regular pancakes, a dusky shade of lavender-gray. One bite delivers the smoky sweetness of the ground roasted blue corn. Note that the recipe calls for the finest grind of blue-corn flour, often called *harina para atole*. This recipe can also be used to make waffles.

1. In a large bowl, combine the blue cornmeal, flour, baking powder, baking soda, and salt. In another bowl, whisk together the eggs, buttermilk, and oil. Combine the mixtures with a few swift strokes. The batter should be the consistency of heavy cream. If too thick, add a few more tablespoons of buttermilk to thin.

2. Heat a griddle or heavy skillet over medium heat until a drop of water dances over the surface. Lightly grease it. Using a scant ¼-cup measure for each pancake, pour the batter onto the griddle. Cook about 2 minutes, or until bubbles form on surface, the edges are dry, and the bottoms are golden brown. Turn once, cooking the opposite side about 1 minute, or until golden. Serve immediately or keep warm in a 200°F oven until ready to serve.

BLUEBERRY–BLUE CORNMEAL PANCAKES: *Sprinkle about 2 tablespoons fresh or unthawed frozen blueberries over the surface of each pancake immediately after pouring onto the griddle. You will need about 1½ cups.*

BLUE CORNMEAL PANCAKES WITH RICE: *Add 1 cup cooked brown rice when mixing the batter in Step 1.*

BLUE CORNMEAL PANCAKES WITH CORN: *Thaw and drain 1 package (10 ounces) frozen baby corn kernels. Spoon 2 to 3 tablespoons of batter onto the griddle and sprinkle immediately with 1 tablespoon of the corn. Serve as a side dish with grilled meat or poultry.*

Whole-Wheat Blueberry Buttermilk Pancakes

Makes sixteen 4-inch pancakes

1 cup unbleached all-purpose flour

3/4 cup whole-wheat flour

1 tablespoon light brown sugar

1 teaspoon baking powder

1 teaspoon baking soda

1/2 teaspoon ground cinnamon

1/4 teaspoon salt

2 cups cultured buttermilk

2 large eggs

1/4 cup vegetable oil

1/4 teaspoon pure vanilla extract

1 1/2 cups fresh or drained canned blueberries, or 1 package (12 ounces) unsweetened, frozen blueberries, unthawed

Whole-wheat pancakes are heartier than pancakes made just with white flour, and blueberries are an important ingredient, giving a counterpoint of taste and texture.

1. In a large bowl, combine the flours, brown sugar, baking powder, baking soda, cinnamon, and salt. In another bowl using a whisk or electric mixer, beat the buttermilk, eggs, oil, and vanilla until foamy. Add the buttermilk mixture to the dry ingredients, stirring just until combined. Do not overmix; the batter will have small lumps. Let the batter stand at room temperature 15 minutes. Gently fold in the blueberries, taking care not to break them.

2. Heat a griddle or heavy skillet over medium heat until a drop of water dances over the surface. Lightly grease it. Using a 1/4-cup measure for each pancake, pour the batter onto the griddle. Cook about 2 minutes, or until bubbles form on the surface, the edges are dry, and the bottoms are golden brown. Turn once, cooking the opposite side, about 1 minute, until golden. The second side will take half the amount of time to cook as the first side. Serve immediately or keep warm in a 200°F oven until ready to serve.

Buckwheat Pancakes

Makes sixteen 4-inch pancakes

1¾ cups unbleached all-purpose flour

¼ cup dark buckwheat flour

2 tablespoons rolled oats

1 teaspoon baking powder

1 teaspoon baking soda

Grated zest of 1 orange

¼ teaspoon salt

1½ cups buttermilk

4 large eggs

3 tablespoons unsalted butter, melted

These light-textured pancakes have wide appeal at breakfast with warm maple syrup as well as for dinner with caviar, smoked salmon, or smoked trout, and a dollop of sour cream. For even lighter pancakes, separate the eggs and fold in the stiffly beaten egg whites last.

1. In a large bowl, combine the flours, rolled oats, baking powder, baking soda, zest, and salt. In another bowl using a whisk or electric mixer, beat the buttermilk, eggs, and melted butter until foamy. Pour the buttermilk mixture into the dry ingredients, stirring just until moistened. Do not overmix; the batter will have small lumps. Let the batter stand at room temperature 15 minutes.

2. Heat a griddle or heavy skillet over medium heat until a drop of water dances over the surface. Lightly grease. Using a ¼-cup measure for each pancake, pour the batter onto the griddle. Cook about 2 minutes, or until bubbles form on the surface, the edges are dry, and the bottoms are golden brown. Turn once, cooking the opposite side about 1 minute, or until golden. The second side will take half the amount of time to cook as the first side. Serve immediately or keep warm in a 200°F oven until ready to serve.

Beer Waffles

Makes 6 to 8 waffles

2 cups unbleached all-purpose flour

1 cup whole-wheat pastry flour

1/4 cup (packed) light brown sugar

Grated zest of 1 lemon

1 teaspoon baking powder

1/2 teaspoon salt

2 3/4 cups beer, not flat

2 large eggs

8 tablespoons (1 stick) unsalted butter, melted

1 tablespoon fresh lemon juice

4 teaspoons pure vanilla extract

Old pioneer cookbooks often contain a recipe for beer "sourdough" pancakes, an easy adaptation of early beer-based starters. These waffles will have a faint flavor of a sourdough and the beer will also serve as a leavening.

1. Preheat the waffle iron to medium-high heat or follow manufacturer's instructions. In a large bowl, combine the all-purpose flour, whole-wheat pastry flour, brown sugar, lemon zest, baking powder, and salt. In another bowl, combine the beer and eggs with a whisk. Pour into the dry mixture, stirring to moisten evenly. Gently stir in the melted butter, lemon juice, and vanilla. Refrigerate for at least 2 hours to overnight.

2. Brush the hot waffle iron grids with melted butter (vegetable oil spray is excellent for this job) and without stirring down the batter, pour about 1 cup of batter for each waffle onto the grid. Close the lid and bake until the waffle is golden brown and crisp, 4 to 5 minutes. Remove from the iron with a fork. Repeat with the remaining batter. Keep the waffles hot in a 200°F oven, uncovered, until ready to serve or serve immediately. *(Waffles may be cooled, transferred to heavy-duty plastic bags, and frozen for up to 2 months.)*

Vanilla Belgian Waffles

Makes 6 to 8 waffles

2 cups unbleached all-purpose flour

1 tablespoon baking powder

1 tablespoon sugar (optional)

Pinch of salt

3 large eggs

8 tablespoons (1 stick) unsalted butter, melted

1½ cups whole milk

1 tablespoon pure vanilla extract

Belgian waffles have a larger, more exaggerated honeycomb grid than standard waffles, which makes for a dramatic pooling of sweet syrups or savory sauces. Although any waffle recipe can be made in a Belgian waffle maker, this recipe is particularly well suited. This batter is wonderful with a cup of fresh blueberries or pitted cherries gently folded in just before baking, and served with pure maple syrup. Belgian waffles can also be topped with a thin piece of soft cheese, then heated in a 350°F oven for about 4 minutes just to melt the cheese. For savory dishes, do not add sugar and vanilla.

1. Preheat the Belgian waffle iron to medium-high or follow manufacturer's instructions. In a bowl, combine the flour, baking powder, sugar, if using, and salt.

2. In another bowl using a whisk or electric mixer, beat the eggs until thick and foamy, about 2 minutes. Add the butter, milk, and vanilla. Add the dry ingredients and beat until smooth. Do not overmix.

3. Brush the waffle iron grids with oil or melted butter. For each waffle, pour about ⅔ to 1 cup of the batter onto the grid, depending on the size of your iron. Close the lid and bake until the waffle is crisp and golden brown, about 4 to 5 minutes. Remove from the iron with a fork to protect your fingers. Repeat with the remaining batter. Keep the waffles warm in a 200°F oven, uncovered until ready to serve, or serve immediately. *(Waffles may be cooled, transferred to heavy-duty plastic bags, and frozen for up to 2 months.)*

NOTE: *Substitute whole-wheat pastry flour for the white flour.*

Crêpes

Makes sixteen to eighteen 7-inch crêpes

3 large eggs

1 cup whole milk

²/₃ cup water or room temperature beer

1 cup plus 2 tablespoons unbleached all-purpose flour

¼ teaspoon salt

5 tablespoons unsalted butter, melted

Cooking spray for greasing the pan

Rolled, stacked, folded, or cut into strips, crêpes are a must-do in a baker's repertoire. The simple batter composed of a high proportion of milk and eggs to flour is quickly beaten, set to rest, and then baked into paper-thin pancakes. I use beer in batter when making meat-filled dishes, like canneloni. Crêpes are usually made the size of your skillet, 6 to 9 inches in diameter; many bakers keep a pan just for making these.

1. Using a blender, food processor, immersion blender, or whisk, combine the eggs, milk, water or beer, flour, and salt, beat until smooth. Scrape down the sides and bottom of the bowl once. Add the melted butter. The batter will be the consistency of cream; adjust the consistency, if necessary. Cover and refrigerate 1 to 2 hours. (The batter may be prepared to this point 1 day ahead and refrigerated until ready to use. Bring the batter back to room temperature and add the butter just before baking.) If your batter is lumpy, strain it.

2. Lightly grease a seasoned crêpe pan or a 9- to 10-inch nonstick frying pan with cooking spray and heat over medium heat until hot. Stir the batter to avoid separation. Working quickly, remove the pan from the heat and pour in about 3 tablespoons of batter, tilting and rotating the pan to completely cover the bottom. If the batter does not spread quickly, it is too thick and needs to be thinned with water. If the batter stiffens when poured into the pan, the pan is too hot. If the crêpes have holes, fill in with a few drops of batter. Plan on a few uneven crêpes at first while regulating the heat of the pan and thickness of the batter.

3. Cook until the bottom is brown and the top dry, less than 1 minute. Turn the crêpe over with a spatula and cook the second side until speckled, about 20 seconds. Slide the crêpe onto paper towels or a clean dish towel. Repeat with the remaining batter, stacking as the crêpes are done and spraying the pan with cooking spray only if there is sticking. (*Crêpes may be cooled, transferred to heavy-duty plastic bags and refrigerated up to 3 days or frozen up to 1 month. Let refrigerated crêpes stand at room temperature 1 hour before filling. Completely defrost frozen crêpes before using.*)

WHOLE-GRAIN CRÊPES: *Substitute ⅓ cup whole wheat, rye, brown rice flour, buckwheat, or fine cornmeal, for ⅓ cup unbleached flour.*

HERB CRÊPES: *Add 2 tablespoons finely chopped fresh herbs, such as dill, thyme, parsley, or marjoram, to the batter.*

SPECIAL DIET CRÊPES: *Substitute buttermilk, plain soy milk, or goat milk for the milk, and use a commercial egg substitute for the eggs. Canola oil can be substituted for the melted butter or the fat can be eliminated.*

DESSERT CRÊPES: *Substitute 3 tablespoons rum, Cognac, or Grand Marnier for an equal amount of the water and add 1 tablespoon of powdered sugar or maple syrup to the batter.*

BAKER'S WISDOM
The Pancake Griddle

Griddle: If you make pancakes regularly, consider investing in a griddle specifically designed for the job. Griddles are also good for cooking eggs, French toast, blintzes, tortillas, and homemade English muffins.

Electric griddle: Very popular backup to stovetop cooking as are waffle irons with a reversible grill/grid. Many ranges used in home kitchens come with an optional griddle built into the top of the stove.

Stovetop griddles: A round or square pan with a low rim. For larger quantities, there are rectangular or oval griddles that fit over two burners, often made of heavy cast aluminum or soapstone.

Soapstone griddles: Made of nonporous, acid-resistant grayish stone that retains heat and needs no greasing. Available in round and oval shapes by mail order (see page 471).

Specialized pans: Used to create uncommon pancakes. These include crêpe pans, Breton crêpe pans for large buckwheat crêpes, blini pans, and cast-iron *plett* pans for making Swedish pancakes.

Cottage Cheese Blintzes

Makes about 30 blintzes

Blintz Wrapper Batter

1½ cups unbleached all-purpose flour or whole-wheat pastry flour

1½ teaspoons baking powder

1⅓ cups whole milk

⅔ cup water

4 large eggs

1 teaspoon pure vanilla extract or grated zest of 1 lemon

½ teaspoon salt

Filling

Two 7½- to 8-ounce containers farmer or pot cheese, or part-skim ricotta

1 pound (2 cups) large-curd creamed cottage cheese

3 large eggs yolks or 3 tablespoons commercial liquid egg substitute

2 teaspoons pure vanilla extract or grated zest of 2 lemons

4 tablespoons (½ stick) unsalted butter

Sweet blintzes are perhaps one of the best known of Jewish holiday dairy foods. They are crêpes with a creamy cheese filling that are baked or fried. The cottage cheese in the filling is drained to remove excess moisture. That prevents a release of moisture during baking or frying. This recipe uses no sugar in the wrappers or filling. The blintzes can be assembled early in the day, chilled, and then baked or fried right before serving. Serve with low-fat sour cream or plain yogurt, and sliced fresh strawberries or whole cherry or blueberry preserves for garnishes.

1. To make the wrappers: Using a blender, food processor, or whisk, combine the batter ingredients and beat until smooth, about 1 minute. Cover and refrigerate 30 minutes to 1 hour.

2. Lightly grease a 6- to 7-inch seasoned crêpe pan or a nonstick frying pan with cooking spray. Heat over medium heat until hot. Stir the batter to avoid separation. Working quickly, remove the pan from the heat and pour in about 2 tablespoons of batter, tilting and rotating the pan to completely cover the bottom. Cook until the bottom is golden brown and the top set, about 30 seconds. Do not turn over. Slide the wrappers in a single layer onto paper towels, cooked side up, next to each other, but not overlapping. Repeat the procedure with the remaining batter. *(The wrappers may be cooled, wrapped in plastic, and refrigerated up to 2 days. Bring back to room temperature before filling.)* Makes about thirty 5- to 6-inch wrappers.

3. To make the filling: Drain the cottage cheese in a fine-mesh strainer over a bowl in the refrigerator for 1 hour. In a food processor, combine the cottage cheese, farmer cheese, egg yolks, and vanilla or lemon zest until just smooth.

4. To assemble: Place 1 heaping tablespoon of the filling at one end of the cooked side of the wrapper. Fold each side over to almost meet in the center; the filling will still be at the end. Fold the blintz up from the bottom to completely enclose the filling, ending with the seam side down, like a plump rectangular packet. The uncooked side of the wrapper will be on the outside. Cover with plastic wrap and refrigerate until ready to cook. *(The blintzes may be frozen in a plastic freezer container. If stacking, place a layer of parchment paper between the layers to prevent sticking.)*

5. To Fry the Blintzes: Melt 1 tablespoon butter in a large skillet over medium-high heat. Place as many blintzes in the pan, seam side down, as will fit. Fry several minutes on each side, or until crisp and golden brown. Add more butter as needed for frying each batch. For frying frozen blintzes, do not thaw.

To Bake the Blintzes: Preheat the oven to 400°F. Parchment-line a baking sheet and butter the paper. Place the baking sheet in the oven to melt the butter. Arrange the packets in a single layer, seam side down, on the baking sheet turn to coat the tops with butter. Bake 15 to 20 minutes, or until golden and heated through. Bake the blintzes without thawing in a 350°F oven for 35 to 40 minutes. Serve immediately.

STRAWBERRY BLINTZES: *Fold in 1 cup sliced fresh strawberries into the filling in Step 3. Use vanilla as the flavoring.*

BLUEBERRY BLINTZES: *Fold in 1 cup fresh or drained, thawed frozen blueberries into the filling in Step 3. Use lemon zest as the flavoring.*

Cornmeal Blini

*Makes about 60 to 80 small
pancakes*

1 tablespoon
(1 package)
active dry yeast

Pinch of sugar, plus
1 teaspoon

¼ cup warm water
(105° to 115°F)

1¼ cups warm milk
(105° to 115°F)

4 large eggs,
separated

1 teaspoon salt

4 tablespoons
(½ stick)
unsalted butter,
melted

⅔ cup fine- or medium-
grind yellow
cornmeal whirled in
a food processor
until fine

1⅓ cups unbleached
all-purpose flour

Melted butter, for
greasing the pan and
brushing

Blini are whole-grain yeasted pancakes. One of the great peasant dishes of the world, blini get lots of attention at parties. Although blini are usually associated with caviar and smoked fish, they can be topped simply with sour cream and chopped hard-cooked eggs, and sprinkled with chives or green onions. For a party, place an assortment of garnishes in separate bowls and allow guests to choose.

1. Pour the warm water in a small bowl. Sprinkle yeast and a pinch of sugar over the surface of the water. Stir to dissolve and let stand at room temperature until foamy, about 10 minutes.

2. In a large bowl using a wire whisk, or using a blender, or food processor, combine the milk, yolks, salt, and remaining 1 teaspoon sugar, butter, and yeast mixture until well blended. Add the cornmeal and flour and blend until smooth with a consistency of heavy cream. Cover with plastic wrap and let stand at room temperature until doubled in bulk, about 1 hour.

3. In a large bowl, beat egg whites into stiff peaks. Fold into batter.

4. Heat a large skillet over medium heat and brush with melted butter. Spoon 1 tablespoon of batter into the skillet. Cook until golden brown on the bottom and bubbles just break on the surface, about 1 minute. Flip over to cook the other side briefly. Stack the blinis on a dry cotton towel and keep warm in an oven on low heat until serving time, covered with aluminum foil. Brush each with a bit of melted butter, if desired. *(Blinis can be made up to 2 days ahead and refrigerated between layers of wax paper or frozen for up to 1 month.)*

NOTE: *Substitute whole-wheat flour or buckwheat flour for the cornmeal.*

Savory Wild Rice Pancakes

Makes twenty 3-inch pancakes

4 tablespoons (½ stick) unsalted butter

1 medium shallot, minced

1 cup unbleached all-purpose flour

1 tablespoon baking powder

½ teaspoon salt

3 large eggs

1 cup whole milk

1½ cups cooked and cooled wild rice (see page 113)

Elegant is the best word to describe these silver dollar–size gems. They nestle nicely next to vegetables and a roasted meat for a very special main course accompaniment.

1. In a medium skillet, melt the butter over medium heat and cook the shallot until tender. Set aside.

2. In a large bowl using a whisk or in the work bowl of a food processor fitted with the metal blade, combine the flour, baking powder, and salt. Add the shallots and butter, eggs, and milk. Beat or process just until smooth, about 1 minute. The batter will be thin. Stir in the wild rice.

3. Heat a griddle or a heavy skillet over medium heat until a drop of water dances over the surface, and lightly grease it. Using a 2-table-spoon measure for each pancake, pour the batter onto the griddle. Cook about 2 minutes or until bubbles form on the surface, the edges are dry, and the bottoms are golden brown. Turn once, cooking the opposite side about 1 minute, or until golden. The second side will take half the amount of time to cook as the first side. Serve immediately or keep warm in a 200°F oven until ready to serve.

Old-fashioned Potato Pancakes

Makes eight 4-inch pancakes

2 tablespoons
unsalted butter

2 medium shallots or
tiny white boiling
onions, finely
chopped

3 large (about 1½
pounds) russet
potatoes

2 large eggs,
lightly beaten

3 tablespoons matzo
meal or fine dry
bread crumbs

Salt to taste

Freshly ground black
pepper, to taste

Canola oil cooking
spray

I make these potato pancakes for myself on Sunday mornings. Use a russet or other high-starch potato to make pancakes that cook up crisp and do not fall apart. Serve very hot, topped with cold unsweetened applesauce and low-fat sour cream.

1. In a large skillet, melt the butter over medium heat. Add the shallot and cook 1 minute to soften. Set aside.

2. Peel and coarsely grate the potatoes for a total of 2½ to 3 cups. Place the grated potatoes in a tea towel and wring out the excess moisture. Place the grated potatoes in a large bowl and immediately add the eggs, matzo meal or bread crumbs, and onions. Stir to combine evenly. Season with salt and pepper.

3. Wipe out the skillet with a paper towel and spray heavily with oil. Heat the skillet over medium-high heat. Using a heaping ¼-cup measure for each pancake, pour the batter into the skillet and flatten each slightly with the back of a spoon. Cook about 5 minutes, turning once, until crisp and golden brown. Serve immediately.

Zucchini Pancakes

Makes sixteen 2-inch pancakes

2 cups (about ¾ pound) unpeeled zucchini or other summer squash, shredded

2 tablespoons chopped Italian flat-leaf parsley

Salt, to taste

Freshly ground black pepper, to taste

1 large egg

½ cup unbleached all-purpose flour

1 teaspoon baking powder

Olive or vegetable oil, for frying

½ cup grated Parmesan, for sprinkling

There is always room for one more recipe using abundant homegrown summer squashes. I sometimes vary this recipe by combining delicious yellow, pale green, and dark green zucchini for a variegated look.

1. Drain the shredded zucchini on paper towels for 10 minutes.

2. In a medium bowl, combine the zucchini, parsley, salt, pepper, and egg. In another bowl, combine the flour and baking powder and stir into the zucchini mixture until combined. Let stand at room temperature 30 minutes.

3. In a small, skillet, heat ½ inch of oil over medium-high heat until hot, but not smoking. Using a tablespoon carefully spoon the batter into the oil. Cook about 2 minutes, or until bubbles form on the surface, the edges are dry, and the bottoms are golden brown. Turn once, cooking the opposite side about 1 minute, or until golden. The second side will take half the amount of time to cook as the first side. Drain briefly on paper towels. Serve immediately or keep warm in a 200°F oven. Serve sprinkled liberally with the Parmesan.

Baked Pancake with Cucumber Salsa

Makes 1 large or
4 small pancakes

4 tablespoons
(½ stick) unsalted
butter

3 large eggs

¾ cup whole milk

⅔ cup unbleached all-
purpose flour

3 tablespoons whole-
wheat flour

½ cup grated Monterey
Jack or crumbled
fresh goat cheese

Cucumber Salsa
(recipe follows)

A baked pancake, or Dutch Baby, is a big, puffy, round pancake that looks and tastes like an oversized popover. This savory version is very popular because it is easy and fast to assemble and ready to serve in twenty minutes. Make the vegetable-laden Cucumber Salsa the night before to develop its flavor.

1. Preheat the oven to 400°F. Place the butter in 1 large or 4 individual gratin dishes, or in a 10-inch cast-iron skillet or deep pie plate. Place the container on a rack in the center of the oven and melt the butter.

2. In a small bowl using a whisk or in the work bowl of a blender or food processor, beat the eggs until foamy, about 1 minute. Add the milk and flours. Beat hard just until smooth.

3. Remove the hot pan from the oven and carefully pour in the batter. The pan will be less than half full. Bake 15 minutes, until puffy and golden. Sprinkle with the cheese and bake 5 minutes longer to melt the cheese. Serve immediately, cut into wedges.

Makes about 1½ cups

1 English cucumber,
seeded and chopped

1 medium tomato,
slightly underripe,
seeded, peeled, and
chopped

1 fresh mild poblano
or Anaheim chile, or
canned minced
roasted green chile

3 tablespoons finely
chopped fresh
cilantro

2 tablespoons olive oil

1 tablespoon red wine
vinegar or apple
cider vinegar

¼ teaspoon crushed
hot pepper flakes, or
to taste

1 small clove garlic,
minced

CUCUMBER SALSA
Mix all the ingredients together in a small bowl. Refrigerate, covered, 2 hours to overnight to meld flavors.

Baked Apple and Pear Oven Pancake

Makes one 12-inch round or 9-by-13-inch rectangle

6 tablespoons unsalted butter

2 medium tart apples, such as Granny Smith, peeled, cored, and sliced

2 medium firm pears, such as Red Bartlett or Comice, peeled, cored, and sliced

1/3 cup (packed) light brown sugar

1 1/2 teaspoons ground cinnamon

Juice of 1 lemon

6 large eggs

1 1/2 cups whole milk

1 1/2 cups unbleached all-purpose flour

1 teaspoon pure vanilla extract

1/4 teaspoon salt

Serve this sweet pancake hot from the oven sprinkled with a mist of powdered sugar and with lemon wedges.

1. Preheat the oven to 425°F. In a large skillet, melt the butter over medium-high heat and sauté the apple and pear slices about 2 minutes, just until tender, but still firm. Sprinkle with the brown sugar, cinnamon, and lemon juice. Stir to combine. Place a 12-inch round or 9-by-13-inch rectangular baking dish in the oven to heat for 2 minutes. Remove the baking dish with oven mitts and scrape the sautéed fruit into it. If the skillet is ovenproof, the fruit may be distributed evenly over the bottom.

2. In a large bowl using a whisk or in the work bowl of a blender or food processor, combine the eggs, milk, flour, vanilla, and salt and beat until well blended and smooth, about 1 minute. Pour the batter over the hot fruit. Place the pancake immediately in the oven and bake for 20 minutes, or until puffed and brown. Let stand 5 minutes before cutting into wedges. Serve immediately.

Mile-High Popovers

Makes 12 popovers

6 large eggs

2 cups whole milk

2 cups unbleached all-purpose flour

4 tablespoons (½ stick) unsalted butter, melted, or vegetable oil

¼ teaspoon salt

Nonstick cooking spray, butter, or oil, for greasing the cups

My girlfriend Julie loves dining in the casually elegant ambiance of the Thunderbird Bookstore & Cafe in Carmel Valley, California, where entrées are served in front of a cozy fireplace, accompanied by fresh-baked, hot popovers as the bread offering. Here is my attempt to recreate a recipe worthy of her description. For a version with less fat, substitute eight egg whites for the six whole eggs. If you want extra protection against sticking, line the bottoms of the popover cups with parchment.

1. In a 1-quart measuring cup with a pouring spout, using a whisk or hand-held rotary beater, or in the work bowl of an electric blender, beat the eggs until foamy. Add the milk, flour, melted butter or oil, and salt. Beat just until smooth. Do not overmix. Cover and refrigerate 1 hour to overnight.

2. Generously grease 12 popover or muffin cups, ramekins, or baba molds. Place the cups so they are not touching on a baking sheet. Pour the batter into each cup until two-thirds full.

3. Place the pans in a cold oven and immediately set the thermostat to 375°F. Bake 30 minutes without opening the oven door. Bake 10 to 15 minutes more, until the popovers are firm and golden brown, piercing the sides of each popover to allow steam to escape during this last phase of baking. Let cool briefly, again piercing each to allow the steam to escape. Remove from the molds by running a knife around the rim and inverting. Serve immediately while hot and puffy. *(Popovers can be made a day ahead. Cool on a rack and store in an airtight plastic bag at room temperature up to 24 hours. To reheat, space the popovers evenly on a baking sheet and bake in a preheated 375°F oven until warm, about 5 to 7 minutes.)*

BRAN POPOVERS: *Add ¼ cup wheat, oat, or rice bran. Continue as directed.*

CORNMEAL POPOVERS: *Substitute ½ cup cornmeal or masa harina (tortilla flour) for ½ cup of the flour. Continue as directed.*

BUCKWHEAT POPOVERS: *Substitute ⅓ cup light or dark buckwheat flour for ⅓ cup flour. Continue as directed.*

SPINACH POPOVERS: Stir ½ cup chopped fresh spinach leaves and ¼ teaspoon freshly grated nutmeg into the batter in Step 1. Continue as directed.

SUN-DRIED TOMATO AND BACON POPOVERS: Stir ⅓ cup crumbled cooked bacon and 3 tablespoons minced sun-dried tomatoes into the batter in Step 1. Continue as directed.

PARMESAN-HERB POPOVERS: Stir ½ cup or grated Parmesan cheese and 2 tablespoons chopped fresh basil, dill, tarragon, or thyme into the batter in Step 1. Continue as directed.

The Best Yorkshire Pudding

Serves 4

⅞ cup unbleached all-purpose flour or whole-wheat pastry flour

¼ teaspoon salt

½ cup whole milk

2 large eggs

½ cup water

About ⅓ cup unsalted butter or roast beef fat, melted

To make the puffiest Yorkshire pudding ever, make sure all the ingredients are at room temperature, the pan is very hot, and follow the recipe to the letter. Do not double or triple the recipe; for the best results, make separate batches.

1. In a 1-quart measuring cup with a pouring spout, using a whisk or hand-held rotary beater or electric blender, combine the flour, salt, and milk. Beat until smooth, about 1 minute. Add the eggs and beat until pale yellow and fluffy, about 1 minute. Add the water and beat on high speed until bubbly. Let stand at room temperature 1 hour.

2. Thirty minutes before baking, preheat the oven to 400°F. Place a 9-by-13-inch rectangular baking dish, yorkshire pudding mold, oval gratin dish, or muffin tin in the oven and heat until hot, 5 to 8 minutes. Carefully remove the pan from the oven and pour in ¼ inch of melted butter or beef fat. Return to the oven and heat until smoking, another 5 to 8 minutes. Watch carefully to avoid burning or splattering.

3. Beat the batter again until bubbly. Carefully remove the hot pan from the oven and pour the batter into the baking container or each cup until two-thirds full. Bake 20 minutes without opening the oven door. Reduce the oven thermostat to 350°F and bake 10 to 15 minutes more, or until the pudding is firm and golden brown. Serve immediately while hot and puffy, by cutting into squares.

SWEET THINGS:
Morning Breads, Sweet Rolls, and Croissants

Good bakers gravitate toward the realm of yeast-raised sweet breads and rolls. No old-time baking day would be complete without a batch of buns or cinnamon rolls. All bakers have their favorite fillings, toppings, and shapes that trademark their kitchens. Dried fruits, such as raisins, apricots, prunes, dates, and figs, lend a colorful line. Almond paste and cream cheese fillings add interest. As fancy as some sweet breads can be, they can also be simple and elegant.

Croissants have roots tracing back to a simple Viennese morning bun, that according to legend was shaped into a crescent-shape roll to commemorate the victory over Turkish invaders. When the Austrian princess Marie Antoinette moved to the French royal court a century later, the roll was part of her baker's repertoire. French bakers developed it into the many-layered croissant we know today.

The same technique as used for croissants is used in creating Danish pastries, another Viennese invention. The hand-formed shapes that inhabit the Danish pastry world read like an exotic menagerie: cockscombs, lion paws, snails, and butterflies—in addition to pinwheels, fans, pockets, and eyeglasses.

When I review my past baking class schedules, I find that sweet breads have been a top request from students for years. These skills have to be practiced often before they are mastered, so be patient.

Since sweet breads and rolls freeze perfectly, stock your freezer with a variety to have on hand for impromptu visitors for breakfast or with tea or coffee.

Old-fashioned Raisin Bread with Molasses Glaze

Makes six 6-by-4-inch loaves

2½ cups warm water
(105° to 115°F)

1 tablespoon
(1 package) active
dry yeast

½ cup plus 1 teaspoon
sugar

8 tablespoons (1 stick)
unsalted butter,
melted

1 large egg, at room
temperature

2 teaspoons salt

5½ to 6 cups unbleached
all-purpose flour or
bread flour

1 cup dark seedless
raisins, plumped in
hot water 10
minutes and drained

Molasses Glaze

1 tablespoon molasses

2 tablespoons hot
water

There is no better bread than homemade raisin bread. It makes glorious morning toast but is also good with a bit of butter for dessert.

1. Pour ½ cup warm water in a small bowl. Sprinkle the yeast and 1 teaspoon sugar over the surface of the water. Stir to dissolve and let stand at room temperature until foamy, about 10 minutes.

2. In a large bowl with a whisk or in the work bowl of a heavy-duty electric mixer fitted with the paddle attachment, combine the remaining water, butter, egg, and yeast mixture. Add the remaining sugar, salt, and 2 cups flour. Beat hard until smooth, about 3 minutes. Add the raisins. Add the flour, ½ cup at a time, to until a shaggy dough that just clears the sides of the bowl is formed. Switch to a wooden spoon if necessary if making by hand.

3. Turn the dough out onto a lightly floured work surface and knead until smooth and elastic, about 5 minutes, dusting with flour only 1 tablespoon at a time as needed to prevent sticking. Push back any raisins that fall out during the kneading.

If kneading by machine, switch from the paddle to the dough hook and knead for 4 to 5 minutes, or until the dough is smooth and springy and springs back when pressed. If desired, transfer the dough to a floured surface and knead briefly by hand.

4. Place the dough in a greased bowl. Turn once to grease the top and cover with plastic wrap. Let rise in a warm place until doubled in bulk, 1 to 1½ hours.

5. Gently deflate the dough. Turn the dough out onto a lightly floured work surface. Grease six 6-by-4-inch loaf pans. Divide the dough into 6 equal portions. Shape each portion into a loaf and place in a loaf pan. With kitchen shears, snip the top of each loaf 5 or 6 times at a 45-degree angle, a full 2 to 3 inches into the dough, to make a jagged pattern. Cover loosely with plastic wrap and let rise until fully doubled in bulk, about 40 minutes. Gently recut the snips for a more pronounced pattern.

6. Twenty minutes before baking, preheat the oven to 350°F. Prepare the glaze by combining the molasses and hot water in a small bowl. Brush the surface of the loaves with the glaze. Brush once more halfway through baking. Place the loaves on a rack in the center of the oven and bake 25 to 30 minutes, or until golden and a cake tester comes out clean. Transfer the loaves immediately to a cooling rack. Cool before slicing.

Honey-Prune Bread

Makes two 9-by-5-inch loaves

1 cup warm water (105° to 115°F)

1 tablespoon (1 package) active dry yeast

Pinch of granulated sugar

1 cup warm milk (105° to 115°F)

3 tablespoons honey

3 tablespoons unsalted butter

2½ teaspoons salt

1½ cups whole-wheat flour

Grated zest of 1 orange

8 ounces moist pitted prunes, coarsely chopped

3 to 3½ cups unbleached all-purpose flour or bread flour

In the United States, the best plums are grown in California's Santa Clara Valley. Prunes are commercially treated with sulfur to preserve color and potassium sorbate to prevent mold. Buy untreated fruit if you have objections or allergies to these additives. Use the moist-pack premium variety, or soften dry prunes by soaking them in warm water for an hour. This loaf is adapted from a recipe by Sharon Cadwallader, who writes the "Naturally" column in the *San Francisco Chronicle*.

1. Pour the warm water in a small bowl. Sprinkle the yeast and sugar over the surface of the water. Stir to dissolve and let stand at room temperature until foamy, about 10 minutes.

2. In a small bowl, combine the milk, honey, and butter. In a large bowl using a whisk or in the work bowl of a heavy-duty electric mixer fitted with the paddle attachment, combine the milk mixture, yeast mixture, salt, and whole-wheat flour. Beat hard until smooth, about 3 minutes. Add the zest, prunes, and the flour, ½ cup at a time, with a wooden spoon until a soft dough that just clears the side of the bowl is formed. Switch to a wooden spoon when necessary if making by hand.

3. Turn the dough out onto a lightly floured work surface and knead until soft and smooth, about 5 minutes. Dough will be just beyond sticky, yet hold its shape.

If kneading by machine, switch from the paddle to the dough hook and knead for 4 to 5 minutes, or until the dough is smooth and springy and springs back when pressed. If desired, transfer the dough to a floured surface and knead briefly by hand.

4. Place the dough in a greased bowl. Turn once to grease the top and cover with plastic wrap. Let rise in a warm area until doubled in bulk, 1 to 1½ hours.

5. Gently deflate the dough. Turn the dough out onto a lightly floured work surface. Grease the loaf pans. Divide the dough into 2 portions. Shape the dough into loaves and place them in the pans. Cover loosely with plastic wrap and let rise until just above the top of the pans, 30 to 40 minutes.

6. Twenty minutes before baking, preheat the oven to 350°F. Place the pans on a rack in the center of the oven and bake 40 to 45 minutes, or until brown and a cake tester inserted in the center comes out clean. Transfer the loaves immediately to a cooling rack. Cool before slicing.

BAKER'S WISDOM
Cutting Dried Fruit

Place the dried fruit on a cutting board. Sprinkle a bit of flour from the recipe onto the fruit and chop with a chef's knife. Kitchen shears work well when sprayed with a nonstick vegetable spray.

Fresh Apple-Walnut Loaf

Makes two 9-by-5-inch loaves

1 tablespoon
(1 package)
active dry yeast

2 tablespoons light
brown sugar

1 cup warm water
(105° to 115°F)

1 cup warm milk
(105° to 115°F)

6 to 6½ cups unbleached all-
purpose flour or
bread flour

2 medium-large tart
cooking apples,
peeled, cored, and
coarsely chopped
(2 to 3 cups)

½ cup dried currants

½ cup walnuts,
coarsely chopped

2 tablespoons walnut
oil

2 large eggs, at room
temperature

2 teaspoons ground
cinnamon

½ teaspoon ground
mace

½ teaspoon ground
allspice

1 tablespoon salt

The dried currants that dot the interior of this loaf are tiny sun-dried grapes, not currant berries. Note that the amount of flour will vary slightly depending on what type of apple you use. This nut-and-spice fruit bread makes such good toast when it is a day old that you will want to tuck away a loaf to save just for that.

1. In a large bowl using a whisk or in the work bowl of a heavy-duty electric mixer fitted with the paddle attachment, combine the yeast, brown sugar, warm water, warm milk, and 2 cups of the flour. Beat until smooth, about 1 minute. Cover the bowl loosely with plastic wrap and let stand at room temperature until foamy, about 1 hour.

2. Add the apples, currants, walnuts, oil, eggs, cinnamon, mace, all-spice, salt, and 1 cup more of the flour. Beat until creamy, about 2 minutes. Add the remaining flour, ½ cup at a time, until a soft dough that just clears the sides of the bowl is formed. Switch to a wooden spoon when necessary if making by hand.

3. Turn the dough out onto a lightly floured work surface and knead until smooth and springy yet firm, about 5 minutes, dusting with flour only 1 tablespoon at a time as needed to prevent sticking. Push back any fruit or nuts that fall out during the kneading.

If kneading by machine, switch from the paddle to the dough hook and knead for 4 to 5 minutes, or until the dough is smooth and springy and springs back when pressed. If desired, transfer the dough to a floured surface and knead briefly by hand.

4. Place the dough in a greased deep container. Turn the dough once to coat the top and cover with plastic wrap. Let rise at room temperature until doubled in bulk, 1½ to 2 hours.

5. Gently deflate the dough. Turn the dough out onto a lightly floured work surface. Grease two 9-by-5-inch loaf pans. Divide the dough into 6 equal portions. Roll each portion into a strip with your palms and lay 3 of the strips together side by side. Braid the strips, taper, and pinch the ends together, and tuck them under. Repeat to make a second loaf. Place the loaves in the loaf pans. Cover loosely with plastic wrap and let rise at room temperature until 1 inch above the rims of the pans, about 45 minutes.

6. Twenty minutes before baking, preheat the oven to 350°F. Place the pans on a rack in the center of the oven and bake 45 to 50 minutes, or until browned and the loaves sound hollow when tapped with your fingers. Transfer the loaves immediately to cooling racks. Cool completely before slicing.

Cashew-Date Bread

Makes two 8½-by-4½-inch loaves, or five 6-by-3½-inch loaves

1 cup plus ¼ cup warm water (105° to 115°F)

2 tablespoons (2 packages) active dry yeast

Pinch of sugar

1 cup warm buttermilk (105° to 115°F)

½ cup honey

½ cup rolled oats

4 tablespoons (1 stick) unsalted butter, melted

1 tablespoon salt

1 teaspoon ground cinnamon

1½ cups whole-wheat flour

¾ cup coarsely chopped pitted dates

¾ cup coarsely chopped raw cashews

About 4 cups unbleached all-purpose flour or bread flour

Nuts and dried fruit have a natural affinity for each other. Besides the cashew and date combination, I have also used dried apples, raisins, and walnuts; dried apricots and pecans; dried pears and hazelnuts; and dried peaches and brazil nuts. The dough is a light wheat-and-oat mixture that makes a rich, sweet morning bread when toasted. The bread is also good sliced thin for a cream cheese tea sandwich.

1. Pour the warm water in a small bowl. Sprinkle the yeast and sugar over the surface of the water. Stir to dissolve and let stand at room temperature until foamy, about 10 minutes.

2. In a large bowl using a whisk or in the work bowl of a heavy-duty electric mixer fitted with the paddle attachment, combine buttermilk, water, honey, oats, butter, salt, and cinnamon in a large bowl. Add the whole-wheat flour and yeast mixture. Beat until creamy and smooth for 3 minutes. Add the dates, cashews, and the flour, ½ cup at a time, stirring with a wooden spoon until a shaggy dough that just clears the sides of the bowl is formed.

3. Turn the dough out onto a lightly floured work surface and knead until smooth, about 5 minutes, dusting with flour only 1 tablespoon at a time as needed to make a soft and springy dough. Take care not to add too much flour. Push back any fruit or nuts that fall out during kneading. The dough will have a slightly dense and sticky quality.

If kneading by machine, switch from the paddle to the dough hook and knead for 4 to 5 minutes, or until the dough is smooth and springy and springs back when pressed. If desired, transfer the dough to a floured surface and knead briefly by hand.

4. Place the dough in a greased bowl. Turn to grease the top and cover with plastic wrap. Let rise in a warm area until doubled in bulk, 1 to 1½ hours.

5. Gently deflate the dough. Turn the dough out onto a lightly floured work surface. Grease the loaf pans. Divide the dough into 2 large or 5 small loaves. Shape the loaves and place them in the pans. Cover loosely with plastic wrap and let rise until level with the tops of the pans, 30 to 40 minutes.

6. Twenty minutes before baking, preheat the oven to 375°F. Bake large loaves 35 to 40 minutes, or until brown and a cake tester inserted in the center comes out clean. Bake the mini loaves 25 to 30 minutes or until brown and a cake tester inserted in the center comes out clean. Transfer immediately to a cooling rack. Cool completely before slicing.

Traditional English Muffins

Makes twelve 3-inch muffins

¼ cup warm water
(105° to 115°F)

1 tablespoon
(1 package) active
dry yeast

Pinch of sugar

4 to 4½ cups unbleached
all-purpose flour

2 teaspoons salt

1 large egg, at room
temperature

1¼ cups warm milk
(105° to 115°F)

2 tablespoons unsalted
butter, melted

½ cup dried currants
(optional)

¼ cup cornmeal or
coarse semolina,
for sprinkling

English muffins really should be called American muffins, because they are the pure Yankee offshoot of griddle-baked crumpets and bannocks. A distant relative of the pancake, they are an unusual but traditional home-baked yeasted little bread. To serve, pull them apart with a fork and toast.

1. Pour the warm water into a small bowl. Sprinkle the yeast and pinch of sugar over the surface of the water. Stir to dissolve and let stand at room temperature until foamy, about 10 minutes.

2. In a large bowl with a whisk or in the work bowl of a heavy-duty electric mixer fitted with the paddle attachment, place 2 cups of the flour and the salt and make a well. Add the egg, milk, butter, and yeast mixture. Beat until creamy, about 2 minutes. Add the remaining flour, ½ cup at a time, and the currants, if desired, until a soft dough that just clears the sides of the bowl is formed. Switch to a wooden spoon when necessary if mixing by hand.

3. Turn the dough out onto a lightly floured work surface and knead until smooth and springy, about 3 minutes, adding 1 tablespoon of flour at a time as needed to prevent sticking. The softer you leave the dough, the lighter the muffin.

If kneading by machine, switch from the paddle to the dough hook and knead for 2 to 3 minutes, or until the dough is smooth and springy and springs back when pressed. If desired, transfer the dough to a floured surface and knead briefly by hand.

4. Place the dough in a greased deep container. Turn once to coat the top and cover with plastic wrap. Let rise at room temperature until doubled in bulk, about 1½ hours.

5. Lightly sprinkle the work surface with cornmeal or semolina. Gently deflate the dough Turn the dough out onto the work surface. Roll the dough into a rectangle about ½ inch thick. Sprinkle the top with cornmeal or semolina to prevent sticking while rolling. Cut the muffins out with a 2 ½- or 3-inch biscuit cutter or drinking glass. Roll out the trimmings and cut out the remaining muffins.

6. Preheat an electric griddle to 350°F or 375°F, or heat a cast-iron stovetop griddle over medium heat until a drop of water sprinkled on the griddle dances across the surface. Lightly grease the surface.

7. Immediately place several muffins on the hot griddle. Cook for about 10 minutes on each side, turning when quite brown. English muffins take time to bake all the way through, and they will swell and be very puffy while baking. Cover the uncooked muffins with a towel or place them in the refrigerator if they are rising too fast while the others are baking. Transfer the baked muffins to a cooling rack. *(Muffins may be stored, tightly wrapped in plastic, in the refrigerator or freezer.)*

Cinnamon Rolls with Irish Cream Glaze

Makes 18 rolls

Dough

- 1 medium russet potato (about 6 ounces), peeled and cut into large chunks
- 2 tablespoons unsalted butter
- 1 tablespoon (1 package) active dry yeast
- ½ cup granulated sugar or ½ cup (packed) light brown sugar
- ¼ cup warm water (105° to 115°F)
- 2 tablespoons vegetable oil
- 1 large egg, at room temperature
- 1 teaspoon salt
- 5 to 5½ cups unbleached all-purpose flour or bread flour

Filling

- 4 tablespoons (½ stick) unsalted butter, melted
- 1¼ cups (packed) light brown sugar
- 1½ tablespoons ground cinnamon

This recipe resides at the apex of the cinnamon roll world. If you cannot eat all the rolls the same day they are made, freeze the rest once they are cool to preserve their light texture.

1. In a medium saucepan, combine the potato chunks with water to cover. Bring to a boil, reduce the heat to low, and cook uncovered, until tender, about 20 minutes. Drain the potato, reserving 1 cup of the liquid. Let the potato water cool to 105° to 115°F. Meanwhile, process the potato with the butter through a food mill placed over a bowl or purée it in a food processor fitted with the metal blade just until smooth. This produces ¾ to 1 cup of purée.

2. Pour the warm water in a small bowl. Sprinkle the yeast and a pinch of the granulated or brown sugar over the surface of the water. Stir to dissolve and let stand at room temperature until foamy, about 10 minutes.

3. In a large mixing bowl with a whisk or in the work bowl of a heavy-duty electric mixer fitted with the paddle attachment, combine the puréed potato, the warm potato water, yeast mixture, the remaining granulated or brown sugar, oil, egg, salt, and 2 cups of the flour. Beat hard to combine, about 1 minute. Add the remaining flour, ½ cup at a time, until a shaggy dough that just clears the sides of the bowl is formed.

4. Turn the dough out onto a lightly floured work surface and knead until smooth and springy, about 4 minutes, dusting with flour only 1 tablespoon at a time as needed to prevent sticking. Take care not to add too much flour, because the dough should be very satiny.

If kneading by machine, switch from the paddle to the dough hook and knead for 3 to 4 minutes, or until the dough is smooth and springy and springs back when pressed. If desired, transfer the dough to a floured surface and knead briefly by hand.

5. Place the dough in a greased deep container. Turn once to coat the top and cover with plastic wrap. Let rise in a warm place until doubled in bulk, 1 to 1½ hours. Gently deflate the dough and let rise a second time until doubled in bulk, 50 minutes to 1 hour.

1 cup dark raisins or dried currants, plumped in hot water 10 minutes and drained (optional)

1 cup (4 ounces) walnuts or pecans, toasted and coarsely ground (optional)

Irish Cream Glaze

1½ cups sifted powdered sugar

4 to 5 tablespoons Irish cream liqueur or milk

6. Gently deflate the dough. Turn the dough out onto a lightly floured work surface. Parchment-line a baking sheet. Divide the dough into 2 equal portions. Roll out each portion into a 10-by-14-inch rectangle at least ¼ inch thick. Brush the surface of each rectangle with the melted butter. Sprinkle the surface of each rectangle evenly with half of the brown sugar and cinnamon, leaving a 1-inch border around the edges. Sprinkle with the raisins or currants and ground nuts, if using. Starting from the long side, roll the dough up jelly-roll fashion. Pinch the seams together and, using a serrated knife or dental floss, cut each roll crosswise into 9 equal portions, each 1 to 1 ½ inches thick. Place each portion cut side up on a parchment-lined baking sheet at least 2 inches apart. Press gently to flatten each swirl slightly. Alternatively, place in 18 greased 3-inch muffin-pan cups for a top-knot effect. Cover loosely with plastic wrap and let rise at room temperature just until puffy, about 20 minutes. *(The rolls may be refrigerated and transferred later to the oven.)*

7. Twenty minutes before baking, preheat the oven to 350°F. Place the baking sheet or muffin cups on a rack in the center of the oven and bake 25 to 30 minutes, or until golden brown and firm to the touch. Using a metal spatula, remove to a rack. Immediately prepare the glaze by combining the powdered sugar and liqueur in a small mixing bowl and whisking until smooth. Adjust the consistency of the glaze by adding more liqueur, a few drops at a time, to make a thin pourable mixture. Dip your fingers or a large spoon into the glaze and drizzle it over the rolls by running your hand or the spoon back and forth over the tops. Or, apply the glaze to the rolls with a brush. Let stand until just warm before eating. *(The rolls may be cooled and frozen in heavy-duty plastic bags up to 3 months.)*

Mexican Morning Buns
Pan Dulce

Makes 16 buns

Dough

1/4 cup warm water (105° to 115°F)

1 tablespoon (1 package) active dry yeast

2/3 cup sugar

2/3 cup warm milk (105° to 115°F)

5 large eggs, at room temperature

2 teaspoons pure vanilla extract

1 teaspoon salt

4 to 4½ cups unbleached all-purpose flour

6 tablespoons (¾ stick) unsalted butter, at room temperature, cut into pieces

Sugar Topping

1 cup unbleached all-purpose flour

1 cup powdered sugar

1 tablespoon pure vanilla extract

1 egg, beaten

1 egg yolk, beaten

8 tablespoons (1 stick) unsalted butter or margarine, at room temperature, cut into pieces

Every Mexican *panadería* north and south of the border has its selection of this round sweet bun in a variety of shapes and sizes with different toppings, from icings to brightly colored pink or red sugar crystals. This homemade *pan dulce* is definitely superior to the bakery version; it's more substantial and less sweet. You can have the buns with a chocolate or cinnamon-vanilla crunchy topping. If you are traveling close to the border, try to find the authentic rustic-looking metal cutters for stamping out designs into the topping. The most common designs are the *concha* (seashell swirl) and the crosshatch; the most common shapes are the *elote* (ear of corn) and the *cuerno* (crescent).

1. To prepare the dough: Pour the water into a small bowl or 1-cup liquid measuring cup. Sprinkle the yeast and a pinch of the sugar over the surface of the water. Stir to dissolve and let stand at room temperature until foamy, about 10 minutes.

2. In a large bowl using a whisk or in the bowl of a heavy-duty electric mixer fitted with the paddle attachment, combine the milk, eggs, vanilla, sugar, salt, and 2 cups of the flour. Add the yeast mixture and beat on medium speed until smooth, about 1 minute. Add the butter pieces and mix on low speed to incorporate, 15 seconds. Add the remaining flour, ½ cup at a time, mixing on low speed until a soft shaggy dough that just clears the sides of the bowl forms. Switch to a wooden spoon when necessary if making by hand.

3. Turn the dough out onto a lightly floured work surface and knead until a soft, smooth, and elastic dough form, 1 to 2 minutes for a machine-mixed dough and 3 to 4 minutes for a hand-mixed dough, dusting with flour only 1 tablespoon at a time, just enough as needed to prevent sticking. The dough will be firm to the touch and springy.

If kneading by machine, switch from the paddle to the dough hook and knead for 3 to 4 minutes, or until the dough is smooth and springy and springs back when pressed. If desired, transfer the dough to a floured surface and knead briefly by hand.

¼ cup unsweetened
cocoa powder

1½ tablespoons ground
cinnamon

1 egg white beaten
with 1 teaspoon
water, for brushing

4. Place the dough in a greased deep container. Turn once to coat the top and cover with plastic wrap. Let rise at room temperature until doubled in bulk, 1 to 1½ hours.

5. To prepare the sugar topping: In a small bowl with your fingers or with a heavy-duty electric mixer or in a food processor, combine the flour and sugar. Sprinkle the vanilla, egg, and egg yolk over the dry mixture and add the butter pieces. Mix or process quickly to make a soft, crumbly mixture. Divide into 2 equal portions, adding the cocoa to one and the cinnamon to the other. Set aside, covered.

6. Grease or parchment-line 1 or 2 large baking sheets. Turn the dough out onto a lightly floured work surface and divide into 16 equal portions.

7. Form each portion into a tight round and press to flatten the round to about 3 inches in diameter. Place all the rolls on the baking sheets. Divide the topping into 16 portions, half chocolate and half cinnamon. Greasing your hands, roll each portion into a ball. Pat or roll each out into a circle that will fit on top of a roll. Press on top of the ball of dough, making certain the circle sticks. Using the tip of a small sharp knife or a *pan dulce* cutter, cut a crisscross or curved shell pattern into the topping. Cover loosely with plastic wrap and let rise at room temperature until puffy, 40 minutes.

8. Twenty minutes before baking, preheat the oven to 375°F. Place the baking sheet on a rack in the center of the oven and bake for 15 to 18 minutes, or until golden brown and firm to the touch. Transfer immediately to a cooling rack. Serve immediately warm or at room temperature.

ELOTES: *Prepare the dough and topping through Step 6. Roll a portion of dough into an elongated oval. Sprinkle with 2 tablespoons of the sugar filling and roll up. Place, seam side down, on the baking sheet and pull up the open lips of dough at one end to form an ear of corn. Slash each ear lengthwise ¼-inch deep with serrated knife to open slightly. Place 2 inches apart on the baking sheet. Continue as directed.*

CUERNOS: *Prepare the dough and topping through Step 6. Roll a portion of the dough into an 8-by-4-inch oval; sprinkle with 2 tablespoons of the filling. Roll up from the long side to make a thick log. Hold both ends and twist in opposite directions, making 6 twists, then curve into a crescent. Place 2 inches apart on the prepared pans. Continue as directed.*

Yeasted Sopaipillas

¼ cup warm water
(105° to 115°F)

1 tablespoon
(1 package) active
dry yeast

2 tablespoons sugar

About 3 cups unbleached
all-purpose flour

1 teaspoon salt

¾ cup milk

1 large egg, at room
temperature

2 tablespoons
shortening or
unsalted butter,
melted

These light little hollow "pillows" of dough are similar to Navajo fry bread (see page 231). Most recipes call for baking powder and frying; this yeast-risen version was originally served at Fred Harvey's La Fonda in Santa Fe. I have adapted it to be baked in the oven, rather than deep-fried. La Fonda offered sopaipillas as an afternoon repast with hot Mexican chocolate or coffee *chango* (cream cheese with guava jelly) and steamed and sugared guava peels.

1. Pour the warm water into a small bowl or 1-cup liquid measuring cup. Sprinkle the yeast and a pinch of sugar over the surface of the water. Stir to dissolve and let stand at room temperature until foamy, about 10 minutes.

2. In a large bowl using a whisk or in the bowl of a heavy-duty electric mixer fitted with the paddle attachment, combine 2¾ cups of the flour, the salt, and 2 tablespoons sugar. Add the yeast, milk, egg, and melted shortening. Beat until smooth, about 1 minute. Switch to a wooden spoon when necessary if making by hand.

3. Turn the dough out onto a lightly floured work surface and knead gently just until smooth, about 10 kneads, dusting with flour only 1 tablespoon at a time as needed to prevent sticking. The dough must remain very soft.

If kneading by machine, switch from the paddle to the dough hook and knead for 1 to 2 minutes, or until the dough is smooth and springy and springs back when pressed. If desired, transfer the dough to a floured surface and knead briefly by hand.

4. Place the dough in a greased deep container, turn once to grease the top, and cover with plastic wrap. Let rise at room temperature for about 45 minutes or in the refrigerator for about 2 hours. *(The dough may be refrigerated at this point for up to 48 hours, but it should be deflated daily.)*

5. Twenty minutes before baking, preheat the oven to 500°F. Parchment-line 2 baking sheets. Gently deflate the dough. Place the dough on a lightly floured work surface and divide it into four. Gently roll each portion of dough out ⅛ to ¼ inch thick. Fold the dough in half and gently reroll it. Do this 2 times. Let the dough rest for a few minutes if it becomes too springy or hard to handle. With a dough wheel or very sharp knife, cut each section of dough into 6 squares, oblongs, triangles, or diamonds. The shapes can be irregular, but they should be about 2 by 3 inches. Place on a lightly floured baking sheet and cover loosely with plastic wrap. If you work quickly, the dough can stay at room temperature for up to 5 minutes; otherwise refrigerate it until ready to bake or up to overnight. Place the dough pieces on the baking sheets, at least I inch apart. Place one baking sheet on a rack in the center of the oven and bake, I pan at a time, 8 to IO minutes until puffed and brown. Serve warm.

VARIATION: *Substitute ½ cup fine white, yellow, or blue cornmeal or mesquite flour for ½ cup of the all-purpose flour.*

Danish Pastries

Makes 20 to 24 individual pastries

¼ cup warm water (105° to 115°F)

1½ tablespoons (1½ packages) active dry yeast

¼ cup (packed) light brown sugar

1 cup half-and-half, light cream, or whole milk, very cold

½ cup (1 stick) unsalted butter, melted and cooled

2 large eggs

1 teaspoon salt

Grated zest of 1 orange

½ teaspoon ground mace or cardamom

1 teaspoon pure vanilla extract

4½ cups unbleached all-purpose flour

1½ cups (3 sticks) unsalted butter, very cold

Egg Glaze

1 egg plus 2 tablespoons water

Fillings

Cheese Envelope Filling (recipe follows)

Prune Crescent Filling (recipe follows)

Known as *Kopenhagener Wienerbrot* in Austria and *Viennabröd* (Vienna bread) in Denmark, these artistically formed individual pastries are a favorite bakery item across America as well as in Europe. The rolling and folding techniques necessary for the multitude of flaky layers are the same as those used in French croissant pastry. Although the technique may seem daunting, it is easily mastered, and the homemade baked pastries make this labor of love worth every minute in the kitchen. Resist the impulse to be over-critical of your shaping if it's uneven or imperfect, as the rising and baking will correct most irregularities, and your personal style will develop with practice.

The most important advice in working with a folded dough is to keep the dough and butter cold every step of the way. Remember also that the dough is mixed and turned the day before shaping and baking. Fillings range from nut to fruit to cheese. I have included directions for my favorites, but mix and match them as you like, or use a can of prune, nut, or poppy seed paste, if that is to your taste. These hand-formed pastries will be smaller in size than most commercial bakery Danish. I learned how to make these pastries from master baker Diane Dexter at Tante Marie's Cooking School in San Francisco.

1. Pour the warm water in a small bowl. Sprinkle the yeast and a pinch of the brown sugar over the surface of the water. Stir to dissolve and let stand at room temperature until foamy, about 10 minutes.

2. In a large bowl using a whisk or in the work bowl of a heavy-duty electric mixer fitted with the paddle attachment, combine the remaining brown sugar, the half-and-half or milk, melted butter, eggs, salt, orange zest, mace, and vanilla. Beat until smooth, about 1 minute. Add the yeast mixture and exactly 4 cups of the flour. Stir until the dough comes together into a shaggy, moist mass and the flour is just absorbed with no dry patches. Switch to a wooden spoon when necessary if making by hand. Do not knead. Add 1 tablespoon of flour at a time as needed to prevent stickiness but no more than a total of 4 tablespoons; this dough should be very soft.

Blueberry Turnover
Filling (recipe
follows)

Almond Crest Filling
(recipe follows)

Apple Danish Filling
(recipe follows)

Finishing Glaze

1/2 cup sifted powdered
sugar

1 tablespoon milk or
cream

1 teaspoon unsalted
butter, melted

1/4 teaspoon lemon,
orange, almond, or
pure vanilla extract

3. Lightly dust an ungreased baking sheet with flour. Place the dough on the sheet and, using your fingers, spread the dough into a large, flat, free-form rectangle about 1 inch thick. The dough will be rough and uneven looking. Cover tightly with plastic wrap, making certain the dough is covered, to avoid dry patches from forming. Refrigerate in the coldest part of the refrigerator until thoroughly chilled, 45 minutes to 1 hour.

4. Using an electric mixer, quickly combine the cold butter with the remaining 1/2 cup of flour until smooth and no hard lumps remain. Or, use a spatula to smear the butter on a work surface, dump the flour on top, and use a chopping motion to combine; knead quickly until the flour is absorbed into the butter. Form the butter into a rough block on the work surface. Pat or roll quickly into a firm, fat rectangle. Wrap in plastic wrap and refrigerate if at all soft or sticky. The butter should be chilled but still pliable. This step is much easier to execute than it sounds.

5. Place the dough on a lightly floured work surface. Roll out into a 20-by-10-inch rectangle about 1/2 inch thick. Divide the butter mixture into 2 equal portions and roll each portion into a 8-by-6-inch rectangle. Place one of the butter portions in the middle third of the dough, working it with your fingers to have it fit. Pull a third of the dough over from the side to cover. Seal the edges to encase the butter. Place the remaining butter portion on top and fold over the remaining third of the dough. Pinch the edges together to seal completely. It is important that the butter not become too soft, or it will seep into the dough rather than form layers.

6. Using firm strokes, roll out the dough into another large, even rectangle and fold again into thirds. Replace on the baking sheet and cover with plastic wrap. Refrigerate for at least 20 but no longer than 30 minutes to chill. If chilled longer than 30 minutes, the butter may harden too much. The chilling period allows the gluten to rest and the butter to firm to allow continued rolling.

7. Repeat the process of rolling out and folding into thirds 2 more times to create the multilayered dough, chilling in between as needed. Take care not to tear the dough or allow the butter to get too soft. Remember to adjust the corners as you are working, to keep them square and tidy, and to move the dough constantly to avoid sticking. Use a soft brush to dust off any excess flour. Chill the dough at any point that it becomes sticky, and remember to keep the folded edge on top.

continues next page

8. Wrap the dough tightly in plastic wrap and refrigerate overnight or for up to 3 days. *(The dough can also be frozen for 1 month at this point, but fresh dough is easier to work with.)*

9. Parchment-line 2 baking sheets or leave ungreased. Gently press the dough to deflate it, and cut it in half with a sharp knife in one downward motion. Do not use a sawing motion; it will destroy the delicate layering. Rewrap 1 section of dough and return it to the refrigerator.

10. For Cheese Envelopes: On a lightly floured work surface, roll out the other half of the chilled pastry into a 16-by-11-inch rectangle ¼ inch thick. Keep lifting and moving the dough to prevent sticking or tearing. Roll the dough back and forth on a diagonal to achieve an even width. Trim the edges, if necessary. With a sharp knife or pastry wheel, cut lengthwise into 3 equal strips, then cut each strip into 4-inch squares. Spoon about 1 heaping tablespoon of the Cheese Envelope Filling into the center of each square. Fold 1 corner of the square over the center of the filling and then fold the others over. Seal with a bit of water.

For Prune Crescents: On a lightly floured work surface, roll out the other half of the chilled pastry into a 16-by-10-inch rectangle ¼ inch thick. Keep lifting and moving the dough to prevent sticking or tearing. Roll the dough back and forth on a diagonal to achieve an even width. Trim the edges, if necessary. With a sharp knife or pastry wheel, cut into six 5-inch squares and then cut each square on the diagonal to make 2 triangles. Place 2 tablespoons of Prune Crescent Filling on the center of the base of each triangle. Roll up from the base edge and then curve the ends to form a crescent.

For Blueberry Turnovers: On a lightly floured work surface, roll out the other half of the chilled pastry into a 15-inch square ¼ inch thick. Keep lifting and moving the dough to prevent sticking or tearing. Roll the dough back and forth on a diagonal to achieve an even width. Trim the edges, if necessary. With a sharp knife or pastry wheel, cut into three 5-inch-wide strips and then cut each strip into three 5-inch squares. Place 2 generous tablespoons of Blueberry Turnover Filling onto the center of each square. Moisten the edges with water and fold in half on the diagonal to make a triangle. Crimp the edges with a folk to seal, and pierce the surface with a knife in 2 places to allow steam to escape.

For Almond Crests: On a lightly floured work surface, roll out the other half of the chilled pastry into a 18-by-12-inch rectangle ¼ inch thick. Keep lifting and moving the dough to prevent sticking or tearing.

Roll the dough back and forth on a diagonal to achieve an even width. Trim the edges, if necessary. With a sharp knife or pastry wheel, cut into three 6-inch-wide strips, then cut each strip into two 6-inch squares. Spread a thin layer of Almond Crest Filling along the center of the bottom half of each, leaving a full ½-inch border around the 3 sides. Fold up the bottom third of the dough over the filling and then fold the top third section over the center to completely enclose the filling. Using a sharp knife, cut ¾-inch-deep slits into a folded edge to make 2 equal-distanced slits, cutting only halfway to the opposite side. Curve slightly to form the crests.

For Apple Danish: On a lightly floured work surface, roll out the other half of the chilled pastry into a 16-by-10-inch rectangle ¼-inch thick. Keep lifting and moving the dough to prevent sticking or tearing. Roll the dough back and forth on a diagonal to achieve an even width. Trim the edges, if necessary. With a sharp knife or pastry wheel, cut lengthwise into 1-inch-wide strips. With your palms on each end of a strip, twist one in the opposite direction from the other at the same time. Form a pinwheel. Tuck the tail underneath. Using your fingertips, press on the center to form an indentation for the filling. Place about 2 table-spoons of the Apple Danish Filling in the center. Sprinkle each pastry with a generous tablespoon of Spice Crumbs to finish.

11. Place the individual shapes on the baking sheet at least 2 inches apart. Do not crowd. Let rise, uncovered, at cool room temperature until doubled in bulk, 1 to 1½ hours. *(The pastries may also be covered with plastic wrap and left to rise in the refrigerator overnight.)*

12. Twenty minutes before baking, preheat the oven to 400°F. When the pastries are light and springy to the touch, brush with the egg glaze. Place a second baking sheet of the same dimensions under the one holding the pastries to double pan and prevent the bottoms from burning. Bake in the center of the oven for 15 to 25 minutes, depending on size.

13. To prepare the finishing glaze: In a small bowl with a whisk, combine the powdered sugar, milk, melted butter, and extract and beat until smooth and thick yet pourable. Using a spatula, transfer the hot pastries to a cooling rack. Glaze the pastries while hot, drizzling the glaze with the end of a spoon, a pastry bag fitted with a small plain tip, or the tips of your fingers. The glaze will set as it cools. Let the pastries cool on the racks for 15 minutes before eating.

VARIATION: *Substitute 3 cups whole-wheat pastry flour for an equal amount of the all-purpose flour. Proceed as directed to mix, shape, and bake.*

CHEESE ENVELOPE FILLING

Makes about 1 1/4 cups filling, enough for 12 pastries

    8 ounces cream cheese, whole-milk ricotta, or farmer cheese

  1/4 cup sugar

1 1/2 tablespoons unbleached all-purpose flour

    1 teaspoon pure vanilla extract

    1 large egg yolk

      Grated zest of 1 lemon

1. In a bowl with a spoon or with an electric mixer, beat the cheese, sugar, flour, vanilla, egg yolk, and lemon zest together until smooth and well combined. Cover and refrigerate for at least 1 hour. *(The filling may be made 24 hours ahead.)*

2. Use as directed in Step 10 of Danish Pastries recipe.

PRUNE CRESCENT FILLING

Makes about 1 1/2 cups filling, enough for 12 pastries

    1 cup finely chopped moist pitted prunes

  1/3 cup orange juice, prune juice, or water

    1 tablespoon fresh lemon juice

  1/4 cup sugar

1. In a small heavy saucepan, combine the prunes, orange juice, lemon juice, and sugar. Simmer, uncovered, until the fruit has absorbed the liquid, about 20 minutes. Remove from the heat and cool before using. *(The filling may be made 48 hours ahead and refrigerated.)*

2. Use as directed in Step 10 of Danish Pastries recipe.

BLUEBERRY TURNOVER FILLING

Makes 1 1/4 cups filling, enough for 9 pastries

1 1/4 cups whole-fruit blueberry preserves

1. Use as directed in Step 10 of Danish Pastries recipe.

ALMOND CREST FILLING

Makes about 1 cup filling, enough for 6 pastries

- 1 cup whole almonds
- 1/3 cup zwieback, biscotti, or shortbread cookie crumbs
- 1/3 cup (packed) light brown sugar
- 4 tablespoons (1/2 stick) unsalted butter, melted
- 1 large egg white
- 1/2 teaspoon pure almond extract

1. Grind the nuts until coarse in a food processor. Add the remaining ingredients and process just until a paste is formed.

2. Use as directed in Step 10 of Danish Pastries recipe.

APPLE DANISH FILLING

Makes about 1 1/2 cups filling, enough for 10 pastries

- 4 tablespoons (1/2 stick) unsalted butter
- 2 1/2 cups sliced and peeled tart cooking apples (about 4 medium apples)
- 1/3 cup (packed) light brown sugar
- 1 tablespoon fresh lemon juice
- 1/2 teaspoon ground cinnamon

Spice Crumbs

- 1/2 cup sugar
- 1/3 cup unbleached all-purpose flour
- 1/2 teaspoon ground cinnamon
- 4 tablespoons (1/2 stick) cold unsalted butter, cut into pieces

1. In a medium skillet, melt the butter over medium heat and add the apples. Cook until apples just begin to soften, 2 to 3 minutes, stirring occasionally. Add the brown sugar, lemon juice, and cinnamon and stir until the sugar dissolves. Let cool or refrigerate for up to 24 hours before using.

2. Combine the spice crumb ingredients in a small bowl and rub the ingredients together with your fingers to make coarse crumbs.

3. Use as directed in Step 10 of Danish Pastries recipe.

Whole-Wheat Croissants

Makes 18 large or 28 small
croissants

1½ tablespoons
(1½ packages)
active dry yeast

¼ cup (packed) brown
sugar

⅓ cup warm water
(105° to 115°F)

¼ cup vegetable oil

2 teaspoons salt

1 cup cold milk

1 large egg

1 cup whole-wheat
pastry flour

4 cups unbleached all-
purpose flour

2 cups (4 sticks) cold
unsalted butter

Rich Egg Glaze
(page 52)

Long the domain of the professional baker, croissants are made
by following a logical set of simple instructions to create a dough
with more than 150 layers. Always use unsalted butter for your
croissants; it has a superior flavor and stays cold longer than
salted butter, which contains a higher percentage of moisture.
And keep the dough and butter cold every step of the way. The
nuttiness of whole-wheat pastry flour gives these croissants a
dense, chewy-texture and a rich flavor.

1. Pour the warm water in a small bowl. Sprinkle the yeast and a pinch
of the brown sugar over the surface of the water. Stir to dissolve and let
stand at room temperature until foamy, about 10 minutes.

2. In a large bowl using a whisk or in the work bowl of a heavy-duty electric mixer fitted with the paddle attachment, combine the oil, remaining brown sugar, salt, milk, egg, and whole-wheat flour. Beat until
smooth. Add the yeast mixture and exactly 3½ cups of the unbleached
flour. Switch to a wooden spoon when necessary if making by hand.
Beat until the dough comes together into a shaggy mass and the flour is
just absorbed with no dry patches. Do not knead. Add 1 tablespoon of
flour at a time as necessary to prevent stickiness, but do not add more
than a total of 4 tablespoons. This dough should be very soft.

3. Lightly dust an ungreased baking sheet with flour. Place the dough
on the sheet and, with your fingers, spread the dough to lie flat in a
large free-form rectangle about 1 inch thick. Cover tightly with plastic
wrap, making certain all the dough is covered to avoid forming dry
patches. Refrigerate until thoroughly chilled, about 45 minutes.

4. Using an electric mixer, quickly combine the cold butter with ½ cup
of the flour until smooth with no hard lumps. Or using a spatula, smear
the butter on a work surface, sprinkle with the flour, and use a chopping motion to combine; knead quickly until the flour is absorbed into
the butter. Form the butter into a rough block shape on the work surface. Pat or roll quickly into a fat rectangle. Wrap in plastic wrap and
refrigerate the butter if it is soft or sticky. The butter should be chilled,
but workable.

5. Turn the dough out on a lightly floured work surface. Roll into a 20-by-10-inch rectangle about ½ inch thick. Divide the butter into 2 equal portions and roll each into a 8-by-6-inch rectangle. Place half the butter in the middle third of the dough. Pull one third over from the side to cover the butter. Seal the edges to encase the butter. Place the remaining butter on top and fold over the remaining third of the dough. Pinch the edges to seal completely.

6. Roll the dough into another large rectangle using firm strokes. Fold again into thirds. Replace the dough on a baking sheet and cover it with plastic wrap. Refrigerate for 20 minutes, but no longer than 30 minutes to chill.

7. Repeat the process of the rolling out and the folding into thirds 2 more times. Take care not to tear the dough or to allow the butter to get too soft. Remember to adjust the corners as you are working, to keep the dough square, and to move the dough constantly to prevent sticking. Use a soft brush to dust off any excess flour. These are the second and third turns. Chill the dough at any point that it becomes sticky.

8. Wrap the dough tightly in plastic wrap, replace it on the baking sheet, and refrigerate it overnight or up to 48 hours. *(The dough also may be frozen for up to 1 month.)*

9. Gently press the dough to deflate it, and cut it in half. Place 1 half back in the refrigerator. Place the other half on a lightly floured work surface and roll it out into a 26-by-15-inch rectangle about ¼ inch thick. Keep lifting and moving the dough to prevent sticking or tearing. Roll the dough on a diagonal to achieve an even width.

10. With a large knife or pastry wheel, cut the dough lengthwise to create 2 long strips. Cut triangles of desired size, taking care to cut cleanly and not pull on the dough. For small croissants, cut 6-by-3-inch triangles, for medium croissants, cut 8-by-4-inch triangles, and for large croissants, cut 10-by-5-inch triangles. Slash a cut no more than 1 inch deep into the center of the base of each triangle.

11. Grease or parchment-line a baking sheet or use a nonstick baking sheet. To shape, pull the points of the triangles to correct their dimensions, if necessary. With the base of a triangle facing you, spread the slit and tightly roll the base up towards the point with one hand, while

continues next page

holding the point and stretching it slightly. Place the croissants on the baking sheet with the top on the bottom, and bend it into a crescent shape by curving the tapered ends toward the center until they are about 2 inches apart. Do not crowd the croissants on the baking sheet. Repeat with the second portion of the dough. Let rise uncovered at room temperature until doubled in bulk, about 1½ hours. (*Formed croissants may be frozen for up to 1 week.*)

12. Twenty minutes before baking, preheat the oven to 425°F. When light and springy to the touch, brush with egg glaze. Place another baking sheet of the same size under the baking sheet to double pan it and protect the bottoms from burning. Place the baking sheet on the center rack of the oven and bake for 15 to 18 minutes or until puffy and golden brown. Remove the croissants to a cooling rack for 15 minutes before eating.

CORNMEAL CROISSANTS: *Substitute ⅔ cup fine yellow cornmeal and ⅓ cup unbleached all purpose flour for the whole-wheat pastry flour.*

PAIN AU CHOCOLAT: *Cut the rolled dough into rectangles instead of triangles. Place 1 tablespoon grated bittersweet chocolate or semisweet chocolate chips on the lower third of the dough. Roll up to form a 5-by-3-inch rectangle and pinch the end seams. Place the rectangle, seam side down, on a greased or parchment-lined baking sheet. Make 2 or 3 diagonal slashes across the top of the dough with a sharp knife. Repeat to make about 18 rolls. Let rise and bake as directed.*

BLUEBERRY OR RASPBERRY WHOLE-WHEAT CROISSANTS: *Place 2 teaspoons blueberry or raspberry preserves at the base of each triangle before rolling. Add 3 or 4 fresh or frozen berries, if desired. Let rise and bake as directed.*

ALMOND CROISSANTS: *Cream 8 tablespoons (1 stick) butter with 1 cup (8 ounces) almond paste. Stir in 2 large eggs, ¼ teaspoon vanilla extract, ¼ teaspoon almond extract, and 1 tablespoon flour, beating until light and fluffy. Place 1 tablespoon filling on the center of the base of each dough triangle before rolling. Roll, let rise, and bake as directed. Dust with powdered sugar before serving.*

Freezing Croissants

Croissants may be frozen before or after they are baked.

To Freeze Baked Croissants: Freeze the croissants in plastic bags as soon as completely cooled. To reheat, place the frozen croissants on a baking sheet in a preheated 400°F oven for about 10 minutes to thaw, warm, and restore flakiness.

To Freeze Unbaked Croissants: Remove the croissants from the freezer and place on a greased or parchment-lined baking sheet. Cover with plastic wrap and let defrost in the refrigerator for 12 to 18 hours or overnight. Let stand, uncovered, at room temperature for about 1 hour. Glaze and bake as described in Step 12 of Croissants recipe.

Pumpkin Brioche

Makes 18 individual rolls

3 tablespoons warm water (105° to 115°F)

1 tablespoon (1 package) active dry yeast

Pinch of sugar

1 cup fresh or canned pumpkin purée at room temperature (see page 165)

3¾ cups unbleached all-purpose flour

¼ cup (packed) light brown sugar

1 teaspoon salt

½ teaspoon ground cinnamon

½ teaspoon grated nutmeg

¼ teaspoon ground cloves

4 large eggs, at room temperature

1 cup (2 sticks) unsalted butter at room temperature, cut into pieces

Pumpkins are popular as food as well as ornamental uses. This is one of my favorite little sweet breads for fall; the rolls are pale orange in color and melt-in-the-mouth tender.

1. Pour the warm water in a small bowl. Sprinkle the yeast and sugar over the surface of the water. Stir to dissolve and let stand at room temperature until foamy, about 10 minutes.

2. In a large bowl using a whisk or in the work bowl of a heavy-duty electric mixer fitted with the paddle attachment, combine the pumpkin, 1 cup of the flour, sugar, salt, and spices. Add the yeast mixture and beat until smooth.

3. Add the eggs, one at a time, beating well after each addition. Gradually add 2 cups more of the flour. Add the butter a few pieces at a time and beat until incorporated. Add exactly ¾ cup more flour and beat until creamy. The dough will be soft, sticky, and batter-like. Switch to a wooden spoon when necessary if making by hand.

4. Scrape the dough into a greased deep container. Cover with plastic wrap and let rise at a cool room temperature until doubled or tripled in bulk, about 3 hours. Gently deflate the dough and cover it tightly with plastic. Refrigerate overnight.

5. Gently deflate the dough. Turn the dough out onto a lightly floured work surface. Grease three ½-inch fluted brioche tins or standard muffin cups. Divide into 3 equal portions. Divide each portion into 6 equal portions. With floured fingers, form each portion into a small ball and place in the tin or muffin cup. Using kitchen shears dipped in flour, snip the top of each ball with an **X** ½ inch deep. Place individual tins on a baking sheet for easier handling. Let rise at a cool room temperature until doubled in bulk, 1 to 1 ½ hours.

6. Twenty minutes before baking, preheat the oven to 400°F. Place the baking sheet on a rack in the center of the oven and bake for 10 minutes. Reduce the thermostat to 350°F and bake 5 to 7 minutes more, or until the buns are golden and a cake tester inserted in the center comes out clean. Transfer immediately to cooling racks. Cool before serving. These buns are best served reheated.

THE CAKE OF BREAD:
Coffee Cakes

Coffee cakes are an American passion, crossing a muffin and a cake, which at the same time are neither too sweet nor too rich. They are never frosted, but may be glazed with jam, dusted with an ethereal layer of powdered sugar, or sport a spice- or walnut-enhanced crumb top. They are excellent showcases for seasonal fresh fruit. Coffee cakes easily satisfy the "I baked it from scratch" urge most cooks get at one time or another.

A coffee cake should be baked immediately after mixing. To avoid overbaking, always set the timer for five to ten minutes before the end of the suggested baking time to start testing with a toothpick or metal tester for doneness. If the edges have pulled away from the sides of the pan, it is a good indication the cake is done. A coffee cake may be quite fragile or very moist coming directly out of the oven, but it sets up as it cools on a rack. A properly cooled cake sets and contracts enough to either turn out of the pan to finish cooling or to cut into serving pieces. To unmold a cake, loosen the sides with a knife or spatula, if necessary. Place a wire cake rack over the top rim of the cake. Place your outstretched palm against the rack to secure it and gently turn the pan upside down onto the rack. The cake will release onto the rack. Carefully remove the pan and allow the cake to finish cooling. A cake left to cool too long will form a crusty outer layer, so a few hours is the maximum time needed. Each recipe will specify the best handling techniques.

Spiced Brown Sugar–Pecan Coffee Cake

Makes one 8-inch cake

Spiced Pecan Crumb Topping

- ¼ cup (packed) light brown sugar
- ¼ cup granulated sugar
- ½ cup unbleached all-purpose flour
- ½ teaspoon ground ginger
- ½ teaspoon ground cinnamon
- ½ teaspoon ground mace
- 6 tablespoons (¾ stick) cold unsalted butter, cut into pieces
- 2 cups (8 ounces) pecans, coarsely chopped

- 4 tablespoons (½ stick) unsalted butter
- ½ cup (packed) light brown sugar
- ½ cup granulated sugar
- 2 large eggs
- 2 teaspoons pure vanilla extract
- 2 cups unbleached all-purpose flour
- 1 teaspoon baking powder
- 1 teaspoon baking soda
- ¼ teaspoon salt
- 1 cup buttermilk

This is a soft-textured buttermilk cake with a crunchy nut topping. I often substitute macadamias or slivered blanched almonds for the pecans. This cake is what used to be called a "keeping cake," because it is naturally preserved by the buttermilk. It can be stored, tightly wrapped in plastic wrap and foil, at room temperature for up to five days before serving.

1. Preheat the oven to 350°F. Parchment-line the bottom of an 8-inch springform pan, an 8-inch fluted ceramic baking dish, or a 2-inch-deep removable-bottom tart pan and grease the sides.

2. To make the crumb topping: Combine the sugars, flour, and spices in a small bowl or the work bowl of a food processor fitted with the steel blade. Cut in the butter with your fingers or process just until the mixture forms coarse crumbs. Add the pecans and set aside.

3. To make the coffee cake: In a bowl using a wooden spoon or in the work bowl of a heavy-duty electric mixer fitted with the paddle attachment, cream the butter and sugars until fluffy. Add the eggs and vanilla extract. Beat until smooth about 1 minute. In another bowl, combine the flour, baking powder, baking soda, and salt. Alternately add the dry mixture and the buttermilk to the creamed mixture. Beat hard until the batter has a creamy consistency, about 1 minute. Do not overbeat or the cake will be tough.

4. Spoon half of the batter into the prepared pan. Sprinkle evenly with half of the crumb topping. Spoon in the remaining batter and sprinkle with the remaining crumb topping. Place the pan on a rack in the center of the oven and bake 40 to 45 minutes, of until a cake tester inserted into the center comes out clean. Remove from the oven to a cooling rack and cool in the pan. To serve, remove the sides of the springform pan or serve from the baking dish, as desired.

Fresh Fruit Cobbler

Makes one 8-inch cake or two 6-inch cakes

4 tablespoons (½ stick) unsalted butter, room temperature

½ cup sugar

1 large egg

1 cup unbleached all-purpose flour

1 teaspoon baking powder

¼ teaspoon salt

½ cup milk

1½ teaspoons pure vanilla extract

About 3 cups pitted and halved or sliced fresh fruit, such as plums, peaches, pears, nectarines, or cherries

Juice of ½ lemon

¼ cup sugar mixed with 1 teaspoon ground cinnamon

This country cake with fresh fruit is among the simplest coffee cakes to make. My favorite fruits for this cake include sweet Tartarian cherries that I get at my local farmers' market. Peeled and pitted ripe summer peaches or nectarines alone, or in combination with plums, apricots, winter pears, or raspberries are also nice. For the adult palate, you could substitute a complementary fruit brandy for 2 tablespoons of the milk.

The cake batter can be doubled and baked in a 13-by-9-inch baking pan.

1. Preheat the oven to 350°F. Grease and flour an 8-inch springform pan, two 6-inch springforms, or an 8-inch square pan. In a bowl using a wooden spoon or in the work bowl of a heavy-duty electric mixer fitted with the paddle attachment, cream the butter and sugar until fluffy. Add the egg and beat well.

2. In another bowl, combine the flour, baking powder, and salt. In a measuring cup, combine the milk and vanilla extract. Alternately beat the dry ingredients and the milk into the creamed mixture in 2 additions. Beat until just smooth and fluffy.

3. Spoon the batter evenly into the prepared pan. Cover with all of the fruit to create a thick layer, and drizzle with the lemon juice. Sprinkle the cinnamon and sugar mixture evenly over the fruit.

4. Place the pan on a rack in the center of the oven and bake until the fruit is bubbly and a cake tester inserted into the center comes out clean, 40 to 45 minutes for an 8-inch pan or 25 to 30 minutes for 6-inch pans. Serve warm or at room temperature, straight from the pan or unmold by slipping off the springform sides. (*The cake may be frozen for up to 2 weeks and reheated.*)

Pear Spice Coffee Cake

Makes one 8-inch cake

Crumb Topping

- ½ cup (packed) light brown sugar
- ⅓ cup unbleached all-purpose flour
- ½ teaspoon ground cinnamon
- 4 tablespoons (½ stick) cold unsalted butter

- 2 cups unbleached all-purpose flour
- 1 cup sugar
- 2 teaspoons baking powder
- ½ teaspoon baking soda
- 1 teaspoon ground cinnamon
- ½ teaspoon ground nutmeg
- ½ teaspoon cloves
- ½ teaspoon allspice
- ½ teaspoon salt
- 1 cup sour cream
- 4 tablespoons (½ stick) unsalted butter, melted
- 2 large eggs
- 2 pears, peeled, cored and finely diced, preferably Bartletts

Fresh pears have a subtle and delicate taste. Choose firm pears that are even in color; a mushy pear just won't do. This cake needs no embellishment since the fruit is so delicious.

1. Preheat the oven to 350°F. Parchment-line the bottom of an 8-inch springform pan and grease sides.

2. To make the topping: In a medium bowl combine the sugar, flour, and cinnamon. Cut in the butter with a pastry cutter or with 2 knives until the mixture forms coarse crumbs.

3. In a large bowl combine the flour, sugar, baking powder, baking soda, and spices. In a large bowl using an electric mixer, combine the sour cream, butter, and eggs. Combine the wet and dry ingredients and beat until smooth and creamy. Fold the pears in, mixing until evenly distributed.

4. Spoon the batter into the pan, smooth, and sprinkle with the crumb topping. Place the pan on a rack in the center of the oven and bake for 55 minutes to 1 hour, or until a cake tester inserted in the center comes out clean.

5. Let the cake cool in the pan for 15 minutes. Remove the sides of the springform pan to cool the cake completely on a rack.

Blueberry Buttermilk Coffee Cake

Makes one 9-inch cake

Crumb Topping

- ¼ cup sugar
- 3 tablespoons unbleached all-purpose flour
- Grated zest of ½ lemon
- 3 tablespoons cold unsalted butter

Cake

- 2½ cups unbleached all-purpose flour
- 2 teaspoons baking powder
- ½ teaspoon baking soda
- 1 cup sugar
- ¼ teaspoon salt
- 1 cup buttermilk
- 2 large eggs
- 8 tablespoons (1 stick) unsalted butter, melted
- 2 cups fresh or unsweetened frozen blueberries, rinsed and dried

Warm Lemon Sauce

- ¼ cup fresh lemon juice
- ½ cup sugar
- Grated zest of 2 lemons
- 1 tablespoon cornstarch
- 3 tablespoons unsalted butter

This is a fantastic blueberry cake to serve in warm wedges with butter or Warm Lemon Sauce. Keep one in the freezer for a special brunch.

1. Preheat the oven to 375°F. Line the bottom of a 9-inch springform pan with parchment paper and grease the sides.

2. To prepare the crumb topping: In a small bowl, combine together the sugar, flour, and zest. Cut in the butter with a pastry cutter or 2 knives until the mixture forms coarse crumbs.

3. To make the cake: In a large bowl combine the flour, baking powder, baking soda, sugar, and salt. In a large bowl using an electric mixer, combine the buttermilk, eggs, and butter. Stir into the dry mixture and beat until well blended. Fold in the blueberries with a few swift strokes.

4. Spoon the batter into the pan, smooth, and sprinkle with the crumb topping. Place the pan on a rack in the center of the oven and bake 50 minutes to 1 hour, or until a cake tester inserted in the center comes out clean.

5. Let the cake cool in the pan 15 minutes. Remove the sides of the springform pan to cool the cake completely.

6. To prepare the warm lemon sauce: Combine the lemon juice, ¼ cup water, sugar, and zest in a medium saucepan over medium heat and heat to just dissolve the sugar.

7. Dissolve the cornstarch in ¼ cup water. Add to the hot lemon mixture. Stir constantly with a small whisk until the mixture comes to a boil, thickens, and turns clear. Remove from the heat and stir in the butter.

8. Serve the cake in a pool of lemon sauce.

Cultured Dairy Products

In the United States, cultured milk products such as sour cream, crème fraîche, yogurt, and buttermilk are made from pasteurized cow's milk, but in many countries they are also made from goat, sheep, buffalo, or yak milk. Goat milk yogurt is also available in natural foods stores in America. The milk is fermented with a bacteria that transforms milk sugar (lactose) into lactic acid, so that the milk curdles naturally into a thick, creamy, tangy product. Sour cream, crème fraîche, and yogurt can be used interchangeably in baking recipes, although the flavor and textures of the final product will vary. There are a variety of low-fat and non-fat buttermilk, yogurt, and sour creams now on the market. They may be used interchangeably with full fat products in baking except where noted in some cake recipes. They are also excellent for use as toppings.

Buttermilk: Once the liquid left over from the churning of butter, modern buttermilk is cultured by the addition of a special bacteria added to nonfat milk. Some brands add some butter to enhance the flavor, but even without it, buttermilk is still thick, tangy, and rich.

Sour cream: Thickened heavy sweet cream. When added to quick breads, results in a dense, moist-textured bread. Low-fat sour cream may be substituted.

Crème fraîche: Made in a similar manner to sour cream but using a different bacteria. It is naturally low in calories and fat and contains no stabilizers or preservatives.

Yogurt: Cultured from whole, low-fat, or nonfat milk. Thinner in consistency and tarter in flavor than sour cream or crème fraîche.

Yogurt cheese: Made by draining yogurt in cheesecloth. A low-fat alternative to cream cheese, it is excellent as a spread on scones. Kefir cheese can be substituted; it has the beneficial acidophilus culture added.

NOTE: Do not freeze dairy products.

Vanilla Sour Cream Coffee Cake

Makes one 10-inch round cake or 12-cup Bundt cake or two 9-by-5-inch loaves

3 cups unbleached all-purpose flour

1½ teaspoons baking powder

1½ teaspoons baking soda

¼ teaspoon salt

¾ cup (1½ sticks) unsalted butter, at room temperature

1½ cups sugar

4 large eggs

2 teaspoons pure vanilla extract

1¼ cups sour cream

¾ cup (packed) light brown sugar

¾ cup (3 ounces) pecans, walnuts, or hazelnuts, finely chopped

2 teaspoons ground cinnamon

⅓ cup Vanilla Powdered Sugar (page 303) or powdered sugar (optional)

This is the quintessential coffee cake, made with pure vanilla extract and layered with nuts. If the cake is baked in a tube pan, spoon strawberries into the center when serving. This cake freezes well.

1. Preheat the oven to 375°F. Grease the cake or loaf pans. In a medium bowl, combine the flour, baking powder, baking soda, and salt. Set aside.

2. In a large bowl using an electric mixer, combine the butter and sugar until smooth and fluffy. Add the eggs, one at a time, beating thoroughly after each addition. Beat in the vanilla and sour cream until just smooth. Gradually add the dry ingredients and beat well until fluffy and light colored. There should be no lumps or dry spots.

3. In a small bowl combine the brown sugar, nuts, and cinnamon. Spoon about one third of the batter into the pan. Sprinkle with one third of the nut mixture. Repeat the process for three layers of batter and ending with a layer of nut mixture.

4. Place the pan on the center rack of the oven and bake 45 minutes to 1 hour, or until a cake tester comes out clean and the top of the cake is not shiny. Let the cake stand in the pan about 15 minutes. Remove from the pan to cool completely on a rack, right side up. Serve on a cake plate, dusted with Vanilla Powdered Sugar, if desired.

Sweet Yeast Dough

Makes 2 free-form braids

Sponge

1½ tablespoons (1½ packages) active dry yeast

1 tablespoon sugar

¼ cup warm water (105° to 115°F)

1¼ cup warm milk (105° to 115°F)

2 cups unbleached all-purpose flour or bread flour

Dough

2 large eggs, at room temperature

Finely grated zest of 1 lemon or orange

2 teaspoons salt

⅓ cup sugar

2½ to 3 cups unbleached all-purpose flour or bread flour

¾ cup (1½ sticks) unsalted butter, at room temperature, cut into small pieces

Rich Egg Glaze (page 52)

Most baking is an act of sustenance, but sweet-bread baking moves into the domain of the artistic. Higher in fat and sugar than everyday loaves, sweet breads are refined and luxurious in both taste and texture. A good, all-purpose sweet dough has a place in every baker's repertoire, because all sweet doughs are minor variations of the same basic proportions, though fillings and shapes will vary. As this bread bakes, the kitchen will fill with intoxicating aromas. The dough is good enough to bake as a simple loaf or decorate it if you wish with silver dragées, bits of angelica, chocolate coffee beans, or glazed nut halves.

1. To make the sponge: In a large bowl using a whisk or in the work bowl of a heavy-duty electric mixer fitted with the paddle attachment, combine the yeast, sugar, water, milk, and 2 cups flour. Beat hard until smooth, about 1 minute. Cover with plastic wrap and let rest at room temperature until bubbly, about 30 minutes.

2. To make the dough: Add the eggs, zest, salt, sugar, and 1 cup flour to the sponge. Beat until smooth. Add the butter, a few pieces at a time, and beat until incorporated. Add the remaining flour, ¼ cup at a time, until a soft dough that just clears the sides of the bowl is formed. Switch to a wooden spoon if necessary when mixing by hand. It is important that this dough be very soft.

3. Turn the dough out onto a lightly floured work surface and knead until smooth, shiny, and soft, about 3 minutes, dusting with flour only 1 tablespoon at a time as needed to prevent sticking. This dough must remain very soft and pliable.

If kneading by machine, switch from the paddle to the dough hook and knead for 3 to 4 minutes, or until the dough is smooth and springy and springs back when pressed. If desired, transfer the dough to a floured surface and knead briefly by hand.

4. Place the dough in a greased deep container. Turn once to coat the top and cover with plastic wrap. Let rise at room temperature until doubled in bulk, 1½ to 2 hours. Gently deflate the dough, re-cover, and refrigerate for 12 to 24 hours.

5. Gently deflate the dough. Turn the dough out onto a lightly floured work surface. Grease or parchment-line a baking sheet. Divide the dough into 6 equal portions. Roll each portion into a strip with your palms and lay 3 of the strips side by side. Braid the strips, taper and pinch the ends together, and tuck them under. Repeat to make a second loaf. Place the loaves on the baking sheet. Cover loosely with plastic wrap and let rise at room temperature until almost doubled in bulk, about 40 minutes. Because of the eggs, this loaf should not completely double during rising, because it will rise a lot in the oven.

6. Twenty minutes before baking, preheat the oven to 350°F. Brush the tops of the loaves with the egg glaze. Place the baking sheet on a rack in the center of the oven and bake 35 to 40 minutes, or until deep golden brown and hollow sounding when tapped. Carefully remove the braids off the baking sheet with a large spatula to a cooling rack. Cool completely before serving.

BAKER'S WISDOM
Sugar

Most morning bread recipes call for regular granulated sugar for sweetening, which also makes for a brown crust and tender crumb.

Superfine sugar: Very finely granulated sugar, also called bar sugar. It can be purchased or made by processing granulated sugar in a food processor for ten seconds. It is called caster or caster sugar in British recipes.

Coarse sugar: Decorator's sugar, used for toppings. Crushed rock sugar or sugar cubes can also be used to create a sweet-crusted top layer.

Powdered sugar: Also known as confectioners' sugar, it is perfect for glazes and decoratively dusting baked sweet loaves. It is best used after sifting.

Brown sugar: A combination of granulated sugar and molasses. I prefer light brown sugar. Dark brown sugar has more molasses added than light brown sugar. Brown sugar must be packed for measuring because it contains a lot of air.

Fresh Apple Coffee Cake

Makes one 10-inch tube cake

4 cups peeled, cored, and coarsely chopped tart cooking apples (about 4 or 5 medium apples)

1/3 cup (packed) light brown sugar

1 1/2 tablespoons ground cinnamon

3 cups unbleached all-purpose flour

1 3/4 cups granulated sugar

1 tablespoon baking powder

1/2 teaspoon salt

Grated zest of 1 orange

4 large eggs

1 cup vegetable oil

1/2 cup fresh or frozen orange juice

This cake is truly extravagant in flavor. Early fall I make it with homegrown Rome Beauty apples, but any firm, tart cooking apple, such as a Granny Smith or Winesap, will do nicely.

1. Preheat the oven to 375°F. Grease and flour a 10-inch tube pan, Bundt pan, or kugelhof mold. In a small bowl, combine the apples with the brown sugar and the cinnamon. Set aside.

2. In a medium bowl, combine the flour, sugar, baking powder, salt, and orange zest. In a large bowl using a whisk or an electric mixer, beat the eggs and oil until thick and creamy, about 2 minutes at high speed. Add the dry ingredients with the orange juice and beat just until moistened, but thoroughly blended. Do not overmix, but there should be no lumps or dry spots.

3. Spoon one third of the batter into the pan. Cover evenly with half the apple mixture and cover with another one third of the batter. Use a spatula to smooth the batter over the apples to cover completely. Repeat with the remaining apples and batter, ending with a smooth layer of batter.

4. Place the pan on a rack in the center of the oven and bake 60 minutes. Cover loosely with a piece of aluminum foil and bake 15 minutes more, or until a cake tester inserted into the center comes out clean. Remove from the oven and cool in the pan on a rack about 1 hour. Invert onto a rack to cool completely before serving. *(This cake freezes well, wrapped tightly in plastic or aluminum foil.)*

Raspberry Braid

Makes 2 medium braids

1 recipe Sweet Yeast Dough (page 294), risen overnight in the refrigerator

Raspberry Filling

2 cups fresh or unthawed frozen unsweetened raspberries

¼ cup sugar

¼ cup cornstarch

2 tablespoons fresh lemon juice or fruit liqueur, such as framboise

Streusel

½ cup sugar

Grated zest of 1 lemon

1 teaspoon ground cinnamon

⅓ cup unbleached all-purpose flour

4 tablespoons (½ stick) cold unsalted butter, cut into pieces

Rich in natural pectin, raspberries it cook into a thick, filling. The shape of this bread is known as a false plait. It is an easy way to form yeast breads so as to showcase colorful fillings.

1. To prepare the filling: In a medium saucepan, combine all the filling ingredients and bring to a boil. Reduce the heat to low and cook until the fruit juices are thick, stirring occasionally and gently to keep the berries as whole as possible. Remove from the heat and set aside to cool.

2. To prepare the streusel: In a small bowl, combine the sugar, zest, cinnamon, and flour. Cut in the butter pieces using your fingers, a pastry cutter, or food processor until coarse crumbs are formed. Set aside.

3. Gently deflate the dough. Turn the Sweet Yeast Dough out onto a lightly floured work surface. Grease or parchment-line a baking sheet. Divide the dough into 2 equal portions. Using a rolling pin, roll each portion into an 8-by-12-inch rectangle. Transfer the dough to the baking sheet and even out the rectangular shapes. Spread half the raspberry filling down the center third of one rectangle. With a sharp knife, cut diagonal strips at 2-inch intervals down the outside edges of the dough, almost through to the filling. Starting at the top, fold the strips alternately from each side at a slight angle to make a crisscross braid. Tuck under any excess dough at the end. Repeat to make the second loaf. Cover loosely with plastic wrap and let rise at room temperature until doubled in bulk, about 45 minutes.

4. Twenty minutes before baking, preheat the oven to 350°F. Sprinkle the top with the streusel. Place the baking sheet on a rack in the center of the oven and bake 35 to 40 minutes, or until the filling is bubbly and the crust is golden brown. Transfer the plaits immediately to a cooling rack. Cool completely before serving.

Maple-Blueberry Whole-Wheat Braid

Makes 2 large braids

Whole-Wheat Sweet Yeast Dough

- ¼ cup warm water (105° to 115°F)
- 1½ tablespoons (1½ packages) active dry yeast
- Pinch of sugar
- Pinch of ground ginger
- 1 cup warm milk (105° to 115°F)
- 6 tablespoons (¾ stick) unsalted butter, melted
- ⅓ cup pure maple syrup
- 2 teaspoons salt
- 2 large eggs
- Grated zest of 1 lemon
- 2 cups whole-wheat flour
- 2½ to 3 cups unbleached all-purpose flour or bread flour

Blueberry Filling

- 1 pint (2 cups) fresh blueberries or 1 package (16 ounces) unsweetened frozen blueberries, unthawed
- ¼ cup pure maple syrup
- ¼ cup cornstarch
- 2 tablespoons fresh lemon juice

Plump, sweet blueberries are sold in familiar pint boxes, which weigh about 14 ounces and yields about 2 cups. It is important to wash blueberries right before using, as they will absorb water if they sit. Make this plaited bread showcasing berries sweetened with maple syrup at the height of the blueberry season, mid to late summer, or during the winter if using frozen berries.

1. To make the dough: Pour the warm water in a small bowl. Sprinkle the yeast, sugar, and ginger, over the surface of the water. Stir to dissolve and let stand at room temperature until foamy, about 10 minutes.

2. In a large bowl using a whisk or in the work bowl of a heavy-duty electric mixer fitted with the paddle attachment, combine the milk, butter, maple syrup, salt, eggs, zest, and whole-wheat flour. Beat until creamy, about 1 minute. Add the yeast mixture and 1 cup of the unbleached flour. Beat for 1 minute. Gradually add the remaining flour, ¼ cup at a time, until a soft dough that just clears the sides of the bowl is formed. Switch to a wooden spoon if necessary when mixing by hand.

3. Turn the dough out onto a lightly floured work surface and knead until smooth, firm, and elastic, about 4 minutes, dusting with flour only 1 tablespoon at a time as needed to prevent sticking. Do not add too much flour. The dough should hold its own shape, but should be soft and pliable.

If kneading by machine, switch from the paddle to the dough hook and knead for 3 to 4 minutes, or until the dough is smooth and elastic and springs back when pressed. If desired, transfer the dough to a floured surface and knead briefly by hand.

4. Place the dough in a greased deep container. Turn once to coat the top and cover with plastic wrap. Let rise at room temperature until doubled in bulk, 1 to 1½ hours.

5. To prepare the filling: In a medium saucepan, combine the blueberries, maple syrup, cornstarch, and lemon juice and bring to a boil. Reduce the heat to low and cook until the blueberry juices are thick, stirring occasionally and gently to keep as many berries whole as possible. Remove from the heat and let cool at room temperature.

Lemon Streusel

1/2 cup sugar

Grated zest of
1 lemon

1 teaspoon ground
cinnamon

1/3 cup unbleached
all-purpose flour

4 tablespoons
(1/2 stick) cold
unsalted butter,
cut into 8 pieces

6. To make the streusel: In a small bowl, combine the sugar, zest, cinnamon, and flour. Cut in the butter pieces using your fingers, a pastry cutter, or food processor until coarse crumbs are formed. Set aside.

7. Gently deflate the dough. Turn the dough out onto a lightly floured work surface. Grease or parchment-line a baking sheet. Divide the dough into 2 equal portions. Using a rolling pin, roll each portion out into a 9-by-15-inch rectangle. Transfer the dough to the baking sheet and even out the rectangle shape. Spread half the blueberry filling down the center third of one rectangle. With a sharp knife, at 2-inch intervals cut diagonal strips down the outside edges of the dough, almost through to the filling. Starting at the top, fold the strips alternately from each side at a slight angle to make a crisscross braid. Tuck under any excess dough at the end. Repeat to make the second loaf. Cover loosely with plastic wrap and let rise at room temperature until doubled in bulk, about 45 minutes.

8. Twenty minutes before baking, preheat the oven to 350°F. Sprinkle the tops evenly with the lemon streusel. Place the baking sheet on a rack in the center of the oven and bake for 40 to 45 minutes or until an even golden brown and a cake tester inserted into the center comes out clean. Remove the loaves immediately to a cooling rack. Cool completely before serving.

Orange Cinnamon Swirl

Makes two 9-by-5-inch loaves

1/4 cup warm water
(105° to 115°F)

1 tablespoon
(1 package) active
dry yeast

Pinch of sugar

1 cup warm milk
(105° to 115°F)

1 cup orange juice

1/2 cup sugar

4 tablespoons
(1/2 stick) unsalted
butter, melted

2 large eggs, at room
temperature

Grated zest of 2
oranges

2 teaspoons salt

6 1/2 to 7 1/2 cups unbleached all-
purpose flour or
bread flour

2/3 cup sugar mixed
with 1 1/2 tablespoons
ground cinnamon

2 tablespoons unsalted
butter, melted, for
brushing

Ground cinnamon,
for dusting
(optional)

What would a bread book be without a recipe for a sugar and spice swirl? This dough is delicately orange flavored from the addition of orange juice and zest. Use ruby-fleshed blood oranges or tangerines to vary the flavor and color. This bread makes very special toast.

1. Pour the warm water in a small bowl. Sprinkle the yeast and the pinch of sugar over the surface of the water. Stir to dissolve and let stand at room temperature until foamy, about 10 minutes.

2. In a large bowl using a whisk or in the work bowl of a heavy-duty electric mixer fitted with the paddle attachment, combine the milk, juice, sugar, butter, eggs, zest, salt and 2 cups of the unbleached flour. Beat until smooth, about 1 minute. Add the yeast mixture and 1 cup more flour. Beat 1 minute more. Add the remaining flour 1/2 cup at a time, until a soft dough that just clears the sides of the bowl is formed. Switch to a wooden spoon if necessary when mixing by hand.

3. Turn the dough out onto a lightly floured work surface and knead until smooth and springy, about 3 minutes, dusting with flour only 1 tablespoon at a time as needed to prevent sticking.

If kneading by machine, switch from the paddle to the dough hook and knead for 2 to 3 minutes, or until the dough is smooth and springy and springs back when pressed. If desired, transfer the dough to a floured surface and knead briefly by hand.

4. Place the dough in a greased deep container. Turn once to coat the top and cover with plastic wrap. Let rise at room temperature until doubled in bulk, 1 to 1 1/2 hours.

5. Gently deflate the dough. Turn the dough out onto a lightly floured work surface. Grease two 9-by-5-inch loaf pans. Divide the dough into 2 equal portions. Roll or pat out each portion into a 8-by-12-inch rectangle. Brush the surface of each rectangle lightly with melted butter and sprinkle with half of the cinnamon sugar, leaving a 1-inch border all around the edge. Starting from the short end, roll the dough up jelly-roll fashion to form a loaf. Pinch the seams to completely seal. Place each loaf, seam-side down, in the loaf pans. Lightly dust the tops with plain ground cinnamon for decoration, if desired. Cover loosely with plastic wrap and let rise at room temperature until 1 inch above the rims of the pans, about 45 minutes.

6. Twenty minutes before baking, preheat the oven to 350°F. Place the loaf pans on a rack in the center of the oven and bake 40 to 45 minutes, or until the loaves sound hollow when tapped with your finger and a cake tester inserted into the center comes out clean. Transfer the loaves immediately to a cooling rack. Cool completely before slicing.

Golden Italian Coffee Cake

Makes two 8-inch Bundt cakes

½ cup warm water (105° to 115°F)

1½ tablespoons (1½ packages) active dry yeast

½ cup sugar

5 cups unbleached all-purpose flour

1 tablespoon grated lemon

1 tablespoon orange zest

2 teaspoons salt

½ cup warm milk (105° to 115°F)

4 large eggs at room temperature

1 teaspoon pure vanilla extract

8 tablespoons (1 stick) unsalted butter at room temperature

⅓ cup powdered sugar or Vanilla Powdered Sugar (recipe follows), for dusting

This is a straightforward name for a fabulous sweet bread redolent of lemon, orange, and vanilla. Reminiscent of *pandoro*, the Italian Christmas bread that is baked in a star mold, this bread is baked in 6-cup mini-Bundt pans. To serve, fill the center with fresh berries and dust the bread with powdered sugar.

1. Pour the warm water in a small bowl. Sprinkle the yeast and a pinch of sugar over the surface of the water. Stir to dissolve and let stand at room temperature until foamy, about 10 minutes.

2. In a large bowl using a whisk or in the work bowl of a heavy-duty electric mixer fitted with the paddle attachment, combine 2 cups of the flour, the remaining sugar, the zests, and salt. Add the milk, eggs, vanilla, and yeast mixture. Beat until smooth, about 1 minute. Add the butter in 4 pieces and 1 cup more of the flour. Beat until smooth, about 1 minute. Add the remaining flour, ½ cup at a time, using exactly 5 cups. Switch to a wooden spoon if necessary when mixing by hand. The dough will be shaggy and just clear the sides of the bowl.

3. Turn the dough out onto an unfloured work surface and knead for about 1 minute, adding no more flour.

If kneading by machine, switch from the paddle to the dough hook and knead for 1 to 2 minutes, or until the dough is smooth and springy and springs back when pressed. If desired, transfer the dough to a floured surface and knead briefly by hand.

4. Place the dough in a greased deep container. Turn once to coat the top and cover with plastic wrap. Let rise at room temperature until doubled in bulk, about 1½ hours.

5. Gently deflate the dough. Turn the dough out onto the work surface. Grease two 6-cup Bundt pans. Divide the dough into 2 equal portions. Roll each portion into 2 fat cylinders with the palms of your hands. Place each in the Bundt pan, filling the pan about half full. Cover loosely with plastic wrap and let rise at room temperature until 1 inch above the rim of the pan, 45 minutes to 1 hour.

6. Twenty minutes before baking, preheat the oven to 350°F. Place the loaf pans on a rack in the center of the oven and bake 35 to 40 minutes or until golden, the loaves sound hollow when tapped with your finger, and a cake tester comes out clean when inserted into the center. Let stand 5 minutes in the pans and turn out immediately to cooling racks. Dust with Vanilla Powdered Sugar before serving.

VANILLA SUGAR/VANILLA POWDERED SUGAR

Makes 2 cups vanilla sugar

- 1 whole or split vanilla bean
- 2 cups sifted granulated or powdered sugar

Bury the vanilla bean in the sugar in an airtight container. Let stand at room temperature for 4 days to 1 week, or until scented as desired. Use the sugar in place of plain sugar. Vanilla sugar keeps indefinitely, covered tightly, at room temperature. Replace the sugar in the container as needed, leaving the bean; replace the bean only when it dries out.

Babka

Makes 1 large tube cake

1 tablespoon
(1 package) active
dry yeast

¼ cup sugar

¼ cup warm water
(105° to 115°F)

8 tablespoons (1 stick)
unsalted butter,
melted

1½ teaspoons salt

2 teaspoons pure
vanilla extract

½ teaspoon almond
extract

¾ cup warm milk
(105° to 115°F)

3 large eggs, at room
temperature

About 4 cups unbleached
all-purpose flour

2 tablespoons unsalted
butter, melted, for
brushing dough

3 tablespoons Vanilla
Powdered Sugar
(page 303), or
powdered sugar

Almond or
Chocolate Filling
(recipes follow)

This babka coffee cake, originally from Poland, can be filled with almond paste or chocolate filling. One recipe of filling is enough for one recipe of babka dough. This babka is adapted from one by Lou Pappas, the food editor of the *Palo Alto Times Tribune*. It is an exemplary coffee cake that freezes well. For best results, use a kugelhopf mold with a nonstick coating, an angel food pan, or any other tube pan with a ten- to twelve-cup capacity. The recipe may also be made into two 9-by-5-inch loaves.

1. Pour the warm water in a small bowl. Sprinkle the yeast and a pinch of sugar over the surface of the water. Stir to dissolve and let stand at room temperature until foamy, about 10 minutes.

2. In a large bowl using a whisk or in the work bowl of a heavy-duty electric mixer fitted with the paddle attachment, combine the butter, the remaining sugar, salt, vanilla, almond, milk, eggs, and 1 cup flour. Beat until smooth. Add yeast mixture. Beat until smooth, about 3 minutes. Add the flour, ½ cup at a time, with a wooden spoon until a soft dough is formed.

3. Turn the dough out onto a lightly floured work surface and knead until smooth and silky, about 5 minutes. Be certain the dough remains soft.

If kneading by machine, switch from the paddle to the dough hook and knead for 4 to 5 minutes, or until the dough is smooth and springy and springs back when pressed. If desired, transfer the dough to a floured surface and knead briefly by hand.

4. Place the dough in a greased bowl. Turn once to grease the top and cover with plastic wrap. Let rise in a warm area until doubled in bulk, about 1½ hours. Meanwhile prepare the filling of choice.

5. Gently deflate the dough. Turn the dough out onto a lightly floured work surface. Generously grease an 8- to 10-cup kugelhopf mold or a tube pan. Roll or pat the dough into a 10-by-12-inch rectangle, and brush with melted butter. Spread with the filling, leaving a ½-inch border all around the edges. Starting from the short end, roll the dough up jelly-roll fashion to form a loaf. Pinch the seams to completely seal. Holding one end of the roll, twist dough about 6 to 8 times to make a rope. Form it into a flat coil and place in the mold or tube pan. The pan should be no more than two-thirds full. Pinch the ends together and pat the dough to lie evenly in the pan. Cover loosely with plastic wrap and let rise until even with the top of the pan, about 45 minutes.

6. Twenty minutes before baking, preheat the oven to 350°F. Place the pan on a rack in the center of the oven and bake for 40 to 45 minutes, or until golden brown and a cake tester inserted into the center comes out clean, and the loaves sound hollow when tapped. Let stand 5 minutes in the pan, and remove the loaves to a cooling rack. Cool completely; let stand 4 hours to overnight, wrapped in plastic, before slicing.

ALMOND FILLING

1 can (8 ounces) almond paste

¼ cup ground blanched almonds

4 tablespoons (½ stick) unsalted butter, softened

1 tablespoon sugar

1 large egg

Combine the ingredients in a bowl and beat until smooth. Set aside.

CHOCOLATE FILLING

¾ cup sugar

⅓ cup unbleached all-purpose flour

3 tablespoons unsweetened powdered cocoa

1 teaspoon ground cinnamon

4 tablespoons (½ stick) unsalted butter, softened and cut into pieces

Combine the sugar, flour, cocoa, and cinnamon and cut in the butter until crumbly. Set aside.

Cinnamon-Walnut Sweet Bread

Makes one 10-inch tube cake, or two 8 1/2-by-4 1/2-inch loaves

2/3 cup (4 ounces) dried cherries

Boiling water

3/4 cup warm water (105° to 115°F)

1 tablespoon (1 package) active dry yeast

1/3 cup sugar

4 1/2 to 5 cups unbleached all-purpose flour

Zest and juice of 1 large lemon

1 teaspoon salt

1 large egg

3/4 cup yogurt

4 tablespoons (1/2 stick) unsalted butter, at room temperature

Spicy Walnut Coating

8 tablespoons (1 stick) unsalted butter

1 cup sugar

1 1/2 tablespoons ground cinnamon

1 1/2 cups (6 ounces) walnuts, finely chopped

This sweet yeast cake is in the European home baking tradition. It is known in Hungarian as *arany galuska,* or "golden dumpling coffeecake," because the balls of dough look like dumplings. The cake can be sliced or pulled apart with your fingers.

1. In a small bowl, combine the dried cherries with boiling water to cover. Set aside to cool to room temperature. In another small bowl, pour in the warm water. Sprinkle the yeast and a pinch of the sugar over the surface of the water. Stir to dissolve and let stand at room temperature until foamy, about 10 minutes.

2. In a large bowl using a whisk or in the work bowl of a heavy-duty electric mixer fitted with the paddle attachment, combine 1 cup of the flour, the remaining sugar, the lemon zest and juice, salt, egg, yogurt, and the yeast mixture. Beat hard until creamy, about 1 minute. Add the room-temperature butter in 3 additions, beating after each addition until incorporated. Add the remaining flour, 1/2 cup at a time, until a soft, shaggy dough that just clears the sides of the bowl is formed. Switch to a wooden spoon if necessary when mixing by hand.

3. Turn the dough out onto a lightly floured work surface and knead quickly until very soft yet quite springy, about 1 minute, dusting with flour only 1 tablespoon at a time as needed to prevent sticking.

If kneading by machine, switch from the paddle to the dough hook and knead for 1 to 2 minutes, or until the dough is soft and quite springy and springs back when pressed. If desired, transfer the dough to a floured surface and knead briefly by hand.

4. Place the dough in a greased deep container. Turn once to coat the top and cover with plastic wrap. Let rise at warm room temperature until doubled in bulk, 1 to 1 1/2 hours.

5. To make the coating: Melt the butter and set aside. In a small bowl, combine the sugar, cinnamon, and walnuts. Drain the dried cherries and pat dry.

6. Gently deflate the dough. Turn the dough out onto a very lightly floured work surface. Generously grease one 10-inch tube pan, or two

8½-by-4½-inch loaf pans. Pull off pieces each about the size of an egg. Roll each piece between your palms to form a uniform ball. Dip the balls, one at a time, into the melted butter, and then roll them in the walnut mixture to coat thickly all over. Place the balls in the prepared pan(s), leaving about ½ inch between them. When you have arranged a full layer, sprinkle evenly with all the dried cherries. Repeat to make a full second layer and sprinkle the top with any remaining walnut mixture and melted butter. Cover with plastic wrap and let rise at room temperature until doubled in bulk, 1 to 1½ hours.

7. Twenty minutes before baking, preheat the oven to 375°F. If using a tube pan with a removable bottom, place it on a sheet of aluminum foil. Place the pan on the rack in the center of the oven and bake 40 to 45 minutes for the tube pan and 30 to 35 minutes for the rectangular loaves or until golden brown, and the loaf sounds hollow when tapped. Cover the top loosely with foil if the loaves are browning too quickly. Remove from the oven and let stand 2 minutes (no longer, as the sugar mixture will tighten as it cools and make unmolding difficult), then invert the bread onto a cooling rack. Let cool at least 20 minutes. Serve warm or at room temperature.

Plum Crumb Cake

Makes one 9-inch cake

¼ cup warm water
(105° to 115°F)

1 tablespoon
(1 package) active
dry yeast

½ cup sugar

½ cup warm buttermilk
(105° to 115°F)

¼ cup vegetable oil

1 large egg

½ teaspoon salt

Grated zest of 1
lemon

2½ cups plus 1
tablespoon
unbleached all-
purpose flour

⅔ cup sour cream

1 teaspoon pure
vanilla extract

Crumb Topping

⅓ cup unbleached all-
purpose flour

¼ cup sugar

½ teaspoon ground
cinnamon

Dash of ground mace

4 tablespoons
(½ stick) cold
unsalted butter, cut
into pieces

2 cups fresh red Santa
Rosa plums or
Italian prune plums,
pitted and sliced

Though this is a yeast coffee cake, the batter is mixed in exactly the same manner as a quick bread. Then it rests for about thirty minutes before baking. It is made here with plums, but you can substitute other firm seasonal or dry frozen fruit such as nectarines, cherries, or blueberries.

1. Pour the warm water in a small bowl. Sprinkle the yeast and a pinch of sugar over the surface of the water. Stir to combine and let stand at room temperature until foamy, about 10 minutes.

2. In a large bowl using a whisk or in the work bowl of a heavy-duty electric mixer fitted with the paddle attachment, combine the buttermilk, ¼ cup sugar, oil, egg, salt, and zest. Add the yeast mixture and 1 cup flour. Beat well, until smooth, about 3 minutes. Add the remaining 1½ cups flour and no more. The batter will be sticky and stiff.

3. Generously grease a 9-inch springform pan, or a 9-inch quiche pan at least 2 inches deep with a removable bottom. With a spatula, scrape the batter into the prepared pan. Spread batter with lightly floured fingers to fill pan evenly. Cover with plastic wrap and let rest in a warm area until slightly puffy, about 30 minutes.

4. In a medium bowl, combine the sour cream, remaining ¼ cup sugar, 1 tablespoon flour, and vanilla. Beat until smooth with a whisk. Set aside.

5. To prepare the topping: In a medium bowl combine the flour, sugar, and spices. Cut the butter in until the mixture is the consistency of coarse crumbs.

6. Twenty minutes before baking, preheat the oven to 400°F. Pour the sour cream layer evenly over the batter. Gently distribute the plums over the sour cream layer. Sprinkle the crumb mixture to completely cover the fruit. Place the pan on the center rack of the oven and bake about 45 minutes, or until top is lightly browned and a cake tester inserted in the center comes out clean. Let the cake cool in the pan 15 minutes. Remove the cake to a cooling rack. Cut in wedges and serve warm or cold. Store leftovers in the refrigerator.

SPUR-OF-THE-MOMENT BAKER:
Quick Breads

Modern quick breads are a pure American product, somewhere between a yeasted bread and a sweet cake. They are leavened with baking powder and/or baking soda or eggs instead of yeast. A large assortment of breads can be made by a simple variation in ingredients, such as seasonal fresh fruit or dried fruit, liqueurs, nuts, cheese, herbs, and spices.

One of the most important techniques in baking quick loaves is beating the wet ingredients with a whisk or electric mixer to aerate them and expand their volume; the mixture doubles, becoming thick and creamy. The dry ingredients are mixed separately, with all the leavenings evenly distributed. The two are then mixed together with a quick and light hand (rarely, if ever, beaten) to avoid activating the gluten in the flour. Most batters are immediately scraped or poured into greased pans to bake in a preheated moderate oven. Breads using baking powder improve in texture and flavor by rising for 15 to 20 minutes at room temperature before going into the oven. Most loaves are best after they have set overnight; this gives time for the crumb to set, making for a firm texture, clean slices, and pronounced flavor.

The proper oven temperature is important for oven spring, the final expanding of the dough when in contact with heat. Quick breads are best baked on the middle shelf with at least two inches of space between each pan to allow the heat to circulate. A quick bread is finished baking when the top looks and feels firm and dry and the edges pull slightly away from the sides of the pan, and when it is evenly browned. A cake tester inserted into the center should come out clean. If the center is still wet, the loaf needs to bake another 5 to 8 minutes. Immediately turn the loaf out of its hot pan onto a wire rack to cool on its side, allowing for air to circulate around it. Loaves that are more cakelike in texture can stand for 15 minutes to firm up slightly before being turned out of their pans.

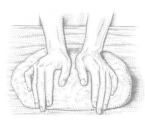

Baking Powder

Baking powder is a versatile leavener that makes quick breads rise and creates a light texture. It starts a chemical reaction between two or more ingredients to create carbon dioxide and guarantees consistent baking results. The leavening is first mixed or sifted with the dry ingredients to distribute it evenly. The dry ingredients are then combined with the wet ingredients and the baking powder is activated, giving off carbon dioxide gas in the form of bubbles. During baking, the flour and egg proteins set with the heat and steam around the bubbles. Many bakers recommend brands that do not contain aluminum, which has a bitter aftertaste. Rumford is an aluminum-free brand.

Double-acting baking powder: A mixture of alkaline and acid ingredients with a stabilizer, baking soda, cornstarch, and phosphate salt. It reacts twice, once when moistened with liquid and again in the hot oven. It can be used in combination with all types of liquid ingredients. Some batters made with double-acting baking powder can sit in the refrigerator for days and still be light textured when baked.

Single-acting baking powder (tartaric acid): It reacts only once, with the liquid ingredients. Single-acting baking powder is no longer commercially available because tartaric acid is expensive, but instructions to bake batters immediately after mixing, a necessity with single-acting baking powder, have remained in many recipes. Many bakers find it results in a finer texture and higher volume, so they mix their own (recipe follows) or add a small amount of cream of tartar (usually ½ teaspoon per 2 cups of flour) to recipes.

Cream of tartar: A naturally fermented leavener contained in the sediment at the bottom of wine barrels. It is combined with baking soda to make single-acting baking powder.

Exact measures are important when using baking powder. Use the guideline of no more than 1½ teaspoons baking powder to 1 cup of flour. When doubling or tripling a recipe, cut back the total amount of leavener by one quarter. For baking at altitudes over 3,500 feet, reduce the baking powder by half the amount to compensate for its ability to expand more quickly at higher altitudes. Baking powder has a shelf life of only 4 months before its effectiveness decreases. Most packages are dated. Test for freshness by placing a teaspoon in a small amount of hot water. If it is fresh, it will fizzle. Quick breads can also be risen by aerating leaveners, such as whole eggs, egg whites, butter, lard, and solid vegetable fats, which produce steam that sets during baking.

Homemade Single-Acting Baking Powder

Combine 1 teaspoon baking soda (alkali) and 2 teaspoons cream of tartar (acid) to substitute for 1 tablespoon baking powder in a recipe's dry ingredients. Bake immediately after mixing. This mixture will not store.

Baking Soda

Bicarbonate of soda, an alkali, is an essential leavener that creates carbon dioxide gas when acid ingredients, such as buttermilk, yogurt, or sour cream, molasses or maple syrup, citrus or vinegar, chocolate, and cream of tartar are used. Batters containing baking soda must be baked immediately after mixing.

Baking soda lends a distinctive flavor to traditional soda breads and darkens baked cocoa-infused batters to a ruddy red. It is often added to recipes just to neutralize the acids, as in some sourdough batters. Too much baking soda gives quick breads a soapy flavor with an acid odor. Modern baking soda is ground very fine and does not need to be dissolved in hot water before adding to the batter. Store baking soda in a cool, dry place.

Lemon–Poppy Seed Bread

Makes one 9-by-5-inch loaf

3 tablespoons fresh poppy seeds

½ cup milk

5 tablespoons unsalted butter, at room temperature

1 cup sugar

2 large eggs

1½ cups unbleached all-purpose flour

1 teaspoon baking powder

Grated zest of 2 lemons

¼ teaspoon salt

Lemon Syrup

¼ cup sugar

¼ cup fresh lemon juice

Poppy seeds are a favorite crunchy addition to quick breads. Soaking the seeds before adding them to the batter heightens their elusive flavor. Poppy seeds can range from a clear slate blue to blue-black in color, with a corresponding range of sweetness. Look for Dutch blue poppy seeds in specialty stores; they are the highest quality and very sweet. Store poppy seeds in the freezer: Since they have a high oil content, they turn rancid quickly. This quick bread needs to stand overnight before cutting.

1. In a small bowl, combine the poppy seeds and milk. Let stand 1 hour to meld the flavors.

2. Preheat the oven to 325°F. Grease a 9-by-5-inch loaf pan. In a large bowl using a whisk or an electric mixer, cream the butter and sugar. Add the eggs, one at a time, beating well after each addition. Combine the flour, baking powder, lemon zest, and salt in a small bowl. Add the dry ingredients alternately with the poppy seed–milk mixture to the creamed mixture in 3 equal portions. Beat just until smooth.

3. Pour the batter into the loaf pan. Place the pan on a rack in the center of the oven and bake 55 to 65 minutes, or until golden brown and a cake tester inserted into the center comes out clean. Place the loaf, in the pan, on a cooling rack.

4. To make the lemon syrup: Combine the sugar and lemon juice in a small saucepan. Cook over low heat just until the sugar dissolves. Pierce the hot loaf about 10 times top to bottom, with a bamboo skewer, or metal cake tester. Immediately pour the hot lemon syrup over the loaf. Cool 30 minutes before turning the loaf out onto a cooling rack to cool completely. Wrap tightly in plastic wrap and let stand at room temperature overnight before serving.

LEMON–POPPY SEED BREAD WITH SAFFRON: *Add ⅛ teaspoon powdered saffron to the milk in Step 1. Continue as directed.*

Dried Apricot–Pecan Bread

Makes two 7½-by-3½-inch loaves

- 1½ cups dried apricot halves
- 1 cup boiling water
- 3 tablespoons unsalted butter
- 1 cup sugar
- 2 cups unbleached all-purpose flour
- 1½ teaspoons baking soda
- ½ teaspoon salt
- ½ cup whole-wheat flour
- 1 cup (4 ounces) pecans, chopped
- 2 large eggs
- ½ cup orange juice, fresh or frozen

This quick bread can be thinly sliced and can be served plain or spread with butter to accompany tea or coffee. It is also good for sandwiches of paper-thin slices of smoked turkey and Black Forest ham. Orange brandy may be substituted for up to half of the orange juice, if you would like a more sophisticated loaf. This loaf needs to stand overnight before cutting.

1. Preheat the oven to 350°F. Grease and flour two 7½-by-3½-inch loaf pans. In the work bowl of a food processor, pulse to coarsely chop the apricots or coarsely chop by hand. Place the pecans in a large bowl and add the boiling water, butter, and sugar. Mix well and set aside to cool to lukewarm.

2. Combine the all-purpose flour, baking soda, and salt. Add to the apricot mixture and stir to combine. Add the whole-wheat flour, pecans, eggs, and orange juice. Beat well with a wooden spoon or electric mixer to make a batter that is evenly combined but slightly lumpy. Do not overmix.

3. Spoon the batter into the loaf pans and let the loaves rest at room temperature for 15 minutes. Place the pans on a rack in the center of the oven and bake 55 to 60 minutes, or until the tops are firm to the touch, the loaves pull away from the sides of the pans, and a cake tester inserted into the centers comes out clean. Transfer the loaves to a cooling rack and cool completely. Wrap tightly in plastic wrap and refrigerate overnight or up to 5 days before serving.

Whole-Wheat Prune Bread

Makes three 5 1/2-by-3-inch loaves

12 ounces moist pitted prunes

1 cup whole-wheat flour

3/4 cup (3 ounces) pecans, chopped

1 cup unbleached all-purpose flour

1 teaspoon baking soda

1/2 teaspoon baking powder

1/4 teaspoon salt

1 teaspoon ground cinnamon

4 tablespoons (1/2 stick) unsalted butter, room temperature

3/4 cup (packed) light brown sugar

1 large egg, at room temperature

1 cup plus 2 tablespoons buttermilk

This is one of the most popular quick breads in my repertoire. When you serve this loaf, be prepared to give out the recipe; at least one person always asks. This loaf needs to stand overnight before cutting.

1. Preheat the oven to 350°F. Grease three 5 1/2-by-3-inch loaf pans. In the work bowl of a food processor, combine the prunes and 1/2 cup of the whole-wheat flour. Pulse to coarsely chop, or coarsely chop by hand. Remove from the work bowl. Add the pecans to the prune mixture. Set aside.

2. In a large bowl, combine the remaining whole-wheat flour, the all-purpose flour, baking soda, baking powder, salt, and cinnamon. Add the prune-nut mixture and toss to blend.

3. In another bowl using a wooden spoon or an electric mixer, cream the butter and brown sugar until fluffy. Add the egg and beat until well combined. Add the flour mixture alternately with the buttermilk to the creamed mixture in 3 equal portions. Beat just until smooth and evenly combined. The batter will be thick.

4. Spoon the batter into the pans. Place the pans on a rack in the center of the oven and bake 40 to 45 minutes, or until a cake tester inserted into the center comes out clean. Cool in the pans 10 minutes before transferring the loaves to a cooling rack. Cool completely. Wrap tightly in plastic wrap and let stand overnight at room temperature or refrigerated before slicing.

Orange-Date Tea Bread

Makes one 8½-by-4½-inch loaf or 6-cup mini Bundt cake

¾ cup chopped pitted dates

¼ cup boiling water

8 tablespoons (1 stick) unsalted butter, at room temperature

1 cup sugar

Grated zest of 1 orange

1 large egg

2 cups unbleached all-purpose flour

1 teaspoon baking powder

1 teaspoon baking soda

¼ teaspoon salt

1 cup milk

1 teaspoon pure vanilla extract

½ cup (2 ounces) pecans, finely chopped

Orange Glaze

⅓ cup sugar

3 tablespoons fresh orange juice

1 teaspoon orange brandy, such as Grand Marnier

This bread is moist and subtly flavored with a hint of orange: an exceptional bread that is not overly rich. Slice it thin for breakfast or serve it alongside a chicken salad. After baking, wrap the bread in plastic and let it stand for one day at room temperature to develop its flavor.

1. Preheat the oven to 350°F. Grease a 8½-by-4½-inch loaf or 6-cup mini Bundt pan. In a small bowl, cover the dates with boiling water and macerate 10 minutes, or until soft.

2. In a large bowl using a wooden spoon or electric mixer, cream the butter, sugar, and zest until fluffy. Add the egg and beat until well combined.

3. In another bowl using a whisk, combine the flour, baking powder, baking soda, and salt. In a third bowl, combine the milk and vanilla.

4. Add the flour mixture alternately with the milk to the creamed mixture, beginning and ending with the flour. Beat well after each addition. Fold in the pecans and the dates with their liquid.

5. Spoon the batter into the loaf pan or mini Bundt pan. Place the pan on a rack in the center of the oven and bake for 40 to 45 minutes, or until the bread pulls away from the side of the pan and a cake tester inserted in the center comes out clean.

6. In a small bowl, combine the sugar, orange juice, and brandy. Immediately after removing the pan from the oven, slowly pour the orange glaze over the hot loaf. Let the loaf stand for 20 minutes to absorb the glaze. Transfer the loaf to a cooling rack to cool completely.

Banana Bread

Makes one 9-by-5-inch loaf or three 5½-by-3-inch loaves

½ cup vegetable oil

1 cup sugar

2 large eggs

1 teaspoon pure vanilla extract

3 medium to large overripe bananas (12 to 14 ounces), slightly mashed

1¼ cups unbleached all-purpose flour

1 teaspoon baking soda

I make banana bread every week and always have backup loaves in the freezer available for quick slicing or gift-giving. Although this bread needs no embellishments, it takes well to dressing up. Add ½ cup chopped nuts; dried cranberries, prunes, figs, or dates; unsweetened crushed pineapple, or shredded coconut to the batter to change the character of the basic loaf. Banana bread should be refrigerated overnight before serving.

1. Preheat the oven to 350°F. Grease and flour a 9-by-5-inch loaf pan or three 5½-by-3-inch pans. In a medium bowl, combine the oil, sugar, and eggs. Beat hard with a whisk or electric mixer until light-colored and creamy, about 2 minutes. Add the vanilla and mashed bananas and beat again until well combined.

2. In a medium bowl, combine the flour and baking soda. Add to the banana-egg mixture and stir to combine. Beat well to make a batter that is evenly combined and creamy in consistency.

3. Spoon the batter into the loaf pan or pans. Place the pans on a rack in the center of the oven and bake for about 50 minutes for the large loaf and 40 minutes for the small loaves, or until the tops are firm to the touch, the loaves pull away from the sides of the pan, and a cake tester inserted into the center comes out clean. Transfer the loaves to a cooling rack and cool completely. Wrap tightly in plastic wrap and refrigerate overnight or up to 5 days before serving.

Mango Bread

Makes two 7½-by-3½-inch loaves

- 2 cups unbleached all-purpose flour
- 2 teaspoons ground cinnamon
- 2 teaspoons baking soda
- ½ teaspoon salt
- ½ cup dried cherries or raisins, plumped in hot water for 10 minutes and drained
- 1 cup sugar
- 2 large eggs
- ⅔ cup vegetable oil
- 1 teaspoon pure vanilla extract
- 2½ cups chopped firm-ripe mangoes (about 3½ pounds)
- 1 tablespoon fresh lemon or lime juice

Mangoes from Mexico and elsewhere hit the market during the spring and summer months, and this bread is an unusual way to use them. They should be ripe but not too tender, so that the flesh holds its shape during baking. Since the pit is stubbornly clingstone, remove the fruit from the pit with a paring knife by cutting down on either side of the pit. Peel the skin off each fruit section with the knife.

1. Preheat the oven to 350°F. Grease two 7½-by-3½-inch loaf pans.

2. In a medium bowl using a whisk, combine the flour, cinnamon, baking soda, and salt. Add the dried cherries and stir until evenly distributed. In another bowl, using a whisk or an electric mixer, beat together the sugar, eggs, and oil until fluffy and light colored, about 3 minutes. Add the vanilla. Add the flour mixture to the sugar mixture and beat just until smooth. Do not overmix. With a large spatula, fold in the mangoes and lemon or lime juice.

3. Spoon the batter into the pans. Place the pans on a rack in the center of the oven and bake 35 to 40 minutes, or until the top is firm, the loaf pulls away from the sides of the pans, and a cake tester inserted into the center comes out clean. Transfer the loaves to a cooling rack to cool completely. Wrap tightly in plastic wrap and let stand at room temperature until serving.

Cranberry-Orange Bread

Makes one 8½-by-4½-inch loaf

1½ cups cranberries, fresh or frozen

1 cup sugar

2 cups unbleached all-purpose flour

1 tablespoon baking powder

¼ teaspoon salt

½ teaspoon freshly grated nutmeg

¼ teaspoon ground ginger

Grated zest of 2 oranges

½ cup (2 ounces) walnuts, chopped

¾ cup orange juice

2 large eggs

1 teaspoon pure vanilla extract

4 tablespoons (½ stick) unsalted butter, melted

Sweetened and cooked cranberries are a boon to creative cooks because of its delightfully tangy flavor, though highly seasonal, cranberries can be frozen in bags and used, unthawed, in any recipe calling for fresh berries, any time of year. Let the bread stand overnight before serving.

1. Preheat the oven to 350°F. Grease and flour a 8½-by-4½-inch loaf pan. In the work bowl of a food processor, combine the cranberries and sugar. Pulse to coarsely chop. Set aside.

2. In a large bowl using a whisk, combine the flour, baking powder, salt, nutmeg, and ginger. Add the orange zest and walnuts. Toss to blend.

3. In a small bowl using a whisk or electric mixer, combine the orange juice and eggs. Beat until frothy. Add the vanilla and the cranberry mixture. Stir to combine. Pour over the dry ingredients and drizzle with the butter. Stir with a large spatula just until moistened and the cranberries are evenly distributed.

4. Spoon the batter into the loaf pan. Place a pan on a rack in the center of the oven and bake 45 to 50 minutes, or until the top is crusty and golden and a cake tester inserted into the center comes out clean. Transfer the loaf to a cooling rack to cool completely. Wrap tightly in plastic wrap and let stand at room temperature overnight before serving.

Carrot and Tangerine Bread

Makes two 9-by-5-inch loaves

- 3 cups unbleached all-purpose flour
- 1½ teaspoons baking powder
- 1½ teaspoons baking soda
- ¼ teaspoon salt
- 2 teaspoons ground cinnamon
- 4 large eggs
- 2 cups sugar
- 1 cup vegetable oil
- 1 teaspoon pure vanilla extract
- 2 tablespoons tangerine juice
- Grated zest of 1 tangerine
- 2 cups finely grated raw carrots

This is a moist loaf with a spicy fragrance and a crisp, sweet crust. It is meant to be very smooth, but it can be enriched with about ½ cup shredded coconut, diced dried apricots, raisins, or finely chopped nuts, if desired. If tangerines are not in season, use oranges and substitute orange juice or an orange liqueur for the tangerine juice. Let the bread stand overnight before slicing.

1. Preheat the oven to 350°F. Grease and flour two 9-by-5-inch loaf pans. In a medium bowl using a whisk, combine the flour, baking powder, baking soda, salt, and cinnamon.

2. In a large bowl using a whisk or electric mixer, beat the eggs and sugar until thick and light colored. Add the oil gradually and beat hard until the mixture is doubled in volume. Add the vanilla, tangerine juice, and zest. Fold in the grated carrots. Stir the dry ingredients into the wet and continue stirring until smooth and well combined.

3. Spoon the batter into the pans, filling each no more than two-thirds full. Place the pans on a rack in the center of the oven and bake 50 to 60 minutes, or until a cake tester comes out clean. Let the loaves stand in the pans 10 minutes. Transfer the loaves to a cooling rack. Cool them lying on their side completely. Wrap tightly in plastic wrap and let stand at room temperature overnight before slicing.

Cream Sherry—Pumpkin Bread

Makes three 8½-by-4½-inch loaves

2 cups granulated sugar

1¼ cups (packed) light brown sugar

3⅔ cups puréed fresh pumpkin (see page 165) or 1 can (29 ounces) pumpkin purée

4 large eggs

1 cup oil, such as walnut, almond, or sunflower seed

4⅔ cups unbleached all-purpose flour

1 tablespoon baking soda

1 teaspoon salt

1½ teaspoons cloves

1½ teaspoons ground cinnamon

1½ teaspoons coriander

½ cup cream sherry

Make your own purée, using a fresh Sugar Pumpkin or other winter squash, such as a large Hubbard, for the best flavor. Canned pumpkin purée is a perfectly acceptable alternative. Be sure to select a good quality cream sherry.

1. Preheat the oven to 350°F. Grease three 8½-by-4½-inch loaf pans. In a large bowl using a whisk or an electric mixer, combine the granulated sugar, brown sugar, pumpkin, eggs, and oil. Beat until smooth, about 1 minute.

2. In a large bowl, using a whisk, combine the flour, baking soda, salt, coriander, cinnamon, and cloves. With a large spatula, combine the wet and dry mixtures and beat until smooth. Stir in the cream sherry. Beat vigorously until thoroughly blended, about 1 to 2 minutes. The batter will be thick and fluffy.

3. Spoon the batter into the loaf pans, filling each no more than three-quarters full. Place the pans on a rack in the center of the oven and bake 65 to 75 minutes, or until the tops are crusty and have a long center crack, and a cake tester inserted into each center comes out clean. Let the loaves stand 5 minutes in the pans. Transfer the loaves to a cooling rack to cool completely. Wrap tightly in plastic wrap and let stand at room temperature overnight or up to 4 days before slicing.

INDIAN PUMPKIN BREAD: *Substitute 1⅓ cups fine yellow, white, or blue cornmeal for an equal amount of unbleached flour.*

BAKER'S WISDOM
Liqueurs and Other Alcoholic Spirits

Distilled spirits add a lavish flavor dimension to quick breads, either infused into the batter or as a glaze. Spirits which are intensely perfumed should be used in small amounts to complement the other ingredients. A nut liqueur, rum, or brandy would go with nuts, for example. Some good flavor combinations are maple syrup and golden rum, nuts with Frangelico (hazelnut liqueur) or Amaretto (almond liqueur), carrots or zucchini with brandy, apricots or peaches with Asti Spumante (sparkling wine), berries and cherries with chambord or cassis, cream sherry with pumpkin, and chocolate- or cream-based liqueurs in glazes. Fruits combine well with corresponding fruit brandies and eau-de-vie. Two classics to have on hand in the kitchen for all-purpose uses are orange-flavored liqueurs, such as Grand Marnier, Triple Sec, or Cointreau, and a good brandy or Cognac. Domestic eaux-de-vie are quite good and less expensive than imported.

Glazed Zucchini Bread

Makes one 9-by-5-inch or three 5½-by-3-inch loaves

¾ cup vegetable oil

1½ cups sugar

3 large eggs

1 teaspoon pure vanilla extract

2 cups grated zucchini

2 cups unbleached all-purpose flour

1½ teaspoons baking soda

1 teaspoon baking powder

¼ teaspoon salt

1 teaspoon ground cinnamon

1 teaspoon ground cloves

1 cup (4 ounces) walnuts, chopped, or golden raisins, plumped and drained

Brandy Glaze

¼ cup sugar

¼ cup brandy or cognac

Zucchini makes a distinguished loaf that is flecked with green. Glazed with a good brandy or cognac, it can be served as a dessert as well as a tea bread. Refrigerate this loaf overnight before serving.

1. Preheat the oven to 350°F. Grease and flour one 9-by-4-inch or three 5½-by-3-inch loaf pans. In a medium bowl using a whisk or electric mixer, combine the oil and sugar. Beat hard until light colored and creamy, about 1 minute. Add the eggs and vanilla extract and beat again until well combined. Fold in the grated zucchini and stir until evenly distributed.

2. In a large bowl, combine the flour, baking soda, baking powder, salt, cinnamon, cloves, and walnuts or raisins. Add the zucchini-egg mixture and stir to combine. Beat just until the batter is evenly combined and creamy in consistency, about 1 minute.

3. Spoon the batter into the pan or pans. Place the pan or pans in the center of the oven and bake 65 to 75 minutes for the large loaf and 40 to 50 minutes for the small loaves, or until the tops are firm, the loaves pull away from the sides of the pans, and a cake tester inserted into the center comes out clean. Let the loaves stand in the pan or pans 5 minutes.

4. To prepare the brandy glaze: Combine the sugar and brandy in a small saucepan. Cook over low heat just until the sugar dissolves. Set aside. Pierce the hot loaf or loaves, top to bottom with a bamboo skewer or metal cake tester about 10 times. Pour over the warm brandy glaze immediately. Cool in the pan 30 minutes before removing to finish cooling on a cooling rack. Wrap tightly in plastic wrap and refrigerate overnight before serving.

Steamed Pecan Corn Bread

Makes two 1-pound loaves

1 cup fine yellow cornmeal, preferably stone ground

2 cups unbleached all-purpose flour

1 cup (4 ounces) pecans, finely chopped

2 teaspoons baking soda

1/2 teaspoon salt

2 cups buttermilk

1/2 cup pure maple syrup

2 large eggs

Steaming corn bread over a hot water bath results in a beautifully moist texture. For an added dimension of flavor, toast the cornmeal lightly on a dry baking sheet or in a heavy, ovenproof skillet in a 325°F oven for 15 to 20 minutes, stirring occasionally until it turns a pale, golden brown. Transfer immediately to a bowl to stop the cooking process. Let it cool completely before making the batter. Steamed breads can also be baked in a 350°F oven for 40 to 50 minutes, but the consistency will be a bit drier and there will be a crusty top surface. Use two 8½-by-4½-inch loaf pans.

1. Generously grease two 1-pound coffee cans and line the bottoms with a circle of parchment paper.

2. In a large bowl, combine the cornmeal, flour, pecans, baking soda, and salt. In a 4-cup measure or large bowl using a whisk or electric mixer, combine the buttermilk, maple syrup, and eggs. Beat well for 1 minute. Pour into the dry ingredients. Beat well until just evenly moistened.

3. Spoon the batter into the prepared containers, filling no more than two-thirds full. Cover each tightly with foil and thick rubber bands or with a lid. Place on a rack in a deep kettle. Add boiling water to a depth of 1 to 2 inches up the sides of the molds. Cover the kettle and reduce the heat to low. Steam about 2½ hours, or until a cake tester inserted into the center comes out clean. Replenish with boiling water as needed.

4. Twenty minutes before baking, preheat oven to 400°F. When the breads are steamed, remove the lids and place the containers in the oven for no more than 5 minutes to dry slightly. Remove from the containers, peel off the parchment paper, and transfer the loaves to a cooling rack to cool on their sides. Serve warm, sliced into rounds. *(The bread may be stored, wrapped in plastic, at room temperature for up to 3 days.)*

Steamed Brown Bread with Dried Blueberries

Makes two 1-pound loaves

- 1 cup dried blueberries
- 3 tablespoons golden rum
- 1 cup medium-grind yellow cornmeal, preferably stone ground
- 1 cup graham or whole-wheat flour
- 1 cup unbleached all-purpose flour
- 2 teaspoons baking soda
- 1/2 teaspoon salt
- 2 cups buttermilk
- 3/4 cup light molasses, warmed slightly for easiest pouring
- 1 large egg

Brown Bread, a cylindrical loaf traditionally made by cooking in a tightly covered mold in simmering water, is pure Americana. Developed during the colonial period to utilize native corn, along with small amounts of locally grown rye and molasses imported from the West Indies, the loaf perfectly complemented a big pot of savory baked beans. Use two one-pound coffee cans topped with foil for the high loaf, or for a more decorative shape, a European-style metal pudding mold with a clamp lid. Steamed breads can also be baked in a 350°F oven for 40 to 50 minutes, but the consistency will be a bit drier and there will be a crusty top surface. Use two 8½-by-4½-inch loaf pans.

1. In a small bowl, combine the blueberries and the rum. Let stand at room temperature I hour to macerate.

2. Generously grease two 1-pound coffee cans and line the bottoms with a circle of parchment paper.

3. In a large bowl, combine the cornmeal, graham flour, all-purpose flour, baking soda, and salt. In a 4-cup measure or large bowl using a whisk or electric mixer, combine the buttermilk, molasses, and egg. Pour into the dry ingredients and add the plumped blueberries. Beat well until evenly moistened.

4. Spoon the batter into the containers, filling each no more than two-thirds full. Cover tightly with foil and thick rubber bands or with a lid. Place on a rack in a deep kettle. Add boiling water to a depth of I to 2 inches up the sides of the molds. Cover the kettle and reduce the heat to low. Steam 2 hours, or until a cake tester inserted into the center comes out clean. Replenish the boiling water, as needed.

5. Twenty minutes before baking, preheat the oven to 400°F. When the breads are steamed, remove the lids and place the containers in the oven for no more than 5 minutes to dry slightly. Remove the loaves from the containers, peel off the parchment paper, and transfer them to a cooling rack and cool them on their sides. Serve the bread warm, sliced into rounds. *(The bread may be stored, wrapped in plastic, at room temperature for up to 3 days.)*

STEAMED APPLESAUCE BROWN BREAD: Substitute 1 cup unsweetened applesauce for 1 cup of the buttermilk. If the dough seems dry, add a few more tablespoons of buttermilk. Continue as directed. Bake as for Steamed Brown Bread with Dried Blueberries.

PURE AMERICANA:
Muffins

The basic techniques for making muffins are very simple. The wet ingredients are beaten and the dry ingredients are mixed in a separate bowl to evenly distribute the leavenings. Then they are combined just until the batter holds together, no more than about 15 seconds. Do not worry about lumps and clumps; they are normal. The less a muffin is beaten, the better. An overbeaten muffin is tough and flat, with undesirable tunnels on the inside. Some oil, melted butter, or fat substitute is necessary to create the tender, coarse crumb typical of most muffins. Some muffin recipes call for creaming the fat and sugar as for a cake, which results in a finer texture. Acidic liquids, such as buttermilk, yogurt, molasses, and citrus, also make for tenderness and balance the flavor. Whole grains and brans soaked in liquid to soften, are often added to the batter.

Although muffins are usually round, they can be made in a wide variety of sizes and shapes. I like to make them in individual heart shapes or the cast-iron gem pans that look like different fruits. My heart mold has 5 cups that hold the same amount of batter (⅓ cup) as a standard 2½-inch cup muffin tin. Look for unusual rectangular-shaped muffin pans, popular in the last century, in antique stores, or substitute miniature bread pans. Standard cups come in pans of 6, 12, and 24 connected cups. The larger pans, easily available from restaurant supply houses, are nice if you have a big family and a big oven. Muffins can also be made in mega 3¼-inch cups or in mini 1⅝-inch cups. Commercial muffin shops make a muffin size that seems to fall in between the oversized and the standard in custom ordered pans. Unless otherwise specified, the muffins in this chapter are standard size. For mega cups, double the recipe; for mini cups, make twice as many muffins. For a muffin cake, bake the entire batter in an 8-inch springform pan.

For thick batters, fill greased, sprayed, or paper-lined muffin cups with a ¼-cup ladle, ice cream scoop, or large spoon until level with the top. For very thin batters, fill the cups three-fourths full to prevent overflowing. If all the cups are not used, fill the empty cups half full with water to keep the muffin tin from buckling and to enlarge the muffins with a bit of added oven moisture. Muffin batters made with only baking powder may be kept in the refrigerator up to

3 days. After that, the leavening will loose its punch and the flour breaks down, resulting in an unappetizing grayish tinge.

Bake muffins in the center of a preheated (never cold) oven. The lower rack browns the bottoms too much, and the top rack cooks the tops faster than the rest of the muffin, so use the middle rack to evenly bake each cup. An oven that is too hot will result in asymmetrical shapes, with the sides of the muffins extending above the cups. Although most muffins bake at about 400°F, temperatures can vary. If a batch of muffins is becoming asymmetrical or browning too quickly, decrease the heat by 25°F. Conversely, muffins will be leaden and will not rise if the oven temperature is too low. Muffins are done when the tops are domed and dry to the touch, the edges have slightly pulled away from the pan, and a tester inserted into the center of a muffin comes out clean. The muffins in the outer cups may bake a few minutes faster than those in the center. After removing from the oven, let the muffins set a minute or two to allow them to shrink a bit from the pan. Remove them from the cups by turning the tin upside down, loosening the muffins with a knife if they do not come out easily. Transfer to a cooling rack. If the muffins stay in the pan, moisture will become trapped and the bottoms will be soggy.

Muffins are best eaten fresh the day they are made, but they freeze perfectly. After they have cooled completely, store in plastic freezer bags in your freezer for up to 3 months. Keep a fresh supply on hand for reheating on the spur of the moment. Reheat the frozen muffins in a microwave oven for a minute or less, or in a 350°F oven, wrapped in foil, for 10 to 15 minutes.

Guide to Muffin Cups

CUP SIZE	BAKING TIME	YIELD
Miniature or gem (1⅝-inch diameter)	10 to 15 minutes	18 to 20
Standard size (2½-inch diameter)	20 to 25 minutes	9 to 10
Oversized muffin (3¼-inch diameter)	25 to 30 minutes	6
Muffin cake (8- to 9-inch diameter)	55 to 65 minutes	1

Fresh Lemon Muffins

Makes 8 muffins

1³/₄ cups unbleached all-purpose flour

¹/₂ cup sugar

1¹/₂ teaspoons baking powder

¹/₂ teaspoon baking soda

¹/₄ teaspoon salt

Grated zest of 2 lemons

8 tablespoons (1 stick) unsalted butter, melted

²/₃ cup fresh lemon juice

1 teaspoon lemon extract (optional)

2 large eggs

Lemon Glaze

¹/₄ cup sugar

¹/₄ cup fresh lemon juice

Through its zest and its juice, the lemon gives freshness and elegance to baked goods. This muffin is an incredible taste treat. Bake it plain, or add a layer of sweetened-to-taste raspberries or cranberries.

1. Preheat the oven to 400°F. Grease or line 8 standard muffin cups. Fill the other 4 cups half way with water. In a large bowl using a whisk, combine flour, sugar, baking powder, soda, salt, and zest.

2. In a large bowl using a whisk or electric mixer, combine the butter, lemon juice, extract, and eggs. Stir the wet mixture into dry ingredients just until moistened. Spoon the batter into the muffin cups, mounding full.

3. Place the muffin tin on a rack in the center of the oven and bake 20 to 25 minutes, or until lightly browned around edges and springy to the touch.

4. To make the lemon glaze: Combine sugar and lemon juice in a small saucepan. Heat to just dissolve the sugar, but do not boil.

5. Pierce the baked muffins in a few places. Pour the warm lemon glaze over the muffins. Cool the muffins in the pan for 5 minutes to absorb the glaze before transferring to a cooling rack. Cool completely.

VARIATION: *Substitute an equal amount of orange zest and orange juice for the lemon zest and juice. Omit the lemon extract.*

Fresh Berry Muffins

Makes 9 muffins

1 cup fresh boysenberries, blackberries, raspberries, or currants

2 to 4 tablespoons sugar, or to taste

6 tablespoons (3/4 stick) unsalted butter, softened

1/4 cup (packed) light brown sugar

2 large eggs

2 cups unbleached all-purpose flour

1 tablespoon baking powder

1/2 teaspoon salt

1 cup half-and-half

1/4 cup granulated sugar mixed with 1 teaspoon ground cinnamon

The layering of the berries in the batter of this basic muffin works perfectly to keep delicate fruits such as boysenberries, blackberries, and raspberries from being crushed during folding. Sweeten the berries to taste before assembling the muffins. Each batch of berries will vary in its acidity-sweetness balance. Try fresh currants in this recipe, if you can find them.

1. Put the berries in a medium bowl and sprinkle the berries with sugar. Let stand for 15 minutes.

2. Grease or line 9 standard muffin cups. Fill the other 3 cups half way with water. In a large bowl using a whisk or electric mixer, combine the butter and sugar and beat until fluffy. Add the eggs, one at a time, and beat until combined, about 1 minute.

3. In a medium bowl using a whisk, combine the flour, baking powder and salt. Add the butter mixture alternately with the half-and-half, mixing until just moistened. Spoon the batter into the muffin cups, filling no more than half full, and sprinkle with fruit. Cover with the remaining batter until level with the top of the pan, and sprinkle with cinnamon and sugar mixture.

4. Place the pan on a rack in the center of the oven and bake 20 to 25 minutes, or until dry and springy to the touch. Cool the muffins in the pan for 5 minutes before removing. Serve warm.

Sour Cream Apple Muffins

Makes 12 muffins

Streusel Topping

- ½ cup (packed) light brown sugar
- ⅓ cup unbleached all-purpose flour
- 4 tablespoons (½ stick) unsalted butter, chilled

- 2 cups unbleached all-purpose flour
- ¾ cup sugar
- 1 tablespoon baking powder
- ¾ teaspoon baking soda
- ¼ teaspoon salt
- 1 teaspoon ground cinnamon
- ¼ teaspoon ground allspice
- ¼ teaspoon nutmeg
- ¼ teaspoon ground cloves
- ½ cup (2 ounces) walnuts, chopped
- 2 tablespoons dried currants
- 2 large eggs
- 4 tablespoons (½ stick) unsalted butter, melted
- 1½ cups sour cream
- 2 cups chopped tart green apples (2 large apples), peeled and cored

Sublime, cakelike apple muffins with a crisp sugar crust, tart chunks of fruit, and the aroma of spices are ever-popular. Be sure to fill cups to the top so that the baked muffins have a high dome.

1. Preheat the oven to 375°F. Grease or line 12 standard muffin cups.

2. To prepare the streusel: In a small bowl with a pastry blender or fork, or in the work bowl of a food processor fitted with the metal blade, combine the sugar and flour. Add the butter in chunks and cut in until coarse crumbs are formed.

3. In a large bowl using a whisk, combine the flour, sugar, baking powder, baking soda, salt, cinnamon, allspice, nutmeg, cloves, walnuts, and currants. In another bowl using a whisk or electric mixer, combine the eggs, melted butter, and sour cream until well blended. Add the chopped apples and egg mixture to the dry ingredients and stir just until evenly moistened, no more than 15 to 20 strokes.

4. Spoon the batter into the muffin cups until level with the tops of the cups. Place the pan on a rack in the center of the oven and bake 20 to 25 minutes, or until browned, the tops feel dry and springy, and a cake tester inserted into the center comes out clean. Do not overbake. Cool the muffins in the pan for 5 minutes before transferring to a cooling rack.

Old-fashioned Prune Muffins

Makes 12 muffins

1 cup unbleached all-purpose flour

1 cup whole-wheat flour

1 cup (packed) brown sugar

1 teaspoon baking powder

1 teaspoon baking soda

1/2 teaspoon salt

1 1/2 teaspoons ground cinnamon

1/2 teaspoon ground mace

8 tablespoons (1 stick) unsalted butter, melted

2 large eggs

1/2 cup buttermilk

1/2 cup prune juice

1 teaspoon pure vanilla extract

12 ounces moist pitted prunes, coarsely chopped

12 walnut or pecan halves

One bite is all it takes to figure out why this moist muffin is so popular. Once a standard bakery item, it has all but disappeared from the commercial scene. But a good prune muffin is worth its weight in gold.

1. Preheat the oven to 375°F. Grease or line 12 standard muffin cups. In a large bowl using a whisk, combine the flours, brown sugar, baking powder, baking soda, salt, cinnamon, and mace.

2. In a medium bowl using a whisk or electric mixer, combine the butter, eggs, buttermilk, prune juice, and vanilla extract and beat until the eggs are thick and light. Add the flour mixture and stir until just moistened, and fold in the prunes.

3. Spoon the batter into the muffin cups until level with the top of the pan. Top each with a nut meat half. Place the pan on a rack in the center of the oven and bake for 20 minutes, or until a cake tester inserted in the middle comes out clean and the tops feel springy. Cool the muffins for 5 minutes in the pan before transferring to a cooling rack.

Banana-Pecan Muffins

Makes 10 muffins

Streusel Topping

1/2 cup sugar

1/3 cup unbleached all-purpose flour

4 tablespoons (1/2 stick) cold unsalted butter

1 cup sugar

1/2 cup vegetable oil

2 large eggs

1 1/2 cups mashed ripe bananas (3 medium bananas)

2 cups unbleached all-purpose flour

1 teaspoon baking powder

1 teaspoon baking soda

1/4 teaspoon salt

1/2 teaspoon ground cinnamon

3/4 cup (3 ounces) pecans, finely chopped

An overripe banana has a black, mottled skin, and the fruit is very sweet and soft, just right for baking. These muffins border on perfection.

1. Preheat the oven to 375°F. Grease or line 10 standard muffin cups. Fill the other 2 cups halfway with water.

2. To prepare the streusel: In a large bowl with a whisk, combine the sugar and flour until blended. Using a pastry blender or in the work bowl of a food processor fitted with the metal blade, cut in the cold butter until coarse crumbs are formed.

3. In a large bowl using a whisk or electric mixer, combine the sugar, oil, and eggs until light colored and foamy. Add mashed banana and beat well. The banana will be incorporated but will still be chunky.

4. In a large bowl using a whisk, combine the flour, baking powder, baking soda, salt, and cinnamon. Add the pecans and the banana mixture and stir with a large spatula until just moistened, about 10 strokes.

5. Spoon into the cups until level with the top of the cup. Place 1 tablespoon streusel on the top of each muffin. Place the pan on a rack in the center of the oven and bake for 20 to 25 minutes, or until a cake tester inserted in the middle comes out clean and the tops feel dry and springy. Cool the muffins in the pan for 5 minutes before transferring to a cooling rack.

Spiced Applesauce Muffins

Makes 9 muffins

1¼ cups unsweetened applesauce

¼ cup (packed) brown sugar

2 large eggs

2 tablespoons vegetable oil

2 cups unbleached all-purpose flour

2 teaspoons baking soda

½ teaspoon powdered instant espresso

½ teaspoon ground cinnamon

½ teaspoon freshly grated nutmeg

¾ cup raisins or chopped nuts (optional)

Applesauce muffins are an American standard, but good recipes are scarce. Bette's Oceanview Diner in Berkeley, California, makes a fabulous one, but I lost the recipe they generously shared with me. So I recreated it as best I could here.

1. Preheat the oven to 375°F. Grease or line 9 standard muffin cups. Fill the other 3 cups half way with water. In a large bowl using a whisk, combine the applesauce, brown sugar, eggs, and oil.

2. In a large bowl using a whisk, combine the flour, baking soda, espresso, and spices. Add to the wet mixture and stir with a large spatula until just moistened, about 10 strokes. Add the raisins or nuts, if desired.

3. Spoon the batter into the cups until level with the top of the pan. Place the pan on a rack in the center of the oven and bake for 20 to 25 minutes, or until a cake tester inserted in the center comes out clean and the tops feel springy. Cool the muffins in the pan for 5 minutes before transferring to a cooling rack.

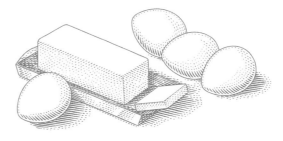

Everyday Maple Bran Muffins

Makes 10 large muffins

1½ cups buttermilk

2 large eggs

4 tablespoons (½ stick) unsalted butter, melted

¼ cup sunflower seed oil or other vegetable oil

¼ cup pure maple syrup

1½ All-Bran whole-grain cereal

1 cup chopped dried apricots

¼ cup dried cranberries

1 cup unbleached all-purpose flour

½ cup wheat or oat bran flakes

¼ cup (packed) light brown sugar

1 teaspoon baking powder

1 teaspoon baking soda

¼ teaspoon salt

½ cup raw sunflower seeds

This bran muffin is made with the unsweetened, high-fiber, whole-bran commercial cereal easily found in supermarkets. The cereal works perfectly, giving the muffins a unique double-bran flavor that is not too sweet for everyday breakfasts. I usually make a double batch to bring to share with friends and neighborhood children.

1. Preheat the oven to 400°F. Grease or line 10 standard muffin cups. Fill the other 2 half way with water. In a large bowl using a whisk or electric mixer, combine the buttermilk, eggs, butter, oil, maple syrup, and cereal. Stir until evenly moistened. Add the dried apricots and cranberries. Let stand at room temperature 5 to 10 minutes.

2. In a large bowl using a whisk, combine the flour, wheat or oat bran flakes, sugar, baking powder, baking soda, salt, and sunflower seeds. Add the dry ingredients to the buttermilk mixture and stir with a large spatula or spoon just until evenly moistened, no more than 15 to 20 strokes.

3. Spoon the batter into each muffin cup until just level with the top of the pan. Place the pan on a rack in the center of the oven and bake 20 to 25 minutes, or until browned, the tops feel dry and springy, and a cake tester inserted into the center comes out clean. Do not overbake. Cool the muffins in the pan for 5 minutes before transferring to a cooling rack.

Raspberry Cornmeal Muffins

Makes 9 muffins

1¼ cups unbleached all-purpose flour

¾ cup fine yellow cornmeal, preferably stone ground

⅔ cup sugar

2 teaspoons baking powder

½ teaspoon baking soda

¼ teaspoon salt

Grated zest of 1 lemon

1 cup milk

2 large eggs

⅓ cup corn oil

1½ cups fresh red or golden raspberries

You may consider this muffin earthy with a touch of glitter. Cornmeal and raspberries: simple and flawless. If your raspberries are very tart, sprinkle them with some of the sugar and macerate for fifteen minutes to sweeten them up before folding into the batter.

1. Preheat the oven to 400°F. Grease or line 9 standard muffin cups. In a large bowl using a whisk, combine the flour, cornmeal, sugar, baking powder, baking soda, salt, and zest.

2. In a large bowl using a whisk or electric mixer, combine the milk, eggs, and corn oil and beat for 1 minute. Pour into the flour mixture and stir with a large spatula just until evenly moistened, no more than 15 to 20 strokes. Gently fold in the raspberries, taking care not to break them up. The batter will be lumpy.

3. Spoon the batter into each muffin cup until just level with the top of the pan. Place the pan on a rack in the center of the oven and bake 20 to 25 minutes, or until browned, the tops feel dry and springy, and a cake tester inserted into the center comes out clean. Do not overbake. Cool the muffins in the pan for 5 minutes before transferring to a cooling rack.

Zucchini Madeleines

Makes about 36 madeleines

- 1½ pounds zucchini, scrubbed and shredded
- ⅓ cup olive oil
- 3 medium shallots, minced
- 5 large eggs
- 2 tablespoons milk or plain yogurt
- 1¼ cups (about 4 ounces) grated Parmesan cheese
- 2 tablespoons (packed) chopped fresh basil leaves
- 1 cup unbleached all-purpose flour
- 1 tablespoon baking powder

Madeleines are small oval cakes with a pretty shell shape molded on one side. They are baked in a traditional rectangular French madeleine pan that bakes eight cakes at a time. I bake two pans at once, flip out the baked ones, regrease and refill until all the batter is used up. I have literally made hundreds of dozens of these as appetizers for catering; they freeze beautifully and taste great at room temperature with wine or champagne.

1. Place the shredded zucchini on layers of paper towels and let drain 20 minutes. Place the olive oil in a skillet over medium heat and sauté the shallots until limp, about 5 minutes.

2. Preheat the oven to 400°F. Grease a 15½-by-7¾-inch madeleine pan with 12 cups with nonstick cooking spray. If making in batches, the last batch may have empty cups. If so, fill these with water after using up all the batter.

3. In a large bowl using a whisk or electric mixer, combine the eggs, milk or yogurt, cheese, and basil. Add the flour and baking powder. Fold in the zucchini and shallots with all the oil using a large spatula until just evenly moistened, no more than 15 to 20 strokes.

4. Spoon the batter into the molds filling two-thirds full, about 1 heaping tablespoon. Place the pan on a rack in the center of the oven and bake 15 to 18 minutes, or until puffy and very lightly browned. Transfer immediately to a cooling rack. Serve hot or room temperature. *(The madeleines may be stored in plastic bags in the refrigerator overnight or frozen up to 2 months.)*

Bacon–Blue Corn Sticks

Makes 28 corn sticks

- 1 cup fine blue cornmeal or *harina para atole*
- 1 cup unbleached all-purpose flour
- 1 tablespoon baking powder
- 1 teaspoon salt
- 1/2 cup (packed) finely chopped fried bacon, at room temperature
- 1 cup sautéed red and green peppers or fresh corn kernels
- 1 1/4 cups plain yogurt
- 2 large eggs, separated
- 2 tablespoons honey, warmed for easy pouring
- 8 tablespoons (1 stick) unsalted butter, melted

Although any baking powder corn bread recipe can be used to make corncob-shape sticks, this recipe reigns supreme. The 7-cup cast-iron pans, relatives of the ceramic molds used by the Aztecs to shape clay corn ears, are sold in specialty food stores. This batter may also be baked in an 8-inch square or 14-by-9-inch rectangular pan and cut into squares to serve. A shell-shaped French madeleine pan makes nice individual hors d'oeuvre bites.

1. Preheat the oven to 450°F. Place 4 cast-iron corncob pans in the oven to heat while mixing the batter.

2. In a large bowl using a whisk, combine the cornmeal, flour, baking powder, and salt. Stir in the bacon and peppers. In another bowl using a whisk or electric mixer, combine the yogurt, egg yolks, honey, and melted butter and beat just until blended. Add the liquid mixture to the dry ingredients and stir with a large spoon or rubber spatula until all ingredients are just moistened, using no more than 15 to 20 strokes.

3. In a clean bowl, beat the egg whites until soft peaks form. Fold into the batter just until no white streaks remain. Take care not to overmix.

4. Using thick oven mitts, carefully remove the hot pans from the oven and spray with nonstick cooking spray (or brush with melted butter or vegetable shortening). Spoon the batter into each mold, filling half to two-thirds full. Immediately return the pans to the oven and bake 15 to 20 minutes, or until puffed in the center, golden brown, and a cake tester inserted into the center comes out clean. Cool the muffins in the pan for 5 minutes before transferring to a cooling rack. Serve warm.

Santa Fe Blue Corn Muffins

Makes 12 muffins

8 tablespoons (1 stick) unsalted butter or margarine, at room temperature

1/2 cup sugar

5 large eggs

1/2 cup milk

1 can (4 ounces) canned green chiles, diced

1 cup blanched fresh or thawed frozen white corn kernels

1 cup coarsely shredded Cheddar cheese

1 cup coarsely shredded Jack cheese

1 cup unbleached all-purpose flour

1 1/4 cups fine blue cornmeal or *harina para atole*

2 teaspoons baking powder

1/2 teaspoon salt

Jacquie Higuera McMahan, author of a number of fantastic cookbooks based on California rancho cooker, adapted these muffins, which she learned to make at New Mexico's Santa Fe School of Cooking, which learned them from Chef Kip McClerin during his stint at La Casa Sena restaurant in Santa Fe. The chef would probably be surprised at how far his recipe has traveled!

1. Preheat the oven to 375°F. Grease or line the cups of 2 standard muffin pans.

2. In a medium bowl using a whisk or electric mixer, combine the butter and sugar until fluffy, 1 minute. Add the eggs, milk, and chiles, beating until well blended. In another bowl, combine the corn, Cheddar and Jack cheeses, flour, cornmeal, baking powder, and salt. Add the corn-flour mixture to the butter mixture, stirring in an additional 1/4 cup flour if the batter is too loose. Beat well to make a thick, creamy batter that falls off the spoon in clumps.

3. Spoon the batter into the muffin tins, filling each cup level with the top. Place the pan on a rack in the center of the oven and bake 20 to 25 minutes, or until golden, they are dry and springy, and a cake tester inserted into the center comes out clean. Cool the muffins in the pan for 5 minutes before removing to a cooling wrack. Serve warm.

Quinoa Whole-Wheat Muffins

Makes 10 muffins

- 1 cup whole-wheat flour
- 1/2 cup unbleached all-purpose flour
- 1/4 cup (packed) light brown sugar
- 1 1/2 teaspoons baking powder
- 1 1/2 teaspoons baking soda
- 1/2 teaspoon salt
- 1 cup buttermilk
- 2 large eggs
- 3 tablespoons sunflower seed oil or other vegetable oil
- 1 1/4 cups cooked and cooled Quinoa (recipe follows)
- 1/2 cup sunflower seeds

Quinoa, the sacred grain of the Incas, is now being grown in the mountains of Colorado and New Mexico. This millet-sized grain has a delicate, sweet flavor. Rinse the grain well before cooking.

1. Preheat the oven to 375°F. Grease or line 10 standard muffin cups. Fill the other 2 cups half way with water.

2. In a medium bowl using a whisk, combine the flours, brown sugar, baking powder, baking soda, and salt. In another bowl using a whisk or electric mixer, combine the buttermilk, eggs, and oil. Add the quinoa and sunflower seeds. Add the milk mixture to the dry ingredients with a large spatula, stirring just until moistened using no more than 15 to 20 strokes.

3. Spoon the batter into the muffin cups, filling each cup level with the top. Place the pan on a rack in the center of the oven and bake 20 to 25 minutes, or until golden, they feel dry and springy, and a cake tester inserted into the center comes out clean. Cool the muffins in the pan for 5 minutes before transferring to a cooling rack. Serve warm.

QUINOA

Makes about 1 1/4 cups

- 1 cup water
- 1/2 cup quinoa, well rinsed

In a small saucepan over high heat, bring the water to a rolling boil. Add the quinoa and reduce the heat as low as possible. Cover and cook until the water is absorbed and the quinoa is tender, about 15 minutes. Remove from the heat and let stand for 10 minutes. Set aside to cool. (*Quinoa may be refrigerated overnight.*)

RED, WHITE, AND BLUE:
Corn Breads

Baking powder corn breads have their place in American cooking. Many bakers specialize in them and astound diners with their versatility. Corn breads can be made from yellow, white, blue, and even red cornmeals, and flavored with fruits, vegetables, herbs, or nuts with equal delectability. There are regional favorites: white corn breads and corn sticks in the South, maple-syrup flavored golden breads in New England, chile breads in the Southwest and Texas, and corn muffins in California. For an elegant dinner, spoon breads are served as a hearty soufflé. For breakfast, leftover corn bread can be reheated and drizzled with maple syrup. Cold, day-old cornbread is also good split, brushed with melted butter, and broiled until lightly toasted. Keep leftover cornbread in the freezer to make stuffing for turkey, chicken, or game hens.

Corn breads are mixed quickly and baked immediately, making them an exceptional last-minute addition to a meal. Mix the dry ingredients in one bowl, the wet in another, and combine them using only a few strokes. Pour into a pan and then place in a hot oven. Nothing more. Meant to be eaten fresh from the oven, corn bread was so aptly described by the late food writer Richard Sax as "hot sunshine."

All types of cornmeal and corn flour can be used in quick breads. Baked goods made with cornmeal are crumbly in texture. Because cornmeal is unique in flavor and texture, there is no substitute for it in baking.

The different grinds of cornmeal contribute to a variety of textures and crumb in the finished baked corn bread (see page 343). The packaged steel-cut cornmeals available on grocery shelves are usually a medium grind, very good in flavor, and keep fresh a long time because they are degerminated. For an exceptional flavor, use very fresh, water-ground meals crushed between heavy granite stones, available from small local mills or natural foods stores; they retain flecks of the flavorful germ and will amaze you with their flavor. Stone-ground cornmeals are usually available in a variety of grinds, and now a variety of colors are appearing. All colors of cornmeal are interchangeable in recipes as long as the grind is similar, but the flavor will vary slightly. Fresh meals will always smell sweet, never sour or rancid.

Wrapped tightly in plastic wrap and then foil, corn breads can be frozen for up to 2 months.

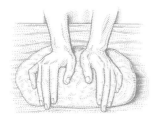

Baking Corn Bread in a Cast-Iron Skillet

The most popular method of baking cornbread is in an 8- or 9-inch square or round pan, but historically, a seasoned 9-inch cast-iron skillet produces the crispest crust (especially on the bottom) and a moist interior. Southern bakers especially like to use round cast-iron skillets that are divided into eight wedge-shaped sections, and cornstick-patterned pans. If you do not have a cast-iron skillet, substitute an 8-by-8-inch square or round pan, or a 9-inch pan for thinner bread. Fourteen corn-shaped sticks or ten 3-inch muffins can also be made.

Heat a 9-inch seasoned cast-iron skillet in a preheated 425°F oven for 5 minutes, remove with thick oven mitts to prevent burns, then swirl with 1 tablespoon solid shortening or butter to grease. Pour in the batter. Immediately return the pan to the hot oven and bake until the top is dry to the touch and the bread separates from the sides. Cast-iron gets very hot; always wear thick oven mitts when handling.

Buttermilk Corn Bread

Makes one 9-inch corn bread

1 cup unbleached
all-purpose flour

1 cup medium-grind
yellow cornmeal

1/4 cup sugar

1 tablespoon baking
powder

1/2 teaspoon salt

2 large eggs

1 cup buttermilk

4 tablespoons
(1/2 stick) unsalted
butter, melted

This corn bread is close to perfect. It is moist and flavorful, the natural mate for a meal of poultry, game, or baked beans, although it seems to complement every kind of food. Served straight out of the oven, it will garner raves.

1. Preheat the oven to 400°F. Grease a 9-inch springform pan or pie plate. In a large bowl, using a whisk, combine the flour, cornmeal, sugar, baking powder, and salt.

2. In another bowl using a whisk or electric mixer, combine the eggs, buttermilk, and butter. Add to the dry ingredients and stir with a large spatula until all the ingredients are just blended, using no more than 15 to 20 strokes.

3. Spoon the batter into the pan or pie plate. Place the pan on a rack in the center of the oven and bake 25 minutes, or until golden around the edges and a cake tester inserted in the center comes out clean. Let stand 15 minutes. Cut into wedges to serve.

VARIATIONS

❧ *Add 1 cup finely chopped pecans*

❧ *Add 1 medium summer squash, grated, with 1/2 teaspoon dried oregano and 1/4 cup freshly grated Parmesan cheese*

❧ *Add grated zest of 2 oranges*

❧ *Add 1 cup grated cheddar cheese*

❧ *Add 1 cup fresh or thawed frozen corn kernels*

❧ *Add 1/2 cup toasted pine nuts*

❧ *Add 1/2 cup canned green chiles with 1/2 teaspoon ground cumin and 1/2 cup grated jack cheese*

❧ *Substitute 1/2 cup puréed cooked carrots for 1/2 cup of the buttermilk*

Cornmeal

Cornmeal has a unique flavor and texture: there is no other grain to substitute for it. It is used for corn bread and muffins and is added to other types of breads and quick breads to give an extra dimension of flavor and texture. For the best flavor, use stone- or water-ground meals.

YELLOW AND WHITE CORNMEALS: Ground from dried yellow or white cornmeal in several varieties of grinds, from fine to coarse.

DEGERMINATED CORNMEAL: Cornmeal with the husk and germ removed for longer supermarket shelf-life.

POLENTA: The Italian name for a very coarsely ground yellow cornmeal imported from Italy. It can sometimes be found mixed with wheat germ or buckwheat flour, and occasionally ground from white corn. Polenta may be substituted for standard yellow cornmeal in recipes but the texture of the finished product will be different.

MASA HARINA: Yellow corn flour made from dried corn kernels treated with a lime solution (calcium hydroxide). It is ground finer than regular cornmeals. It is used to make corn tortilla doughs; it is also very good in corn bread.

BLUE CORNMEAL: Slightly grainier and sweeter, more intensely corn-flavored than other color meals, it makes purple-pink– to blue-green– to lavender-tinged baked products, depending on the liquid ingredients it is combined with. Baked goods made with blue cornmeal need a bit more fat per recipe, because it contains about 7 percent less fat than other colored meals. Ground from dried blue corn, it comes in several grinds.

HARINA PARA ATOLE: Roasted blue corn flour, especially good in pancakes.

HARINILLA: Lime-treated blue cornmeal, haranilla is a coarse grind used especially for tortilla making.

Store fresh cornmeal, tightly covered, in a cool, dry place, in the refrigerator up to 6 to 8 months, or in the freezer for 1 year.

Yogurt Corn Bread

Makes one 8-inch corn bread

- 1 cup fine yellow or white cornmeal, preferably stone ground
- 1 cup unbleached all-purpose flour
- 2 tablespoons sugar or maple syrup
- ½ teaspoon salt
- ½ teaspoon baking soda
- Grated zest of 1 large orange
- 2 large eggs
- ¼ cup buttermilk
- 1¼ cups plain yogurt
- ¼ cup corn oil

The combination of buttermilk and yogurt give a wonderful flavor to stone-ground cornmeal. This bread is light and particularly moist. With blueberries, it bakes into one of the most satisfying breakfast breads.

1. Preheat the oven to 425°F. Grease a springform or deep cake pan. In a large bowl using a whisk, combine the cornmeal, flour, sugar, salt, baking soda, and orange zest.

2. In a small bowl using a whisk, combine the eggs, buttermilk, and yogurt. Add to the dry ingredients and pour the oil over the top of the batter. Stir with a large spatula just until moistened yet thoroughly blended. Take care not to overmix.

3. Spoon the batter into the pan. Place the pan in the center of the oven and bake 20 to 25 minutes, or until golden around the edges and a cake tester inserted into the center comes out clean. Let stand 15 minutes. Cut into thick wedges to serve.

BACON CORN BREAD: *In a medium skillet, cook 1 cup diced smoked bacon or Italian pancetta (4 or 5 slices) until crisp. Drain on paper towels and add to the batter in Step 2. Bake as directed.*

BERRY CORN BREAD: *Fold 1½ cups rinsed fresh raspberries, blueberries, or blackberries into the batter in Step 2. Bake as directed.*

BLACK OLIVE CORN BREAD: *Add 1 cup chopped California or imported black olives to the batter in Step 2. Scrape the batter into a 9-by-5-inch loaf pan. Bake about 35 to 40 minutes, or until bread tests done.*

APPLE CORN BREAD: *Add 1½ cups peeled, cored, and coarsely chopped tart cooking apples (about 2 whole apples) to the batter in Step 2. Bake as directed.*

RICE CORN BREAD: *Add 1 cup cold cooked brown, white, or wild rice to the batter in Step 2. Bake as directed.*

Savory Corn Bread Stuffing

Makes about 6 cups, enough to stuff a 12- to 14-pound turkey

1 recipe Buttermilk Corn Bread (page 342), Yogurt Corn Bread (page 344), or other corn bread, cooled

3 tablespoons olive oil

1 large onion, chopped

3 ribs celery, chopped

2 medium-size tart cooking apples, peeled, cored, and chopped, or 6 ounces dried apples, plumped in hot water and chopped

1/2 cup pine nuts or pecans

1/3 cup chopped fresh parsley

2 teaspoons poultry seasoning or 3/4 teaspoon each dried thyme, marjoram, and rosemary, crumbled

1 teaspoon dried sage or 1 tablespoon thinly sliced fresh sage leaves

Freshly ground black pepper, to taste

2 tablespoons Madeira or dry sherry

About 1/4 cup canned chicken broth

Any homemade corn bread can be the basis for poultry stuffing. Vary plain corn bread by adding 1 cup chopped cooked bacon, crumbled cooked sausage, or chopped prosciutto, or substituting 1 cup chopped dried fruit, such as raisins or dried apricots, pears, raisins, cherries, or cranberries, soaked in Calvados or Madeira. Substitute chopped walnuts, pecans, or vacuum-packed roasted chestnuts for the pine nuts. Make the corn bread the day before assembling the stuffing for best results. Use for chicken, game hens, or turkey.

1. Cut the cooled corn bread into 3/4-inch cubes and place on a baking sheet. Cover with a clean dish towel and let stand at room temperature overnight to dry out.

2. In a large skillet, heat the olive oil over medium heat. Cook the onion and celery until soft, about 5 minutes. Remove from the heat. Add the corn bread cubes, apples, pine nuts, parsley, poultry seasoning, sage, and pepper. Add the Madeira and broth and toss until just moistened; the stuffing should be on the dry side; it will moisten more from the meat juices during roasting.

VARIATION: *Taste to adjust seasonings. Use immediately or refrigerate until stuffing the poultry just before roasting. To bake the stuffing separately, spoon into a buttered baking dish. Dot with butter and sprinkle with more chicken broth. Cover with foil and bake in a preheated 325°F oven for 35 to 45 minutes. Uncover and bake the last 15 minutes more to crisp the top.*

Blue Corn Bread

Makes one 9-inch corn bread

1 cup unbleached all-purpose flour

1 cup fine blue cornmeal or *harina para atole*

2 teaspoons baking powder

1/2 teaspoon baking soda

1/2 teaspoon salt

1 1/4 cups sour cream

1/4 cup corn oil

2 large eggs

Here is a good corn bread that is not sweet, yet is still moist and full of flavor. For a rustic container, use this technique: line the greased baking pan with a layer of corn husks, leaving about three inches standing up above the sides of the pan. Turn the baked bread out of the pan in its own wrapping.

1. Preheat the oven to 375°F. Grease a 9-inch springform pan or pie plate.

2. In a medium bowl using a whisk, combine the flour, cornmeal, baking powder, baking soda, and salt. In another bowl using a whisk, combine the sour cream, oil, and eggs. Add to the dry ingredients and stir with a spoon or rubber spatula until the ingredients are just blended. The batter will be very thick. Take care not to overmix.

3. Spoon the batter into the pan. Place the pan in the center of the oven and bake 25 to 30 minutes, or until it is golden around the edges, feels dry and springy to the touch, and a cake tester inserted into the center comes out clean. Let stand 15 minutes. Cut into wedges to serve.

CHERRY–BLUE CORN BREAD: *Gently fold 1 can (16 ounces) drained pitted sour pie cherries into the batter in Step 2.*

Green and Red Pepper Corn Bread

Makes one 8-inch corn bread

2 tablespoons corn oil

1/2 red bell pepper, cored, seeded, and cut into thin strips about 1 inch long

1/2 mild green chile pepper, such as Anaheim, New Mexico, or poblano, cored, seeded, and cut into thin strips about 1 inch long

1/2 small hot green pepper, such as a jalapeño, cored, seeded, deveined, and minced

3/4 cup unbleached all-purpose flour

3/4 cup fine yellow cornmeal, preferably stone ground, or *masa harina*

3 tablespoons sugar

2 teaspoons baking powder

1/2 teaspoon baking soda

1/2 teaspoon salt

1/2 teaspoon ground cumin

1 large egg

1 cup sour cream

1/2 cup (4 ounces) shredded Jack cheese

This sour-cream corn bread includes sweet red bell peppers with a mild green chile and a dash of jalapeños. For a more authentic Southwest flavor, use *masa harina*, the cornmeal used for making tortillas; it is available in the flour section of many supermarkets or in ethnic grocery stores.

1. Preheat the oven to 400°F. Grease an 8-inch springform pan or pie pan, or a 9-inch cast-iron skillet. Heat the corn oil in a small skillet and add the bell pepper and chiles. Cover and cook over low heat until tender, about 5 minutes. Remove from the heat.

2. In a large bowl using a whisk, combine the flour, cornmeal, sugar, baking powder, baking soda, salt, and cumin. In a small bowl using a whisk or electric mixer, beat together the egg, sour cream, and cooked chiles with any excess oil. Add to the dry ingredients and stir with a spoon or spatula until blended. The batter will be lumpy. Take care not to overmix.

3. Spoon the batter into the pan, pie pan, or cast-iron skillet. Place the pan in the center of the oven and bake 15 minutes. Sprinkle with the shredded cheese and return to the oven for 10 minutes longer, or until golden around the edges and a cake tester inserted into the center comes out clean. Let stand 15 minutes. Cut into wedges to serve.

Maple Whole-Wheat Johnnycake with Blueberries

Makes one 9-inch johnnycake

1¼ cups fine yellow cornmeal, preferably stone ground

1 cup whole-wheat pastry flour

1 tablespoon baking powder

½ teaspoon salt

2 large eggs

¾ cup buttermilk

¼ cup pure maple syrup

4 tablespoons (½ stick) unsalted butter, melted

1½ cups fresh or unthawed frozen blueberries

Whole-wheat johnnycakes are popular in Nova Scotia and New England, where sugar maples grow profusely. Locals say maple sweetening is unequaled by any other in the world, and they are a common addition to corn breads from those areas. Corn bread does not keep well, so plan to serve the bread the same day it is made.

1. Preheat the oven to 400°F. Grease a springform or a 9-inch cake pan. In a large bowl, using a whisk, combine the cornmeal, flour, baking powder, and salt.

2. In a small bowl using a whisk, combine the eggs, buttermilk, and maple syrup. Add to the dry ingredients and pour over the melted butter. Stir with a wooden spoon just until moistened and thoroughly blended. Take care not to overmix. Using a spatula, gently fold in the blueberries.

3. Pour the batter into the pan. Place the pan in the center of the oven and bake 20 to 25 minutes, or until golden around the edges and a cake tester inserted into the center comes out clean. Let stand 15 minutes. Cut into wedges to serve.

SUGAR AND SPICE:
Gingerbread

One of the greatest pleasures of gingerbread is the intoxicating fragrance that pervades the kitchen—the whole house, in fact—while baking. Ground spices are combined with ground ginger for just the right blend. Always use plenty of ground ginger (buy a new bottle every 6 to 9 months) for the best flavor. About ¼ cup finely grated ginger may be substituted for one tablespoon ground ginger, but the flavor will be quite different since ground ginger has a more concentrated, hot flavor.

Besides the intensely aromatic spices, the true heart of good gingerbread is the molasses, which lends its characteristic flavor, color, and soft texture to the bread. Use unsulfured molasses rather than blackstrap, which is bitter. To make a white gingerbread, substitute sugar, maple syrup, or honey for the molasses.

Gingerbreads can be delicately pale and spicy with just cinnamon and ginger, or dark and aromatically piquant with a subtle blend of ground sweet-hot spices that enhance each other. Blends can include ground black or white pepper, allspice, cloves, coriander, mace, and powdered mustard in combination with cinnamon and ginger. It is not unusual to find old recipes with ingredients ranging from vinegar, rose water, and orange juice to aniseed, crystallized ginger, and ground almonds.

Gingerbreads can be baked successfully into a moist, spongy, spicy loaf in a wide variety of metal, clay, porcelain, or glass baking pans. They can be eaten straight from an oven-to-table baking dish, or turned out and drizzled with glaze. Cutting large, thin gingerbread into individual rounds with a biscuit cutter is very convenient for serving dessert to large groups. Gingerbread's intense flavor mellows nicely after a day or two, but it is just as good eaten warm from the oven.

This is a cake you will rarely find in a bakery—it is a real homemade treat. It dresses up well with puréed fruit, sweet custard sauces, layers of good jam, chocolate glazes, fluffy lemon frosting, whipped cream, and cream cheese spreads.

Gingerbread with Lemon and Raspberry Sauces

Makes one 9-inch round or square cake or twelve 3-inch round cakes

2½ cups unbleached all-purpose flour

2 tablespoons instant espresso powder

1 tablespoon ground ginger

1 teaspoon ground cinnamon

½ teaspoon ground cloves

½ teaspoon freshly grated nutmeg

¼ teaspoon freshly ground black pepper

¼ teaspoon salt

Grated zest of 1 lemon

8 tablespoons (1 stick) unsalted butter

½ cup (packed) light brown sugar

½ cup unsulfured molasses

½ cup pure maple syrup

2 large eggs

2 teaspoons baking soda

1 cup boiling water

Raspberry Sauce (recipe follows), for serving

Lemon Sauce (recipe follows), for serving

For sophisticated diners, serve this English-style moist spice cake napped with lemon and raspberry sauces, dollops of cold crème fraîche, and fresh berries or serve it more simply, with warm, unsweetened applesauce.

1. Preheat the oven to 350°F. Grease a 9-inch square or round cake pan, a springform pan, or grease and parchment-line a 15-by-10-by-1-inch pan. In a large mixing bowl using a whisk, combine the flour, espresso, spices, salt, and lemon zest. In a small saucepan, combine the butter, brown sugar, molasses, and maple syrup. Stir constantly over low heat until the butter is melted. Remove from the heat.

2. Make a well in the center of the dry ingredients and pour in the hot butter mixture. Add the eggs and immediately beat with a wooden spoon or electric mixer until smooth. Combine the baking soda and boiling water. Pour over the batter and stir gently just until evenly incorporated.

3. For 1 Large Cake: Pour the batter into the square, round, or springform pan. Place the pan in the center of the oven and bake 35 to 40 minutes, or until the top springs back when touched and a cake tester inserted into the center comes out clean. Let cool in the pan on a rack. Cut into wedges or squares to serve.

For Individual Cake Rounds: Spread the batter into a greased and parchment-lined jelly-roll pan. Place the pan in the center of the oven and bake for 25 to 30 minutes. Let cool in the pan on a rack. Cut out 12 rounds with a 3-inch round biscuit or other decorative cutter, saving the excess cake for snacks. Top with cold crème fraîche, fresh raspberries, and a mint sprig.

RASPBERRY SAUCE

Makes about 2 cups

- 2 cups fresh
  raspberries or
  1 package
  (12 ounces) thawed
  unsweetened frozen
  raspberries

- 3 tablespoons
  raspberry vinegar

- ¼ cup sugar, or to taste

In a small bowl, sprinkle the berries with the vinegar and sugar. Let stand 1 hour at room temperature. Pass through a sieve to remove seeds. Refrigerate until ready to serve.

LEMON SAUCE

Makes about 1⅓ cups

- ¼ cup fresh lemon juice

- ½ cup water

- ½ cup sugar

  Grated zest of 2
  lemons

- 1 tablespoon
  cornstarch

- 3 tablespoons unsalted
  butter

Combine the lemon juice, ¼ cup water, sugar, and zest in a medium saucepan. Cook over medium-high heat just until the sugar is dissolved. In a small bowl, dissolve the cornstarch in the remaining ¼ cup water. Add to hot lemon mixture. Stir constantly with a whisk over medium-high heat until the mixture comes to a full boil, thickens, and becomes clear. Remove from the heat and stir in the butter. Serve warm or at room temperature.

Peach Upside-Down Ginger Cake

Makes one 9-inch cake

6 firm, ripe large peaches

4 tablespoons (½ stick) unsalted butter

¾ cup (packed) light brown sugar

¼ teaspoon finely grated nutmeg

¼ teaspoon ground cinnamon

¼ teaspoon ground ginger

8 tablespoons (1 stick) unsalted butter, at room temperature

½ cup sugar

2 large eggs

3 tablespoons unsulfured molasses

1 teaspoon pure vanilla extract

1½ cups unbleached all-purpose flour

½ teaspoon baking soda

¼ teaspoon salt

1½ teaspoons ground ginger

½ teaspoon ground cinnamon

¼ teaspoon ground cloves

¼ teaspoon freshly grated nutmeg

¼ cup boiling water

Amaretto Cream (recipe follows)

Upside-down cakes have a reputation of being cloyingly sweet, which they need not be. Every summer I take advantage of the bounty of fresh fruit to make one or more. This cake, which uses fresh peaches, is also excellent made with nectarines, plums, apples, apricots, cherries, fresh pineapple, or papaya. Serve with Amaretto Cream (following), a delicate French custard sauce.

1. Preheat the oven to 350°F. Peel, pit, and thickly slice the peaches; you should have 2 to 3 cups.

2. Melt the 4 tablespoons butter in a 9-inch ceramic or metal cake or springform pan in the oven or over low heat. When melted, stir in the brown sugar, nutmeg, cinnamon, and ginger. Heat just until the brown sugar is melted. Remove from the heat and arrange the peach slices in a single layer over the melted sugar. Set aside.

3. In a large bowl using a whisk or electric mixer, cream the butter and sugar. Beat in the eggs, molasses, and vanilla until light and fluffy. In another bowl using a whisk, combine the flour, baking soda, salt, and spices. Add the boiling water and flour mixture alternately to the creamed mixture, mixing just until creamy. Do not overbeat.

4. Carefully spoon the batter over the peaches in the pan. Place the pan in the center of the oven and bake 30 to 40 minutes, or until a cake tester inserted into the center of the cake comes out clean. Cool the cake in the pan for 5 minutes, inverting onto a serving plate. Serve warm or at room temperature accompanied by the cold Amaretto Cream.

AMARETTO CREAM

Makes about 3 cups

  2 cups heavy cream

  1/2 cup sugar

  3 large eggs

  1/4 cup Amaretto or
almond liqueur

In a saucepan or a microwave oven, scald the heavy cream. In a mixing bowl or food processor, combine the sugar and the eggs. Beat hard with a whisk or process until light colored and foamy. Whisking constantly, or through the feed tube with the food processor running, add the hot cream very slowly. Pour the sauce into a medium saucepan. Cook over medium heat, stirring constantly, until just slightly thickened. Pour into a bowl and stir in the liqueur. Cool slightly. Refrigerate, covered, until serving time.

Blueberry Gingerbread

Makes one 8-inch cake

1½ cups fresh
    blueberries

2 tablespoons
    granulated sugar

3 tablespoons
    blueberry vinegar

1½ cups unbleached all-
    purpose flour

½ cup (packed) light
    brown sugar

1 teaspoon baking
    soda

¼ teaspoon salt

2 teaspoons ground
    ginger

¼ teaspoon ground
    cinnamon

¼ teaspoon ground
    mace

½ cup sour cream

8 tablespoons (1 stick)
    unsalted butter,
    melted

2 large eggs

2 tablespoons pure
    maple syrup

Cinnamon Ice Cream
    (recipe follows),
    for serving

Blueberry gingerbread is a really special summer dessert when served with ice cream and additional fresh berries. This cake is moist, spicy, and fruity. With ice cream it is quite ethereal.

1. In a medium bowl, gently toss the blueberries with the granulated sugar and vinegar. Let stand at room temperature 1 hour.

2. Preheat the oven to 350°F. Grease an 8-inch square, heart-shaped, or springform pan. In a large bowl using a whisk or electric mixer, combine the flour, brown sugar, baking soda, salt, ginger, cinnamon, and mace. Drain the berries, reserving the juices, and set aside. In another bowl using a whisk, combine the reserved juices and the sour cream. Add the melted butter, eggs, and maple syrup. Add ½ cup of the flour mixture and beat until smooth. Add the remaining flour mixture and beat just until smooth and fluffy, about 1 minute.

3. Spread two thirds of the batter into the pan. Arrange the macerated berries over the top. Spoon over the remaining batter without completely covering the fruit. Place the pan in the center of the oven and bake 45 to 50 minutes, or until the top is dry and springy and a cake tester inserted into the center comes out clean. Cool on a rack until serving time. Serve cut into wedges and with one or two scoops of Cinnamon Ice Cream and additional fresh berries spooned over the cake.

CINNAMON ICE CREAM

Makes 1 quart

1 quart vanilla ice
    cream

2 tablespoons ground
    cinnamon

Let the ice cream soften slightly at room temperature for 10 to 15 minutes. With an electric mixer or by hand with a wooden spoon, beat the ice cream until just creamy. Add the cinnamon and blend until evenly distributed. Working quickly, scrape the ice cream back into the carton with a large spatula. Refreeze for at least 6 hours before serving.

Fresh Apricot Gingerbread

Makes one 10-inch tube cake

1 cup sour cream

8 tablespoons (1 stick) unsalted butter, softened

²/₃ cup unsulfured molasses

¹/₂ cup sugar

2 large eggs

3¹/₂ cups unbleached all-purpose flour

2 teaspoons baking soda

¹/₂ teaspoon cream of tartar

¹/₄ teaspoon salt

1 tablespoon ground ginger

1 teaspoon ground mace

1 teaspoon ground cinnamon

12 ripe fresh apricots, halved, stoned, and each snipped into 4 pieces

¹/₂ cup (2 ounces) pecans, chopped

2 pieces crystallized ginger, finely chopped

Powdered sugar, for dusting (optional)

This early country-style gingerbread, with a batter embellished with ripe fresh apricots, is a marriage of spices and fruit that is quite unusual, but exceptionally complementary. Crystallized preserved ginger is a confection rather than a spice and is available in gourmet food stores.

1. Preheat the oven to 350°F. Grease a 10-inch fluted or springform tube pan. In a mixing bowl using a spoon or electric mixer, combine the sour cream, butter, molasses, sugar, and eggs. Beat hard until smooth and well blended, about 1 minute.

2. In another bowl using a whisk, combine the flour, baking soda, cream of tartar, salt, ginger, mace, and cinnamon. Beat into the sour cream mixture until light and fluffy. Using a large spatula, fold in the apricots, pecans, and crystallized ginger.

3. Spoon the batter into the pan. Place the pan in the center of the oven and bake 45 to 50 minutes, or until the top springs back when touched and a cake tester inserted into the center comes out clean. Let stand in the pan 10 minutes before turning the cake out onto a cooling rack to cool completely before slicing. Dust with powdered sugar, if desired.

A SLICE OF DIVINITY:
Celebration and Dessert Breads

The American baking tradition includes religion, folk art, history, culture, and fantasy. Ceremonial breads mark harvest time, seasonal changes, birth, death, and gratitude to the gods.

Over the centuries, sweet bread recipes, complete with specific directions for shaping and decorating, have been handed down within families and communities. With recipes updated for today's ingredients, baking these breads is satisfying, and it gives bakers an opportunity to showcase their art. These festive creations never go out of style, because they are based on time-tested formulas and result in loaves that look and taste fabulous. They have universal appeal.

Avoid the disappointment of dry and tasteless commercial versions of these classic breads. As with all handmade foods, you have control over your ingredients when you make special breads at home.

BAKER'S WISDOM
Hints for Perfect Celebration and Dessert Breads

When making embellished sweet breads, keep in mind the following tips.

- Avoid commercial brands of candied fruit peels. They are laced with preservatives and artificial colors and lack the intense bittersweet flavor and texture of homemade. Make your own candied peels or substitute dried fruits. You can keep a variety of dried fruits on hand in the freezer for up to one year.

- Rework the dough if you are not satisfied with the shapes you have formed: Allow the dough to rest on the work surface, covered with a towel or plastic wrap, for about ten minutes to relax, then re-form. Bread dough is sturdy and forgiving, so experiment until you get the shape you want.

- The dough will rise double in the last rise and then again in the oven, so fussy details in shaping and decorating do not remain distinct. Simple classic shapes are the most successful.

🐝 Bake loaves well ahead of the occasion and freeze them for up to one month. Defrost on the day needed, adding the final glazing and decorative touches at that time. The loaf will taste and slice as perfectly as the day it was baked.

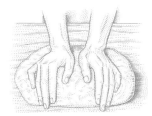

BAKER'S WISDOM
About Chocolate

Chocolate is by far one of the most popular ingredients added to breads. Its sensuous quality adds flavor not only to bread dough, but also to a myriad of fillings and glazes. Chocolate is made from the fruit of the cacao tree, which only grows in lands around the equator. After drying and fermentation in the field, the beans are shipped to manufacturers around the world, each having their own special methods—from roasting to conching—for achieving a characteristic flavor and aroma.

Roasting the cacao beans is a subtle art. The process releases elusive volatile compounds that determine the final flavor, much like roasting coffee beans. Next comes the blending of the beans; this is where the alchemical proportions of adding this and that is comparable to the blending of grapes to make wine. The beans are then processed into a thick paste known as chocolate liquor. The chocolate liquor is processed to make the familiar commercial varieties of chocolate, from bitter to milk, depending on the amount of sugar added. The conching process removes any grittiness, so your tongue gets a rich smooth chocolate sensation without any distractions. This smooth texture is what gives chocolate its sensual appeal. After aging, the chocolate is ready for the consumer.

All brands of chocolate vary in taste and quality, despite similar labeling. They have different amounts of sugar, cocoa butter, and vanilla. Experiment to find the ones you like best. Also take care to only use the type of chocolate called for in a recipe. For example, milk chocolate cannot be substituted for unsweetened or bittersweet; your recipe would not taste the way it was intended.

Unsweetened Chocolate: Contains chocolate liquor with at least 50 percent cocoa butter.

Bittersweet and Semisweet Dark Chocolate: Contain up to 35 percent chocolate liquor and, depending on the manufacturer, different amounts of cocoa butter.

Milk Chocolate: Contains 10 percent liquor and a large amount of cocoa butter and milk solids. It is very sensitive to heat.

White Chocolate: Not a true chocolate, but a combination of sugar, cocoa butter, milk solids, and vanilla flavoring.

Couverture: Thin coating chocolate, used mainly for candy making, dipping fruits, and glazing, though it can be substituted for bittersweet and semisweet chocolate. It melts and spreads beautifully. When using this chocolate in a recipe, use less fat per recipe than for regular dark chocolates, since couverture contains 39 percent cocoa butter.

Quality brands of dark, milk, and white chocolate are Lindt, Ghirardelli, Maillard, Scharffen Berger, Callebaut, Tobler, Valrhona, and Nestlé. Store solid chocolate tightly wrapped in a cool, dry place up to 6 months. Chocolate sometimes develops a thin white surface coating, known as bloom, when it has been stored at too warm a temperature. Bloom is harmless, and the chocolate may be used as needed.

Unsweetened Cocoa Powder: Chocolate liquor that has had some of the cocoa butter pressed out and is then ground to a fine powder. It is a good choice in baking for fat- and cholesterol-restricted diets. Dutch process cocoa is alkaline-treated, and therefore darker in color, less bitter, and richer in flavor than nonalkalized cocoa. Quick-bread recipes utilizing Dutch process cocoa require slightly more baking powder to maintain the proper acid-alkaline balance. For nonalkalized natural cocoa, such as Hershey's (in the brown can), baking soda is an important ingredient for balancing the natural acids. Good brands of Dutch-processed cocoa are Dröste, Poulain, Baker's, van Houten, Hershey's European-style (in the silver can), and Ghirardelli. Cocoa keeps indefinitely in an airtight container. To substitute cocoa powder for baking chocolate, use 3 tablespoons cocoa and 1 tablespoon vegetable oil or butter for every 1-ounce square of baking chocolate. Do not substitute instant cocoa powder in recipes: it is precooked and sweetened.

BAKER'S WISDOM
Melting Chocolate

The key to melting chocolate successfully is to melt it slowly over low heat and not to allow it to come into contact with water. You can do this on the stovetop, in the oven, or in the microwave. Whichever method you use, first coarsely chop the chocolate for uniform melting. The container in which it is melted must be dry. Chocolate burns very easily, so keep the temperature below 125°F. If it is overheated, chocolate will become grainy and taste scorched. All types and brands of chocolate melt at different rates and have different consistencies. Semisweet and milk chocolates tend to hold their shape when melted and must be stirred with a whisk or rubber spatula to create a smooth consistency.

Melting Chocolate on the Stovetop: Place the coarsely chopped chocolate in a double boiler over hot, but not simmering, water. Let the chocolate stand until melted, stirring occasionally. If melting milk chocolate or white chocolate, which are very heat sensitive, remove the double boiler from the heat after the water is hot and let stand until the chocolate is melted. Keep the temperature below 115°F.

Melting Chocolate in a Conventional Oven: Place the chocolate in an oven-proof baking dish in a preheated 300° to 350°F oven. Check every 5 minutes until melted.

Melting in a Microwave Oven: Place the chocolate in a microwave-safe container and partially cover with plastic wrap. Microwave at 50 percent power for 1 minute, depending on the amount, until shiny and slightly melted. Stir at 30-second to 1-minute intervals throughout the melting process until completely melted. Milk and white chocolates take less time than dark chocolates.

Pernod Panettone

Makes 2 medium round loaves or 1 tall loaf

- ½ cup golden raisins
- ½ cup snipped dried apricots
- ½ cup plus 2 tablespoons Pernod liqueur
- ¼ cup warm water (105° to 115°F)
- 1 tablespoon (1 package) active dry yeast
- ⅓ cup sugar
- 1 cup warm milk (105° to 115°F)
- 8 tablespoons (1 stick) unsalted butter, melted
- 1 teaspoon salt
- 2 large eggs
- About 4 cups unbleached all-purpose flour
- ¼ cup pine nuts
- ¼ cup slivered blanched almonds
- 3 tablespoons sugar, for glaze

Panettone is a Christmas specialty of Milan, Italy. This rich, fancy, candied fruit—studded pane is one of my signature loaves, permeated with the Mediterranean licorice flavor of anise. To achieve the classic cylindrical mushroom shape and characteristic porous texture, use a charlotte mold with extended aluminum foil sides, a two-pound coffee can, a tall panettone tube mold (which looks like an elongated angel food cake pan), or the traditional panettone paper molds available at specialty cookware shops like Williams Sonoma. Stale panettone—if you ever have any!—can be used for a great bread pudding. To make *panettoncinos*, this recipe will make ten individual loaves baked in clean 8-ounce pineapple cans with foil collars.

1. In a medium bowl, combine the dried fruits and the ½ cup Pernod. Let stand for 1 hour to macerate.

2. Pour the warm water in another small bowl. Sprinkle the yeast and a pinch of sugar over the surface of the water. Stir to dissolve, and let stand at room temperature until foamy, about 10 minutes.

3. In a large bowl with a whisk or in the work bowl of a heavy-duty electric mixer fitted with the paddle attachment, combine the warm milk, butter, the remaining sugar, and salt. Add the eggs, the 2 remaining tablespoons Pernod, and 1 cup of the flour, and beat until smooth and creamy, about 1 minute. Add the yeast mixture and 1 cup more of the flour. Beat 1 minute longer. Drain the fruits, reserving the liqueur for the glaze. Add the fruits, pine nuts, and almonds. Add the remaining flour, ½ cup at a time, until a soft dough that just clears the sides of the bowl is formed, with the solids evenly distributed. Switch to a wooden spoon when necessary if making by hand.

4. Turn the dough out onto a lightly floured work surface and knead until smooth and springy, about 3 minutes, dusting with flour only 1 tablespoon at a time as needed to prevent sticking. Push back any fruits that fall out of the dough during kneading. The dough should remain soft.

If kneading by machine, switch from the paddle to the dough hook and knead for 2 to 3 minutes, or until the dough is smooth and springy

and springs back when pressed. If desired, transfer the dough to a floured surface and knead briefly by hand.

5. Place the dough in a greased deep container. Turn once to coat the top and cover with plastic wrap. Let rise at room temperature until doubled in bulk, about 2 hours.

6. Turn the dough out onto the work surface. Grease or parchment-line a baking sheet or grease a panettone mold or a 2-pound coffee can for a cylindrical loaf. Divide the dough into 2 equal portions for round loaves, or leave the dough in 1 piece for a tall loaf. To make free form loaves, shape each of the 2 portions into a tight round ball and place them at least 3 inches apart on the baking sheet. Using a serrated knife, slash an **X** ½ inch deep into the top of each loaf. To make a cylindrical loaf, place all the dough in the panettone mold or coffee can. Cover with plastic wrap and let rise again at room temperature until doubled in bulk, about 45 minutes.

7. Twenty minutes before baking, preheat the oven to 375°F. Place the baking sheet or pan on the low center rack of the oven and bake 40 to 45 minutes or until browned and the loaf sounds hollow tapped on the bottom with your finger. Transfer the loaves immediately to a cooling rack.

8. While the bread is still warm, prepare the glaze. Combine the reserved liqueur and add enough water to equal ¼ cup. (If all the liqueur has been absorbed by the fruits, combine 2 tablespoons water with 2 tablespoons Pernod.) Place in a small saucepan and add the 3 tablespoons sugar. Heat, stirring just until the sugar dissolves. Brush the warm bread twice all over and let stand to dry completely before serving.

Stollen with Dried Cherries and Pineapple

Makes 2 large flat loaves

¹/₂ cup dried cherries

¹/₂ cup dried currants

¹/₂ cup dried pineapple

¹/₂ cup golden raisins

Boiling water

Sponge

1 cup warm milk
(105° to 115°F)

¹/₂ cup sugar

1 tablespoon
(1 package) active
dry yeast

1 cup unbleached
all-purpose flour

Dough

2 large eggs

2 tablespoons Cognac

Grated zest of 1
lemon

¹/₂ teaspoon freshly
grated nutmeg

1 teaspoon salt

3¹/₂ to 4 cups unbleached all-
purpose flour

³/₄ cup (1¹/₂ sticks)
unsalted butter, at
room temperature,
cut into 12 pieces

The large, tapered shape symbolizes the Christ child in swaddling clothes. The traditional flat loaf works best, since the dough is rich in dried fruits and butter with a rather firm, dry texture.

1. Place the dried fruit in a medium bowl, and cover with boiling water to plump. Set aside to cool.

2. To make the sponge: In a large bowl using a whisk or in the work bowl of a heavy-duty electric mixer fitted with the paddle attachment, combine the milk and sugar. Sprinkle with the yeast and stir to dissolve. Let stand for 5 minutes. Sprinkle with 1 cup of the flour and beat until smooth, 1 minute. Scrape down the sides and cover with plastic wrap. Let stand at room temperature until bubbly, about 1 hour.

3. To make the dough: Drain the dried fruit. Add the fruit, eggs, Cognac, lemon zest, nutmeg, salt, and 1 cup of the flour to the sponge. Beat until combined. Add the butter a few pieces at a time, beating after each addition. Continue to add the flour, ¹/₂ cup at a time, until a dough that just clears the sides of the bowl is formed. Switch to a wooden spoon when necessary if mixing by hand.

4. Turn the dough out onto a lightly floured work surface and knead until smooth and springy, about 2 to 3 minutes, dusting with flour only 1 tablespoon at a time as needed to prevent sticking. Push back in any fruits that fall out while kneading.

If kneading by machine, switch from the paddle to the dough hook and knead for 2 to 3 minutes, or until the dough is smooth and springy and springs back when pressed. If desired, transfer the dough to a floured surface and knead briefly by hand.

5. Cover the dough with a towel and let rest on the work surface for 10 minutes.

6. Gently deflate the dough. Turn the dough out onto a floured work surface. Grease or parchment-line a baking sheet. Divide the dough

4 tablespoons
(½ stick) unsalted
butter, melted

2 tablespoons sugar
mixed with
½ teaspoon ground
cinnamon

Sifted powdered
sugar, for dusting

into 2 equal portions. Roll or pat the dough out into a 12-by-8-inch oval about ½ inch thick. Dust the work surface with only enough flour to prevent sticking. Brush each oval with melted butter and sprinkle each with half of the cinnamon sugar. Make a crease down the center of the oval and, without stretching it, fold one of the long sides over the center crease to within ¾ inch of the opposite side. This forms a long, narrow loaf with tapered ends. Press the top edge lightly to seal. Repeat the procedure to form the second stollen. Place the stollens on the baking sheet and cover loosely with plastic wrap. Let rise again in a warm place until almost doubled in bulk, about 1 hour.

7. Twenty minutes before baking, preheat the oven to 375°F. Place the baking sheet on a rack in the center of the oven and bake 35 to 40 minutes, or until lightly browned. If the tops are browning too fast, cover loosely with aluminum foil. Take care not to overbake. Transfer the loaves to a cooling rack. Dust with powdered sugar. Cut into thin slices to serve. *(Stollen will keep, wrapped in plastic, for 2 weeks at room temperature.)*

Saffron Bread with Scented Geranium Powdered Sugar

Makes 1 large braided or round wreath

1 cup dried currants

¼ cup cream sherry

½ teaspoon saffron threads, crumbled

1 cup warm milk (105° to 115°F)

1 tablespoon (1 package) active dry yeast

¼ cup sugar

2 large eggs

2 teaspoons salt

4 to 4½ cups unbleached all-purpose flour or bread flour

8 tablespoons (1 stick) unsalted butter, at room temperature, cut into 8 pieces

Scented Geranium Powdered Sugar (recipe follows), for dusting

Tinted yellow with saffron, this loaf is part of the repertoire of both English and Scandinavian bakers, who add saffron to dough to make up for the lack of egg yolks as well as for the distinctive flavor. To gild the lily, dust this barely sweet saffron bread with your own scented powdered sugar. To make this bread in a bread machine, see page 463.

1. In a small bowl, toss the currants with the sherry. Set aside and let macerate for about 1 hour.

2. In a small saucepan, sprinkle the saffron over ⅓ cup water, bring to a simmer, and remove from the heat. Let stand at room temperature for 30 minutes.

3. In a large bowl using a whisk or in the work bowl of a heavy-duty electric mixer fitted with the paddle attachment, pour in the milk. Sprinkle the yeast and sugar over the surface of the milk. Stir to dissolve and let stand at room temperature until foamy, about 10 minutes.

4. Add the eggs, sugar, salt, and 1 cup of the flour to the yeast mixture and beat until creamy, 1 minute. Add the saffron water, currants, and sherry, and 1 cup more of the flour. Beat for 1 minute. Add the butter, a few pieces at a time, beating well after each addition to incorporate. Add the remaining flour, ½ cup at a time, until a soft dough that just clears the sides of the bowl is formed. Switch to a wooden spoon when necessary if mixing by hand.

5. Turn the dough out onto a lightly floured work surface and knead until smooth and springy, about 3 minutes, dusting with flour only 1 tablespoon at a time as needed to prevent sticking.

If kneading by machine, switch from the paddle to the dough hook and knead for 2 to 3 minutes, or until the dough is smooth and springy and springs back when pressed. If desired, transfer the dough to a floured surface and knead briefly by hand.

6. Place the dough in a greased deep container. Turn once to coat the top and cover with plastic wrap. Let rise at room temperature until doubled in bulk, about 1½ hours.

7. Gently deflate the dough. Turn the dough out onto a floured work surface. Divide into 3 equal portions. Form each portion into a 14-inch-long fat rope. Place the 3 ropes parallel to each other. Begin braiding, starting in the center rather than at the ends for a more even shape. Take one of the outside ropes and fold it over the center rope, then repeat the movement from the opposite side. Continue by alternating the outside ropes over the center rope. When complete, turn the dough around and repeat the procedure. Pinch the ends together and tuck them under. The dough may also be connected at both ends to form a round braid. It may also be formed without braiding by forming it into one thick log and connecting both ends to make a circle. Using floured kitchen shears, make 2-inch-deep parallel cuts at 1-inch intervals on the top of the loaf. Cover loosely with plastic wrap and let rise at room temperature until doubled in bulk, about 45 minutes.

8. Twenty minutes before baking, preheat the oven to 375°F. Place the baking sheet on a rack in the center of the oven and bake 35 to 40 minutes, or until browned and hollow sounding when tapped with your finger. Transfer the loaves to a cooling rack. Just before serving, dust with Scented Geranium Powdered Sugar.

SCENTED GERANIUM POWDERED SUGAR

Makes 2 cups scented sugar

- 2 cups sifted powdered sugar
- 6 scented geranium leaves of a single variety, rinsed and dried on paper towels

In an airtight container, place a bottom layer of about ½ cup of the powdered sugar. Lay 2 of the geranium leaves on top of the sugar. Continue to layer sugar and leaves 20 more times, ending with a layer of sugar. Cover tightly and let stand at room temperature 1 week before using. (*Scented sugar will keep for 3 months at room temperature.*)

Bohemian Sweet Rolls

Kolacki

Makes 24 rolls

- 1 tablespoon (1 package) active dry yeast
- 3 tablespoons sugar
- ½ cup warm water (105° to 115°F)
- 1½ cups milk (105° to 115°F)
- Grated zest of 1 lemon
- 2 large eggs
- 1½ teaspoons salt
- 6 to 6½ cups unbleached all-purpose flour
- 8 tablespoons (1 stick) unsalted butter, at room temperature, cut into pieces

Dried Fruit Filling

- 8 ounces dried fruit, such as dried sour cherries, cranberries, apricots, peaches, or prunes
- 2 tablespoons fruit brandy
- ⅓ cup sugar
- Grated zest and juice of 1 lemon
- 2 tablespoons unsalted butter

Luckily for us, Czech bakers have passed along a jewel of yeast pastry tradition, the *kolack*. These puffy, round, feather-light buns, which conceal a dried fruit or cheese filling, are, along with gingerbread figures, favorite holiday tree ornaments. Be warned though: One bite and you'll be hooked. My favorite filling is made with dried sour cherries, but any other dried fruit filling or cheese is also wonderful. Each batch of filling makes enough for 2 dozen rolls.

1. Pour the warm water in a small bowl. Sprinkle the yeast and a pinch of the sugar over the surface of the water. Stir to dissolve and let stand at room temperature until foamy, about 10 minutes.

2. In a large bowl with a whisk or in the work bowl of a heavy-duty electric mixer fitted with the paddle attachment, combine the remaining sugar, the warm milk, lemon zest, eggs, salt, and 2 cups of the flour. Beat hard for 1 minute. Add the yeast mixture and ½ cup more of the flour. Beat again for 1 minute. Add the butter pieces and beat until incorporated. Add the remaining flour, ½ cup at a time, until a soft dough that just clears the sides of the bowl is formed. Switch to a wooden spoon when necessary if making by hand.

3. Turn the dough out onto a lightly floured work surface and knead until smooth and elastic, 1 to 2 minutes, dusting with flour only 1 tablespoon at a time as needed to prevent sticking. Do not add too much flour or the bread will be dry.

If kneading by machine, switch from the paddle to the dough hook and knead for 1 to 2 minutes, or until the dough is smooth and elastic and springs back when pressed. If desired, transfer the dough to a floured surface and knead briefly by hand.

4. Place the dough in a greased deep container. Turn once to coat the top and cover with plastic wrap. Let rise at room temperature until doubled in bulk, 1 to 1½ hours.

Fresh Cheese Filling

1½ cups (12 ounces)
ricotta cheese or
fromage blanc

½ cup sugar

1 large egg

1 teaspoon pure
vanilla extract

Grated zest of 1
lemon

5. Meanwhile, prepare the fruit or cheese filling. To make the fruit filling, in a small saucepan, combine the dried fruit of your choice with a corresponding fruit brandy and water to cover. Bring to a boil, cover, and reduce the heat to low. Cook until tender, about 20 minutes. Drain, reserving ¼ cup of the liquid. Combine the warm fruit, reserved liquid, sugar, lemon zest, lemon juice, and butter in a food processor fitted with the metal blade and process until just smooth. To make the cheese filling, combine all the ingredients in a food processor and purée just until smooth. Set aside or cover and refrigerate until needed.

6. Gently deflate the dough. Turn the dough out onto a floured work surface. Grease or parchment-line 2 baking sheets. Divide into 2 equal portions. Divide each portion into 12 equal portions. Form each portion into a round ball. Flatten each ball into a disk about 3 inches in diameter. Place the disks about 2 inches apart on the baking sheets. Cover loosely with plastic wrap and let rise at room temperature until puffy, about 30 minutes. (The pastries may also rise overnight in the refrigerator.)

7. Twenty minutes before baking, preheat the oven to 350°F. With your thumb or the back of a large spoon, press an indentation into the center of each roll to form a hollow. Spoon a heaping tablespoon of filling into each hollow. Place one pan at a time on a rack in the center of the oven and bake 20 to 25 minutes or until the rolls are golden brown. Transfer to a cooling rack. Serve warm or at room temperature.

Portuguese Sweet Bread with Honey

Makes 2 round loaves

Sponge

1½ tablespoons (1½ packages) active dry yeast

½ cup warm water (105° to 115°F)

1 cup warm milk (105° to 115°F)

¼ cup sugar

2 cups unbleached all-purpose flour or bread flour

Dough

8 tablespoons (1 stick) unsalted butter, at room temperature, cut into small pieces

½ cup honey

2 teaspoons salt

3 large eggs, at room temperature

3½ to 4 cups unbleached all-purpose flour or bread flour

Rich Egg Glaze (page 52)

From the Azores to Cape Cod to the Hawaiian Islands, Portuguese Sweet Bread appears on Easter tables and in bakeries halfway around the world from its place of origin. A simple egg bread traditionally topped with hard-cooked eggs and a cross made of dough, it is just as appealing plain.

1. To make the sponge: In a large bowl using a whisk or in the work bowl of a heavy-duty electric mixer fitted with the paddle attachment, combine the yeast, water, milk, sugar, and flour and beat until smooth. Scrape down the sides and cover with plastic wrap. Let stand at room temperature until bubbly, about 1 hour.

2. To make the dough: Stir down the sponge and add the butter, honey, salt, eggs, and 1 cup of the flour. Beat hard until creamy, about 1 minute. Continue to add the flour ½ cup at a time, until a soft dough that just clears the sides of the bowl is formed. Switch to a wooden spoon when necessary if making by hand.

3. Turn the dough out onto a lightly floured work surface and knead for about 2 to 3 minutes, or until a soft, smooth, and springy dough is formed, dusting with flour only 1 tablespoon at a time as needed to prevent sticking.

If kneading by machine, switch from the paddle to the dough hook and knead for 2 to 3 minutes, or until the dough is soft, smooth, and springy, and springs back when pressed. If desired, transfer the dough to a floured surface and knead briefly by hand.

4. Place the dough in a greased deep container. Turn once to coat the top and cover with plastic wrap. Let rise at room temperature until doubled in bulk, about 1½ hours.

5. Gently deflate the dough. Turn the dough out onto a floured work surface. Grease or parchment-line a baking sheet. Divide the dough into 2 equal portions. Form each portion into a tight, round loaf and place on the baking sheet. Cover loosely with plastic and let rise at room temperature until puffy, but not quite doubled in bulk, about 30 minutes.

6. Twenty minutes before baking, preheat the oven to 375°F. Brush the loaves with the egg glaze. Place the baking sheet on a rack in the center of the oven and bake 35 to 40 minutes, or until golden brown and the loaves sound hollow when tapped with your finger. Transfer the loaves to a cooling rack. Cool before slicing.

Italian Anise Easter Bread

Makes three 9-by-5-inch or freestanding braided loaves

- 1 cup milk
- 1 cup sugar
- 6 tablespoons (³/₄ stick) unsalted butter
- 2 teaspoons active dry yeast
- Pinch of sugar
- ¹/₄ cup warm water (105° to 115°F)
- 6 to 6¹/₂ cups unbleached all-purpose flour
- 1¹/₂ teaspoons salt
- 2 teaspoons baking powder
- 4 large eggs
- 2 tablespoons pure anise extract
- 1 egg, beaten, for glaze
- 1 tablespoon aniseed, or fennel seeds, for sprinkling

Here is a special family recipe from my friend Lisa Warren. The austere bread is infused with the strongly scented oil of anise, a plant also known for its soothing digestive qualities. Lisa's recipe is triple this one; she uses a full five pounds of flour to make extra braids for gift giving. Note that the dough rises slowly at room temperature before a final rise and shaping. The crust of this bread is dark and glossy and sprinkled with fennel seeds. You may add a cup or two of golden raisins to the dough, if you wish. This bread freezes well.

1. In a medium saucepan or microwave-proof bowl, combine the milk, the 1 cup sugar, and butter. Heat, stirring occasionally, until the butter is melted. Let the mixture cool until warm, 105° to 115°F. Pour the warm water in a small bowl. Sprinkle the yeast and the pinch of sugar over the surface of the water. Stir to dissolve and let stand at room temperature until foamy, about 10 minutes.

2. In a large bowl using a whisk or in the work bowl of a heavy-duty electric mixer fitted with the paddle attachment, combine 3 cups of the flour, salt, and baking powder. Make a well in the center and break the 4 eggs into the well. Gradually mix a few tablespoons of the flour into the eggs, add the anise extract and yeast and milk mixtures, and beat until soft, smooth, and sticky, about 2 minutes. Add the remaining flour, ½ cup at a time, until a soft dough that just clears the sides of the bowl is formed. Switch to a wooden spoon when necessary if making by hand.

3. Turn the dough out onto a lightly floured work surface and knead until smooth and elastic, 4 to 5 minutes, dusting with flour only 1 tablespoon at a time as needed to prevent sticking. It is important that this dough remain very soft and springy.

If kneading by machine, switch from the paddle to the dough hook and knead for 4 to 5 minutes, or until the dough is smooth and springy and springs back when pressed. If desired, transfer the dough to a floured surface and knead briefly by hand.

4. Place the dough in a greased deep container. Turn once to coat the top and cover tightly with plastic wrap. Let rise at cool room temperature until doubled in bulk, about 12 hours or as long as overnight.

5. Gently deflate the dough and let rise again at room temperature until doubled in bulk, 1 to 1½ hours. Gently deflate the dough. Turn the dough out onto a lightly floured work surface. Grease the loaf pans or parchment-line a baking sheet. Divide the dough into 9 equal portions. Roll each portion into a rope 12 inches long. Place 3 ropes parallel to each other. Begin braiding, starting in the center rather than at the ends for a more even shape. Take one of the outside ropes and fold it over the center rope, then repeat the movement from the opposite side. Continue by alternating the outside ropes over the center ropes. When completed, turn the dough around and repeat the procedure. Pinch the ends together and tuck them under. Repeat to make 2 more braids. Place each braid into a greased 9-by-5-inch loaf pan, or on the baking sheet. Cover loosely with plastic wrap and let rise at room temperature until doubled in bulk or 1 inch above the rims of the pans, 45 minutes to 1 hour.

6. Twenty minutes before baking, preheat the oven to 350°F. Brush the tops with the egg glaze, taking care not to let it drip down the sides of the pan. Sprinkle with the fennel seeds. Place the pans or baking sheet on a rack in the center of the oven and bake 35 to 40 minutes, or until deep golden brown, and the loaves sound hollow when tapped with your finger. Transfer to a cooling rack. Cool completely.

Hungarian Nut Rolls

Diós Tekeres

Makes 4 rolls

- 1 tablespoon (1 package) active dry yeast
- ½ cup sugar
- 1 cup warm milk (105° to 115°F)
- 8 tablespoons (1 stick) unsalted butter, at room temperature
- 1 large egg
- Grated zest of 1 lemon
- ½ teaspoon salt
- 3¾ to 4½ cups unbleached all-purpose flour

Walnut Paste

- 4 cups (1 pound) walnuts
- ½ cup sugar
- 1½ teaspoons ground cinnamon
- 2 tablespoons Cognac
- About ⅓ cup hot milk (120°F)
- 1 whole egg, beaten, for glaze

Recipes for Hungarian rolls have graced many a handwritten cookbook, reflecting the strong baking tradition of the Austro-Hungarian Empire. They are tremendously popular in Hungary, appearing for Easter and Christmas holidays, filled with poppy seeds and raisins as well as ground nuts. Every home and pastry shop has its own recipe for these rolls, known familiarly as *beigli*.

1. Pour ⅓ cup of the warm milk in a small bowl. Sprinkle the yeast and the pinch of sugar over the surface of the milk. Stir to dissolve and let stand at room temperature until foamy, about 10 minutes.

2. In a large bowl using a wooden spoon or in the work bowl of a heavy-duty electric mixer fitted with the paddle attachment, beat together the butter and sugar until fluffy. Add the egg and beat vigorously for 1 minute. Beat in the remaining ⅔ cup milk, the lemon zest, salt, and 1 cup of the flour. Then beat in the remaining flour, ½ cup at a time, until a soft dough that just clears the sides of the bowl is formed.

3. Turn the dough out onto a lightly floured work surface and knead until smooth and pliable, about 3 minutes, dusting with flour only 1 tablespoon at a time as needed to prevent sticking. The dough will be very soft but not sticky.

If kneading by machine, switch from the paddle to the dough hook and knead for 2 to 3 minutes, or until the dough is smooth and springy and springs back when pressed. If desired, transfer the dough to a floured surface and knead briefly by hand.

4. Place the dough in a greased deep container. Turn once to coat the top and cover with plastic wrap. Let rise at cool room temperature for 4 to 6 hours, deflating once or twice, or as long as overnight in the refrigerator.

5. Gently deflate the dough. Turn the dough out onto a floured work surface and divide into 4 equal portions. Form each portion into a thick rectangle, place on loosely floured parchment paper, cover loosely with a clean tea towel, and let rest for 30 minutes.

6. Meanwhile, make the filling: Combine the walnuts, sugar, and cinnamon in a food processor fitted with the metal blade. Process until finely ground. Combine the Cognac and milk and, with the motor running, pour the mixture through the feed tube in a slow, steady stream, processing until a thick, spreadable paste is formed. (The filling may be made ahead and stored, tightly covered, in the refrigerator.)

7. Grease or parchment-line a baking sheet. Using a floured rolling pin on a very lightly floured work surface to minimize sticking, roll or pat out each dough portion into a 13-by-7-inch rectangle about ⅛ inch thick. Spread the surface of each rectangle evenly with one-fourth of the nut paste. Working with 1 rectangle at a time and starting from a long side, fold over a 2-inch section. Continue to fold the dough in this manner to create a flattish oval (rather than round) long log of dough. Pinch the seams and place the dough, seam side down, on the baking sheet, fitting all 4 rolls horizontally on the pan about 2 inches apart. Brush with the egg glaze and prick all over with a fork. Let rest, uncovered, at room temperature about 20 minutes.

8. Twenty minutes before baking, preheat the oven to 350°F. Brush once more with the beaten egg. Place the baking sheet on a rack in the center of the oven and bake 30 to 40 minutes, or until golden and the loaves sound hollow when tapped with your finger. (If using 2 baking sheets, change the rack positions halfway through baking.) Let rest on the baking sheet 10 minutes. Using a large spatula, transfer the loaves to a cooling rack. Cool completely. Handle the hot breads carefully, because they are quite delicate.

VARIATION: *Substitute 1 tablespoon unsweetened cocoa powder for the cinnamon in the filling. Though not authentic, pecans or hazelnuts can be substituted for the walnuts.*

BAKER'S WISDOM
Nuts and Seeds

A recipe's flavor can be easily altered by the adding or changing nuts or seeds. Good nuts for baking are almonds, hazelnuts, pecans, walnuts, macadamias, pistachios, cashews, and pine nuts. Sesame, pumpkin, and sunflower seeds can be used for extra flavor, texture, and nutrition.

Measure nuts in a dry measuring cup or by weight. Chop nuts by hand with a chef's knife, in a nut grinder, or in a food processor, taking care not to overprocess or the nuts will become a paste. Nuts may be chopped in sizes ranging from chunky to quite fine. Coarsely chopped nuts are slightly larger than a raisin, finely chopped nuts are about the size of a currant. Coarsely ground nuts look rather like polenta, and finely ground nuts a powder the consistency of coarse whole-wheat flour. For best results, grind nuts with a few tablespoons flour or sugar from the recipe. Buy fresh or vacuum-packed nuts. To keep nuts from turning rancid, store in the refrigerator for up to 9 months or in the freezer for up to 2.

Toasting Nuts
Toasting nuts significantly enhances their flavor. You may toast them in a skillet, in the oven, or in a microwave oven.

To toast nuts in a skillet
Place the nuts in a dry skillet over medium heat and toast, shaking, until golden. This method is especially good for pine nuts, sesame seeds, and rolled oats. They will crisp as they cool.

To toast nuts in the oven
Place on an ungreased baking sheet in the center of a preheated 325 to 350°F oven and toast until golden brown. Do not bake nuts to the point that they are dark in color, as they will taste burnt.

To toast nuts in a microwave oven
Place the nuts in a single layer on paper towels or on a microwave safe plate, uncovered. Microwave on high for 1 to 4 minutes, stirring twice, until nuts are golden brown.

ALMONDS: Can be purchased whole, with or without skins, slivered or sliced. Toast for 5 to 10 minutes, with sliced almonds cooking faster. To blanch whole almonds, cover with 1 inch boiling water. Let stand 1 to 2 minutes. Drain and squeeze each nut to pop off the skin. Dry and recrisp in a 200°F oven for 12 to 15 minutes.

HAZELNUTS: Bought whole. May be marketed as filberts. Toast for 10 to 14 minutes, or until the skins blister. Immediately wrap the nuts in a clean dish towel and let stand for 1 minute. Rub off the skins. Let cool.

WALNUTS, PECANS, CASHEWS, AND MACADAMIAS: Can be bought in halves or pieces. Toast for 5 to 8 minutes.

PISTACHIOS: Can be bought whole or shelled. To blanch pistachios, cover with 1 inch of boiling water. Let stand 1 minute. Drain and wrap the nuts in a clean dish towel and rub off the skins. Place on an ungreased baking sheet and dry at 300°F for 10 minutes. Cool thoroughly.

PINE NUTS, SUNFLOWER SEEDS, AND PUMPKIN SEEDS: Toast for 7 to 10 minutes.

Alpine Easter Bread

Makes one 10-inch round loaf

1/2 cup milk

8 tablespoons (1 stick) unsalted butter

1/2 cup warm water (105° to 115°F)

1 1/2 tablespoons (1 1/2 packages) active dry yeast

2/3 cup sugar

4 to 4 1/2 cups unbleached all-purpose flour

2 teaspoons grated lemon zest

1 1/2 teaspoons salt

3 large eggs

1 1/2 teaspoons pure vanilla extract or 1 vanilla bean, split and scraped

1/2 teaspoon lemon extract

Nut Liqueur Glaze

1 cup sifted powdered sugar

1 tablespoon unsalted butter, melted

2 to 3 tablespoons nut liqueur, such as Pistacha, Amaretto, Frangelico, or Nocino

10 whole toasted, chocolate-coated or silver-coated almonds, for garnish

Baked into a round loaf, this Easter bread is light, rich, and delicate. Egg breads are often associated with spring and rebirth. The round shape represents the sun and the rhythm of the seasons. The aroma of this loaf is so intoxicating that legend says it has healing powers.

1. In a small saucepan, combine the milk and butter. Heat until the butter is melted. Let cool to 105° to 115°F, about 20 minutes.

2. Pour the warm water in a small bowl. Sprinkle the yeast and a pinch of the sugar over the surface of the water. Stir to dissolve and let stand at room temperature until foamy, about 10 minutes.

3. In a large bowl using a whisk or in the work bowl of a heavy-duty electric mixer fitted with the paddle attachment, combine 1 1/2 cups of the flour, the remaining sugar, lemon zest, and salt. Add the yeast and milk mixtures, eggs, and extracts. Beat until creamy, about 2 minutes. Add the remaining flour, 1/2 cup at a time, on low speed until a soft dough that just clears the sides of the bowl is formed. Switch to a wooden spoon when necessary if mixing by hand.

4. Turn the dough out onto a lightly floured work surface and knead until the dough is soft and springy, about 3 minutes, dusting with flour only 1 tablespoon at a time as needed to prevent sticking. The dough should not be dry.

If kneading by machine, switch from the paddle to the dough hook and knead for 2 to 3 minutes, or until the dough is smooth and springy and springs back when pressed. If desired, transfer the dough to a floured surface and knead briefly by hand.

5. Place the dough in a greased deep container. Turn once to coat the top and cover with plastic wrap. Let rise at warm room temperature until doubled in bulk, about 2 hours. Do not rush this dough, as the full rising time is important to develop flavor and texture.

6. Gently deflate the dough. Turn the dough out onto a floured work surface and shape into a smooth, round loaf. Grease a 10-inch springform pan or a 10-inch round cake pan 4 inches deep. Place the dough in the pan. Cover loosely with plastic wrap and let rise at warm room temperature until doubled in bulk, about 1 hour.

7. Twenty minutes before baking, preheat the oven to 350°F. Bake 50 to 60 minutes or until brown and a cake tester comes out clean when inserted into the center. Transfer the loaf from the pan to a cooling rack. Place the rack over a plate or a sheet of wax paper to catch the drips.

8. To prepare the glaze: In a small bowl, combine the ingredients and whisk until smooth. Adjust the consistency of the glaze by adding hot water a few drops at a time as needed. Drizzle the glaze over the warm loaf, letting it drip down the sides. Stud the outer edge with whole almonds, if desired. The glaze will set as the loaf cools.

Byzantine Easter Bread

Makes 4 round loaves

- 1 cup warm milk (105° to 115°F)
- 3/4 cup (1½ sticks) unsalted butter
- 1½ tablespoons (1½ packages) active dry yeast
- 1½ cups sugar
- 6 large eggs
- 1/3 cup olive oil
- 1 tablespoon pure vanilla extract
- 1 tablespoon salt
- 2 teaspoons *nigella* or fennel seeds
- 1 teaspoon lightly crushed *mahlep* seeds or 2 teaspoons lightly crushed aniseed and 1 teaspoon ground cinnamon
- 3/4 teaspoon mastic granules, pulverized in a mortar with 1/2 teaspoon sugar, or 1 teaspoon ground allspice
- 6 to 6½ cups unbleached all-purpose flour or bread flour
- 1 large egg beaten with 1 tablespoon honey and 1 tablespoon milk, for glaze
- 1/3 cup sesame seeds

They may be flavored in a number of ways—lemon, orange, vanilla, aniseed, or *pekmez* (boiled down grape must)—and are sprinkled with sesame seeds or almonds. The exotic spices used in this loaf are *nigella* (related to fennel), mastic, and *mahlep,* the crushed pits of St. Lucy's cherries (named for the convent where the trees were first planted). All are native to Asia Minor, and they are readily available at Middle Eastern or Greek markets for flavoring your baking items. Springtide motifs, such as flowers, leaves, or berries, fashioned from excess dough will transform these rich festival loaves into objects of art.

1. In a medium saucepan or microwave-safe bowl, combine ½ cup of the milk and all the butter. Heat on the stove top or in the microwave, stirring occasionally, until the butter is melted. Let the mixture cool until warm, 105° to 115°F. Pour the remaining ½ cup warm milk in a small bowl. Sprinkle the yeast and a pinch of sugar over the surface of the milk. Stir to dissolve and let stand at room temperature until foamy, about 10 minutes.

2. In a large bowl using a whisk or in the work bowl of a heavy-duty electric mixer fitted with the paddle attachment, beat the remaining sugar and the eggs until light colored, about 1 minute. Add the olive oil, vanilla, salt, *nigella*, *mahlep*, and mastic, the warm milk-butter mixture, yeast mixture, and 2 cups of the flour. Beat for 2 minutes. Add the remaining flour; ½ cup at a time, until a soft dough forms that just clears the sides of the bowl. Switch to a wooden spoon when necessary if making by hand.

3. Turn the dough out onto a lightly floured work surface and knead until smooth, translucent, and elastic, about 3 minutes, dusting with flour only 1 tablespoon at a time as needed to prevent sticking. It is important that this dough remain soft and springy.

If kneading by machine, switch from the paddle to the dough hook and knead for 2 to 3 minutes, or until the dough is smooth and elastic and springs back when pressed. If desired, transfer the dough to a floured surface and knead briefly by hand.

4. Place the dough in a greased deep container. Turn once to coat the top and cover tightly with plastic wrap. Let rise at cool temperature about 6 hours, deflating 3 times or as necessary.

5. Gently deflate the dough. Turn the dough out on a lightly floured work surface. Grease or parchment-line two baking sheets. Divide the dough into 4 equal portions. Form each portion into a smooth, tight, round loaf. Place the loaves on the baking sheets (these loaves will rise to almost triple in bulk during baking). Cover loosely with plastic wrap and let rise at room temperature until doubled in bulk, 45 minutes to 1 hour.

6. Twenty minutes before baking, preheat the oven to 350°F. Brush the loaves with the egg glaze and sprinkle with the sesame seeds. Place the baking sheets on center racks of the oven and bake both trays as close to the center of the oven as possible, switching positions halfway during baking, for 35 to 40 minutes, or until browned and a cake tester inserted into the center comes out clean. Or, bake on 1 sheet at a time and keep the other baking sheet refrigerated for 30 minutes before baking. Transfer the loaves to a cooling rack. Cool completely before slicing.

Kulich with Almonds and Ginger
Russian Easter Coffee Cake

Makes two 7-inch tall loaves

1/4 cup golden raisins

1/4 cup dried cherries

1/4 cup finely chopped dried apricots or unsweetened, unsulfured dried papaya

1/4 cup orange brandy, Grand Marnier, or flavored vodka

Sponge

1 tablespoon (1 package) active dry yeast

1/4 cup lukewarm water (100°F)

1/2 cup lukewarm milk or light cream (100°F)

1 cup unbleached all-purpose flour

Dough

3 large eggs

2 teaspoons pure vanilla extract

2 teaspoons salt

1/2 cup sugar

2 3/4 to 3 1/4 cups unbleached all-purpose flour

Kulich, a classic coffee cake made for the Russian Orthodox Easter, has a tall shape rather like a puffy mushroom. It is served by slicing off the top puff and placing it on a serving plate. Then the body is sliced in half vertically, each half is cut into 1/2-inch-thick slices, and the slices are arranged around the top piece. Serve the bread with Paskha (recipe follows), the uncooked cheese cake traditionally served with kulich for the Orthodox Easter.

1. In a small bowl, combine the raisins, cherries, and apricots with the brandy. Cover and macerate at room temperature while preparing the sponge, about 1 hour.

2. To prepare the sponge: In a large bowl with a whisk or in the work bowl of a heavy-duty electric mixer fitted with the paddle attachment, combine the yeast, warm water, warm milk, and flour. Beat hard until smooth, about 1 minute. Cover with plastic wrap and let rest at room temperature until bubbly, about 1 hour.

3. To prepare the dough: Add the eggs, vanilla, salt, sugar, and 1 cup of the flour to the sponge. Beat until smooth. Add the butter, a few pieces at a time, and beat until incorporated. Stir in the macerated fruit and its liquor. Add the remaining flour, 1/2 cup at a time, until a soft dough that just clears the sides of the bowl is formed. Switch to a wooden spoon when necessary if making by hand.

4. Turn the dough out onto a lightly floured work surface and knead until smooth, shiny, and soft, 2 to 3 minutes, dusting with flour only 1 tablespoon at a time as needed to prevent sticking. It is important that this dough remain very soft and pliable.

If kneading by machine, switch from the paddle to the dough hook and knead for 2 to 3 minutes, or until the dough is smooth, shiny and soft, and springs back when pressed. If desired, transfer the dough to a floured surface and knead briefly by hand.

4 tablespoons
(½ stick) unsalted
butter, at room
temperature, cut
into pieces

½ cup (2 ounces)
almonds, lightly
toasted and chopped

⅓ cup finely chopped
crystallized ginger
(about 1½ ounces)

1 tablespoon unsalted
butter, melted,
for brushing

Powdered sugar,
for dusting

Paskha (recipe
follows), for serving
(optional)

5. Place the dough in a greased deep container. Turn once to coat the top and cover with plastic wrap. Let rise at room temperature until doubled in bulk, 1½ to 2 hours.

6. Gently deflate the dough. Turn the dough out onto a floured work surface. Grease two 7-inch charlotte molds, 5-pound honey tins, or 2-pound coffee cans. Pat the dough into a fat rectangle. Sprinkle with the almonds and ginger. Fold the dough over and knead gently to distribute the nuts and ginger evenly. Divide the dough into 2 equal portions. Place each portion in a greased mold, tin, or can. Cover loosely with buttered plastic wrap and let rise until about ½ inch above the rims of the pans, about 40 minutes.

7. Twenty minutes before baking, preheat the oven to 350°F. Place the pans on the lowest rack of the oven and bake 35 to 40 minutes, or until golden brown and a cake tester inserted into the center comes out clean. If the tops brown too quickly, cover loosely with a piece of aluminum foil. Transfer the loaves immediately to a cooling rack. *(At this point, kulich may be wrapped airtight and frozen up to 3 months. Thaw in the wrapping and rewarm in a 350°F oven for 20 minutes, then decorate.)* Brush the warm tops with melted butter and dust with powdered sugar. Cool completely and serve at room temperature.

1 cup heavy cream

1½ teaspoons pure vanilla extract or finely minced vanilla bean

2 tablespoons fruit liqueur, such as apricot, pear, or raspberry

2½ pounds fresh farmer cheese

1 cup (2 sticks) unsalted butter at room temperature

2 large egg yolks or commercial liquid egg substitute equivalent

1 cup superfine sugar

Grated zest of 1 orange and 1 lemon

¼ cup dried currants

¼ cup golden raisins

¼ cup minced dried apricots

¼ cup minced dried pineapple

½ cup (2 ounces) slivered blanched almonds

PASKHA

In lieu of a carved, truncated wooden paskha mold, a mesh or metal colander with the capacity of about 2½ quarts will do nicely. A cone-shaped chinois strainer is close to the traditional shape, right down to its planed tip. Paskha must sit in the refrigerator for 2 days. It will drain off a surprising amount of liquid, so place the mold over a shallow bowl and cover it with plastic wrap to protect the delicate flavors.

1. In a large bowl, pour in the cream and whip with the vanilla and liqueur until soft peaks form. Set aside. In another large bowl using a spoon or electric mixer, combine the cheese and butter, beating until fluffy and well blended. Add the yolks, one at a time, and beat in the sugar. Add the whipped cream mixture and the zests, fruits, and nuts. Mix just to combine evenly.

2. Line a traditional paskha mold or clean flower pot with 2 layers of damp cheesecloth, with the excess cloth hanging over the edge. Spoon the cheese mixture into the mold, filling it to the brim. Fold the edges of the cloth over the cheese. Cover with plastic wrap and place a heavy object, such as a foil-wrapped brick, on the cheese. Place over a shallow bowl and refrigerate from overnight to 2 days.

3. To unmold, place a serving plate over the mold and invert. Gently lift off the mold and remove the cheesecloth. Stud the sides with slivered blanched almonds radiating down the sides from the top. Serve immediately or refrigerate until serving time. (*Refrigerate any leftovers immediately and store, tightly wrapped, for up to 4 days.*)

American Chocolate Bread

Makes eight 4½-by-2½-inch loaves

Sponge

2 tablespoons (2 packages) active dry yeast

2 tablespoons sugar

1 cup warm water (105° to 115°F)

1½ cups unbleached all-purpose flour or bread flour

Dough

1 cup warm milk (105° to 115°F)

5 tablespoons unsalted butter, melted

1 tablespoon salt

4 to 4½ cups unbleached all-purpose flour or bread flour

8 ounces semisweet chocolate

3 tablespoons Vanilla Powdered Sugar (page 303), or powdered sugar

Chocolate bread is more of a little morning loaf than Bread with Three Chocolates. It is less rich than pain au chocolat made from croissant dough (page 284). If you like, spread a tablespoon of seedless raspberry preserves under each piece of chocolate before forming the loaf. The small pans make perfect individual loaves.

1. In a large bowl using a whisk or in the work bowl of a heavy-duty electric mixer fitted with the paddle attachment, place the yeast, sugar, water, and 1½ cups flour. Beat until smooth, about 3 minutes. Cover and let stand in a warm place until doubled in bulk, about 1 hour.

2. Stir down the sponge with a wooden spoon. Add 1 cup milk, 3 tablespoons butter, salt, and 1 cup flour. Beat hard until smooth, about 2 minutes. Add the flour, ½ cup at a time, to form a soft dough.

3. Turn the dough out onto a lightly floured work surface and knead for about 5 minutes, adding 1 tablespoon of flour at a time as necessary until dough just loses its stickiness. It will be soft and springy.

If kneading by machine, switch from the paddle to the dough hook and knead for 4 to 5 minutes, or until the dough is smooth and springy and springs back when pressed. If desired, transfer the dough to a floured surface and knead briefly by hand.

4. Place the dough in a greased bowl. Turn once to coat top and cover with plastic wrap. Let rise in a warm place until doubled in bulk, about 1 hour.

5. Grease eight 4½-by-2½-inch loaf pans. Cut the chocolate into 1-ounce portions. Gently deflate dough. Turn the dough out on a lightly floured work surface and divide into 8 equal portions. Pat each portion out into a 7-by-4-inch rectangle about ¾ inch to 1 inch thick. Place a piece of chocolate at short edge of each dough portion and roll the dough up jelly roll fashion. Pinch the edges to seal and completely enclose chocolate. Arrange each roll in a loaf pan, cover loosely with plastic wrap, and let rise until almost doubled, about 15 minutes.

6. Twenty minutes before baking, preheat the oven to 375°F. Brush the loaves with the remaining 2 tablespoons butter and sprinkle with about 1 teaspoon sugar to sparkle the crust. Place the pans in the oven and bake 20 to 25 minutes, or until a delicate brown. Transfer the loaves to a cooling rack for 20 minutes. Serve warm.

Hot Cross Buns with Dried Fruit and Two Glazes

Makes 18 buns

3/4 cup warm water (105° to 115°F)

1 tablespoon (1 package) active dry yeast

1/3 cup sugar

1 cup warm milk (105° to 115°F)

8 tablespoons (1 stick) unsalted butter, melted

1 teaspoon salt

3 large eggs

3 1/2 to 4 cups unbleached all-purpose flour

1 cup dried currants

1/2 cup chopped dried apricots

1/2 teaspoon ground mace

1/2 teaspoon pure vanilla extract

Sugar Glaze

1/4 cup sugar

1/2 cup water

Lemon Icing

1 cup sifted powdered sugar

1 teaspoon fresh lemon juice

1 teaspoon grated lemon zest

1 1/2 tablespoons milk

Little Celtic breads decorated with a Greek-style cross are a very old tradition. The symbolic gesture of the cross can be emphasized by layering thin bands of pastry over the top. Decorate the buns with lemon icing over a shiny sugar glaze for Easter weekend. This is a traditional home-baked English specialty popular since the Elizabethan era.

1. Pour the warm water in a small bowl. Sprinkle the yeast and a pinch of sugar over the surface of the water. Stir to dissolve and let stand at room temperature until foamy, about 10 minutes.

2. In a large bowl using a whisk or in the work bowl of a heavy-duty electric mixer fitted with the paddle attachment, combine the milk, butter, sugar, salt, eggs, and 1 cup of the flour. Beat hard for 1 minute. Add the yeast mixture, dried fruits, spice, vanilla, and 1 cup more flour. Beat until well mixed, about 1 minute. Add the remaining flour, 1/2 cup at a time, until a soft dough that just clears the sides of the bowl is formed. Switch to a wooden spoon when necessary if mixing by hand.

3. Turn the dough out onto a lightly floured work surface and knead until soft, smooth, and springy, about 3 minutes, dusting with flour only 1 tablespoon at a time as needed to prevent sticking. Push back in any fruit that falls out during needing.

If kneading by machine, switch from the paddle to the dough hook and knead for 2 to 3 minutes, or until the dough is soft, smooth, and springy and springs back when pressed. If desired, transfer the dough to a floured surface and knead briefly by hand.

4. Place the dough in a greased deep container. Turn once to coat the top and cover with plastic wrap. Let rise at room temperature until doubled in bulk, 1 to 1 1/2 hours.

5. Meanwhile, prepare the sugar glaze: In a heavy saucepan, combine the sugar and water. Boil, uncovered, for 5 minutes. Use immediately, or store in a covered jar in the refrigerator, then reheat to boiling before using.

6. To prepare the lemon icing: In a small bowl, combine the powdered sugar, lemon juice, lemon zest, and milk. Beat hard with a whisk until smooth. The icing should be a bit firm for piping.

7. Gently deflate the dough. Turn the dough out onto the floured work surface. Grease or parchment-line a baking sheet. Divide the dough into 2 equal portions. Roll each portion into a 10-inch-long log and, with a sharp knife, cut into 9 equal portions. Form each portion into a round bun and place each bun about 1½ inches apart on the baking sheet. Let rise, uncovered, at room temperature until doubled in bulk, about 30 minutes.

8. Twenty minutes before baking, preheat the oven to 375°F. With a sharp knife, cut a cross no more than ½ inch deep over the surface of each bun. Place the baking sheet on a rack in the center of the oven and bake for 15 to 20 minutes, or until browned and the buns sound hollow when tapped with your finger. Remove the buns immediately to a cooling rack. Brush the buns immediately with the glaze. Let cool. When the glaze is dry, place the icing in a pastry bag fitted with a small, plain tip and pipe a cross over the top of each bun. Let stand for at least 20 minutes to set.

Golden Rum Babas

Makes 12 babas

½ cup dried currants or dried cherries

3 tablespoons golden rum

Dough

1 tablespoon (1 package) active dry yeast

1 tablespoon granulated sugar

¼ cup warm water (105° to 115°F)

2 cups unbleached all-purpose flour

4 large eggs, at room temperature

1 teaspoon salt

8 tablespoons (1 stick) unsalted butter, cut into 16 pieces

Soaking Syrup

1¼ cups sugar

½ cup golden rum

Apricot Glaze

1 cup apricot jam

1 tablespoon golden rum

Vanilla Whipped Cream

¾ cup heavy cream, chilled

1 tablespoon powdered or superfine sugar

½ teaspoon pure vanilla extract

The baba, invented by King Stanilas Lezzinki, was named after Ali Baba, the hero of Arabian Nights fame. Here is the classic version with rum, but other popular variations call for orange or peach brandy, framboise, or kirsch. The baba and its near relative, the savarin, are light and spongy, moist and delicate. They are remarkably easy to prepare, because they require no kneading. Babas are baked in small 3-inch molds that look like the Turkish cap called a fez. The molds are readily available in specialty cookware stores. To make this dough in a bread machine, see page 465.

1. Place the currants or dried cherries in a small jar or bowl and add the rum. Let stand from 1 hour to as long as overnight at room temperature to macerate.

2. To prepare the dough: Pour the warm water in a small bowl. Sprinkle the yeast and a pinch of sugar over the surface of the water. Stir to dissolve and let stand at room temperature until foamy, about 10 minutes.

3. In a large bowl using a whisk, or in the work bowl of a heavy-duty electric mixer fitted with the paddle attachment, add the flour and make a well in the center. Add the eggs, sugar, and salt to the well. Gradually mix a few tablespoons of the flour into the eggs. Add the yeast mixture and beat until a soft, sticky dough is formed. Beat until smooth, about 3 minutes.

4. Place the dough in a greased container and sprinkle the butter pieces over the top. Cover with plastic wrap and let rise at room temperature until doubled in bulk, about 1 hour.

5. Fold the butter into the dough and gently slap the dough against the sides of the bowl until completely incorporated. The dough and butter will be about the same temperature during the mixing. Fold in the macerated fruit with its liquid.

6. Generously grease twelve ½-cup baba molds or standard muffin cups. Spoon enough batter in to fill each mold one-third to one-half full (about 3 tablespoons). Do not overfill or the babas will not rise and expand properly during baking. Press the dough lightly into the bottom of each mold. If using baba molds, arrange them on a baking sheet about 2 inches apart. Let the dough rise, uncovered, at room temperature until even with the rims of the molds, about 45 minutes.

7. Twenty minutes before baking, preheat the oven to 375°F. Place the baking sheet on the center rack of the preheated oven and bake the babas 15 minutes, or until a cake tester inserted into the center comes out clean and the sides are brown and have shrunk from the molds slightly. Unmold the babas onto a rack and let cool completely. *(The babas may be wrapped and stored at room temperature up to 2 days at this point.)*

8. To prepare the soaking syrup: In a medium, heavy saucepan, combine 2 cups water and the sugar. Heat slowly over low heat until the sugar dissolves, swirling occasionally. Raise the heat and bring to a boil. Immediately remove from the heat and pour into a heatproof bowl. Place a cooled baba into the hot syrup and ladle the syrup gradually over the cake to moisten the surface evenly. Do this only for about 5 seconds or the baba will be soggy. Using a slotted spoon, transfer the baba to a rack placed over a baking sheet to catch the drips. Repeat with the remaining babas, reheating the syrup, if necessary, because the syrup is more easily absorbed when hot. Let the babas stand at room temperature for 30 minutes to dry.

9. Place the babas on a large plate and spoon about 2 teaspoons rum over each one. Put back on the rack to dry.

10. Meanwhile, prepare the apricot glaze: Purée the apricot jam in a blender or a food processor until smooth. Transfer to a small, heavy saucepan and add 2 tablespoons water and the rum. Heat just until warm. Using a small brush, apply the glaze over the entire surface of each baba to seal in the liquor. Place the babas on a serving platter as each one is finished. Refrigerate, tightly covered, until ready to serve.

11. One hour before serving, make the vanilla whipped cream. In a small bowl, whip the cream with the sugar and vanilla until soft peaks form. Scoop into a pastry bag fitted with a large star tip. Pipe a large rosette of cream on top of each baba. *(Babas are best served the day they are made, but will keep refrigerated up to 2 days.)*

Orange Savarin with Berries

Makes one 9-inch ring cake

- 1 tablespoon (1 package) active dry yeast
- 4 teaspoons sugar
- 1/4 cup warm water (105° to 115°F)
- 2 cups unbleached all-purpose flour
- 4 large eggs
- 1 teaspoon salt
- 8 tablespoons (1 stick) unsalted butter, cut into 16 pieces, softened

Orange Syrup

- 3/4 cup sugar
- 1/2 cup fresh orange juice

Apricot Glaze

- 1 cup apricot jam

Berries

- 2 1/2 cups strawberries, cherries, raspberries, blueberries, or blackberries or a combination
- 1/4 cup sugar
- 1/4 cup rum or fruit liqueur or spirit

Whipped Cream

- 1 cup heavy cream
- 1 tablespoon sugar
- 1 tablespoon rum or fruit liqueur or spirit

Savarin is a superb French yeast cake soaked in spirits and served as dessert after a light meal. It should be eaten the day it is made, when it is moist and quite delicate. Savarin is good by itself with just whipped cream. If you use berries, match them with a complementary spirit, such as Grand Marnier with strawberries, kirsch with cherries, Chambord, rum, or framboise with raspberries.

1. Pour the warm water in a small bowl. Sprinkle the yeast and 1 teaspoon of the sugar over the surface of the water. Stir to dissolve and let stand at room temperature until foamy, about 10 minutes.

2. In a large bowl using a whisk or in the work bowl of a heavy-duty electric mixer using the paddle attachment, place the flour and make a well in center. Add the eggs, the remaining sugar, and salt. Gradually mix a few tablespoons of flour into the eggs. Add the yeast mixture and beat until a sticky, soft dough is formed. Beat until smooth, about 3 minutes.

3. Place the dough in a greased bowl and sprinkle butter pieces over the top. Cover with plastic wrap and let rise at room temperature until doubled in bulk, about 1 hour.

4. Fold the butter into dough and gently slap the dough against the sides of the bowl until incorporated completely. The dough and butter will be about the same temperature during mixing.

5. Generously grease a 5-cup savarin or 9-inch metal ring mold. Spoon enough batter in to full the mold one half full. Cover with plastic wrap and let rise at room temperature about 25 minutes, until even with the rim of the pan. Remove the plastic wrap and let rise 20 minutes more.

6. Twenty minutes before baking, preheat the oven to 375°F. Place the mold on a rack in the center of the oven and bake 30 to 35 minutes, or until a cake tester inserted in the center comes out clean. Cool in the pan 5 minutes. Loosen the edges and turn out onto a rack to cool completely. *(The cake may be wrapped and stored at room temperature up to 3 days at this point.)*

7. To make the orange syrup: Combine the sugar and ¾ cup water in a small pan and heat until the sugar is dissolved, about 5 minutes. Add the orange juice. Heat to boiling and ladle over the cake until the syrup is absorbed. Let stand at room temperature about 1 hour.

8. To make the apricot glaze: Whirl the apricot jam in a blender or food processor until smooth. In a small pan, heat the jam to a boil. Brush the cake with the hot apricot glaze to seal in the moisture. Slide the cake (or use 2 spatulas to lift the cake) onto a serving platter. It can be refrigerated at this time for a few hours before serving.

9. Combine the berries, sugar, and liqueur in a medium bowl. Let stand about 10 minutes. Whip the cream with the sugar and liqueur until soft peaks form. To serve, spoon berry mixture into the center of the savarin. Garnish the top of berries with whipped cream.

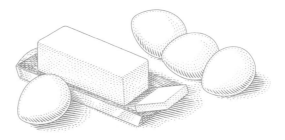

Hungarian Sweet Cheese Bread

Makes 2 small Bundt cakes

Dough

1½ tablespoons (1½ packages) active dry yeast

½ cup sugar

½ cup warm water (105° to 115°F)

1 cup (2 sticks) unsalted butter, at room temperature

4 large eggs

1 cup (8 ounces) sour cream

1 teaspoon salt

Grated zest of 1 lemon

5½ to 6 cups unbleached all-purpose flour

Cheese Filling

8 ounces cream cheese, at room temperature

8 ounces fresh goat cheese, at room temperature

1 cup sugar or Vanilla Sugar (see page 303)

4 large eggs

1 tablespoon fresh lemon juice

This recipe became a standard in my teaching repertoire and was consistently voted the favorite sweet bread. Do not worry about the shaping technique; the dough is pliable and easily handled. Sour cream is a common ingredient in European sweet doughs; its acidity and richness lend a unique tangy flavor and smooth texture.

1. Pour the warm water in a small bowl. Sprinkle the yeast and a pinch of the sugar over the surface of the water. Stir to dissolve and let stand at room temperature until foamy, about 10 minutes.

2. In a large bowl using a wooden spoon or in the bowl of a heavy-duty electric mixer fitted with the paddle attachment, cream the butter with the sugar until smooth. Add the eggs, one at a time, and beat until incorporated. Add the yeast mixture, the sour cream, salt, lemon zest, and 2 cups of the flour. Beat until a smooth batter is formed, about 2 minutes. Add the remaining flour, ½ cup at a time, until a soft dough that just clears the sides of the bowl is formed. Switch to a wooden spoon when necessary if making by hand.

3. Turn the dough out onto a lightly floured work surface and knead until a very soft, springy dough is formed, 4 to 5 minutes for a hand-mixed dough, 1 to 3 minutes for a machine-mixed dough, dusting with flour only 1 tablespoon at a time, just enough to prevent sticking. This dough is very rich and does not require a long kneading time; it can easily absorb too much flour. Take care to keep the dough as soft as possible.

If kneading by machine, switch from the paddle to the dough hook and knead for 4 to 5 minutes, or until the dough is smooth and springy and springs back when pressed. If desired, transfer the dough to a floured surface and knead briefly by hand.

4. Place the dough in a greased deep container. Turn once to coat the top and cover with plastic wrap. Let rise at room temperature until doubled in bulk, about 1½ hours.

5. To prepare the cheese filling: In a medium bowl with a wooden spoon or the an electric mixer, beat the cheeses until smooth. Add the

3/4 cup apricot jam,
    puréed in a blender
    or food processor
    until smooth

3 tablespoons brandy,
    Cognac, or orange
    liqueur

sugar and beat until fluffy. Add the eggs, one at a time, beating well after each addition. Add the lemon juice. Refrigerate until needed.

6. Gently deflate the dough. Generously brush 2 mini Bundt pans with melted butter. Turn the dough out onto a floured work surface. Divide the dough in half. With a rolling pin, roll 1 portion of the dough into a 12-inch circle about ½ to ¾ inch thick. Fold in half and place over half of the prepared pan. Unfold the dough and carefully fit it into the bottom with 2 to 3 inches of dough hanging over the edge of the mold. The center tube will be covered by the dough. Repeat the procedure with the other portion of the dough. Divide the cheese filling between the 2 pans and spread out evenly. Lift the overhanging dough back over the filling and place in overlapping folds to cover it. Press the folded edges against the inside tube to encase the filling. Using kitchen shears, cut an **X** in the dough covering the center tube. Fold each triangle back over the folds of the dough. Repeat with the second pan. Cover loosely with plastic wrap and set aside at room temperature to rise for 30 minutes, or until dough comes to ¼ inch below the top rim of the pans.

7. Twenty minutes before baking, preheat the oven to 350°F. Place the pans on a rack in the center of the oven and bake 35 to 40 minutes, or until quite brown and a cake tester inserted in the center comes out clean. Let cool in the pan for 10 minutes. While the cake is cooling in the pan, prepare the glaze. Combine the jam and brandy in a small saucepan and heat to boiling. Turn the loaves out onto a cooling rack. After turning the cake out of the pan, immediately brush the glaze over the entire surface of the warm pastry two times. Let cool for at least 1 hour before slicing.

Bread with Three Chocolates

Makes 2 round loaves

1 cup warm water
(105° to 115°F)

1 tablespoon
(1 package)
dry active yeast

½ cup sugar

5½ to 6 cups unbleached all-
purpose flour or
bread flour

½ cup unsweetened
Dutch process cocoa
powder

2 teaspoons instant
espresso powder

2 teaspoons salt

1 cup warm milk (105°
to 115°F)

6 tablespoons (¾
stick) unsalted
butter, melted

2 large eggs

5 ounces semisweet or
bittersweet
chocolate, chopped

2 ounces milk
chocolate, chopped

The first bread I bought at Il Fornaio bakery in San Francisco was a yeasted Italian chocolate loaf. In my desire to duplicate its unusual flavor and texture, this special-occasion bread was born. Use only the best chocolate for this: good brands include Callebaut, Tobler, Sharffen Berger, Perugina, Van Houten, and Dröste.

1. Pour ½ cup warm water in a small bowl. Sprinkle the yeast and a pinch of the sugar over the surface of the water. Stir to dissolve and let stand at room temperature until foamy, about 10 minutes.

2. In a large bowl using a whisk or in the work bowl of a heavy-duty electric mixer fitted with the paddle attachment, combine 2 cups flour, the remaining sugar, cocoa, espresso, and salt. Add remaining the warm water, the milk, butter, and eggs. Beat hard until smooth and add the yeast mixture. Beat until smooth, about 2 minutes. Add the chopped chocolate with a wooden spoon. Add the remaining flour, ½ cup at a time, until a shaggy dough that just clears the sides of the bowl is formed. Take care not to break up chocolate too much.

3. Turn the dough out onto a lightly floured work surface and knead for about 5 minutes, dusting with flour only 1 tablespoon at a time as needed to make a smooth, silky dough.

If kneading by machine, switch from the paddle to the dough hook and knead for 4 to 5 minutes, or until the dough is smooth and springy and springs back when pressed. If desired, transfer the dough to a floured surface and knead briefly by hand.

4. Place the dough in a greased bowl. Turn once to grease the top and cover with plastic wrap. Let rise in a warm place until doubled in bulk, 1 to 1½ hours.

5. Gently deflate the dough. Turn the dough out onto a lightly floured work surface. Grease two 6-cup charlotte molds, 8-inch ovenproof casseroles, or springform pans. Divide the dough into 2 equal portions. Shape the portions into round loaves and place the loaves in the molds, casseroles or pans. Cover loosely with plastic wrap and let rise to 1 inch above the rim of the pans, about 30 minutes.

6. Twenty minutes before baking, preheat the oven to 375°F. Place the containers on a rack in the center of the oven and bake 40 to 45 minutes, or until crusty and a cake tester inserted in the center comes out clean. Transfer the loaves to a cooling rack. Cut into wedges to serve.

FAST AND BEAUTIFUL:
Food Processor Breads

If you don't own a heavy-duty electric mixer, avoid hand kneading at all costs, and haven't been able to connect with an electronic bread machine, a food processor might be just your tool for mixing yeast doughs. Your work space stays incredibly clean; the dough is mixed in just a few minutes; and the method fits right into the fast-paced preparation time we have come to expect in today's kitchen. The food processor is perfect for making one or two small loaves and very efficient for mixing otherwise very stiff whole-grain rich doughs.

A dough that would take ten to fifteen minutes to make and knead by hand and five to eight minutes with a heavy-duty electric mixer is done in one to two minutes with the processor. The dough still has to rise, be shaped, and rise again (a second rise is important for developing texture), and, of course, be baked. The machine does the work while you retain maximum creative license.

Check the manufacturer's instructions for specifics on your machine before making dough in it, because some processors have a motor that is too weak for bread dough. Also, be sure your machine can process the amount of dough you want to make. A small processor can handle about 3 to 4 cups of flour and up to 1½ cups of liquid, for one medium or two small loaves. The capacity of a standard-size food processor is 6 to 7 cups total of flour and 2½ cups of liquid. The following "Big Four" make the size machine that is best for home baking: Cuisinart, Sunbeam, KitchenAid, and Robot Coupe. Never exceed the directed amounts, because the machine will not be able to mix the dough properly. If you own the largest machine, which handles up to 10 cups of flour and is marketed by Cuisinart, the recipes that follow can be tripled. Otherwise, the recipes can be made as written or doubled.

The following techniques are critical for successful food processor bread doughs.

- All types of flour are measured by the dip-and-sweep method: Spoon the flour from its bag into a dry measuring cup as a heaping measure (this aerates it slightly; no need to ever sift) and level off the top with a knife; never tap, shake, or compress the flour in the measuring cup. Since the amount of moisture that flour retains varies, you may need a little more or less flour than called for in the recipe. You may also need a little more or less liquid.

- Cool or lukewarm water (80° to 100°F) is used for the dough. This may seem unusual for a yeast dough but the fast action of the processor blade raises the temperature of the dough rapidly. Doughs can overheat and kill the delicate yeast and end its leavening power.

- If a dough is too sticky (the machine may slow down and sound like it is straining), stop the machine and let the dough rest for five to eight minutes to absorb some of the moisture. Scrape the dough from the sides into the center and sprinkle with 1 to 2 tablespoons of flour and process until a smooth ball is formed. Whole-grain doughs will always be stickier than all-white flour doughs.

- Unless otherwise instructed, add liquids as slowly as possible in a steady stream through the feed tube, otherwise the dough can become moist at the bottom and dry at the top. Pouring slowly allows you the most control over the consistency of the dough batter.

- If the dough gets too dry and stiff, remove it and cut it into quarters, return it to the machine, and sprinkle with 1 to 2 tablespoons of liquid; process, adding more liquid in increments, until smooth. This is important to produce a bread that is not too dense.

- If the machine shuts down, unplug it immediately and remove the dough to finish kneading by hand. (Food processors are designed to shut down temporarily when they overheat. They can be turned back on after a short rest.)

When a recipe calls for dotting an ingredient, such as butter, in a circle around the work bowl, that assures it will be evenly distributed during the mixing. Dried fruit and nuts, though, should be folded in or kneaded in after the dough is removed from the machine. The processing action of the machine makes using whole spices and herbs very easy.

I find finishing off with a few hand kneads assures me, by my sense of touch, that the dough is as smooth and silky as I desire, and any adjustments can easily be made by hand.

Use the metal all-purpose blade, rather than the plastic dough blade, for maximum efficiency in mixing yeast doughs. Use a plastic spatula for scraping down the sides of the work bowl and a plastic dough card for removing the dough ball, taking care to secure the blade by putting your fingers in the casing underneath to anchor it. If there are two pulse options on your machine, use the normal pulsing action. Count "One Mississippi, two Mississippi," et cetera, for each second, or keep a clock with a sweep second hand nearby.

BAKER'S WISDOM
Mixing Dough in the Food Processor

Each recipe will direct you to mix the dough by one of these two methods:

The Liquid Sponge Method: This can be done two ways. The direct method is to dissolve the yeast in part of the liquid and let it proof until foamy. The yeast mixture is then added to the dry ingredients with the remaining liquids through the feed tube. In the sponge starter method, the yeast is combined with some liquid and flour and left to ferment for 2 to 12 hours before the sponge is added to the dry ingredients and remaining liquids. This batter technique adds flavor and texture to a dough.

The Dry Mix Method: Also known as RapidMix, this method calls for combining the yeast with all of the remaining dry ingredients. Very warm liquid (110° to 120°) is added in a slow stream through the feed tube to process the dough.

Milling Whole Grains in the Food Processor

Home milling is a subject all serious bakers touch upon one time or another. Because home grinders, both electric and hand, are bulky and expensive (except for the grain-grinding attachment to the KitchenAid stand mixer), most bakers make do with commercial flours and processed whole grains. But there is a technique, unique to the food processor, that allows soaking and processing very hard whole grains such as wheat berries before adding them as a "dry" ingredient. The technique also works with commercially grown wild rice, jasmine rice, cracked wheat, cracked millet, oat groats, rye berries, partially cooked hominy, whole pearled barley, and coarse cracked-grain cereal blends.

To Process Whole Grains
Soak ½ to I cup whole grains in half the amount of boiling water (¼ to ½ cup) for at least 3 to 4 hours, or as long as overnight at room temperature. Process in the food processor until the grains are finely ground or form a sticky purée. Remove from the work bowl and set aside until needed. Dot the processed grain in a circle on top of the dry ingredients in the work bowl, or process initially with a small amount of flour, then add with all of the dry ingredients.

Sesame White Bread

¾ cup lukewarm milk (105° to 115°F)

2½ teaspoons active dry yeast

½ teaspoon sugar

3 cups bread flour

1 teaspoon salt

2 tablespoons unsalted butter, at room temperature, cut into pieces

1 large egg

3 tablespoons sesame seeds

The combination of strong motor-driven kneading and the rising power of egg results in a white bread that is rich in flavor and close textured. Sesame seeds add flavor and crunch to this simple loaf. Bake it in a clay pan if you have one; it will produce a thicker, crispier crust than a metal pan. This is old-fashioned American baking at its best.

1. In a 2-cup liquid measure, pour in the lukewarm milk. Sprinkle the yeast and sugar over the surface of the warm milk. Stir to dissolve and let stand at room temperature, until foamy, about 10 minutes.

2. In the work bowl of the food processor fitted with the metal blade, combine the flour, and salt. Dot the top with the butter pieces. Process for 5 seconds. With the motor running, immediately pour the yeast-milk mixture and the egg through the feed tube in a steady stream as fast as the flour mixture will absorb it. After the dough forms a soft, elastic ball and clears the sides of the bowl, process 45 seconds more to knead. If the dough is too sticky, add flour by the tablespoonful. If it is too dry, add water by the teaspoonful.

3. Using a plastic dough scraper, transfer the dough ball to a clean work surface and give a few kneads by hand to even out the dough consistency.

4. Place the dough into a lightly greased container. Turn once to grease the top and cover with plastic wrap. Let rise at room temperature until doubled in bulk, about 1 hour.

5. Turn the dough out onto a floured work surface. Grease an 8½-by-4½-inch clay or metal loaf pan. Shape the dough into an oblong loaf. Place the sesame seeds on a piece of wax paper or a plate and roll the entire loaf in the seeds, coating it heavily. Place the loaf in the pan. Cover loosely with plastic wrap and let rise again at room temperature until it reaches 1 inch above the top of the pan, 45 minutes.

6. Twenty minutes before baking, preheat the oven to 375°F. Using a sharp knife, slash 1 long crease lengthwise across the top, no more than ½ inch deep. Place the pan on the center rack of the oven and bake 40 to 45 minutes, or until lightly browned and the bottom sounds hollow when tapped with your finger. Transfer the loaf immediately to a cooling rack. Cool before slicing.

Buttermilk Whole-Wheat Bread

Makes one 8½-by-4½-inch loaf

- ¼ cup lukewarm water (105° to 115°F)
- 2½ teaspoons active dry yeast
- ½ teaspoon sugar
- 2 cups whole-wheat flour
- 1 cup bread flour
- ¼ cup dry buttermilk powder
- 1 teaspoon salt
- 3 tablespoons unsalted butter, room temperature, cut into pieces
- 3 tablespoons unsulfured molasses
- ¾ cup cool water (80°F)

Shaping the dough into a two-strand twist, one of the most enticing ways to form a loaf, seems to help it rise higher. Using buttermilk powder makes it possible to assemble this loaf on the spur of the moment from pantry ingredients. This is your toast and sandwich loaf.

1. In a 2-cup liquid measure, pour in the lukewarm water. Sprinkle the yeast and sugar over the surface of the water. Stir to dissolve and let stand at room temperature 10 minutes.

2. In the work bowl of the food processor fitted with the metal blade, combine the flours, buttermilk powder, and salt. Dot the top with the butter pieces. Process for 5 seconds. Add the molasses and cool water to the yeast mixture. With the motor running, immediately pour the liquid through the feed tube in a steady stream as fast as the flour mixture will absorb it. After the dough forms a soft, elastic ball and clears the sides of the bowl, process 45 seconds more to knead. If the dough is too sticky, add flour by the tablespoonful. If it is too dry, add water by the teaspoonful.

3. Using a plastic dough scraper, transfer the dough ball to a clean work surface. Give a few kneads by hand to even out the dough consistency.

4. Place the dough in a lightly greased container. Turn once to grease the top and cover with plastic wrap. Let rise at room temperature until doubled in bulk, about 1 hour.

5. Turn the dough out onto a floured work surface. Grease an 8½-by-4½-inch clay or metal loaf pan. Divide the dough into 2 equal portions. Pat the dough into fat logs about 8 inches long. Twist the 2 sections around each other and tuck the ends under. Place in the pan. Cover loosely with plastic wrap. Let rise again at room temperature until it reaches 1 inch above the top of the pan, about 45 minutes.

6. Twenty minutes before baking, preheat the oven to 375°F. Place the pan on a rack in the center of the oven and bake 35 to 40 minutes, or until lightly browned and the bottom sounds hollow when tapped with your finger. Transfer the loaves immediately to a cooling rack. Cool before slicing.

French Bread

Made in the Food Processor

Makes 1 round boule, 2 bâtards, 4 baguettes, or 8 petits pains

- 2½ teaspoons active dry yeast
- ½ teaspoon sugar
- ⅔ cup lukewarm water (105° to 115°F)
- 2½ cups all-purpose flour
- 1 cup unbleached bread flour
- ½ cup semolina flour
- 2 teaspoons salt
- 1 cup cool water (80°F)

    Yellow cornmeal, for sprinkling

- 1 egg white beaten with 1 teaspoon water, for glaze

This was the first bread my mom and I learned to make in the food processor. We took a class at Barbara Powers' cooking school in Saratoga, California, in the early 1980s and have made this bread and the Italian Whole Wheat (page 404) ever since. I added the semolina flour for extra flavor and texture.

1. In a 2-cup liquid measure, pour in the warm water. Stir the yeast and sugar over the surface of the water. Stir to dissolve and let stand at room temperature about 10 minutes.

2. In the work bowl of the food processor fitted with the metal blade, combine the all-purpose bread and semolina flours and salt. With the motor running, immediately pour the yeast mixture and the cool water through the feed tube in a steady stream as fast as the flour mixture will absorb it. After the dough forms a soft, elastic ball and clears the sides of the bowl, process 45 to 60 seconds more to knead. If the dough is too sticky, add flour by the tablespoonful. If it is too dry, add water by the teaspoonful.

3. Using a plastic dough scraper, transfer the dough ball to a clean work surface. Give a few kneads by hand to even out dough consistency.

4. Place the dough in a lightly greased container and turn once to grease the top. Cover with plastic wrap and let rise at room temperature until tripled in bulk, 1½ to 2 hours. The dough can be refrigerated overnight.

5. Turn the dough out onto a floured work surface. The boule, bâtards, and petits pains are best baked on a parchment-lined baking sheet sprinkled with cornmeal; the baguettes are best in well-greased baguette pans, sprinkled with cornmeal. Shape the dough into the desired loaves. Place on the baking sheet or baguette pan. Place the dough round, seam side up, on a clean floured dish towel or in a cloth-lined banneton, cover with the edges of the towel, and let rise. Cover loosely with plastic wrap, and let rest again at room temperature until tripled in bulk, about 1 hour 15 minutes.

6. Twenty minutes before baking, preheat the oven to 450°F, placing a baking stone on the lower third shelf. If rising on the towel or in a banneton, turn the dough out onto a wooden peel heavily sprinkled with cornmeal. Using a pastry brush, brush the tops of all the loaves with the egg glaze. Using a sharp knife, slash the surface a few times diagonally across the top, no more than ½ inch deep. Place the baking sheet or baguette pans directly on the stone, or with a quick action of the wrist, slide the loaf onto the baking stone. Reduce the oven thermostat to 425°F. Bake 1 round boule 35 to 40 minutes; the 2 bâtards bake 25 to 30 minutes; the baguettes bake 20 to 25 minutes; and the 8 petits pains bake 18 to 24 minutes, or until golden brown and the loaf sounds hollow when tapped with your finger. Transfer to a cooling rack. Eat the bread warm, or the same day it is baked.

TO SHAPE BAGUETTES: *Divide the dough into 4 equal portions. Flatten each into a thin 10-by-5-inch rectangle with the palm of your hand. Starting at the long end, roll each up each rectangle, using your thumbs to help roll tightly. With the side of your hand, define a depression lengthwise down the center of the dough. Fold over and pinch seams to seal. Roll back and forth from the center out to adjust the dough and make a tight cylinder slightly shorter than your baking sheet or pan. Gently transfer, seam side down, to the prepared pans.*

TO SHAPE BÂTARDS (OBLONG TORPEDO-SHAPED LOAVES THAT LOOK LIKE SHORT, FAT BAGUETTES): *Divide the dough into 2 equal portions. Pat each portion into a rectangle and roll up tightly, as for baguettes, but shape each roll into an 8-inch elongated oval with tapered ends and a thick middle section. Gently transfer, seam side down, to a prepared baking sheet. With a serrated knife, slash the top 3 times on the diagonal, no deeper than ¼ inch, or make 1 long slash down the middle of each loaf.*

TO SHAPE A BOULE (A SMALL ROUND COUNTRY LOAF): *Pat the dough into a thick, uneven circle. Pull up the sides and knead to form the dough into a tight round. Pull the sides down into the bottom seam to create a ball with surface tension. Place seam side down on the prepared baking sheet. Let rise. Glaze, and using a serrated knife or kitchen shears, slash an* **X** *on top no deeper than ¼ inch.*

TO SHAPE PETITS PAINS (CRUSTY LITTLE FRENCH ROLLS): *Divide the dough into 8 equal portions. Form into small rounds or ovals. With the rounds, form into tight balls as for miniature boules. Pinch the ends to form a spindle shape with a thick middle and tapered ends. Using a serrated knife or kitchen shears, slash the tops of the rounds with a cross and the ovals once down middle, no deeper than ¼ inch. Place seam side down on the prepared baking sheets. Let rise only 15 minutes.*

Pain de Campagne
Made in the Food Processor

Makes 1 round loaf

Sponge

- ½ teaspoon active dry yeast
- ¾ cup brut champagne, at room temperature
- 1 cup bread flour

Dough

- 2½ cups bread flour
- ¼ cup instant nonfat dry milk
- 1½ teaspoons (½ package) active dry yeast
- 1½ teaspoons salt
- ½ cup cool water (80°F)
- 2 tablespoons walnut oil

This country bread is flavored by the sparkling wine used to make the sponge starter. Use this bread for crostini and croutons. This is the queen of peasant loaves.

1. To make the sponge, in a 1-quart container, whisk together the yeast, sparkling wine, and flour until smooth; the mixture will be thick. Cover loosely with plastic wrap and let stand at room temperature until bubbly and fermented, about 12 hours.

2. To make the dough, in the work bowl of the food processor fitted with the metal blade, combine the sponge, the flour, milk powder, yeast, and salt and process 15 seconds. With the motor running, immediately pour the water and oil through the feed tube in a steady stream as fast as the flour mixture will absorb it. After the dough forms a soft, elastic ball and clears the sides of the bowl, process 60 seconds more to knead. If the dough is too sticky, add flour by the tablespoonful. If it is too dry, add water by the teaspoonful.

3. Using a plastic dough scraper, transfer the dough ball to a clean work surface. Give a few kneads by hand to even out dough consistency.

4. Place the dough in a lightly greased container, and turn once to grease the top. Cover with plastic wrap and let rise at room temperature until doubled in bulk, about 1½ hours.

5. Turn the dough out onto a clean work surface. Parchment-line a baking sheet and sprinkle with flour. Shape the dough into a tight round. Place the dough on the baking sheet, and cover loosely with plastic wrap. Let rise again at room temperature until fully doubled, about 1 hour. Or place the dough round, seam side up, on a clean floured dish towel or in a cloth-lined banneton, cover with the edges of the towel, and let rise.

6. Twenty minutes before baking, preheat the oven to 450°F, placing a baking stone on the lower third shelf. If rising on the towel or in a banneton, turn the dough out onto a wooden peel heavily sprinkled with flour. Using a sharp knife, slash the surface a few times diagonally across the top, no more than ½ inch deep. With a quick action of the wrist, slide the loaf onto the baking stone, or place the baking sheet directly on the stone. Reduce the oven thermostat to 425°F. Bake 35 to 40 minutes, or until golden brown and the loaf sounds hollow when tapped with your finger. Transfer to a cooling rack and cool. Eat the bread the same day it is baked.

Italian Whole-Wheat Bread

Makes 1 round loaf

Sponge

2½ teaspoons active
dry yeast

²/₃ cup lukewarm water
(105° to 115°F)

1 cup cool water
(80°F)

1 cup unbleached
all-purpose flour

1½ cups whole-wheat
flour

Dough

1½ cups unbleached
all-purpose flour

1 tablespoon sugar

2 teaspoons salt

Yellow cornmeal,
for sprinkling

The dough for this traditional *pane integrale* can also be shaped
into two long, thin loaves and baked in a baguette frame for 20
to 25 minutes. Serve this exceptional bread with Marinated Goat
Cheese, a recipe that is too good to miss.

1. To make the sponge, in a 4-quart container, whisk together the yeast
and warm water. When the yeast is dissolved, add the cool water and the
all-purpose and whole-wheat flours. Whisk until smooth. Cover loosely
with plastic wrap and let stand at room temperature until bubbly and
fermenting, 4 hours to overnight.

2. In the work bowl of the food processor fitted with the metal blade,
combine the sponge, 1½ cups unbleached flour, sugar, and salt and
process 15 seconds. After the dough forms a soft, elastic ball and clears
the sides of the bowl, process 60 seconds more to knead. If the dough is
too sticky, add flour by the tablespoonful. If it is too dry, add water by
the teaspoonful.

3. Using a plastic dough scraper, transfer the dough ball to a clean work
surface. Give a few kneads by hand to even out dough consistency.

4. Place the dough in a lightly greased container. Turn once to grease
the top and cover with plastic wrap. Let rise at room temperature 30
minutes.

5. Turn the dough out onto a floured work surface. Parchment-line a
baking sheet and sprinkle it with cornmeal. Shape the dough into a tight
round. Place on the baking sheet and cover loosely with plastic wrap and
let rise again at room temperature until almost tripled in bulk, 1 to 1½
hours. Alternately, place the dough round, seam side up, on a clean
floured dish towel or in a lined banneton, cover with the edges of the
towel, and let rise.

6. Twenty minutes before baking, preheat the oven to 450°F, placing a
baking stone on the lower third shelf. If rising on the towel or in a banneton, turn the risen bread out onto a wooden peel heavily sprinkled
with cornmeal. Using a sharp knife, slash the surface once down the
center, no more than ½ inch deep. With a quick action of the wrist,

slide the loaf onto the baking stone, or place the baking sheet directly on the stone. Reduce the oven thermostat to 425°F. Bake 35 to 40 minutes, or until golden brown and the top sounds hollow when tapped with your finger. The loaf will not be very dark brown because of the wheat flour and small amount of sugar. Transfer to a cooling rack and cool at least 20 minutes before slicing.

BAKED MARINATED GOAT CHEESE

1 teaspoon dried thyme leaves

1 teaspoon dried savory leaves

1/2 teaspoon dried oregano leaves

1/2 teaspoon freshly ground black pepper

11 ounces French Montrachet or domestic chabis

1/2 cup extra-virgin olive oil

1. Mix the herbs and pepper together and press into the surface of the cheese log, covering the entire surface. Place in a plastic container and pour the olive oil over the cheese. Cover tightly and refrigerate for 5 days to 1 week to meld flavors.

2. To serve, remove the log from the oil and slice into 6 equal pieces. Place in a small shallow gratin dish. Cover with the oil. Bake in a preheated 400°F oven for 5 to 8 minutes, or until just hot. Serve immediately out of the baking dish.

Sour Rye Bread

Makes 1 round loaf

Starter

1 teaspoon active dry yeast

½ cup lukewarm water (110° to 115°F)

½ cup medium rye flour

1 teaspoon minced onion

Sponge

½ cup cool water (80°F)

½ cup medium rye flour

Dough

1½ teaspoons (½ package) active dry yeast

Pinch of sugar

3 tablespoons lukewarm water (110° to 115°F)

2 cups bread flour

2 tablespoons vegetable oil

1¼ teaspoons salt

1 teaspoon caraway seeds

1 teaspoons fennel seeds

¼ teaspoon ground coriander

2 tablespoons rye flour plus ½ teaspoon caraway seeds, for sprinkling

Flavored with a haunting blend of spices, this Scandinavian-style rye bread is dense and smooth-textured. You will need to start the sour sponge a full day before baking. You can make the starter in the morning, and the sponge in the evening. Let it rest overnight, and make the dough the next morning.

1. To make the starter: In a 1-quart container, whisk together the yeast, water, rye flour, and the onion until smooth. The mixture will be thick. Cover loosely with plastic wrap and let stand at room temperature until bubbly and fermenting, about 8 hours.

2. To make the sponge: Add the water and rye flour to the starter. Whisk until smooth. Cover loosely with plastic wrap and let stand at room temperature for at least 8 hours or overnight.

3. In a 1-cup liquid measure, pour in the warm water. Sprinkle the yeast and sugar over the surface of the water. Stir to dissolve. Let stand at room temperature until foamy, about 10 minutes.

4. In the work bowl of the food processor fitted with the metal blade, combine the sponge, yeast mixture, the unbleached flour, oil, salt, caraway, fennel, and coriander and process 15 seconds. After the dough forms a soft, elastic ball and clears the sides of the bowl, process 1 minute more to knead. If the dough is too sticky, add flour by the tablespoonful. If it is too dry, add water by the teaspoonful.

5. Using a plastic dough scraper, transfer the dough ball to a clean surface. Give a few kneads by hand to even out dough consistency.

6. Place the dough in a lightly greased container. Turn once to grease the top and cover with plastic wrap. Let rise at room temperature 30 minutes.

7. Turn the dough out onto a floured work surface. Parchment-line a baking sheet and sprinkle with rye flour and caraway seeds. Shape the dough into a tight round. Place on the baking sheet and roll the dough around in the flour and seeds. Cover loosely with plastic wrap and let rise again at room temperature until fully doubled in bulk, about 1 hour.

8. Twenty minutes before baking, preheat the oven to 425°F, placing a baking stone on the lower third shelf. Using a sharp knife, slash the surface a few times across the top, no more than ½ inch deep. Place the baking sheet directly on the stone. Reduce the oven thermostat to 400°F. Bake 35 to 45 minutes, or until golden brown and the top sounds hollow when tapped with your finger. Transfer to a cooling rack and let cool. Eat the bread the same day it is baked.

Four-Seed Whole-Wheat Bread

Makes 2 small round loaves

- ⅓ cup lukewarm water (105° to 115°F)
- 2½ teaspoons active dry yeast
- ¼ cup honey
- 2¾ cups bread flour
- 1 cup whole-wheat flour
- ½ cup cracked wheat
- 1½ teaspoons salt
- ¼ cup sunflower seed oil
- 1 cup cool water (80°F)
- 1 cup raw sunflower seeds
- 2 tablespoons sesame seeds
- 2 tablespoons poppy seeds
- ½ cup plus 3 tablespoons pumpkin seeds

When heated, the seeds exude their aromatic oils into the bread; they make it taste very special. This bread is a compact loaf with lots of seeds in every bite. Serve it in thick slices with soups.

1. In a 2-cup liquid measure, pour in the lukewarm water. Sprinkle the yeast and honey over the surface of the water. Stir to dissolve and let stand until foamy, about 10 minutes.

2. In the work bowl of the food processor fitted with the metal blade, combine the bread and whole-wheat flours, the cracked wheat, and salt, and pulse to mix. Add the oil and water to the yeast mixture and, with the motor running, immediately pour the liquid through the feed tube in a steady stream as fast as the flour mixture will absorb it. After the dough forms a soft, elastic ball and clears the sides of the bowl, process 45 seconds more to knead. If the dough is too sticky, add flour by the tablespoonful. If it is too dry, add water by the teaspoonful.

3. Using a plastic dough scraper, transfer the dough ball to a lightly greased container. Turn once to grease the top and cover with plastic wrap. Let rise at room temperature until doubled in bulk, about 1½ hours. Meanwhile, clean the work bowl and blade.

4. Turn the dough out onto a clean work surface. Parchment-line a baking sheet. Give a few kneads by hand to even out dough consistency. Pat into an oval. Sprinkle with the sunflower seeds, sesame seeds, poppy seeds, and ½ cup pumpkin seeds and fold in half. Knead gently to distribute evenly. Divide the dough in half and shape each portion into a tight round. Process the remaining 3 tablespoons pumpkin seeds until coarsely chopped, about 10 pulses. Roll each round in the chopped seeds, coating the tops. Place on the baking sheet, cover loosely with plastic wrap, and let rise again at room temperature until doubled in bulk, 45 minutes to 1 hour.

5. Twenty minutes before baking, preheat the oven to 375°F. Place the baking sheet on a rack in the center of the oven and bake 35 to 40 minutes, or until lightly browned and the loaves sound hollow when tapped with your finger. Transfer to a cooling rack. Cool before slicing.

Rosemary Raisin Bread

Makes 1 round loaf

- ½ cup lukewarm water (105° to 115°F)
- 2½ teaspoons active dry yeast
- ¼ cup sugar
- ⅓ cup nonfat dry milk powder
- 2¾ cups bread flour
- 1½ teaspoons salt
- 1 teaspoon dried rosemary leaves
- ¼ cup olive oil, preferably Italian
- 2 large eggs
- 2 to 4 tablespoons cool water (80°F)
- ½ cup dark raisins

A small amount of rosemary adds a distinctive herbal flavor to this unusual Italian egg bread. It requires only one rise before baking, making it a very quick yeast bread to mix and bake.

1. In a 2-cup liquid measure, pour in the warm water. Sprinkle the yeast and pinch of the sugar over the surface of the water. Stir to dissolve. Let stand at room temperature until foamy, about 10 minutes.

2. In the work bowl of the food processor fitted with the metal blade, combine the dry milk, flour, the remaining sugar, salt, and rosemary. Pulse to mix. With the motor running, immediately pour the yeast mixture, oil, and eggs through the feed tube in a steady stream as fast as the flour mixture will absorb it. Process 10 seconds to blend. In a steady stream, drizzle in a few tablespoons of the cool water just until the dough forms a soft, elastic ball and clears the sides of the bowl. Process 30 seconds more to knead. If the dough is too sticky, add flour by the tablespoonful. If it is too dry, add water by the teaspoonful. Turn off the motor and let the dough rest 5 minutes.

3. Turn on the processor, drizzle with a few more teaspoons of water to soften the dough slightly to make a smooth, but not sticky, ball. Process the dough ball another 15 seconds; it will circle the bowl.

4. Parchment-line a baking sheet. Using a plastic dough scraper, turn the dough out onto a clean work surface; give a few kneads by hand to even out dough consistency. Pat the dough into an oval. Sprinkle with the raisins and fold in half. Knead gently to distribute the raisins evenly. Shape the dough into a tight round. Place the dough on the baking sheet and brush the top with olive oil. Cover loosely with plastic wrap and let rise at room temperature until doubled in bulk, 45 minutes to 1 hour.

5. Twenty minutes before baking, preheat the oven to 350°F. Brush the top again with olive oil and using a sharp knife, slash an **X** on the top, no more than ½ inch deep. Place the baking sheet on a rack in the center of the oven and bake 30 to 35 minutes, or until lightly browned and the loaf sounds hollow when tapped with your finger. Transfer to a cooling rack. Cool before slicing.

Multi-Grain Wild Rice Bread

Makes one 8¹⁄₂-by-4¹⁄₂-inch loaf

- ¹⁄₃ cup lukewarm water (105° to 115°F)
- 2¹⁄₂ teaspoons active dry yeast
- ¹⁄₂ teaspoon light brown sugar
- 2 cups bread flour
- ¹⁄₄ cup whole-wheat flour
- ¹⁄₄ cup rye flour
- ¹⁄₄ cup toasted wheat germ or wheat bran
- 3 tablespoons rolled oats
- ¹⁄₄ cup cooked wild rice (see page 113)
- 2 tablespoons light brown sugar
- 1¹⁄₂ teaspoons salt
- 1 tablespoon unsalted butter, at room temperature, cut into pieces
- ³⁄₄ cup cool water (80°F)
- Melted butter, for brushing

After the Italian Whole-Wheat, this is my most requested recipe using the food processor. You combine six grains and end up with an exceptional loaf. I guarantee you will make this loaf many times.

1. In a 2-cup liquid measure, pour in the warm water. Sprinkle the yeast and sugar over the surface of the water. Stir to dissolve and let stand at room temperature until foamy, about 10 minutes.

2. In the work bowl of the food processor fitted with the metal blade, combine all of the flours, wheat germ, oats, wild rice, brown sugar, and salt. Dot the top with the butter pieces. Process 10 seconds. Add the cool water to the yeast mixture and, with the motor running, immediately pour the mixture through the feed tube in a steady stream as fast as the flour mixture will absorb it. After the dough forms a soft, elastic ball and clears the sides of the bowl, process 45 seconds more to knead. If the dough is too sticky, add flour by the tablespoonful. If it is too dry, add water by the teaspoonful.

3. Using a plastic dough scraper, transfer the dough ball to a lightly floured work surface. Give a few kneads by hand to even out dough consistency. Place the dough in a lightly greased container. Turn once to grease the top and cover with plastic wrap. Let rise at room temperature until doubled in bulk, about 1¹⁄₂ hours.

4. Turn the dough out onto a clean work surface. Grease an 8¹⁄₂-by-4¹⁄₂-inch clay or metal loaf pan. Shape the dough into an oblong loaf. Place in the pan, cover loosely with plastic wrap, and let rise again at room temperature until it reaches the top of the pan, 45 minutes to 1 hour.

5. Twenty minutes before baking, preheat the oven to 375°F. Brush the top with melted butter and using a sharp knife, slash 3 times on the diagonal across the top, no more than ¹⁄₂ inch deep. Place the loaf pan on a rack in the center of the oven and bake 35 to 40 minutes, or until lightly browned and the bottom sounds hollow when tapped with your finger. Remove from the oven and brush once more with melted butter. Transfer the loaf to a cooling rack. Cool before slicing.

Pepper Cheese Bread

Makes one 8½-by-4½-inch loaf

3 ounces extra-sharp cheddar cheese

2½ teaspoons active dry yeast

½ teaspoon sugar

⅓ cup lukewarm water (105° to 115°F)

2½ cups unbleached bread flour

½ cup whole-wheat flour

1¼ teaspoons freshly ground black pepper

1 teaspoon salt

4 tablespoons (½ stick) unsalted butter, at room temperature, cut into pieces

¾ cup cool water (80°F)

1 teaspoon hot pepper sauce

This bread is streaked with cheese and touched with the heat of the black and red peppers. It is perfect alone or toasted.

1. Process the cheese using the medium shredding disc in the food processor. Remove and set aside. In a 2-cup liquid measure, pour in the warm water. Sprinkle the yeast and sugar over the surface of the water. Stir to dissolve and let stand at room temperature until foamy, about 10 minutes.

2. In the work bowl of the food processor fitted with the metal blade, combine the bread flour, whole-wheat flour, pepper, and salt and pulse to combine. Dot the top with the butter pieces. Process 10 seconds. Add the water to the yeast mixture and, with the motor running, immediately pour the mixture and hot pepper sauce through the feed tube in a steady stream as fast as the flour mixture will absorb it. After the dough forms a soft, elastic ball and clears the sides of the bowl, add the cheese and process 45 seconds more to knead. If the dough is too sticky, add flour by the tablespoonful. If it is too dry, add water by the teaspoonful.

3. Using a plastic dough scraper, transfer the dough ball to a floured work surface. Give a few kneads by hand to even out dough consistency. Place the dough in a lightly greased container. Turn once to grease the top and cover with plastic wrap. Let rise at room temperature until doubled in bulk, about 1 hour.

4. Turn the dough out onto a clean work surface. Grease an 8½-by-4½-inch loaf pan. Shape the dough into an oblong loaf. Place in the pan, cover loosely with plastic wrap, and let rise again at room temperature until it reaches 1 inch above the top of the pan, 1 to 1½ hours.

5. Twenty minutes before baking, preheat the oven to 375°F. Using a sharp knife, slash 3 times on the diagonal across the top, no more than ½ inch deep. Place the pan on a rack in the center of the oven and bake 35 to 40 minutes, or until lightly browned and the bottom sounds hollow when tapped with your finger. Transfer to a cooling rack. Cool before slicing.

Sour Cream Braid

Makes 1 braided loaf

Dough

- ¼ cup lukewarm water (105° to 115°F)
- 2½ teaspoons active dry yeast
- 2 tablespoons plus ½ teaspoon sugar
- ½ cup cold milk
- ⅓ cup sour cream
- 1 large egg
- 1 teaspoon pure vanilla extract
- ½ teaspoon almond extract
- 3 cups unbleached all-purpose flour
- ½ teaspoon salt
- 4 tablespoons (½ stick) unsalted butter, at room temperature, cut into pieces

Sugar Crust

- 1 egg beaten with 1 teaspoon water, for glazing
- 1 heaping tablespoon sugar
- ¼ teaspoon ground cardamom

Although it has a sugar crust, this bread is not sweet. The crust is touched with the distinctive flavor of crushed cardamom seeds. Excellent for holidays—and it freezes perfectly.

1. In a 1-cup liquid measure, pour in the warm water. Sprinkle the yeast and ½ teaspoon sugar over the surface of the water. Stir to dissolve. Let stand until foamy, 10 minutes. In a small bowl, whisk together the milk, sour cream, egg, vanilla, and almond extract. Add the yeast mixture and stir to combine.

2. In the work bowl of the food processor fitted with the metal blade, combine the flour, 2 tablespoons sugar, and salt. Dot the top with the butter pieces. Process 10 seconds. With the motor running, immediately pour the yeast-milk mixture through the feed tube in a steady stream as fast as the flour mixture will absorb it. After the dough forms a soft, elastic ball and clears the sides of the bowl, process 45 seconds more to knead. If the dough is too sticky, add flour by the tablespoonful. If it is too dry, add water by the teaspoonful.

3. Using a plastic dough scraper, transfer the dough ball to a lightly floured work surface. Give a few kneads by hand to even out dough consistency. Place the dough in a lightly greased container. Turn once to grease the top and cover with plastic wrap. Let rise at room temperature until doubled in bulk, about 1 hour.

4. Turn the dough out onto a clean work surface. Parchment-line a baking sheet. Divide the dough into 3 equal portions. Shape each portion into a 12-inch-long rope tapered at each end. Be sure the ropes are of equal size and shape. Place the 3 ropes parallel to each other. Begin braiding, starting in the center rather than at the ends for a more even shape. Take one of the outside ropes and fold it over the center rope, then repeat the movement from the opposite side. Continue by alternating the outside ropes over the center rope. When complete, turn the dough around and repeat the procedure from the center out to the other end. Tuck the ends under and place on the baking sheet. Cover loosely with plastic wrap, and let rise again at room temperature until doubled in bulk, about 45 minutes.

5. Twenty minutes before baking, preheat the oven to 375°F. Brush the surface with the egg glaze. Combine the sugar and cardamom and sprinkle on the surface evenly. Place the baking sheet on a rack in the center of the oven and bake 35 to 40 minutes, or until lightly browned and the bottom sounds hollow when tapped with your finger. Transfer the loaf immediately to a cooling rack. Cool before slicing.

NOTE: *Substitute 1 cup whole-wheat flour for 1 cup of the all-purpose flour if you wish.*

SOUR CREAM RAISIN BRAID: *In step 4, pat the dough into a fat rectangle. Sprinkle with 1 cup of golden raisins and 2 teaspoons minced dried lemon peel. Fold the dough over and knead to distribute evenly. Let stand, covered, on the work surface 10 minutes before dividing the dough and shaping as directed.*

Alsatian Kugelhopf

Makes 1 tube cake

- ½ cup golden raisins
- ¼ cup currants
- ¼ cup dried blueberries
- ¼ cup golden rum
- 2½ teaspoons active dry yeast
- ⅓ cup plus ½ teaspoon sugar
- ¼ cup lukewarm water (105° to 115°F)
- ⅓ cup blanched almonds
- 2½ cups unbleached all-purpose flour
- Zest of ½ lemon, cut off in strips
- Zest of ¼ orange, cut off in strips
- 6 tablespoons (¾ stick) unsalted butter, at room temperature
- 2 large eggs
- ½ teaspoon salt
- ½ cup lukewarm milk (90° to 100°F)
- 10 whole blanched almonds, for garnish
- Plain or Vanilla Powdered Sugar (page 303), for dusting

Nordic Ware makes a 6-cup mini Bundt pan, readily available in good kitchenware stores, which is perfect for this sweet bread. The bread is crowned with whole almonds and studded with dried fruits. Fill the center with whole fresh berries and serve on a beautiful pedestal cake plate.

1. In a small bowl, combine the raisins, currants, and blueberries with the rum. Macerate 30 minutes. In a 2-cup liquid measure, pour in the warm water. Sprinkle the yeast and the ½ teaspoon sugar over the surface of the water. Stir to dissolve and let stand at room temperature until foamy, about 10 minutes.

2. In the work bowl of the food processor fitted with the metal blade, combine the almonds and ½ cup of the flour and process to a fine meal. Remove and set aside. Place the citrus zest strips and ⅓ cup sugar in the work bowl and process until finely chopped. Add the butter and process 15 seconds, until fluffy. Add the eggs and process 10 seconds. Add the nut meal, remaining all-purpose flour, and salt. Pulse 5 times. Add the yeast mixture and the milk through the feed tube; process until a smooth batter is formed.

3. Using a large plastic spatula, transfer the batter to a greased mixing bowl. Fold in the macerated dried fruit. Cover the bowl with plastic wrap and let rise at room temperature until fully doubled in bulk, about 1½ hours.

4. Generously butter a 6-cup kugelhopf mold or mini Bundt pan. Arrange the whole almonds in the indentations around the bottom of the mold. Stir down the batter and scrape into the mold. Cover the mold with plastic wrap and let rise again at room temperature until it reaches the top of the pan, 45 minutes to 1 hour.

5. Twenty minutes before baking, preheat the oven to 375°F. Preheat to 350°F if using a pan with a dark finish. Place the mold on a rack in the center of the oven and bake 40 to 50 minutes, or until lightly browned and a cake tester inserted into the center comes out clean. Remove from the pan to a cooling rack. Cool, then dust with powdered sugar.

ROBOTIC KNEADS:
The Bread Machine

The electronic bread machine is an all-in-one baking appliance. I have to admit I never thought I would bake bread in an automatic machine and say I enjoyed it. Bread making by hand or food processor was always efficient enough for me, but I have found that the bread machine creates satisfying, full-flavored yeast breads with no compromise of standards when time is an important consideration. Included in this chapter are some of my best recipes adapted for the machine.

Bread machines have hit the home baker's kitchen by storm, with dozens of models with different features and sizes to choose from. They are revolutionizing the age-old art of yeast baking. In a machine the size of a bread box is an internal motor that turns a kneading blade, a nonstick mixing and baking canister, an electric coil to bake the loaf, and a microcomputer. Sophisticated electronics control the motor, temperature, humidity, all the timing, and often even store a recipe in the machine's memory bank.

The shape of the loaf is determined by the shape of the mixing cylinder: an oval, or cubed, long horizontal rectangle, or tall loaf. Every loaf has the distinctive mark of the bread machine: a bottom hole that is created by the kneading paddle. The electronic process differs from hand bread making in that rising and baking times are fixed, rather than being variable, and that there is no series of risings. The entire process takes about three to four hours, unless programmed otherwise. The timer may be set on a delayed cycle for up to thirteen hours, which will give you fresh bread for breakfast or an evening meal. The recipe booklets accompanying most models include a wide variety of plain, specialty, exotic, and even bizarre bread recipes that will appeal to a wide range of home-baking needs. Once the basic recipe has been mastered, you should feel free to substitute and experiment with it. In adapting your own recipes, allow for some trial and error as you adjust the timing to your particular machine. Or try some of the following recipes from my repertoire.

BAKER'S WISDOM

Hints for Successful Bread Machine Baking

The following list will acquaint you with the most important rules of bread machine baking. They apply for all machine models.

❧ Read your recipe carefully and never exceed the capacity of your machine for best results. It is important, especially initially, to follow exactly the manufacturer's instructions and recipe guide-lines for your model. Check my recipe format against your book-let; some models take a dash more or less yeast, or a tablespoon or two more liquid.

❧ Layer the ingredients according to the manufacturer's instruc-tions. In the delayed cycle, layer so that the yeast and dry milk are in the bottom of the baking cylinder. It is important that they do not touch the liquid.

❧ The small machines make a 1-pound loaf, about eight slices (per-fect for two people), and have a capacity of ¾ to 1 cup of liquid and 2 to 3 cups flour, which means dividing most traditional yeast bread recipes calling for 5 to 6 cups of flour in half. This total amount of flour includes any other dry ingredients such as bran, whole-wheat flour, oatmeal, and other specialty flours, but not dry milk powder. The larger machines use about 1½ cups liquid to 4 cups flour, making close to a 1½-pound loaf, about 12 slices. To make a 2-pound loaf in the largest machines, double the 1-pound recipe measurements.

❧ Milk and eggs are extremely perishable and should not be used in delayed cycles, but are perfectly fine in the regular cycles. To pre-vent rancidity, use water and dried milk powder instead of fresh milk. Use 2 tablespoons to ⅓ cup nonfat dry milk powder or dry buttermilk powder for each cup of water. Experiment with other liquids. Powdered and liquid egg substitutes can be substituted beautifully for fresh eggs. One large egg equals ¼ cup liquid.

❧ Fat brings out the flavor and makes the texture of bread softer. Use butter for delicate, rich breads; vegetable oil, such as sunflower, walnut, corn, or canola, for hearty, whole-grain breads; olive oil for Italian or low-cholesterol breads; or lecithin granules. Cut butter into pieces before placing in the canister.

- Substituting honey, molasses, maple syrup, or barley malt syrup for sugar can make a crust exceptionally dark or even cause it to burn. Turn down the crust crisp control for these breads.

- If the dough rises too high, then collapses back into the mixing cylinder, check your rising time. Either the dough has risen too long, or the total amount of dough in the recipe was too large for your model. You might also try cutting back the amount of liquid by 2 tablespoons and the yeast by ½ teaspoon.

- Measure the ingredients exactly as specified in recipes to avoid the overflowing of the dough onto the heating element or having the top portion of the loaf underbaked. If the dough does overflow, clean the container and element with warm soapy water and dry thoroughly. If there is still a burnt smell, lay a clean towel in the bottom of the container and cover it with a layer of baking soda. Close the lid and let stand for about 2 days to clean the smell out of the system.

- Remove the loaf from the pan as soon as possible and cool on a rack, especially if your model does not have a cool cycle to remove the warm, moist air at the end of the baking cycle.

- Bread machine breads are best eaten the same day they are made; this method produces loaves that dry out quickly.

BAKER'S WISDOM
Bread Machine Settings

The terms cycle, setting, and mode are used interchangeably. These different setting will all produce different results on each machine, so following the manufacturer's guide is best.

Crust Color: Some models offer a setting that gives the choice of a light, medium, or dark crust. I usually use the light setting for basic, sweet, and whole-grain breads, but check to make sure the bread bakes all the way through the first time you use it to make certain it is the correct setting. Use medium for lean country breads. I find the dark setting often burns, so I never use it. Some models have a Bake (Light) mode or Bake (Rapid) mode for speeding up or slowing down the regular cycle.

Basic Bread: This is the all-purpose setting you'll probably use most often for white and light whole-grain breads. Some models have a Tender bread setting for the same type of breads with fat added.

French Bread: Some models have this for lean country breads baked with no fat or sugar. There is often a Crisp setting for the same purpose.

Whole-Wheat Bread: This setting allows heavy whole-grain flours an extra and longer rising time. If your machine lacks this, use the basic cycle, reset after the rise to allow the dough to rise a second time. If you make this type of bread often be sure to search out a model with this option.

Fruit and Nut Bread: Also known as the Raisin Bread or Mix Bread cycles, this mode allows for the addition of dried fruit, nuts, seeds, and chocolate chips so as to avoid overmixing and pulverizing them into the batter. Add at the beep.

Sweet Bread: Breads with a high sugar content or cheese rise slower than basic breads and the crust browns more quickly. This translates to a longer rise and lower baking temperature. Some models have a Special setting for doughs that are removed after the rise cycle, filled and rolled, then returned to the pan for baking. If your model lacks this setting, simply remove the kneading blade.

Quick Bread: This setting is for nonyeast batters, cakes, and doughs with no kneading or rise time.

Rise: On some models the rise is called the Dough or Manual setting. This is the setting to use when making a dough that will not be baked in the machine. Remove the dough at the beep and proceed to shape by hand as directed. Bake in a traditional oven or return the dough to the canister after shaping to finish the bake cycle.

BAKER'S WISDOM
Adapting Traditional Bread Recipes to the Bread Machine

Although the market is now replete with baking books devoted to the bread machine, there comes a time when the baker begins to think of adapting old recipes to the new technology. Since the unit is small, recipes have to be reduced to fit the dry and liquid capacities of the machine. Although minor adjustments on fractions, such as ¼ or ⅓ teaspoon of a ground spice or yeast, are tolerable, the following basic guidelines and accurate measuring are very important to avoid an over-flowing loaf or a small and unpalatable one. Eggs are counted as liquid and small amounts of dry ingredients, such as bran, are counted in the total dry. For a 2-pound loaf, double the 1-pound measurements.

For the best results, always have the ingredients at room temperature and place them in the pan according to the manufacturer's instructions.

1½-pound loaf	1-pound loaf
1⅛ to 1½ cups liquid	¾ to 1 cup liquid
3 to 4 cups flour	2 to 2⅔ cups flour
3 to 6 teaspoons gluten	1 to 4 teaspoons gluten
1 to 4 tablespoons fat	2 teaspoons to 3 tablespoons fat
1 to 4 tablespoons sweetener	2 teaspoons to 3 tablespoons sweetener
½ to 1½ teaspoons salt	¼ to 1 teaspoon salt
½ to 3 teaspoons bread machine yeast	¼ to 2 teaspoons bread machine yeast

Special Ingredients for the Bread Machine

Yeast
All bread machine models require the use of active dry yeast, which does not need preliminary fermentation. There is now a special yeast on the market developed for the bread machine by both Fleischmann's and Red Star, although regular active dry, RapidRise, and SAF instant yeasts also work fine. The recipes in this chapter call for bread machine yeast.

Water
Use spring or bottled water, as the hardness or softness of tap water can affect the final loaf by inhibiting or stimulating the yeast.

Salt

I use a fine sun-evaporated sea salt in recipes. If you reduce the amount of salt be sure to reduce the yeast proportionately, as the yeast will make the dough rise too fast without the salt to inhibit it. This is especially important in the bread machine.

Flour

The best bread machine loaves are made with a high proportion of bread flour, rather than all whole-wheat flour or all-purpose flour; this high-gluten flour helps to ensure a loaf that is not too dense. King Arthur's Baker's Catalogue (see page 471) even offers a Special for Machines Bread Flour ringing in at 12.7 percent gluten. I add 1½ teaspoons to 1 tablespoon of gluten per cup of flour to offset heavier and nongluten flours called for in some recipes. Loaves with some whole-grain flours or meals will always be more compact in texture than all-white-flour loaves. Since humidity affects the exact volume of flour, check your dough consistency after the first 10 minutes in the machine. If the dough is too moist, add an additional 1 to 2 tablespoons of flour.

Dough Enhancers

The ideal bread machine loaf is light and high, and using gluten, malted barley flour, ascorbic acid, and lecithin are ways to get it. Although this is new terminology for most bakers, professional bakers have utilized dough enhancers for decades. Food professional Lora Brody is market-ing a dough enhancer that includes most of these ingredients, but you can certainly mix your own. I use some gluten in all my bread machine recipes.

Gluten: A pure plant protein, not a flour, gluten is dried, ground, and marketed as a powdered extract known as vital wheat gluten or just plain gluten. The recommended amount is 1 teaspoon per 1 cup of white flour and 1½ teaspoons of whole-grain flour. If using vital wheat gluten flour (a mixture of gluten mixed with all-purpose flour), use 1 tablespoon per 1 cup flour. Store vital wheat gluten in the refrigerator for up to 1 year.

Lecithin: A soybean-based emulsifier that contributes to a more efficient mixing, which is often used in professional bakeries. It is excellent for low-fat breads. Lecithin also enhances gluten activity. Widely available in health food stores, it comes in granules or liquid form. Substitute exactly for the oil or butter measurement if using the granules; use half the measurement if using the liquid, which is more concentrated. Use about ¼ teaspoon per I cup of flour. Store in the refrigerator

Malted Barley Flour: Also called diastatic malt powder. This is sprouted barley that has been roasted, ground, and dried. It is a favorite of professional bakers because it helps break down the starch in flour, improves texture, and acts as a sugar. Add a scant ½ teaspoon for a I½-pound loaf and a heaping ¼ teaspoon for a I-pound loaf. This is powerful stuff.

Ascorbic Acid or Vitamin C: Vitamin C strengthens weak flours and yeast loves it; a small pinch per 6 cups flour is all that is necessary (that is no more than ⅓ teaspoon for a I½-pound loaf). Buy in bulk or crush your vitamin tablets. Two tablespoons of vinegar or lemon juice, often added to heavy whole-grain doughs such as pumpernickel, or acid ingredients such as buttermilk and yogurt, have the same effect. Never add ascorbic acid if a recipe has acid ingredients; it's overkill.

HOMEMADE PERFORMANCE PLUS BREAD MACHINE FLOUR

Makes about 7½ cups

6 cups unbleached bread flour or whole-wheat flour, as desired

1 cup dry buttermilk powder

2 tablespoons gluten (3 tablespoons if using whole-wheat flour) or ⅓ cup vital wheat gluten flour

2 teaspoons diastatic malt powder

½ teaspoon ascorbic acid crystals

In a plastic container with an airtight lid, combine all the ingredients and stir with a large whisk to evenly distribute. Store in a cool, dry place for up to 6 months.

Cuban Bread

Originally made popular in the late James Beard's Oregon cooking classes, this bread is crusty on the outside, tender and chewy on the inside. The crisp crust is made by giving the dough a second kneading cycle to develop the gluten.

Makes 1 loaf

1 ½-pound loaf	*1-pound loaf*
1¼ cups water	¾ cup water
3¼ cups bread flour	2 cups bread flour
3 teaspoons gluten	2 teaspoons gluten
1 tablespoon sugar	2 teaspoons sugar
1 teaspoon salt	½ teaspoon salt
1½ teaspoons bread machine yeast	1 teaspoon bread machine yeast

1. Place the ingredients in the bread machine according to manufacturer's instructions. Set crust on medium, program for French Bread cycle, and press Start. After the Kneading cycle, reset, allowing the dough to be kneaded a second time.

2. After the baking cycle ends, remove the bread immediately from the machine to a cooling rack. Cool to room temperature before slicing.

Cottage Cheese–Dill Bread

This bread has successfully made the transition from a traditional yeast bread and casserole loaf to the bread machine. The texture is quite moist and delicate, and the bread makes great toast.

Makes 1 loaf

1 ½-pound loaf

- 1 minced shallot
- 2 tablespoons olive oil
- ²/₃ cup water
- ³/₄ cup small curd cottage cheese
- 1 large egg
- 3 cups bread flour
- 3 teaspoons gluten
- 1½ tablespoons nonfat dry milk powder
- 2 tablespoons chopped fresh dill or 1 tablespoon dried dillweed
- 2 tablespoons sugar
- 1 teaspoons salt
- 1³/₄ teaspoons bread machine yeast

1-pound loaf

- 1 small minced shallot
- 1 tablespoon olive oil
- ¹/₃ cup water
- ¹/₃ cup small curd cottage cheese
- 1 large egg
- 2 cups bread flour
- 2 teaspoons gluten
- 1 tablespoon nonfat dry milk powder
- 1 tablespoon plus 1 teaspoon chopped fresh dill or 2 teaspoons dried dillweed
- 1 tablespoon sugar
- ¹/₂ teaspoon salt
- 1¹/₄ teaspoons bread machine yeast

1. In a small skillet, cook the shallot in the oil over medium heat until translucent. Set aside to cool to room temperature.

2. Layer all of the ingredients in the bread machine according to manufacturer's instructions. Set Crust on light, program for Basic or Tender Bread, and press Start.

3. After the baking cycle ends, remove the bread immediately from the machine to a cooling rack. Cool to room temperature before slicing.

Sweet Swirled Breads

Makes 1 loaf

One recipe
Buttermilk Honey
Bread (page 430),
or Egg Bread
(page 426)

Choice of filling
(see variations that
follow)

Vanilla Sugar or
Vanilla Powdered
Sugar (optional)
(page 303)

I have adapted these filling ideas from the kitchen of my friend Kat Wilson; they make wonderful breakfast breads. The dough is removed from the machine, spread with filling and rolled up, and either put back into the machine or into the oven for baking.

1. Program the bread machine for Basic Bread or the Dough cycle. After the Rising cycle ends, at the beep immediately remove the dough and place on a lightly floured work surface and pat into an 8-by-12-inch fat rectangle. Sprinkle or brush with the desired filling, leaving a 1-inch space all the way around. Starting at the short edge, roll up jelly-roll fashion. Tuck the ends under, pinch the bottom seam, and coat the bottom with nonstick cooking spray. If using the Basic Bread cycle, remove the kneading blade and place the dough back in the pan. Press Start to continue to rise and bake.

2. To bake the loaf in your kitchen oven, grease an 8½-by-4½-inch loaf pan for the 1½-pound loaf, or a 7½-by-3½-inch loaf for the 1-pound loaf. Spray the top with nonstick cooking spray and cover lightly with plastic wrap. Let rise at room temperature until doubled in bulk, about 50 minutes.

3. Twenty minutes before baking, preheat the oven to 350°F. Place the pan on a rack in the center of the oven and bake 30 to 35 minutes, or until golden brown, the sides have slightly contracted from the pan, and the loaf sounds hollow when tapped with your finger. Remove to a cooling rack. Cool and dust with Vanilla Sugar, if desired.

KAT'S FAVORITE CHERRY-CHEESE FILLING: *Combine 6 to 8 ounces cream cheese and 1 to 2 tablespoons milk or sour cream to a smooth, thick, spreadable consistency. Spread the dough rectangle with the cheese. Top with ½ to ¾ cup canned cherry pie filling. Continue as directed.*

SPICE FILLING: *Brush the dough rectangle with 1 to 2 tablespoons melted unsalted butter. Combine ½ cup (packed) light brown sugar or granulated maple sugar and 2½ teaspoons ground cinnamon or cardamom and sprinkle over the rectangle. Continue as directed.*

ALMOND FILLING: *Spread with ½ to ¾ cup Solo brand almond filling, or ½ recipe Almond Crème, page 74. Continue as directed.*

HONEY DATE FILLING: Gently heat 1 to 2 tablespoons unsalted butter, and 3 tablespoons honey together. Brush the dough rectangle with the honey-butter mixture. Sprinkle with 1½ teaspoons ground cinnamon and ⅓ to ½ cup chopped pitted dates. Continue as directed.

APPLE-NUTMEG FILLING: Brush the dough rectangle with 1 to 2 tablespoons melted unsalted butter. Combine ⅓ cup light brown sugar, 1 teaspoon freshly grated nutmeg and ¼ teaspoon ground allspice and sprinkle over the rectangle. Evenly scatter ¾ cup chopped peeled and cored fresh apple and ¼ cup chopped walnuts. Continue as directed.

GRANOLA-BLUEBERRY FILLING: Brush the dough rectangle with 1 to 2 tablespoons melted unsalted butter. Sprinkle with ⅓ to ½ cup sweetened granola. Scatter ½ to ⅔ cup fresh blueberries on top. Continue as directed.

ORANGE-PECAN FILLING: Brush the dough rectangle with 1 to 2 tablespoons melted unsalted butter. Spread with ½ to ⅔ cup imported rough-cut orange marmalade. Sprinkle ⅓ to ½ cup chopped pecans on top. Continue as directed.

APRICOT AND WHITE CHOCOLATE FILLING: Brush the dough rectangle with 1 to 2 tablespoons melted unsalted butter. Sprinkle ½ to ¾ cup white chocolate chips and ½ to ¾ cup snipped dried apricots (soaked first in hot water 20 minutes, drained and patted dry with paper towels), and 3 tablespoons chopped walnuts on top. Continue as directed.

Egg Bread

Another basic bread, good for toast or grilled sandwiches. Round and long rolls are easy to make from this dough (recipe follows).

Makes 1 loaf

1½-pound loaf		*1-pound loaf*	
½	cup milk	½	cup milk
½	cup water	¼	cup water
1	large egg plus 1 yolk	1	large egg
3	tablespoons unsalted butter, melted	2	tablespoons unsalted butter, melted
3	cups bread flour	2	cups bread flour
3	teaspoons gluten	2	teaspoons gluten
1	teaspoon salt	¾	teaspoon salt
1¾	teaspoons bread machine yeast	1¼	teaspoons bread machine yeast

1. Place the ingredients in the bread machine according to manufacturer's instructions. Set Crust on light, program for Basic or Tender Bread, and press Start.

2. After the baking cycle ends, immediately remove the bread from the machine to a cooling rack. Cool to room temperature before slicing.

HAMBURGER, HOT DOG, LONG ROLLS, AND SANDWICH BUNS

Dough for 1-pound loaf makes 6 round and 8 long rolls

Dough for 1½-pound loaf makes 8 round and 10 long rolls

1 recipe Egg Bread (above)

1. Place the ingredients in the bread machine according to manufacturer's instructions. Program for the Dough cycle and press Start.

2. Parchment-line a baking sheet. After the Rising cycle ends, at the beep immediately remove the dough and place on a lightly floured work surface. Divide the 1-pound dough into 6 equal portions for hamburger or sandwich buns, 7 equal portions for hot dog or long rolls. Divide the 1½-pound dough into 8 equal portions for hamburger or sandwich buns, and 10 equal portions for hot dog or long rolls. Form the hamburger buns into tight rounds; form the long rolls by flattening the dough into ovals and rolling up each portion tightly from the long end to form a cylinder. Place the rolls on the baking sheet at least 1 inch apart. Cover lightly with plastic wrap and let rise 30 minutes.

3. Twenty minutes before baking, preheat the oven to 375°F. Place the baking sheet on a rack in the center of the oven and bake until lightly browned, for 15 to 22 minutes depending on the size of the roll. Remove immediately to a cooling rack. Cool thoroughly before slicing.

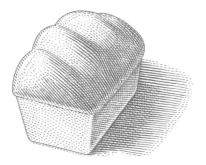

Challah
Made in the Bread Machine

Challah, the traditional Jewish egg bread, has no peer. This dough can be baked inside the machine or removed to be shaped and baked in the oven. For a conventional recipe for this bread, see page 63.

Makes 1 loaf

1½-pound loaf	1-pound loaf
¾ cup water	½ cup water
2 large eggs	1 large egg
1 large egg yolk	1 large egg yolk
3 tablespoons vegetable oil	2 tablespoons vegetable oil
2¾ cups bread flour	2 cups bread flour
2 tablespoons sugar	1 tablespoon sugar
3 teaspoons gluten	2 teaspoon gluten
1 teaspoon salt	¾ teaspoon salt
1¾ teaspoons bread machine yeast	1¼ teaspoons bread machine yeast
1 tablespoon poppy or sesame seeds, for sprinkling	1 tablespoon poppy or sesame seeds, for sprinkling

1. Place the ingredients in the bread machine according to manufacturer's instructions. Set Crust on light, program for Basic or Tender Bread and press Start. After the Rise cycle, carefully lift the lid and sprinkle with the poppy or sesame seeds. Close the lid and continue.

2. After the baking cycle ends, remove the bread immediately from the machine to a cooling rack. Cool before slicing.

TO SHAPE THE CHALLAH IN THE TRADITIONAL MANNER: *Program for Dough. After the Rising cycle ends, at the beep immediately remove the dough and place on a lightly floured work surface. Parchment-line a baking sheet. Divide the dough into 3 equal portions. Shape each portion into a rope tapered at the end. Be sure the ropes are of equal size and shape. Place the 3 ropes parallel to each other. Begin braiding, starting in the center rather than at the ends for a more even shape. Take one of the outside ropes and fold it over the center rope, then* repeat the movement from the opposite side. Continue by alternating the outside ropes over the center rope. When completed, turn the dough around and repeat the procedure from the center out to the other end. Place the braid onto the baking sheet, or in an 8½-by-4½-inch loaf pan (for the 1 ½ pound loaf) or 7 ½-by-3 ½-inch loaf pan (for the 1-pound loaf). Sprinkle the top with poppy or sesame seeds and cover lightly with plastic wrap. Let rise at room temperature until doubled in bulk, about 40 minutes. Twenty minutes before baking, preheat the oven to 350°F and bake for 25 to 30 minutes, or until golden brown and the loaf sounds hollow when tapped with your finger. Remove immediately to a cooling rack.

Buttermilk Honey Bread
Made in the Bread Machine

This is a basic white bread, especially nice for toast and sandwiches. It is also the basis for various swirled breads (see page 424). For a conventional recipe for this bread, see page 54.

Makes 1 loaf

1½-pound loaf

- 1 cup plus 3 tablespoons water
- 2 tablespoons unsalted butter, melted
- 3 tablespoons honey
- 3 cups bread flour
- ⅓ cup dry buttermilk powder
- 5 teaspoons gluten
- 1 teaspoon salt
- 1¾ teaspoons bread machine yeast

1-pound loaf

- ⅞ cup water
- 1½ tablespoons unsalted butter, melted
- 2 tablespoons honey
- 2 cups bread flour
- ¼ cup dry buttermilk powder
- 3 teaspoons gluten
- ¾ teaspoon salt
- 1¼ teaspoons bread machine yeast

1. Place the ingredients in the bread machine according to manufacturer's instructions. Set Crust on light, program for Basic Bread, and press Start.

2. After the baking cycle ends, remove the bread immediately from the machine and place on cooling rack. Cool to room temperature before slicing.

Brioche with Cheese and Walnuts

This is a recipe adapted from Madge Rosenberg's *The Best Bread Machine Book Ever* (HarperCollins, 1992) made with what I consider one of the best cheeses in the world: Emmenthaler from the Jura Mountains in France. The classic tall shape is easily imitated in the bread machine. This is a picnic bread par excellence.

Makes 1 loaf

1 1/2-pound loaf

- 3/4 cup water
- 3 large eggs, at room temperature
- 8 tablespoons (1 stick) unsalted butter, at room temperature
- 2 2/3 cups bread flour
- 1 tablespoon sugar
- 2 teaspoons gluten
- 1 teaspoon salt
- 1 3/4 teaspoons bread machine yeast
- 3/4 cup finely diced Emmenthaler or Swiss cheese
- 3 tablespoons chopped walnuts

1-pound loaf

- 1/2 cup water
- 2 large eggs, at room temperature
- 6 tablespoons (3/4 stick) unsalted butter, at room temperature
- 1 3/4 cups bread flour
- 2 teaspoons sugar
- 1 1/2 teaspoons gluten
- 3/4 teaspoon salt
- 1 1/4 teaspoons bread machine yeast
- 1/2 cup finely diced Emmenthaler or Swiss cheese
- 2 tablespoons chopped walnuts

1. Place the ingredients, except the cheese and walnuts, in the bread machine according to manufacturer's instructions. Set Crust on light, program for Fruit and Nut Bread, and press Start. At the beep add the cheese and walnuts.

2. After the baking cycle ends, remove the bread immediately from the machine to a cooling rack. Cool to room temperature before slicing.

Honey Whole-Wheat Bread

All bakers want a good all-purpose whole-wheat bread in their repertoire. You can substitute white whole-wheat flour for the regular whole-wheat flour. The type of honey you use will add its own character.

Makes 1 loaf

1½-pound loaf	**1-pound loaf**
1¼ cups water	⅞ cup water
2 tablespoons vegetable oil	1½ tablespoons vegetable oil
¼ cup honey	3 tablespoons honey
2 cups bread flour	1½ cups bread flour
1 cup plus 2 tablespoons whole-wheat flour	⅔ cup whole-wheat flour
¼ cup nonfat dry milk powder	3 tablespoons nonfat dry milk powder
5 teaspoons gluten	1 tablespoon gluten
1 teaspoon salt	¾ teaspoon salt
1¼ teaspoons bread machine yeast	1 teaspoon bread machine yeast

1. Place the ingredients in the bread machine according to manufacturer's instructions. Set Crust on light, program for Basic or Whole-Wheat Bread and press Start.

2. After the baking cycle ends, remove the bread immediately from to a cooling rack. Cool to room temperature before slicing.

THREE SEED HONEY WHOLE-WHEAT BREAD: *For the 1-pound loaf, add ¼ cup sunflower seeds, 4 teaspoons sesame seeds, and 1 heaping teaspoon poppy seeds to the flour. For the 1½-pound loaf, add ⅓ cup sunflower seeds, 2 tablespoons sesame seeds, and 2 teaspoons poppy seeds to the flour.*

FRESH HERB HONEY WHOLE-WHEAT BREAD: For the 1-pound loaf, add ¼ teaspoon grated lemon zest, 2 tablespoons chopped walnuts or pine nuts, and ¼ cup chopped fresh herbs. For the 1½-pound loaf, add ½ teaspoon grated lemon zest, 3 tablespoons chopped walnuts or pine nuts, and ⅓ cup chopped fresh herbs. Use one or any combination of parsley, basil, chervil, oregano, dill, chives, mint, thyme, lovage, or marjoram. This loaf is especially nice made with all fresh basil.

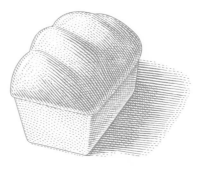

100 Percent Whole-Wheat Bread
Made in the Bread Machine

This fiber-rich loaf is moist and hearty. The dough rises twice to make a palatable loaf. If you have a whole-wheat bread cycle, use it; otherwise, reset for the second rise. For a conventional recipe for this bread, see page 84.

Makes 1 loaf

1 1/2-pound loaf	1-pound loaf
1 1/3 cups water	7/8 cup water
1/4 cup vegetable oil	3 tablespoons vegetable oil
3 tablespoons honey	2 tablespoons honey
3 1/2 cups whole-wheat flour	2 1/3 cups whole-wheat flour
1/3 cup dry buttermilk powder	1/4 cup dry buttermilk powder
2 tablespoons gluten	1 1/2 tablespoons gluten
1 1/4 teaspoons salt	3/4 teaspoon salt
2 1/4 teaspoons bread machine yeast	1 3/4 teaspoons bread machine yeast

1. Place the ingredients in the bread machine according to manufacturer's instructions. Set Crust on light, program for Whole-Wheat Bread, and press Start. If using the Basic Bread cycle, after the Rising cycle, reset to allow the dough to rise a second time.

2. After the baking cycle ends, remove the bread immediately from the machine to a cooling rack. Cool to room temperature before slicing.

Sesame Semolina Bread

Be sure to use the finely ground semolina flour that is used for making pasta, rather than the coarser grind that is similar to farina. The flavor of this bread is wonderful.

Makes 1 loaf

1 1/2-pound loaf		1-pound loaf	
1 1/3	cups water	1	cup water
2	tablespoons olive oil	1 1/2	tablespoons olive oil
1	tablespoon sugar	2	teaspoons sugar
1 1/2	cups bread flour	1	cups bread flour
1 1/2	cups semolina flour	1	cup semolina flour
1 1/2	tablespoons sesame seeds	1	tablespoon sesame seeds
3	teaspoons gluten	2	teaspoons gluten
1	teaspoon salt	3/4	teaspoon salt
1 3/4	teaspoons bread machine yeast	1 1/4	teaspoons bread machine yeast

1. Place the ingredients in the bread machine according to manufacturer's instructions. Set Crust on light, program for Basic Bread cycle, and press Start.

2. After the baking cycle ends, remove the bread immediately from the machine to a cooling rack. Cool to room temperature before slicing.

Cracked Wheat Bread
Made in the Bread Machine

Cracked wheat bread is an old-time favorite. The combination of molasses and honey gives this loaf a unique flavor. For a conventional recipe for this bread, see page 88.

Makes 1 loaf

1½-pound loaf	1-pound loaf
1¼ cups boiling water	1 cup boiling water
½ cup cracked wheat or bulgur	⅓ cup cracked wheat or bulgur
2 tablespoons molasses	2 tablespoons molasses
2 teaspoons honey	1½ teaspoons honey
3 tablespoons unsalted butter	2 tablespoons unsalted butter
1⅔ cups bread flour	1 cup bread flour
1 cup whole-wheat flour	⅔ cup whole-wheat flour
⅓ cup dry buttermilk powder	¼ cup dry buttermilk powder
2 tablespoons gluten	1½ tablespoons gluten
1¼ teaspoons salt	¾ teaspoon salt
2¼ teaspoons bread machine yeast	2 teaspoons bread machine yeast

1. In a mixing bowl, pour the boiling water over the cracked wheat. Add the molasses, honey, and butter. Let stand 1 hour to soften the wheat.

2. Place the remaining ingredients and the soaked grain in the bread machine according to manufacturer's instructions. Set Crust on light, program for Basic Bread or Whole-Wheat Bread, and press Start.

3. After the Baking cycle ends, remove the bread immediately from the machine to a cooling rack. Cool to room temperature before slicing.

Bran-Molasses-Sunflower Bread
Made in the Bread Machine

This bread is another of my signature breads adapted from the recipe I developed during my restaurant baking years. It appeared on the cover of *Bon Appétit* magazine. For a conventional recipe for this bread, see page 92.

Makes 1 loaf

1 1/2-pound loaf		1-pound loaf	
1 1/4	cups water	7/8	cup water
2	tablespoons butter, melted	1 1/2	tablespoons butter, melted
3	tablespoons molasses	2	tablespoons molasses
3	cups bread flour	2	cups bread flour
1/2	cup wheat bran	1/3	cup wheat bran
1/4	cup raw sunflower seeds	3	tablespoons raw sunflower seeds
1/4	cup nonfat dry milk powder	3	tablespoons nonfat dry milk powder
5	teaspoons gluten	3	teaspoons gluten
1	teaspoon salt	3/4	teaspoon salt
1 3/4	teaspoons bread machine yeast	1 1/2	teaspoons bread machine yeast

1. Place the ingredients in the bread machine according to manufacturer's instructions. Set Crust on light, program for Basic Bread cycle, and press Start.

2. After the baking cycle ends, remove the bread immediately from the machine to a cooling rack. Cool to room temperature before slicing.

Graham Granola Bread

Granola bread has been one of my favorites ever since someone brought me a loaf of store-bought in the early 1970s. I just had to make it myself. Now I've adapted it to the bread machine, which does a fine job.

Makes 1 loaf

1½-pound loaf	*1-pound loaf*
1¼ cups water	7/8 cup water
2 tablespoons unsalted butter, softened	1½ tablespoons unsalted butter, softened
1 large egg, at room temperature	1 large egg, at room temperature
2 cups bread flour	1½ cups bread flour
1 cup granola	¾ cup granola
½ cup graham flour	⅓ cup graham flour
¼ cup dry buttermilk powder	3 tablespoons dry buttermilk powder
4 teaspoons gluten	3 teaspoons gluten
1 teaspoon salt	¾ teaspoon salt
2 teaspoons bread machine yeast	1½ teaspoon bread machine yeast

1. Place the ingredients in the bread machine according to manufacturer's instructions. Set Crust on light, program for Basic Bread or Whole-Wheat Bread, and press Start.

2. After the baking cycle ends, remove the bread immediately from the pan to a cooling rack. Cool to room temperature before slicing.

Old-fashioned Oatmeal Bread

Use quick-cooking imported Irish oatmeal for this recipe. The flavor of Irish oats is the richest of any I ever tasted and the loaf retains a nubby texture.

Makes 1 loaf

1 1/2-pound loaf		1-pound loaf	
1 1/3	cups water	1	cup water
2	tablespoons vegetable oil	1 1/2	tablespoons vegetable oil
1/4	cup honey	3	tablespoons honey
3	cups bread flour	2	cups bread flour
1	cup rolled oats	3/4	cup rolled oats
1/4	cup nonfat dry milk powder	3	tablespoons nonfat dry milk powder
5	teaspoons gluten	1	tablespoon gluten
1	teaspoon salt	3/4	teaspoon salt
1 3/4	teaspoons bread machine yeast	1 1/4	teaspoons bread machine yeast
	Rolled oats, for sprinkling		Rolled oats, for sprinkling

1. Place the ingredients in the bread machine according to manufacturer's instructions. Set Crust on light, program for Basic Bread, and press Start. After the Rising cycle, carefully lift the lid and sprinkle with the extra rolled oats. Close the lid and continue the bake cycle.

2. After the baking cycle ends, remove the bread immediately from the machine to a cooling rack. Cool to room temperature before slicing.

Country Bread

This bread can also be made in the La Cloche (see page 133).

Makes 1 loaf

1½-pound loaf	*1-pound loaf*
1¼ cups water	¾ cup water
¼ cup plain yogurt	3 tablespoons plain yogurt
1½ tablespoons vegetable or nut oil	1 tablespoon vegetable or nut oil
2⅔ cups bread flour	1¾ cups bread flour
⅓ cup whole-wheat flour	¼ cup whole-wheat flour
⅓ cup medium rye flour	¼ cup medium rye flour
3 teaspoons gluten	2 teaspoons gluten
1 teaspoon salt	½ teaspoon salt
2¼ teaspoons bread machine yeast	1¾ teaspoons bread machine yeast

1. Place the ingredients in the bread machine according to manufacturer's instructions. Set Crust on medium, program for French Bread, and press Start. After the Kneading cycle, reset, allowing the dough to be kneaded a second time.

2. After the baking cycle ends, remove the bread immediately from the machine to a cooling rack. Cool to room temperature before slicing.

COUNTRY BREAD WITH RAISINS AND WALNUTS: *Set Crust on light, program for French Bread or Fruit and Nut Bread, and press Start. If using French Bread, mix into the flour ¼ cup golden raisins and 3 tablespoons chopped walnuts for the 1-pound loaf, and ⅓ cup golden raisins and ¼ cup chopped walnuts for the 1½-pound loaf. If using Fruit and Nut Bread, add the fruit and nuts at the beep. Continue as directed.*

COUNTRY BREAD WITH DRIED FIGS: *Set Crust on light, program for French Bread or Fruit and Nut Bread, and press start. If using French Bread, mix ¼ cup chopped dried figs for the 1-pound loaf and ⅓ cup chopped dried figs for the 1½-pound loaf into the flour. If using Fruit and Nut bread, add the figs at the beep. Continue as directed.*

Narsai's Light Rye Bread

Food professional Narsai David of San Francisco is a dedicated home baker. In May 1989 he published some of the first bread machine recipes. I still make this rye, but with the addition of gluten and a bit of orange zest to make a loaf that is the best of its genre.

Makes 1 loaf

1½-pound loaf	*1-pound loaf*
1 cup water	¾ cup water
3 tablespoons molasses	2 tablespoons molasses
2 tablespoons vegetable oil	1 tablespoon vegetable oil
2 cups bread flour	1½ cups bread flour
¾ cup medium rye flour	½ cup medium rye flour
5 teaspoons gluten	1 tablespoon gluten
1 tablespoon caraway seeds	2 teaspoons caraway seeds
1 teaspoon grated orange zest	½ teaspoon grated orange zest
1 teaspoon salt	¾ teaspoon salt
2 teaspoons bread machine yeast	1¾ teaspoons bread machine yeast

1. Place the ingredients in the bread machine according to manufacturer's instructions. Set Crust on light, program for Basic Bread cycle, and press Start.

2. After the baking cycle ends, remove the bread immediately from the machine to a cooling rack. Cool to room temperature before slicing.

Black Russian Rye Bread

Made in the Bread Machine

This bread is dense, rich, and textured. It stays fresh for days. For a conventional recipe for this bread, see page 102.

Makes 1 loaf

1 ½-pound loaf	1-pound loaf
1⅛ cups water	⅞ cup water
3 tablespoons molasses	2 tablespoons molasses
2 tablespoons apple cider vinegar	1 tablespoon apple cider vinegar
2 tablespoons unsalted butter, melted	1½ tablespoons unsalted butter, melted
2 cups bread flour	1⅓ cups bread flour
1 cup medium rye flour	⅔ cup medium rye flour
¼ cup whole-wheat flour	3 tablespoons whole-wheat flour
¼ cup wheat bran	3 tablespoons wheat bran
2 tablespoons medium-grind yellow cornmeal	1½ tablespoons medium-grind yellow cornmeal
2½ tablespoons unsweetened cocoa powder	1½ tablespoons unsweetened cocoa powder
5 teaspoons gluten	1 tablespoon gluten
1 teaspoon instant espresso powder	¾ teaspoon instant espresso powder
2 teaspoons minced shallot	1 teaspoon minced shallot
2 teaspoons caraway seeds	1 teaspoon caraway seeds
¼ teaspoon fennel seeds	⅛ teaspoon fennel seeds
1¼ teaspoons salt	1 teaspoon salt
2¼ teaspoons bread machine yeast	2 teaspoons bread machine yeast

1. Place the ingredients in the bread machine according to manufacturer's instructions. Set Crust on light, program for Basic Bread or Whole-Wheat Bread, and press Start. If using Basic Bread, after the rising cycle, reset, to allow the dough to rise a second time.

2. After the baking cycle ends, remove the bread immediately from the machine to a cooling rack. Cool to room temperature before slicing.

Cornmeal-Millet Bread

Adding cornmeal to yeast doughs makes for a sweet, grainy textured bread. If you're used to making only baking powder corn breads you are in for a great surprise. The combination of millet and stone-ground cornmeal was first introduced in the landmark *Tassajara Bread Book* in the early 1970s and fast became a homemade-bread favorite.

Makes 1 loaf

1½-pound loaf		1-pound loaf	
1¼	cups water	¾	cup water
2	tablespoons honey	1½	tablespoons honey
1½	tablespoons unsalted butter, melted	1	tablespoon unsalted butter, melted
3	cups bread flour	2	cups bread flour
½	cup medium-grind yellow cornmeal	⅓	cup medium-grind yellow cornmeal
3	tablespoons whole raw millet	1½	tablespoons whole raw millet
⅓	cup dry buttermilk powder	¼	cup dry buttermilk powder
4	teaspoons gluten	3	teaspoons gluten
1	teaspoon salt	¾	teaspoon salt
1¾	teaspoons bread machine yeast	1¼	teaspoons bread machine yeast

1. Place the ingredients in the bread machine according to manufacturer's instructions. Set Crust on light, program for Basic or Whole-Wheat Bread cycle; press Start.

2. After the baking cycle ends, remove the bread immediately from the machine to a cooling rack. Cool to room temperature before slicing.

CORNMEAL CRESCENT DINNER ROLLS

Makes 16 Rolls

1 recipe Cornmeal-
Millet Bread

1. Place the ingredients in the bread machine according to manufacturer's instructions. Program for the Dough cycle and press Start.

2. Parchment-line a baking sheet. After the Rising cycle ends, at the beep immediately remove the dough and place on a lightly floured work surface. Divide into 2 equal portions. Roll into an 8-inch round for the 1-pound loaf and a 10-inch round for the 1½-pound loaf. Using a pastry wheel, cut each round into 8 wedges. Roll up each from the wide edge and place 1 inch apart on the baking sheet, point side down. Cover lightly with plastic wrap and let rise at room temperature until doubled in bulk, about 30 minutes.

3. Twenty minutes before baking, preheat the oven to 375°F. Place the baking sheet on a rack in the center of the oven and bake 15 to 18 minutes, or until lightly browned. Serve warm.

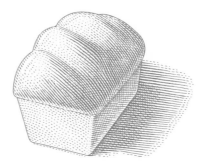

Squaw Bread
Made in the Bread Machine

Whole wheat and rye Squaw Bread is one of my signature breads. It is sweetened with "raisin water." For a conventional recipe for this bread, see page 106.

Makes 1 loaf

1 1/2-pound loaf	1-pound loaf
1 1/3 cups water	1 cup water
3 tablespoons oil	2 tablespoons oil
3 tablespoons honey	2 tablespoons honey
2 tablespoons dark raisins	1 1/2 tablespoons dark raisins
2 tablespoons brown sugar	1 1/2 tablespoons brown sugar
1 1/2 cups bread flour	1 cup bread flour
1 1/4 cups whole-wheat flour	3/4 cup whole-wheat flour
3/4 cup medium rye flour	1/2 cup medium rye flour
1/4 cup nonfat dry milk powder	3 tablespoons nonfat dry milk powder
2 tablespoons gluten	1 1/2 tablespoons gluten
1 teaspoon salt	3/4 teaspoon salt
1 3/4 teaspoons bread machine yeast	1 1/4 teaspoons bread machine yeast

1. In a blender or food processor, combine 1/2 cup of the water, the oil, honey, raisins, and brown sugar. Let stand for 5 minutes to soften the raisins, then process. Add the remaining water and process again.

2. Place the raisin water and the remaining ingredients in the bread machine according to manufacturer's instructions. Set Crust on light, program for Whole-Wheat Bread, and press Start.

3. After the baking cycle ends, remove the bread immediately from the machine to a cooling rack. Cool to room temperature before slicing.

Italian Olive Oil Bread
Made in the Bread Machine

Although I usually make this low-fat *pane casalingo,* or homemade Italian bread, by hand with an eight-hour starter, I find it bakes up nicely in the bread machine. I use raw Roman Meal cereal, a combination of wheat and rye flakes, bran, and flaxseed. For a conventional recipe for this bread, see page 122.

Makes 1 loaf

1½-pound loaf		1-pound loaf	
1	cup water	¾	cup water
¾	cup Bread Machine Sponge Starter (page 448)	½	cup Bread Machine Sponge Starter (page 448)
2	tablespoons olive oil	1½	tablespoons olive oil
2	cups bread flour	1⅓	cups bread flour
1	cup whole-wheat flour	⅔	cup whole-wheat flour
2½	tablespoons Roman Meal flakes, wheat bran, or wheat germ	2	tablespoons Roman Meal flakes, wheat bran, or wheat germ
5	teaspoons gluten	3	teaspoons gluten
1	teaspoon salt	¾	teaspoon salt
2	teaspoons bread machine yeast	1¼	teaspoons bread machine yeast

1. Place the ingredients in the bread machine according to manufacturer's instructions. Set Crust on medium, program for Basic Bread or French Bread, and press Start. After the Kneading cycle, reset, to allow the dough to be kneaded a second time.

2. After the baking cycle ends, remove the bread immediately from the machine to a cooling rack. Cool to room temperature before slicing.

BREAD MACHINE SPONGE STARTER

3/4 cup bread flour or 1/2 cup bread flour and 1/4 cup whole-wheat flour, preferably organic

1/3 teaspoon bread machine yeast

2/3 cup spring or bottled water

Combine the flour, yeast, and water in the bread machine. Set program on the Dough cycle and let it expand and ferment in the machine. The sponge starter is ready to use after 2 hours and can stay in the machine up to 8 hours before proceeding with the recipe. *(The sponge starter can be removed from the pan and refrigerated overnight before use. Bring back to room temperature before using.)* Make a new batch of starter each time you make bread. Makes about 3/4 cup starter.

Tuscan Peasant Bread
Made in the Bread Machine

Tuscan Peasant Bread, called *pane toscano* in Italian, has been made for centuries, designed without the taste of salt to complement saltier foods. For a conventional recipe for this bread, see page 50.

Makes 1 loaf

1 1/2-pound loaf	1-pound loaf
3/4 cup water	1/2 cup water
3/4 cup Bread Machine Sponge Starter (page 448)	1/2 cup Bread Machine Sponge Starter (page 448)
2 3/4 cups bread flour	1 7/8 cups bread flour
1/4 cup whole-wheat flour	2 tablespoons whole-wheat flour
3 teaspoons gluten	2 teaspoons gluten
Pinch of sugar	Pinch of sugar
Pinch of salt	Pinch of salt
1 1/2 teaspoons bread machine yeast	1 teaspoon bread machine yeast

1. Place the ingredients in the bread machine according to manufacturer's instructions. Set Crust on medium, program for French Bread, and press Start. After the Kneading cycle, reset, to allow the dough to be kneaded a second time.

2. After the baking cycle ends, remove the bread immediately from the machine to a cooling rack. Cool to room temperature before slicing.

TUSCAN PEASANT BREAD WITH OLIVES MADE IN THE BREAD MACHINE: *Add green or black olives, imported or domestic, after the dough is kneaded a second time, 1/4 cup for a 1-pound loaf, and 1/3 cup for a 1 1/2-pound loaf.*

Buttermilk Potato Bread
Made in the Bread Machine

Mashed potatoes give bread fluffy texture and tangy flavor. This dough also makes great dinner rolls. For a conventional recipe for this bread see page 138.

Makes 1 loaf

1½-pound loaf		1-pound loaf	
1	medium potato (about 6 ounces)	1	medium potato (about 6 ounces)
1	tablespoon unsalted butter, melted	2	teaspoons unsalted butter, melted
1	tablespoons sugar	2	teaspoons sugar
3¼	cups bread flour	2¼	cups bread flour
¼	cup dry buttermilk powder	3	tablespoons dry buttermilk powder
3	teaspoons gluten	2	teaspoons gluten
1	teaspoon salt	¾	teaspoon salt
1½	teaspoons bread machine yeast	1	teaspoon bread machine yeast

1. Peel and cut up the potato. In a small saucepan, combine the potato and water to cover. Cook, covered, over medium-low heat until the potato is tender, 10 to 20 minutes, depending on the size of the pieces. Drain, reserving the potato water. Add more water to make ⅞ cup total for the 1-pound loaf and 1⅓ cups total for the 1½-pound loaf. Mash the potato to make ⅓ cup for a 1-pound loaf and ½ cup for the 1½-pound loaf. Let both the potato water and mashed potato cool to room temperature.

2. Place the ingredients in the bread machine according to manufacturer's instructions. Set Crust on light, program for Basic Bread or Tender Bread and press Start.

3. After the baking cycle ends, remove the bread immediately from the machine to a cooling rack. Cool to room temperature before slicing.

PULL-APART POTATO DINNER ROLLS

Makes 12 to 16 rolls

1 recipe Buttermilk
Potato Bread Made
in the Bread
Machine

1. Prepare the mashed potato and potato water as directed on page 450 and let cool to room temperature. Place the ingredients in the bread machine according to manufacturer's instructions. Program for the Dough cycle and press Start.

2. Grease or parchment-line a round cake pan, 9-inch for the 1-pound loaf, or 10-inch for the 1½-pound loaf. After the Rising cycle ends, at the beep immediately remove the dough and place on a lightly floured work surface. Divide the 1-pound loaf into 12 equals portions, or the 1½-pound loaf into 16 equal portions. Shape each into a tight ball and place in the pan. Dust the top heavily with flour and cover lightly with plastic wrap. Let rise at room temperature until doubled in bulk, about 30 minutes.

3. Twenty minutes before baking, preheat the oven to 375°F. Bake for 25 to 30 minutes or until golden brown and the sides have shrunk slightly from the pan. Serve warm.

Wild Rice–Molasses Bread
Made in the Bread Machine

This bread is a real surprise; the wild rice and the molasses are a dynamite duo. To cook the wild rice, see page 113. You will have more than you need. Save the extra for salad or pancakes (see page 251). For a conventional recipe for this bread, see page 112.

Makes 1 loaf

1½-pound loaf	1-pound loaf
1¼ cups water	⅞ cup water
¼ cup walnut oil	3 tablespoons walnut oil
¼ cup molasses	3 tablespoons molasses
2 cups bread flour	1½ cups bread flour
1 cup plus 2 tablespoons whole-wheat flour	⅔ cup whole-wheat flour
¼ cup nonfat dry milk powder	3 tablespoons nonfat dry milk powder
5 teaspoons gluten	1 tablespoon gluten
1 teaspoon salt	¾ teaspoon salt
1¾ teaspoons bread machine yeast	1¼ teaspoons bread machine yeast
½ cup cooked wild rice	⅓ cup cooked wild rice

1. Place the ingredients, except the wild rice, in the bread machine according to manufacturer's instructions. Set Crust on light, program for Fruit and Nut Bread, and press Start. Add the wild rice at the beep.

2. After the baking cycle ends, remove the bread immediately from the machine to a cooling rack. Cool to room temperature before slicing.

Sourdough Farm Bread

This loaf, adapted from a recipe that appeared in *Sunset Magazine* in the early 1990s, is moist with the pleasant tang of the sourdough. Make the sourdough starter at least two days before making this dough.

Makes 1 loaf

1½-pound loaf		*1-pound loaf*	
1	cup water	⅔	cup water
1	cup Classic Sourdough Starter (page 120)	¾	cup Classic Sourdough Starter (page 120)
3½	cups bread flour	2½	cups bread flour
2	tablespoons sugar	1	tablespoon sugar
4	teaspoons gluten	3	teaspoons gluten
1	teaspoon salt	¾	teaspoon salt
1¾	teaspoons bread machine yeast	1¼	teaspoons bread machine yeast

1. Place the ingredients in the bread machine according to manufacturer's instructions. Set crust on Light, program for Basic Bread, and press Start.

2. After the baking cycle ends, remove the bread immediately from the machine to a cooling rack. Cool to room temperature before slicing.

Pain de Campagne

Made in the Bread Machine

Also called French Whole-Wheat Country Bread, this is an earthy loaf that contains no fat. If you decide to shape this loaf by hand and finish baking in the oven, you can use the La Cloche baking dish (see page 133). Prepare the sponge starter in the bread machine and let it ferment for 4 hours before mixing the dough. For a conventional recipe for this bread, see page 128.

Makes 1 loaf

1½-pound loaf	1-pound loaf
¾ cup water	½ cup water
1 cup Bread Machine Sponge Starter (page 448)	¾ cup Bread Machine Sponge Starter (page 448)
2 cups whole-wheat flour	1¼ cup whole-wheat flour
1 cup bread flour	¾ cup bread flour
5 teaspoons gluten	3 teaspoons gluten
1 teaspoon salt	¾ teaspoon salt
1¾ teaspoons bread machine yeast	1¼ teaspoons bread machine yeast

1. Place the ingredients in the bread machine according to manufacturer's instructions. Set Crust on medium and program for French Bread, and press Start. After the Kneading cycle, reset, to allow the dough to be kneaded a second time.

2. After the baking cycle ends, remove the bread immediately from the machine to a cooling rack. Cool to room temperature before slicing.

FRENCH ROUND BOULE OR LONG BÂTARD

Makes 1 loaf

1 recipe Pain de
Campagne Made in
the Bread Machine

1. Place the ingredients in the bread machine according to manufacturer's instructions. Program for the Dough cycle and press Start.

2. Parchment-line a baking sheet with parchment paper and sprinkle with cornmeal. After the Rising cycle ends, at the beep immediately remove the dough and place on a lightly floured work surface. Form into a tight round or pat into a thick rectangle and roll up from the long edge to form a thick cylinder. Dust the top with flour. Transfer, seam side down, to the baking sheet. Cover loosely with plastic wrap and let rise at room temperature until doubled in bulk, about 45 minutes.

3. Twenty minutes before baking, preheat the oven to 400°F, with a baking stone on the lower third rack. With a sharp knife, slash the round loaf with an **X** or the long loaf with 3 parallel lines, no more than ¼ inch deep. Place the pan directly on the stone in the oven and bake 25 to 30 minutes, or until the crust is brown and crisp and the loaf sounds hollow when tapped with your finger. Remove the loaf to a cooling rack.

Basic Pizza Dough
Made in the Bread Machine

Pizza dough is mixed and risen in the machine, then shaped by hand, topped as desired, and baked in the oven. This method makes homemade pizza easier than ever. For a conventional recipe for pizza dough as well as sauce and topping suggestions, see page 213.

Dough for the 1 1/2-pound loaf makes one 14-inch round, one 11-by-17-inch rectangular, or three 8-inch round pizzas.

1 1/2-pound loaf

- 1 cup water
- 3 tablespoons olive oil
- 3 cups unbleached bread flour
- 3 teaspoons gluten
- 2 teaspoons sugar
- 1 teaspoon salt
- 1 3/4 teaspoons bread machine yeast

  Cornmeal or coarse semolina, for sprinkling

Dough for the 1-pound loaf makes one 10- or 12-inch round, one 9-inch square, or two 8-inch round pizzas.

1-pound loaf

- 3/4 cup water
- 2 tablespoons olive oil
- 2 cups unbleached bread flour
- 2 teaspoons gluten
- 1 teaspoon sugar
- 3/4 teaspoon salt
- 1 1/2 teaspoons bread machine yeast

  Cornmeal or coarse semolina, for sprinkling

1. Place the ingredients in the bread machine according to manufacturer's instructions. Program for the Dough cycle and press Start.

2. Preheat the oven to 500°F, with a baking stone on the center rack. Sprinkle a pizza pan with cornmeal or semolina. After the Rising cycle ends, at the beep immediately remove the dough and place on a lightly floured work surface. Flatten the dough into a disk. With a rolling pin or by pressing with your fingers, roll the dough out from the center, rotating as you roll to get an even circle. Place the dough round on the pizza pan. Top with sauce, cheese, and any other topping, as desired.

3. For a thin crust, immediately place the pan directly on the stone in the oven and bake 15 to 20 minutes, or until the crust is brown and crisp. For a thick crust, let rise at room temperature until the dough is doubled in bulk, about 40 minutes, before topping and baking. Check the underside of the crust to be sure it is browned. Transfer the pizza to a cutting board and cut into wedges with a pizza wheel or serrated knife. Serve hot!

WHOLE-WHEAT PIZZA DOUGH: *Substitute ½ to 1½ cups whole-wheat flour for an equal amount of unbleached flour. The more whole-wheat flour, the harder the dough will be to roll out, so be prepared to patch up holes.*

CORNMEAL PIZZA DOUGH: *Substitute ¼ cup polenta or yellow, white, or blue cornmeal for ¼ cup unbleached flour.*

HERBED PIZZA DOUGH: *Add 1 to 2 tablespoons mixed chopped fresh herbs, such as basil, tarragon, sage, rosemary, chervil, oregano, parsley, or marjoram to the dough during mixing.*

GARLIC PIZZA DOUGH: *Add 1 clove sautéed, finely chopped garlic to the dough during mixing.*

SEMOLINA PIZZA DOUGH: *Substitute ½ to 1 cup semolina flour for ½ to 1 cup unbleached flour.*

SAFFRON PIZZA DOUGH: *Add ¼ teaspoon saffron threads to ¾ to 1 cup boiling water. Let cool to 105°F to 115°F, then substitute for plain water.*

SUZANNE'S SOURDOUGH PIZZA: *Add ¼ cup Classic Sourdough Starter (page 120) or Bread Machine Sponge Starter (page 448) for each cup of liquid. Combine the water, starter, yeast, olive oil, and sugar in the bread machine and whisk to combine. Leaving the machine off, close the lid and let the mixture rise and form a sponge for 30 minutes. Add the flour, gluten, and salt; program for the Dough cycle, and press Start.*

Cinnamon-Raisin-Currant Bread

This is my sister Meg's favorite breakfast bread dressed up a bit.

Makes 1 loaf

1 1/2-pound loaf		1-pound loaf	
1 1/4	cups water	7/8	cup water
2	tablespoons unsalted butter, melted	1	tablespoon unsalted butter, melted
2	tablespoons brown sugar	1 1/2	tablespoons brown sugar
3	cups bread flour	2	cups bread flour
1/4	cup nonfat dry milk powder	3	tablespoons nonfat dry milk powder
5	teaspoons gluten	3	teaspoons gluten
1	teaspoon salt	1/2	teaspoon salt
1	teaspoon ground cinnamon	3/4	teaspoon ground cinnamon
2	teaspoons bread machine yeast	1 1/2	teaspoons bread machine yeast
1/2	cup raisins	1/4	cup raisins
1/2	cup currants	1/3	cup currants

1. Place the ingredients, except the raisins and currants, in the bread machine according to manufacturer's instructions. Set Crust on light, program for Fruit and Nut Bread, and press Start. At the beep add the fruits. (You may also mix all the ingredients together and program for Sweet Bread.)

2. After the baking cycle ends, remove the bread immediately from the machine to a cooling rack. Cool to room temperature before slicing.

Maple Pecan Bread

Maple and pecans are a favorite sweet bread combination. It makes a simple bread taste rich and complex.

Makes 1 loaf

1 1/2-pound loaf	1-pound loaf
1 cup water	3/4 cup water
1/3 cup maple syrup	1/4 cup maple syrup
2 tablespoons unsalted butter, melted	1 tablespoon unsalted butter, melted
1/4 cup nonfat dry milk powder	3 tablespoons nonfat dry milk powder
3 cups bread flour	2 cups bread flour
4 teaspoons gluten	3 teaspoons gluten
1 teaspoon salt	1/2 teaspoon salt
2 teaspoons bread machine yeast	1 1/2 teaspoons bread machine yeast
1/2 cup chopped pecans	1/3 cup chopped pecans

1. Place the ingredients, except the pecans, in the bread machine according to manufacturer's instructions. Set Crust on light, program for Fruit and Nut Bread and press Start. At the beep add the nuts. (You may also mix all the ingredients together and program for Sweet Bread.)

2. After the baking cycle ends, remove the bread immediately from the machine to a cooling rack. Cool to room temperature before slicing.

Pernod Panettone
Made in the Bread Machine

Panettone, an Italian Christmas tradition, is perfect for brunch or for dessert. Use day-old slices in bread pudding. For a conventional recipe for this bread, see page 360.

Makes 1 loaf

1 ½-pound loaf	1-pound loaf
⅓ cup golden raisins	¼ cup golden raisins
⅓ cup snipped dried apricots	¼ cup snipped dried apricots
⅓ cup Pernod	¼ cup Pernod
1 cup water	¾ cup water
6 tablespoons (¾ stick) unsalted butter, melted	4 tablespoons (½ stick) unsalted butter, melted
4 tablespoons sugar	3 tablespoons sugar
3 cups bread flour	2 cups bread flour
¼ cup nonfat dry milk powder	3 tablespoons nonfat dry milk powder
3 teaspoons gluten	2 teaspoons gluten
1 teaspoon salt	½ teaspoon salt
2¼ teaspoons bread machine yeast	1½ teaspoons bread machine yeast
3 tablespoons pine nuts	2 tablespoons pine nuts
3 tablespoons slivered blanched almonds	2 tablespoons slivered blanched almonds
3 tablespoons sugar, for glazing	3 tablespoons sugar, for glazing

1. In a small bowl, combine the raisins, apricots, and Pernod. Macerate for 1 hour. Drain and reserve any liquid. Set aside.

2. Place the ingredients, except the fruit, in the bread machine according to manufacturer's instructions. Set Crust on light, program for

Fruit and Nut Bread, and press Start. At the beep add the drained fruit. (You may also mix all the ingredients together and program for Sweet Bread.)

3. After the baking cycle ends, remove the bread immediately from the machine to a cooling rack.

4. Prepare a glaze by combining the reserved liqueur with enough water to make ¼ cup. Place in a small saucepan and add the sugar. Heat until the sugar is dissolved. Brush the warm bread all over twice. Cool to room temperature before slicing in wedges.

Mexican Chocolate Bread

This is a variation on my Bread with Three Chocolates (page 392) reflecting my love of Southwestern and Mexican baking. It is highlighted with a hint of cinnamon and orange. Dried orange peel is available on the spice shelf at the supermarket.

Makes 1 loaf

1½-pound loaf	*1-pound loaf*
½ cup milk	½ cup milk
½ cup water	¼ cup water
1 large egg plus 1 yolk, at room temperature	1 large egg, at room temperature
3 tablespoons unsalted butter, melted	2 tablespoons unsalted butter, melted
¼ cup sugar	3 tablespoons sugar
2½ cups bread flour	2 cups bread flour
3 tablespoons unsweetened Dutch-process cocoa powder	2 tablespoons unsweetened Dutch-process cocoa powder
5 teaspoons gluten	1 tablespoon gluten
1 teaspoon instant espresso powder	¾ teaspoon instant espresso powder
1 teaspoon salt	¾ teaspoon salt
¾ teaspoon ground cinnamon	½ teaspoon ground cinnamon
½ teaspoon dried orange peel	¼ teaspoon dried orange peel
2 ounces bittersweet chocolate chips	1½ ounces bittersweet chocolate chips
2 teaspoons bread machine yeast	1½ teaspoons bread machine yeast

1. Place the ingredients in the bread machine according to manufacturer's instructions. Set Crust on light, program for Sweet Bread, and press Start.

2. After the baking cycle ends, remove the bread immediately from the machine to a cooling rack. Cool to room temperature before slicing.

Saffron Bread
Made in the Bread Machine

Saffron breads, favorites of Scandinavian and English bakers, date back to the seventeenth century. They can be made easily in the bread machine. For a conventional recipe for this bread, see page 364. Dust with powdered sugar or Scented Geranium Powdered Sugar, page 365.

Makes 1 loaf

1 1/2-pound loaf

- 1/3 cup currants
- 1 tablespoon cream sherry
- 1/4 teaspoon saffron threads, crumbled
- 1/2 cup warm water
- 1/2 cup milk
- 1 large egg plus 1 yolk, at room temperature
- 4 tablespoons unsalted butter, softened
- 3 cups bread flour
- 1/4 cup sugar
- 3 teaspoons gluten
- 1 teaspoon salt
- 3/4 teaspoon ground cardamom
- 2 teaspoons bread machine yeast
- Powdered sugar, for dusting

1-pound loaf

- 1/4 cup currants
- 1 tablespoon cream sherry
- 1/8 teaspoon saffron threads, crumbled
- 1/4 cup warm water
- 1/4 cup milk
- 1 large egg, at room temperature
- 3 tablespoons unsalted butter, softened
- 2 cups bread flour
- 3 tablespoons sugar
- 2 teaspoons gluten
- 3/4 teaspoon salt
- 1/2 teaspoon ground cardamom
- 1 1/2 teaspoons bread machine yeast
- Powdered sugar, for dusting

1. In a small bowl, combine the currants and sherry. Macerate at room temperature 1 hour. Sprinkle the saffron over the surface of the water and let stand 30 minutes.

continues next page

2. Place all of the ingredients in the bread machine according to manufacturer's instructions. Set Crust on light, program for Sweet Bread, and press Start.

3. After the baking cycle ends, remove the bread immediately from the machine to a cooling rack. Cool to room temperature before dusting with powdered sugar and slicing.

Grand Baba

The cylindrical shape of the baba is perfect for the bread machine. This is a Grand Baba, compared to the individual babas on page 386. It, too, however, is soaked in a spirited syrup, glazed, and served with sweetened whipped cream.

Makes 1 loaf

1½-pound loaf	*1-pound loaf*
⅓ cup water	¼ cup water
3 large eggs, at room temperature	2 large eggs, at room temperature
8 tablespoons (1 stick) unsalted butter, melted	5 tablespoons unsalted butter, melted
2 cups bread flour	1½ cups bread flour
2 tablespoons sugar	1 tablespoon sugar
½ teaspoon grated lemon zest	⅓ teaspoon grated lemon zest
2 teaspoons gluten	1½ teaspoons gluten
½ teaspoon salt	⅓ teaspoon salt
1¼ teaspoons bread machine yeast	1 teaspoon bread machine yeast

Rum Syrup

½ cup (packed) light brown sugar

½ cup granulated sugar

1 cup water

¼ cup golden rum

Cherry Glaze

¼ pound dried cherries, soaked in hot water 1 hour

⅓ cup sugar

1. Place the ingredients in the bread machine according to manufacturer's instructions. Set Crust on light, program for Sweet Bread and press Start. The dough will be batterlike.

2. Make the rum syrup: Combine the sugars and water in a small saucepan and heat until the sugar is dissolved, about 5 minutes. Cool to warm. Add the rum and set aside.

3. After the Baking cycle ends, remove the pan and place on a rack. Pierce the top in a few places with a bamboo skewer. Turn out of the pan onto a deep plate. Slowly pour the rum glaze all over the cake and let it stand to absorb the glaze that collects at the base. Cover with plastic wrap. Prepare the cherry glaze.

continues next page

Sweetened whipped cream, for serving

4. Drain off the water and purée the cherries with a food mill or in a food processor. Combine with an equal amount of sugar in a small saucepan and boil 5 minutes to reduce slightly and thicken. Brush cake all over with hot cherry glaze to seal in moisture. Cool and transfer to a clean serving plate before slicing. Store in the refrigerator.

BAKING EQUIPMENT

Bread making is a culinary art requiring very little equipment: a bowl, a spoon, and an oven. But there are very nice tools that help make bread making easier and more enjoyable. Buy good quality equipment; the bread they produce is worth the few extra pennies.

Choose a work surface in the kitchen that is a comfortable height and is large enough for working with dough. Place a clean wood, marble, or plastic work surface on the counter for easy cleanup. Keep your work board just for making bread and pastry; strong odors are hard to scrub off and can impart a taste to dough. Keep dry and liquid measuring cups and spoons, spatulas, dough scraper, thermometers, and a wet towel close at hand while working.

In this book, each recipe lists the equipment needed for that particular recipe. The following list is a general list.

- Baguette tray pans

- Baking pans and molds: heavy aluminum, European tinned steel, glass, earthenware, or nonstick

- Baking sheets: heavy aluminum or steel in several sizes that fit in your oven.

- Bannetons, or muslin-lined baskets for rising European-style free-form breads

- Biscuit cutters and pastry wheel

- Bowls: crockery, glass, stainless steel or aluminum, and deep plastic buckets in a variety of sizes from small to over-sized, for mixing and rising

- Chef's knife, citrus grater, kitchen shears

- Cooling racks: stainless steel, wire, or wood

- Dough scrapers: 6-inch flexible plastic for scraping bowls and a stainless steel bench knife scraper with a wooden handle for cleaning the work surface and dividing pieces of dough

- Food processor

- Heavy-duty electric stand mixer with three attachments: the flat paddle, the wire whip, and the dough hook

- Heavy-duty oven mitts, to protect the lower arms

- Loaf pans in several sizes, individual or frames

- Long serrated bread knife, for slicing bread loaves, cutting sweet roll dough, and for decorative slashing before baking

- Measuring cups, liquid and dry

- Measuring spoons

- Molds: fluted brioche molds, charlotte molds, pie pans, popover pans

- Muffin tins

- Parchment paper for lining pans

- Pastry brushes: several, 1 to 3 inches wide, with natural bristles for applying glazes, and a large clean paint brush for dusting off the work space

- Pizza pans

- Plastic wrap, in the widest width available, for covering doughs during rising

- Pullman pans

- Rolling pin, preferably the large ball-bearing type

- Scale: beam-balance, electronic, or spring

- Spatulas: plastic and metal, one extra-wide

- Spoons: wooden and metal

- Springform pans

- Tape measure

- Thermometers: oven and instant-read yeast

- Timer

- Tube pans: plain and fluted (Bundt, Turk's head, Kugelhopf, panettone, savarin ring)

- Unbleached muslin cheesecloth

- Unglazed tiles or commercial baking stone and a short-handled wooden baker's peel

- Whisks: mini, regular, and large balloon type

- Work space: wooden board, marble slab, or plastic cutting board, no smaller than 15 by 21 inches, for kneading and forming

HIGH-ALTITUDE BAKING GUIDE

Altitudes over 3,000 feet affect baking procedures. The atmosphere is drier, due to lower air pressure, and flours dry out; bread recipes require slightly more liquid to produce a soft, silky yeast dough. Water usually takes longer to boil. Sugar and chocolate tend to become more concentrated in batters, and liquid evaporates quickly. The scientist in you will need to closely observe results and experiment to get the proper dough consistencies for your yeast breads. Asking a neighbor or coworker for first-hand information is the best way to go. There are also special reference books devoted to the art of high-altitude baking for people who live at altitudes higher than 3,000 feet.

Fermentation and rising is faster the higher you go as the leavening carbon dioxide gases are able to expand faster due to the thinner air, and rising times will be decreased up to one-half. Overrising causes a finished loaf to be coarse in texture. For bread baking there is really only one technique to remember: To avoid overrising, reduce yeast by ½ teaspoon for every tablespoon or package called for in the recipe. A second rise to just nearly double in bulk is recommended for the best flavor and texture. No temperature adjustment of liquids is necessary.

Oven Temperature: Increase by 25°F to compensate for faster rising in the oven and slower heating. The same rules apply to sourdough and quick-bread baking.

Liquids: For each cup, increase the amount by 1 tablespoon at more than 3,000 feet; 2 to 3 tablespoons at 5,000 feet; and 3 to 4 tablespoons at 7,000 to 8,000 feet.

Sugar: For each cup, decrease the amount by 1 tablespoon at more than 3,000 feet; 2 tablespoons at 5,000 feet; and 3 tablespoons at 7,000 to 8,000 feet.

Flour: For each cup, increase flour by 1 tablespoon at more than 3,000 feet; 2 tablespoons at 5,000 feet; and 3 tablespoons at more than 6,500 feet. Store flour in airtight containers.

MAIL-ORDER SOURCES

Although this book was written to utilize ingredients widely available in ordinary super-markets and natural foods stores, included here is a list of reliable mail-order sources for exceptional grains, hard-to-find ingredients, and special equipment. Consider the investment in good pans, hand tools, and mixers a lifetime investment and a joy to work with.

Mail-order sources for flour and grains offer their own catalogs and take telephone orders. The prices are moderate, but shipping is extra, and grains can be very heavy. The following suppliers all have outstanding products for baking. Please note that all stone-ground products should be stored in the refrigerator or freezer on arrival.

Bob's Red Mill
Natural Foods, Inc.
5209 S.E. International Way
Milwaukie, OR 97222
503-645-3215
Organic flours and grains, including blue cornmeal, teff, gluten, kamut, and spelt.

Gibbs Wild Rice
10400 Billings Road
Live Oak, CA 95053
Mild-flavored, paddy-grown wild rice.

Gray's Grist Mill
P.O. Box 422
Adamsville, RI 02801
401-783-4054
Stone-ground local cornmeal and flours.

King Arthur Baker's Catalog
P.O. Box 876
Norwich, VT 05055
800-827-6836
Grains (whole and cracked cereal blends, and flours including spelt and kamut), European instant yeast, and baking equip-ment. This is the best source for one-stop shopping.

Pamela's Products, Inc. (Guisto's Mail Order Source for the Home Baker)
156 Utah Avenue
South San Francisco, CA 94080
415-952-4546
Freshly ground organic flours and grains.

Sur La Table
1765 Sixth Avenue South
Seattle, WA 98134-1608
800-243-0852
An enviable variety of tools and equipment for bread bakers.

Teals Super Value
P.O. Box 660
Cass Lake, MN 56633
Traditional hand-harvested wild rice.

The Vermont Country Store
P.O. Box 3000
Manchester Center, VT 05225-3000
Maple sugar products.

Vermont Soapstone Company
Box 168
Perkinsville, VT 05151
A source of soapstone griddles.

Walnut Acres
Walnut Acres Road
Penns Creek, PA 17862
800-344-9025
Whole-grain flours, amaranth, and quinoa.

White Lily Foods Company
P.O. Box 871
Knoxville, TN 37901
615-546-5511
The flour of the South: self-rising and pastry flour for biscuits.

Williams-Sonoma
P.O. Box 7456
San Francisco, CA 94120-7456
800-541-2233
A cook's catalog for fine kitchen equipment.

INDEX

A Alcoholic spirits, 321

Almonds

Almond Crème, 74

Almond Crests, 281

Almond Croissants, 284

Almond Filling, 424

Alsatian Kugelhof (food processor), 414

Babka, 304–5

blanching, 375

Kulich with Almonds and Ginger (Russian Easter Coffee Cake), 380–81

Marzipan Brioche with Apricot Brandy Glaze, 74–75

Paskha, 382

Sweet Swirled Breads (bread machine), 424–25

toasting, 375

Alpine Easter Bread, 376–77

Alsatian Kugelhof (food processor), 414

Altitudes, baking at high, 470

Amaretto Cream, 353

American Chocolate Bread, 383

Anadama Bread with Tillamook Cheddar Cheese, 108–9

Apples

Apple Corn Bread, 344

Apple Danish, 281

Apple-Nutmeg Filling, 425

Baked Apple and Pear Oven Pancake, 255

Fresh Apple Coffee Cake, 296

Fresh Apple-Walnut Loaf, 264–65

Savory Corn Bread Stuffing, 345

Sour Cream Apple Muffins, 330

Sweet Swirled Breads (bread machine), 424–25

Applesauce

Spiced Applesauce Muffins, 333

Steamed Applesauce Brown Bread, 325

Apricots

Apricot and White Chocolate Filling, 425

Apricot Brandy Glaze, 74, 391

Apricot Glaze, 386–87, 388–89

Dried Apricot–Pecan Bread, 313

Fresh Apricot Gingerbread, 355

Hot Cross Bun with Dried Fruit, 384–85

Kulich with Almonds and Ginger (Russian Easter Coffee Cake), 380–81

Paskha, 382

Pernod Panettone, 360–61

Pernod Panettone (bread machine), 460–61

Sweet Swirled Breads (bread machine), 424–25

Arany galuska, 306

Artichoke Pie, Eggplant, Pepper, and, 208–9

Ascorbic acid, 421

B Babas

Golden Rum Babas, 386–87

Grand Baba (bread machine), 465–66

Babka, 304–5

Bacon

Bacon–Blue Corn Sticks, 337

Bacon Corn Bread, 344

Pancetta-Onion Gruyère Ring, 200–201

Sun-Dried Tomato and Bacon Popovers, 257

Bagels

about, 157

Cinnamon-Raisin Bagels, 180

Egg Bagels, 178–79

freezing, 32

Onion Bagels, 180

Orange-Oatmeal Bagels, 180

Pumpernickel Bagels, 180

Whole-Wheat Bagels, 180

Baked Apple and Pear Oven Pancake, 255

Baked Marinated Goat Cheese, 405

Baked Pancake with Cucumber Salsa, 254

Baking, about, 29–31

Baking powder, 310–11

Baking soda, 311

Baking stones, 121, 212

Bananas

Banana Bread, 316

Banana-Pecan Muffins, 332

Basic Pizza Dough, 213–15

Basic Pizza Dough (bread machine), 456–57

Basil
    Tomato-Basil Sauce for Pizza, 215
    Whole-Wheat Basil Bread, 140–41
Beer
    Beer Waffles, 244
    Potato and Rye Vienna Twist, 104–5
Beigli, 372
Belgian Waffles, Vanilla, 245
Bell peppers
    Bacon–Blue Corn Sticks, 337
    Eggplant, Pepper, and Artichoke Pie, 208–9
    Green and Red Pepper Corn Bread, 347
Berries. *See also individual berries*
    Berry Corn Bread, 344
    Fresh Berry Muffins, 329
    Orange Savarin with Berries, 388–89
Best Yorkshire Pudding, 258
Biscuits
    Blueberry Biscuits, 183
    Classic Buttermilk Biscuits, 182
    Cornmeal-Orange Biscuits, 185
    freezing, 33
    Jalapeño Biscuits, 182
    making, 181
    making, in a food processor, 183
    Old-fashioned Shortcake Biscuits, 186
    Pecan Biscuits, 182
    Sweet Potato Biscuits, 184
    Whole-Wheat Biscuits, 183
    Wild Rice Biscuits, 182
Blackberries
    Berry Corn Bread, 344
    Fresh Berry Muffins, 329
    Orange Savarin with Berries, 388–89
Black breads
    Black Bread Rolls, 168
    Black Russian Rye Bread, 102–3
    Black Russian Rye Bread (bread machine), 442–43
    Black Olive Corn Bread, 344
Blini, Cornmeal, 250

Blintzes
    Blueberry Blintzes, 249
    Cottage Cheese Blintzes, 248–49
    Strawberry Blintzes, 249
Blueberries
    Alsatian Kugelhof (food processor), 414
    Berry Corn Bread, 344
    Blueberry Biscuits, 183
    Blueberry Blintzes, 249
    Blueberry–Blue Cornmeal Pancakes, 241
    Blueberry Buttermilk Coffee Cake, 291
    Blueberry Danish Turnovers, 280
    Blueberry Gingerbread, 354
    Blueberry Whole-Wheat Croissants, 284
    Granola-Blueberry Filling, 425
    Maple-Blueberry Whole-Wheat Braid, 298
    Maple Whole-Wheat Johnnycake with Blueberries, 348
    Orange Savarin with Berries, 388–89
    Steamed Brown Bread with Dried Blueberries, 324–25
    Sweet Swirled Breads (bread machine), 424–25
    Whole-Wheat Blueberry Buttermilk Pancakes, 242
Blue Corn Bread, 346
Blue Cornmeal Pancakes, 241
Blue Cornmeal Pancakes with Corn, 241
Blue Cornmeal Pancakes with Rice, 241
Blue Corn Tortillas (Tortillas de Maíz Azul), 230
Bohemian Sweet Rolls (Kolacki), 366–67
Bolillos (French-Style Mexican Hard Rolls), 162–63
Boule de Poîlane, 128
Bow Knots and Rosettes, 159
Braided Rolls, 159
Bran
    about, 38, 93
    Black Russian Rye Bread, 102–3
    Black Russian Rye Bread (bread machine), 442–43
    Bran, Molasses, and Sunflower Bread (bread machine), 437
    Bran-Molasses-Sunflower Bread, 92–93
    Bran Popovers, 256

Everyday Maple Bran Muffins, 334

Whole-Wheat Bran Bread with Dates, 193

Brandy Glaze, 322

Bread crumbs, 59

Bread machine recipes

    Basic Pizza Dough, 456–57

    Black Russian Rye Bread, 442–43

    Bran, Molasses, and Sunflower Bread, 437

    Bread Machine Sponge Starter, 448

    Brioche with Cheese and Walnuts, 431

    Buttermilk Honey Bread, 430

    Buttermilk Potato Bread, 450

    Challah, 428–29

    Cinnamon-Raisin-Currant Bread, 458

    Cornmeal Crescent Dinner Rolls, 444–45

    Cornmeal-Millet Bread, 444

    Cornmeal Pizza Dough, 457

    Cottage Cheese–Dill Bread, 423

    Country Bread, 440

    Country Bread with Dried Figs, 440

    Country Bread with Raisins and Walnuts, 440

    Cracked Wheat Bread, 436

    Cuban Bread, 422

    Egg Bread, 426

    French Long Bâtard, 454–55

    French Round Boule, 454–55

    Fresh Herb Honey Whole-Wheat Bread, 433

    Garlic Pizza Dough, 457

    Graham Granola Bread, 438

    Grand Baba, 465–66

    hamburger, hot dog, long rolls, and sandwich buns,
        426–27

    Herbed Pizza Dough, 457

    Homemade Performance Plus Bread Machine Flour,
        421

    Honey Whole-Wheat Bread, 432

    Italian Olive Oil Bread, 447

    Maple Pecan Bread, 459

    Mexican Chocolate Bread, 462

    Narsai's Light Rye Bread, 441

    Old-fashioned Oatmeal Bread, 439

    100 Percent Whole-Wheat Bread, 434

    Pain de Campagne, 454–55

    Pernod Panettone, 460–61

    Pull-Apart Potato Dinner Rolls, 451

    Saffron Bread, 463–64

    Saffron Pizza Dough, 457

    Semolina Pizza Dough, 457

    Sesame Semolina Bread, 435

    Sourdough Farm Bread, 453

    Squaw Bread, 446

    Suzanne's Sourdough Pizza, 457

    Sweet Swirled Breads, 424–25

    Three-Seed Honey Whole-Wheat Bread, 432

    Tuscan Peasant Bread, 449

    Tuscan Peasant Bread with Olives, 449

    Whole-Wheat Pizza Dough, 457

    Wild Rice–Molasses Bread, 452

Bread machines

    adapting traditional recipes to, 419

    convenience of, 415

    hints for, 416–17

    mixing dough in, 21

    settings for, 417–18

    special ingredients for, 419–21

Bread sticks

    about, 157

    Cheese Bread Sticks, 145

    Italian Bread Sticks (Grissini), 174–75

    Wild Rice Bread Sticks, 176–77

    Bread with Three Chocolates, 392–93

Brie cheese

    Brie in Brioche, 78

    croutons, 60

Brioche

    basic recipe, 70–72

    Brie in Brioche, 78

    Brioche with Cheese and Walnuts (bread machine),
        431

    Cornmeal Brioche, 76–77

    Cornmeal Brioche with Capers, 77

Cornmeal Brioche with Sun-Dried Tomatoes, 77

    croustade, 71

grosse, à tête, 71

making dough by hand, 73

Marzipan Brioche with Apricot Brandy Glaze, 74–75

nanterre, 72

pain brioche, 71–72

parisienne, 72

Pumpkin Brioche, 286

yields and baking times, 72

Brown bread

    Steamed Applesauce Brown Bread, 325

    Steamed Brown Bread with Dried Blueberries, 324–25

Brown Rice Bread with Dutch Crunch Topping, 110–11

Bruschetta, 61

Buckwheat flour

    about, 99

    Buckwheat Pancakes, 243

    Buckwheat Popovers, 256

    Rain and Sun, 98–99

Bulgur

    about, 96

    Cracked Wheat Bread, 88–89

    Cracked Wheat Bread (bread machine), 436

    Oatmeal-Bulgur Bread, 96–97

Buns. *See also* Rolls

    hamburger and hot dog (bread machine), 426–27

    Hot Cross Bun with Dried Fruit and Two Glazes, 384–85

    Mexican Morning Buns (Pan Dulce), 272–73

    sandwich (bread machine), 426–27

    Sesame Burger Buns, 170–71

Butter

    about, 75

    Nasturtium Butter, 69

Butterfly Rolls, 159

Buttermilk

    about, 55, 292

    Blueberry Buttermilk Coffee Cake, 291

    Blue Cornmeal Pancakes, 241

Buckwheat Pancakes, 243

Buttermilk Corn Bread, 342

Buttermilk Honey Bread, 54–55

Buttermilk Honey Bread (bread machine), 430

Buttermilk Potato Bread, 138–39

Buttermilk Potato Bread (bread machine), 450

Buttermilk Potato Rolls, 139

Buttermilk Waffles, 238

Buttermilk Waffles with Rice, 238

Buttermilk Whole-Wheat Bread (food processor), 399

Celeste's Sunflower-Oatmeal Bread, 156

Classic Buttermilk Biscuits, 182

Cornmeal-Orange Biscuits, 185

Cracked Wheat Bread, 88–89

Everyday Maple Bran Muffins, 334

Fig-Walnut Scones, 189

Graham Scones with Pine Nuts and Raisins, 190

Irish Soda Bread with Caraway and Drambuie, 191

Lemon Buttermilk Waffles, 238

Maple Whole-Wheat Johnnycake with Blueberries, 348

My Favorite Buttermilk Dinner Rolls, 158–59

Old-fashioned Buttermilk Pancakes, 237

Old-fashioned 100 Percent Whole-Wheat Bread, 84–85

Pull-Apart Potato Dinner Rolls (bread machine), 451

Rain and Sun, 98–99

Seven-Grain Buttermilk Waffles, 239

Sour Cream Buttermilk Waffles, 238

Spiced Brown Sugar–Pecan Coffee Cake, 288

Steamed Applesauce Brown Bread, 325

Steamed Brown Bread with Dried Blueberries, 324–25

Steamed Pecan Corn Bread, 323

Super Whole-Grain Buttermilk Waffles, 238

Whole-Wheat Blueberry Buttermilk Pancakes, 242

Whole-Wheat Bran Bread with Dates, 193

Whole-Wheat Irish Herb Bread, 192

Whole-Wheat Prune Bread, 314

Yogurt Corn Bread, 344

Byzantine Easter Bread, 378–79

C California Olive Rolls, 173

California Walnut Bread, 150–51

Calzone

    about, 212

    Spinach Calzone, 222–23

Campers Pizza, 216–17

Caraway seeds

    Black Russian Rye Bread, 102–3

    Black Russian Rye Bread (bread machine), 442–43

    Irish Soda Bread with Caraway and Drambuie, 191

    Narsai's Light Rye Bread (bread machine), 441

    Pain de Seigle, 132–33

    Sour Poppy Seed Rye, 134–35

Carrot and Tangerine Bread, 319

Cashews

    Cashew-Date Bread, 266–67

    toasting, 375

Celeste's Sunflower-Oatmeal Bread, 156

Cereals, mixed-grain

    about, 40

    Seven-Grain Buttermilk Waffles, 239

    Seven-Grain Honey Bread, 114–15

Challah (Jewish Egg Braid)

    basic recipe, 63–64

    bread machine recipe, 428–29

    freeze now/bake later, 65

    Sweet Vanilla Challah, 66–67

    variations, 65

Cheddar cheese

    Anadama Bread with Tillamook Cheddar Cheese, 108–9

    Cheddar Cheese Bread with Toasted Sesame Seeds, 142–43

    Pepper Cheese Breads (food processor), 411

    Santa Fe Blue Corn Muffins, 338

Cheese

    Anadama Bread with Tillamook Cheddar Cheese, 108–9

    Baked Marinated Goat Cheese, 405

    Blueberry Blintzes, 249

    Bohemian Sweet Rolls (Kolacki), 366–67

Brie croutons, 60

Brie in Brioche, 78

Brioche with Cheese and Walnuts (bread machine), 431

Cheddar Cheese Bread with Toasted Sesame Seeds, 142–43

Cheese Bread Sticks, 145

Cheese Danish Envelopes, 280

Cottage Cheese Blintzes, 248–49

Cottage Cheese–Dill Bread (bread machine), 423

Crescia al Formaggio, 198–99

Deep Dish Pizza with Sausage and Mozzarella, 218–20

Eggplant, Pepper, and Artichoke Pie, 208–9

Garlic and Mozzarella Stromboli, 202–3

Green and Red Pepper Corn Bread, 347

Grilled Herb and Cheese Flatbread, 48

Gruyère Pullman Loaf, 144–45

Hungarian Sweet Cheese Bread, 390–91

Italian-Style Herb Bread, 204–5

Kat's Favorite Cherry-Cheese Filling, 424

Parmesan-Herb Popovers, 257

Paskha, 382

Pepper Cheese Breads (food processor), 411

Pizza Pie with Cheese (Pane al Pizza con Formaggio), 221

Santa Fe Blue Corn Muffins, 338

Spinach Calzone, 222–23

Strawberry Blintzes, 249

Sweet Swirled Breads (bread machine), 424–25

Torta d'Erbe (Italian Green Tort), 206–7

Zucchini Madeleines, 336

Cherries

    Cherry–Blue Corn Bread, 346

    Cherry Glaze, 465–66

    Cinnamon-Walnut Sweet Bread, 306–7

    Golden Rum Babas, 386–87

    Kat's Favorite Cherry-Cheese Filling, 424

    Kulich with Almonds and Ginger (Russian Easter Coffee Cake), 380–81

    Stollen with Dried Cherries and Pineapple, 362–63

    Sweet Swirled Breads (bread machine), 424–25

Chestnuts
    flour, 154
    Roasted Chestnut Bread, 154–55
Chiles
    Green and Red Pepper Corn Bread, 347
    Jalapeño Biscuits, 182
    Santa Fe Blue Corn Muffins, 338
Chocolate. *See also* White chocolate
    about, 357–58
    American Chocolate Bread, 383
    Babka, 304–5
    Bread with Three Chocolates, 392–93
    melting, 359
    Mexican Chocolate Bread (bread machine), 462
    Pain au Chocolat, 284
    substitutions, 358
    varieties of, 357–58
Christmas breads
    Bohemian Sweet Rolls (Kolacki), 366–67
    Hungarian Nut Roll (Diós Tekeres), 372–73
    Pernod Panettone, 360–61
    Pernod Panettone (bread machine), 460–61
    Stollen with Dried Cherries and Pineapple, 362–63
Cinnamon Ice Cream, 354
Cinnamon-Raisin Bagels, 180
Cinnamon-Raisin-Currant Bread (bread machine), 458
Cinnamon Rolls with Irish Cream Glaze, 270–71
Cinnamon-Walnut Sweet Bread, 306–7
Classic Buttermilk Biscuits, 182
Classic Sourdough Starter, 120
Cloverleaf Rolls, 159
Cobbler, Fresh Fruit, 289
Cocoa powder, 358
Coffee cakes. *See also* Sweet breads
    Babka, 304–5
    baking and cooling, 287
    Blueberry Buttermilk Coffee Cake, 291
    freezing, 32–33
    Fresh Apple Coffee Cake, 296
    Fresh Fruit Cobbler, 289
    Golden Italian Coffee Cake, 302–3

    Kulich with Almonds and Ginger (Russian Easter Coffee Cake), 380–81
    Pear Spice Coffee Cake, 290
    Plum Crumb Cake, 308
    Spiced Brown Sugar–Pecan Coffee Cake, 288
    Vanilla Sour Cream Coffee Cake, 293
Cooling, 31
Corn
    Bacon–Blue Corn Sticks, 337
    Blue Cornmeal Pancakes with Corn, 241
Corn breads
    about, 340
    Apple Corn Bread, 344
    Bacon–Blue Corn Sticks, 337
    Bacon Corn Bread, 344
    baking, in a cast-iron skillet, 341
    Berry Corn Bread, 344
    Black Olive Corn Bread, 344
    Blue Corn Bread, 346
    Buttermilk Corn Bread, 342
    Cherry–Blue Corn Bread, 346
    Green and Red Pepper Corn Bread, 347
    Maple Whole-Wheat Johnnycake with Blueberries, 348
    Rice Corn Bread, 344
    Savory Corn Bread Stuffing, 345
    Steamed Pecan Corn Bread, 323
    storing, 340
    Yogurt Corn Bread, 344
Cornmeal. *See also* Corn breads; Masa harina
    about, 343
    Anadama Bread with Tillamook Cheddar Cheese, 108–9
    Blueberry–Blue Cornmeal Pancakes, 241
    Blue Cornmeal Pancakes, 241
    Blue Cornmeal Pancakes with Corn, 241
    Blue Cornmeal Pancakes with Rice, 241
    Cornmeal Blini, 250
    Cornmeal Brioche, 76–77
    Cornmeal Brioche with Capers, 77
    Cornmeal Brioche with Sun-Dried Tomatoes, 77

Cornmeal Crescent Dinner Rolls (bread machine),
  444–45
Cornmeal Croissants, 284
Cornmeal-Millet Bread (bread machine), 444
Cornmeal-Orange Biscuits, 185
Cornmeal Pizza Dough, 215
Cornmeal Pizza Dough (bread machine), 457
Cornmeal Popovers, 256
Indian Pumpkin Bread, 320
Rain and Sun, 98–99
Raspberry Cornmeal Muffins, 335
Santa Fe Blue Corn Muffins, 338
Steamed Applesauce Brown Bread, 325
Steamed Brown Bread with Dried Blueberries,
  324–25
Cottage cheese
  Blueberry Blintzes, 249
  Cottage Cheese Blintzes, 248–49
  Cottage Cheese–Dill Bread (bread machine), 423
  Strawberry Blintzes, 249
Country breads
  about, 116
  baking, in a Dutch oven, 117
  Country Bread (bread machine), 440
  Country Bread with Dried Figs (bread machine), 440
  Country Bread with Raisins and Walnuts (bread
    machine), 440
  Farmstead Sourdough Bread, 118–19
  Italian Olive Oil Bread, 122–23
  Italian Olive Oil Bread (bread machine), 447
  Pain de Campagnard, 130–31
  Pain de Campagne, 128–29
  Pain de Campagne (bread machine), 454–55
  Pain de Campagne (food processor), 402–3
  Pain de Seigle, 132–33
  Semolina Sesame Seed Twist, 124–25
  Sourdough Farm Bread, 453
  Sour Four-Seed Rye, 135
  Sour Poppy Seed Rye, 134–35
  Vienna Bread, 126–27
Country-Style Whole-Wheat Pita, 234–35

Couverture, 358
Cracked Wheat Bread, 88–89
Cracked Wheat Bread (bread machine), 436
Cranberries
  Cranberry-Orange Bread, 318
  Everyday Maple Bran Muffins, 334
Cream cheese
  Cheese Danish Envelopes, 280
  Hungarian Sweet Cheese Bread, 390–91
  Kat's Favorite Cherry-Cheese Filling, 424
  Pancetta-Onion Gruyère Ring, 200–201
  Sweet Swirled Breads (bread machine), 424–25
Cream of tartar, 310
Cream Sherry–Pumpkin Bread, 320
Crème fraîche, 292
Crêpes
  basic recipe, 246
  Dessert Crêpes, 247
  freezing, 33
  Herb Crêpes, 247
  Special Diet Crêpes, 247
  Whole-Grain Crêpes, 247
Crescent Rolls, 159
Crescia al Formaggio, 198–99
Croissants
  about, 259
  Almond Croissants, 284
  Blueberry Whole-Wheat Croissants, 284
  Cornmeal Croissants, 284
  freezing, 32, 285
  Raspberry Whole-Wheat Croissants, 284
  Whole-Wheat Croissants, 282–84
Crostini, 61
Croustade, 71
Croutons
  Brie, 60
  garlic, 60
  large, 60
  small, 59–60
Cuban Bread (bread machine), 422
Cucumber Salsa, 254

Cuernos, 272, 273
Currants
    Alsatian Kugelhof (food processor), 414
    Cinnamon-Raisin-Currant Bread (bread machine),
        458
    Cinnamon Rolls with Irish Cream Glaze, 270–71
    Fresh Apple-Walnut Loaf, 264–65
    Fresh Berry Muffins, 329
    Golden Rum Babas, 386–87
    Hot Cross Bun with Dried Fruit and Two Glazes,
        384–85
    Paskha, 382
    Saffron Bread (bread machine), 463–64
    Saffron Bread with Scented-Geranium Powdered
        Sugar, 364–65
    Stollen with Dried Cherries and Pineapple, 362–63
    Whole-Wheat Irish Herb Bread, 192

D Dairy products, 40, 292
Danish Pastries, 259, 276–81
Dates
    Cashew-Date Bread, 266–67
    Honey Date Filling, 425
    Orange-Date Tea Bread, 315
    Sweet Swirled Breads (bread machine), 424–25
    Whole-Wheat Bran Bread with Dates, 193
Deep Dish Pizza with Sausage and Mozzarella, 218–20
Dessert Crêpes, 247
Dessert rusks, 61
Diastatic malt powder, 421
Dill
    about, 137
    Cottage Cheese–Dill Bread (bread machine), 423
    Seeded Dill Rye, 137
Double Crescent Rolls, 159–60
Dough
    deflating, 27
    different types of, 23–24
    enhancers, 420–21
    forming, into loaf, 27–28

    freezing, 24
    kneading, 21–23
    mixing, 19–21
    mixing, in the food processor, 397
    rising, 24–27, 28
Dried Apricot–Pecan Bread, 313
Dutch Baby, 254
Dutch Crunch Topping, 110–11
Dutch ovens, 117

E Easter breads
    Alpine Easter Bread, 376–77
    Byzantine Easter Bread, 378–79
    Hot Cross Bun with Dried Fruit and Two Glazes,
        384–85
    Hungarian Nut Roll (Diós Tekeres), 372–73
    Italian Anise Easter Bread, 370–71
    Kulich with Almonds and Ginger (Russian Easter
        Coffee Cake), 380–81
    Portuguese Sweet Bread with Honey, 368–69
Eggplant, Pepper, and Artichoke Pie, 208–9
Eggs. *See also* Brioche
    about, 62
    Alpine Easter Bread, 376–77
    Byzantine Easter Bread, 378–79
    Challah (bread machine), 428–29
    Egg Bagels, 178–79
    Egg Bread (bread machine), 426
    Egg Glaze, 276
    Jewish Egg Braid (Challah), 63–65
    Lemon Whole-Wheat Egg Bread with Nasturtium
        Butter, 68–69
    Onion Tart, 210–11
    Portuguese Sweet Bread with Honey, 368–69
    Rich Egg Glaze, 52–53
    Rosemary Raisin Bread (food processor), 409
    storing, 67
    substitutions, 67
    Sweet Vanilla Challah, 66–67
    Vanilla Egg Glaze, 66–67

Elotes, 272, 273

Emmenthaler cheese

    Brioche with Cheese and Walnuts (bread machine),
        431

    Crescia al Formaggio, 198–99

English Muffins, Traditional, 268–69

Equipment, 467–69

    baking stones, 121, 212

    Dutch ovens, 117

    La Cloche, 133

    mixers, 19–20

    ovens, 30–31

    pancake griddles, 239, 247

    for pizza, 212

    power pans, 212

    waffle irons, 239

Everyday Maple Bran Muffins, 334

F   Farmer cheese

    Cheese Danish Envelopes, 280

    Paskha, 382

Farmstead Sourdough Bread, 118–19

Farm-Style White Bread with Cardamom, 56–57

Fat, 41

Fermentation, 18–19

Figs

    Country Bread with Dried Figs (bread machine), 440

    Fig-Walnut Scones, 189

Finishing Glaze, 277

Flatbreads

    about, 227

    Blue Corn Tortillas (Tortillas de Maíz Azul), 230

    Corn Tortillas (Tortillas de Maíz), 228–29

    Country-Style Whole-Wheat Pita, 234–35

    Flour Tortillas (Tortillas de Harina), 232–33

    Garden Flatbreads, 48–49

    Grilled Herb and Cheese Flatbread, 48

    Honey Indian Fry Bread, 231

    Indian Fry Bread, 231

    Low-Fat Flour Tortillas, 233

    Mesquite Flour Tortillas, 233

Flour

    all-purpose, 38

    bread, 38

    for bread machines, 420, 421

    cake, pastry, or "instant," 38

    chestnut, 154

    gluten, 39, 420

    graham, 39, 81

    harina para atole, 241

    Homemade Performance Plus Bread Machine Flour,
        421

    measuring, 37

    self-rising, 39

    semolina, 39–40, 125

    spelt, 39

    wheat, 37

    whole-wheat, 39, 81

Flour tortillas

    Flour Tortillas (Tortillas de Harina), 232–33

    Low-Fat Flour Tortillas, 233

    Mesquite Flour Tortillas, 233

Focaccia

    about, 212

    Herbed Focaccia, 226

    Olive Focaccia, 224

Food processor breads

    Alsatian Kugelhof, 414

    Buttermilk Whole-Wheat Bread, 399

    Four-Seed Whole-Wheat Bread, 408

    French Bread, 400–401

    Italian Whole-Wheat Bread, 404–5

    Multi-Grain Wild Rice Bread, 410

    Pain de Campagne, 402–3

    Pepper Cheese Breads, 411

    Rosemary Raisin Bread, 409

    Sesame White Bread, 398

    Sour Cream Braid, 412–13

    Sour Cream Raisin Bread, 413

    Sour Rye Bread, 406–7

Food processors

advantages of, 394

best, for baking, 394

making biscuits and shortcakes in, 183

making tortilla dough in, 233

mixing dough in, 20–21, 397

techniques with, 394–97

Freezer Rolls, 160–61

Freezing

bread, 31–33

dough, 24

French Bread (food processor), 400–401

French Bread (Pain Ordinaire), 46–47

French Long Bâtard (bread machine), 454–55

French Nut Bread, 148–49

French Round Boule (bread machine), 454–55

French-Style Mexican Hard Rolls (Bolillos), 162–63

French Whole-Wheat Country Bread. *See* Pain de Campagne

Fresh Apple Coffee Cake, 296

Fresh Apple-Walnut Loaf, 264–65

Fresh Apricot Gingerbread, 355

Fresh Berry Muffins, 329

Fresh Fruit Cobbler, 289

Fresh Lemon Muffins, 328

Fruit, dried. *See also individual fruits*

Alsatian Kugelhof (food processor), 414

Bohemian Sweet Rolls (Kolacki), 366–67

Cashew-Date Bread, 266–67

cutting, 263

Golden Rum Babas, 386–87

Hot Cross Bun with Dried Fruit and Two Glazes, 384–85

Kulich with Almonds and Ginger (Russian Easter Coffee Cake), 380–81

Paskha, 382

Pernod Panettone, 360–61

Pernod Panettone (bread machine), 460–61

Stollen with Dried Cherries and Pineapple, 362–63

Fruit, fresh. *See also individual fruits*

Fresh Fruit Cobbler, 289

Peach Upside-Down Ginger Cake, 352

Plum Crumb Cake, 308

Fry breads

about, 227

Honey Indian Fry Bread, 231

Indian Fry Bread, 231

G Garden Flatbreads, 48–49

Garlic

croutons, 60

Garlic and Mozzarella Stromboli, 202–3

Garlic Pizza Dough, 215

Garlic Pizza Dough (bread machine), 457

Gingerbread and ginger cake

about, 349

Blueberry Gingerbread, 354

Fresh Apricot Gingerbread, 355

Gingerbread with Lemon and Raspberry Sauces, 350

Peach Upside-Down Ginger Cake, 352

Glazed Zucchini Bread, 322

Glazes

about, 28–29

Apricot Brandy Glaze, 74, 391

Apricot Glaze, 386–87, 388–89

Brandy Glaze, 322

Cherry Glaze, 465–66

Egg Glaze, 276

Finishing Glaze, 277

Irish Cream Glaze, 271

Lemon Glaze, 328

Lemon Icing, 384–85

Molasses Glaze, 260–61

Nut Liqueur Glaze, 376–77

Orange Glaze, 315

Rich Egg Glaze, 52–53

Sugar Glaze, 384–85

Vanilla Egg Glaze, 66–67

Gluten, 39, 420

Goat cheese

Baked Marinated Goat Cheese, 405

Hungarian Sweet Cheese Bread, 390–91

Golden Italian Coffee Cake, 302–3

Golden Rum Babas, 386–87

Graham flour

about, 39, 81

Graham Bread, 90–91

Graham Granola Bread (bread machine), 438

Graham Scones with Pine Nuts and Raisins, 190

Grains, whole. *See also individual grains*

advantages of, 79

baking with, 80

milling, in the food processor, 397

processing, 397

storing, 80

Grand Baba (bread machine), 465–66

Grand Marnier Strawberries and Crème Chantilly, 187

Granola

Graham Granola Bread (bread machine), 438

Granola-Blueberry Filling, 425

Green and Red Pepper Corn Bread, 347

Grilled Herb and Cheese Flatbread, 48

Grill-Top Baked Pizza, 217

Grissini (Italian Bread Sticks), 174–75

Grosse brioche à tête, 71

Gruyère cheese

Cheese Bread Sticks, 145

Crescia al Formaggio, 198–99

Eggplant, Pepper, and Artichoke Pie, 208–9

Gruyère Pullman Loaf, 144–45

Pancetta-Onion Gruyère Ring, 200–201

H Hamburger buns, 426–27

Harina para atole, 241, 343

Harinilla, 230, 343

Hazelnuts

French Nut Bread, 148–49

Prune-Nut Filling, 425

Sweet Swirled Breads (bread machine), 424–25

toasting, 375

Herbs

fresh, 136

Fresh Herb Honey Whole-Wheat Bread (bread machine), 433

Herb Crêpes, 247

Herbed Focaccia, 226

Herbed Pizza Dough, 215

Herbed Pizza Dough (bread machine), 457

Homemade Brown-and-Serve Rolls, 161

Homemade Performance Plus Bread Machine Flour, 421

Homestyle White Bread with Poppy Seeds, 52–53

Honey

Buttermilk Honey Bread, 54–55

Buttermilk Honey Bread (bread machine), 430

Fresh Herb Honey Whole-Wheat Bread (bread machine), 433

Honey and Seed Bread, 58

Honey Date Filling, 425

Honey Indian Fry Bread, 231

Honey-Prune Bread, 262–63

Honey Whole-Wheat Bread (bread machine), 432

Portuguese Sweet Bread with Honey, 368–69

Seven-Grain Honey Bread, 114–15

substituted for sugar, 41

Three-Seed Honey Whole-Wheat Bread (bread machine), 432

Hot Cross Bun with Dried Fruit and Two Glazes, 384–85

Hot dog buns, 426–27

Hungarian Nut Roll (Diós Tekeres), 372–73

Hungarian Sweet Cheese Bread, 390–91

I Ice Cream, Cinnamon, 354

Indian Fry Bread, 231

Indian Pumpkin Bread, 320

Irish Cream Glaze, 271

Irish Soda Bread with Caraway and Drambuie, 191

Italian Anise Easter Bread, 370–71

Italian Bread Sticks (Grissini), 174–75

Italian Green Tort (Torta d'Erbe), 206–7

Italian Olive Oil Bread, 122–23

Italian Olive Oil Bread (bread machine), 447

Italian-Style Herb Bread, 204–5

Italian Walnut-Raisin Whole-Wheat Bread, 86–87

Italian Whole-Wheat Bread (food processor), 404–5

J Jack cheese

Green and Red Pepper Corn Bread, 347

Santa Fe Blue Corn Muffins, 338

Jalapeño Biscuits, 182

Jewish Egg Braid. *See* Challah

Johnnycake. *See* Corn breads

K Kamut, 81

Kat's Favorite Cherry-Cheese Filling, 424

Kneading, 21–23

Kolacki (Bohemian Sweet Rolls), 366–67

Kugelhof, Alsatian (food processor), 414

Kulich with Almonds and Ginger (Russian Easter Coffee
Cake), 380–81

L La Cloche, 133

Leavening, 18–19

Lecithin, 420–21

Lemons and lemon juice

Fresh Lemon Muffins, 328

Lemon Buttermilk Waffles, 238

Lemon Cream Scones, 188

Lemon Glaze, 328

Lemon Icing, 384–85

Lemon–Poppy Seed Bread, 312

Lemon–Poppy Seed Bread with Saffron, 312

Lemon Sauce, 351

Lemon Syrup, 312

Lemon Whole-Wheat Egg Bread with Nasturtium
Butter, 68–69

Warm Lemon Sauce, 291

Liqueurs, 321

Liquids, 40

Low-Fat Flour Tortillas, 233

M Macadamia nuts

Pain Hawaiian, 152–53

toasting, 375

Madeleines, Zucchini, 336

Malted barley flour, 421

Mangoes

Mango Bread, 317

removing pit from, 317

Maple syrup

Everyday Maple Bran Muffins, 334

Gingerbread with Lemon and Raspberry Sauces, 350

Maple-Blueberry Whole-Wheat Braid, 298

Maple Pecan Bread (bread machine), 459

Maple Whole-Wheat Johnnycake with Blueberries,
348

Steamed Pecan Corn Bread, 323

Marzipan Brioche with Apricot Brandy Glaze, 74–75

Masa harina

about, 343

Blue Corn Tortillas (Tortillas de Maíz Azul), 230

Corn Tortillas (Tortillas de Maíz), 228–29

Melba toast, 60

Mesquite Flour Tortillas, 233

Mexican Chocolate Bread (bread machine), 462

Mexican Flat Rolls (Teleras), 163

Mexican Morning Buns (Pan Dulce), 272–73

Mile-High Popovers, 256

Millet

Cornmeal Crescent Dinner Rolls (bread machine),
444–45

Cornmeal-Millet Bread (bread machine), 444

Honey and Seed Bread, 58

Mixing, about, 19–21

Molasses

Black Russian Rye Bread, 102–3

Black Russian Rye Bread (bread machine), 442–43

Bran, Molasses, and Sunflower Bread (bread
machine), 437

Bran-Molasses-Sunflower Bread, 92–93

Buttermilk Whole-Wheat Bread (food processor), 399

Fresh Apricot Gingerbread, 355

Gingerbread with Lemon and Raspberry Sauces, 350

Graham Bread, 90–91

Molasses Glaze, 260–61

Steamed Brown Bread with Dried Blueberries, 324–25

Swedish Rye Bread, 100–101

Wild Rice–Molasses Bread, 112–13

Wild Rice–Molasses Bread (bread machine), 452

Mozzarella cheese

    Deep Dish Pizza with Sausage and Mozzarella, 218–20

    Garlic and Mozzarella Stromboli, 202–3

    Italian-Style Herb Bread, 204–5

    Pizza Pie with Cheese (Pane al Pizza con Formaggio), 221

    Spinach Calzone, 222–23

    Torta d'Erbe (Italian Green Tort), 206–7

Muffins

    Bacon–Blue Corn Sticks, 337

    Banana-Pecan Muffins, 332

    cups, 327

    Everyday Maple Bran Muffins, 334

    freezing, 33

    Fresh Berry Muffins, 329

    Fresh Lemon Muffins, 328

    Old-fashioned Prune Muffins, 331

    Quinoa Whole-Wheat Muffins, 339

    Raspberry Cornmeal Muffins, 335

    Santa Fe Blue Corn Muffins, 338

    Sour Cream Apple Muffins, 330

    Spiced Applesauce Muffins, 333

    techniques for, 326–27

    Traditional English Muffins, 268–69

    Zucchini Madeleines, 336

Multi-grain breads

    Multi-Grain Wild Rice Bread (food processor), 410

    Seven-Grain Buttermilk Waffles, 239

    Seven-Grain Honey Bread, 114–15

My Favorite Buttermilk Dinner Rolls, 158–59

N Nasturtium Butter, 69

Nut Liqueur Glaze, 376–77

Nuts. *See also individual nuts*

    about, 374–75

    chopping, 374

    French Nut Bread, 148–49

    Hungarian Nut Roll (Diós Tekeres), 372–73

    Prune-Nut Filling, 425

    purchasing, 374

    toasting, 374–75

    Vanilla Sour Cream Coffee Cake, 293

O Oats

    about, 95

    Cashew-Date Bread, 266–67

    Celeste's Sunflower-Oatmeal Bread, 156

    Oatmeal-Bulgur Bread, 96–97

    Oatmeal-Potato Bread, 94–95

    Old-fashioned Oatmeal Bread (bread machine), 439

    Orange-Oatmeal Bagels, 180

Old-fashioned Buttermilk Pancakes, 237

Old-fashioned 100 Percent Whole-Wheat Bread, 84–85

Old-fashioned Potato Pancakes, 252

Old-fashioned Prune Muffins, 331

Old-fashioned Raisin Bread with Molasses Glaze, 260–61

Old-fashioned Shortcake Biscuits, 186

Olives

    Black Olive Corn Bread, 344

    California Olive Rolls, 173

    Olive Bread, 146–47

    Olive Focaccia, 224

    Olive Pesto, 225

    Olive Toasts for Hors d'Oeuvres, 147

    Tuscan Peasant Bread with Olives, 51

    Tuscan Peasant Bread with Olives (bread machine), 449

Onions

    Onion Bagels, 180

    Onion Rolls, 47

    Onion Tart, 210–11

    Pancetta-Onion Gruyère Ring, 200–201

Oranges and orange juice
  Cornmeal-Orange Biscuits, 185
  Cranberry-Orange Bread, 318
  Dried Apricot—Pecan Bread, 313
  Fresh Apple Coffee Cake, 296
  Orange Cinnamon Swirl, 300–301
  Orange-Date Tea Bread, 315
  Orange Glaze, 315
  Orange-Oatmeal Bagels, 180
  Orange-Pecan Filling, 425
  Orange Savarin with Berries, 388–89
  Orange Syrup, 388–89
  Sweet Swirled Breads (bread machine), 424–25
Ovens, 30–31

P Pain au Chocolat, 284
  Pain brioche, 71–72
  Pain de Campagnard, 130–31
  Pain de Campagne, 128–29
  Pain de Campagne (bread machine), 454–55
  Pain de Campagne (food processor), 402–3
  Pain de mie, 144
  Pain de Seigle, 132–33
  Pain Hawaiian, 152–53
  Pain Ordinaire (French Bread), 46–47
  Pancake griddles, 239, 247
  Pancakes
    about, 236
    Baked Apple and Pear Oven Pancake, 255
    Baked Pancake with Cucumber Salsa, 254
    Blueberry—Blue Cornmeal Pancakes, 241
    Blue Cornmeal Pancakes, 241
    Blue Cornmeal Pancakes with Corn, 241
    Blue Cornmeal Pancakes with Rice, 241
    Buckwheat Pancakes, 243
    Cornmeal Blini, 250
    freezing, 33
    Old-fashioned Buttermilk Pancakes, 237
    Old-fashioned Potato Pancakes, 252
    Savory Wild Rice Pancakes, 251

    Sourdough Pancakes, 240
    Whole-Wheat Blueberry Buttermilk Pancakes, 242
    Zucchini Pancakes, 253
Pancetta-Onion Gruyère Ring, 200–201
Pandoro, 302
Pan Dulce (Mexican Morning Buns), 272–73
Pane alle noci e uva, 86
Pane al Pizza con Formaggio (Pizza Pie with Cheese), 221
Pane casalingo, 122, 447
Pane integrale, 404
Pane sciocco, 50
Pane toscano, 50, 449
Panettone
  Pernod Panettone, 360–61
  Pernod Panettone (bread machine), 460–61
Parker House Rolls, 160
Parmesan cheese
  Parmesan-Herb Popovers, 257
  Zucchini Madeleines, 336
Paskha, 382
Pastries. *See also* Croissants
  Almond Crests, 281
  Apple Danish, 281
  Blueberry Danish Turnovers, 280
  Cheese Danish Envelopes, 280
  Danish Pastries, 259, 276–81
  Prune Crescents, 280
  Yeasted Sopaipillas, 274–75
Peach Upside-Down Ginger Cake, 352
Pears
  Baked Apple and Pear Oven Pancake, 255
  Pear Spice Coffee Cake, 290
Pecans
  Banana-Pecan Muffins, 332
  Cinnamon Rolls with Irish Cream Glaze, 270–71
  Dried Apricot—Pecan Bread, 313
  Fresh Apricot Gingerbread, 355
  Maple Pecan Bread (bread machine), 459
  Orange-Date Tea Bread, 315
  Orange-Pecan Filling, 425
  Pecan Biscuits, 182

Spiced Brown Sugar–Pecan Coffee Cake, 288

Steamed Pecan Corn Bread, 323

Sweet Swirled Breads (bread machine), 424–25

toasting, 375

Whole-Wheat Prune Bread, 314

Pepper Cheese Breads (food processor), 411

Pernod Panettone, 360–61

Pernod Panettone (bread machine), 460–61

Pesto, Olive, 225

Petits Pains au Lait, 166–67

Petits Pains (Crusty Little French Rolls), 401

Pineapple, dried

Paskha, 382

Stollen with Dried Cherries and Pineapple, 362–63

Pine nuts

Graham Scones with Pine Nuts and Raisins, 190

toasting, 375

Pistachios, 375

Pita, Country-Style Whole-Wheat, 234–35

Pizza

about, 212

Basic Pizza Dough, 213–15

Basic Pizza Dough (bread machine), 456–57

Campers Pizza, 216–17

Cornmeal Pizza Dough, 215

Cornmeal Pizza Dough (bread machine), 457

Deep Dish Pizza with Sausage and Mozzarella, 218–20

equipment for, 212

Garlic Pizza Dough, 215

Garlic Pizza Dough (bread machine), 457

Grill-Top Baked Pizza, 217

Herbed Pizza Dough, 215

Herbed Pizza Dough (bread machine), 457

Pizza Pie with Cheese (Pane al Pizza con Formaggio), 221

rustica, 218

Saffron Pizza Dough, 215

Saffron Pizza Dough (bread machine), 457

Semolina Pizza Dough, 215

Semolina Pizza Dough (bread machine), 457

Suzanne's Sourdough Pizza (bread machine), 457

tips, 216

Tomato-Basil Sauce for Pizza, 215

toppings, 216

Whole-Wheat Pizza Dough, 215

Whole-Wheat Pizza Dough (bread machine), 457

Plum Crumb Cake, 308

Polenta, 343. *See also* Cornmeal

Popovers

Bran Popovers, 256

Buckwheat Popovers, 256

Cornmeal Popovers, 256

freezing, 33

Mile-High Popovers, 256

Parmesan-Herb Popovers, 257

Spinach Popovers, 257

Sun-Dried Tomato and Bacon Popovers, 257

Poppy seeds

about, 312

Homestyle White Bread with Poppy Seeds, 52–53

Honey and Seed Bread, 58

Lemon–Poppy Seed Bread, 312

Lemon–Poppy Seed Bread with Saffron, 312

Shallot and Poppy Seed Bread, 196–97

Sour Poppy Seed Rye, 134–35

Portuguese Sweet Bread with Honey, 368–69

Potatoes

Buttermilk Potato Bread, 138–39

Buttermilk Potato Bread (bread machine), 450

Buttermilk Potato Rolls, 139

Cinnamon Rolls with Irish Cream Glaze, 270–71

Oatmeal-Potato Bread, 94–95

Old-fashioned Potato Pancakes, 252

Potato and Rye Vienna Twist, 104–5

Pull-Apart Potato Dinner Rolls (bread machine), 451

Power pans, 212

Prunes

about, 262

Honey-Prune Bread, 262–63

Old-fashioned Prune Muffins, 331

Prune Crescents, 280

Prune-Nut Filling, 425

Sweet Swirled Breads (bread machine), 424–25

Whole-Wheat Prune Bread, 314

Pull-Apart Potato Dinner Rolls (bread machine), 451

Pullman Loaf, Gruyère, 144–45

Pumpernickel breads

 Black Russian Rye Bread, 102–3

 Black Russian Rye Bread (bread machine), 442–43

 Pumpernickel Bagels, 180

Pumpkin

 Cream Sherry–Pumpkin Bread, 320

 Indian Pumpkin Bread, 320

 Pumpkin Brioche, 286

 purée, 165

 Refrigerator Squash Cloverleafs, 165

 Squash Cloverleafs, 164–65

Pumpkin seeds

 Four-Seed Whole-Wheat Bread (food processor), 408

 toasting, 375

Q Quick breads

 baking, 30

 Banana Bread, 316

 Carrot and Tangerine Bread, 319

 Cranberry-Orange Bread, 318

 Cream Sherry–Pumpkin Bread, 320

 Dried Apricot–Pecan Bread, 313

 freezing, 33

 Glazed Zucchini Bread, 322

 Indian Pumpkin Bread, 320

 Lemon–Poppy Seed Bread, 312

 Lemon–Poppy Seed Bread with Saffron, 312

 Mango Bread, 317

 Orange-Date Tea Bread, 315

 Steamed Applesauce Brown Bread, 325

 Steamed Brown Bread with Dried Blueberries, 324–25

 Steamed Pecan Corn Bread, 323

 techniques for, 309

 Whole-Wheat Prune Bread, 314

Quinoa

 cooking, 339

 Quinoa Whole-Wheat Muffins, 339

R Rain and Sun, 98–99

Raisins

 Alsatian Kugelhof (food processor), 414

 Cinnamon-Raisin Bagels, 180

 Cinnamon-Raisin-Currant Bread (bread machine), 458

 Cinnamon Rolls with Irish Cream Glaze, 270–71

 Country Bread with Raisins and Walnuts (bread machine), 440

 Glazed Zucchini Bread, 322

 Graham Scones with Pine Nuts and Raisins, 190

 Irish Soda Bread with Caraway and Drambuie, 191

 Italian Walnut-Raisin Whole-Wheat Bread, 86–87

 Kulich with Almonds and Ginger (Russian Easter Coffee Cake), 380–81

 Old-fashioned Raisin Bread with Molasses Glaze, 260–61

 Paskha, 382

 Pernod Panettone, 360–61

 Pernod Panettone (bread machine), 460–61

 Rosemary Raisin Bread (food processor), 409

 Sour Cream Raisin Bread (food processor), 413

 Squaw Bread, 106–7

 Squaw Bread (bread machine), 446

 Stollen with Dried Cherries and Pineapple, 362–63

Raspberries

 Berry Corn Bread, 344

 Fresh Berry Muffins, 329

 Orange Savarin with Berries, 388–89

 Raspberry Braid, 297

 Raspberry Cornmeal Muffins, 335

 Raspberry Sauce, 351

 Raspberry Whole-Wheat Croissants, 284

Refrigerator Rolls, 160

Refrigerator Squash Cloverleafs, 165

Reheating, 31

Rice. *See also* Wild rice
    Blue Cornmeal Pancakes with Rice, 241
    Brown Rice Bread with Dutch Crunch Topping,
        110–11
    Buttermilk Waffles with Rice, 238
    Rice Corn Bread, 344
Rich Egg Glaze, 52–53
Ricotta cheese
    Blueberry Blintzes, 249
    Bohemian Sweet Rolls (Kolacki), 366–67
    Cheese Danish Envelopes, 280
    Cottage Cheese Blintzes, 248–49
    Deep Dish Pizza with Sausage and Mozzarella, 218–20
    Spinach Calzone, 222–23
    Strawberry Blintzes, 249
    Torta d'Erbe (Italian Green Tort), 206–7
Rising, 24–27, 28
Roasted Chestnut Bread, 154–55
Rolls. *See also* Buns
    about, 157
    Black Bread Rolls, 168
    Bohemian Sweet Rolls (Kolacki), 366–67
    Bow Knots and Rosettes, 159
    Braided Rolls, 159
    Butterfly Rolls, 159
    Buttermilk Potato Rolls, 139
    California Olive Rolls, 173
    Cinnamon Rolls with Irish Cream Glaze, 270–71
    Cloverleaf Rolls, 159
    Cornmeal Crescent Dinner Rolls (bread machine),
        444–45
    Crescent Rolls, 159
    Double Crescent Rolls, 159–60
    Freezer Rolls, 160–61
    freezing, 32–33
    French-Style Mexican Hard Rolls (Bolillos), 162–63
    Homemade Brown-and-Serve Rolls, 161
    Hungarian Nut Roll (Diós Tekeres), 372–73
    long (bread machine), 426–27
    Mexican Flat Rolls (Teleras), 163
    My Favorite Buttermilk Dinner Rolls, 158–59

    Onion Rolls, 47
    Parker House Rolls, 160
    Petits Pains au Lait, 166–67
    Petits Pains (Crusty Little French Rolls), 401
    Pull-Apart Potato Dinner Rolls (bread machine), 451
    Refrigerator Rolls, 160
    Refrigerator Squash Cloverleafs, 165
    Sesame Whole-Wheat Long Rolls, 172
    Snails, 160
    Squash Cloverleafs, 164–65
    Walnut Rolls, 151
    Water Rolls, 169
Rosemary Raisin Bread (food processor), 409
Rum Syrup, 465
Rusks, dessert, 61
Russian Easter Coffee Cake (Kulich with Almonds and
    Ginger), 380–81
Rye breads. *See also* Black breads; Pumpernickel breads
    Narsai's Light Rye Bread (bread machine), 441
    Pain de Campagnard, 130–31
    Pain de Seigle, 132–33
    Potato and Rye Vienna Twist, 104–5
    Seeded Dill Rye, 137
    Sour Four-Seed Rye, 135
    Sour Poppy Seed Rye, 134–35
    Sour Rye Bread (food processor), 406–7
    Squaw Bread, 106–7
    Squaw Bread (bread machine), 446
    Swedish Rye Bread, 100–101

S Saffron Bread (bread machine), 463–64
Saffron Bread with Scented-Geranium Powdered Sugar,
    364–65
Saffron Pizza Dough, 215
Saffron Pizza Dough (bread machine), 457
Salsa, Cucumber, 254
Salt, 41, 420
Santa Fe Blue Corn Muffins, 338
Sauces
    Amaretto Cream, 353

Lemon Sauce, 351

Olive Pesto, 225

Raspberry Sauce, 351

Tomato-Basil Sauce for Pizza, 215

Warm Lemon Sauce, 291

Sausage

Deep Dish Pizza with Sausage and Mozzarella, 218–20

Italian-Style Herb Bread, 204–5

Sausage Bread, 195

Savarin, Orange, with Berries, 388–89

Savory Corn Bread Stuffing, 345

Scented-Geranium Powdered Sugar, 365

Scones

Fig-Walnut Scones, 189

freezing, 33

Graham Scones with Pine Nuts and Raisins, 190

Lemon Cream Scones, 188

making, 181

Seeds. *See also individual seeds*

Four-Seed Whole-Wheat Bread (food processor), 408

Seeded Dill Rye, 137

Sour Four-Seed Rye, 135

Sour Poppy Seed Rye, 134–35

Three-Seed Honey Whole-Wheat Bread (bread machine), 432

toasting, 375

Semolina flour

about, 39–40, 125

Italian Bread Sticks (Grissini), 174–75

Semolina Pizza Dough, 215

Semolina Pizza Dough (bread machine), 457

Semolina Sesame Seed Twist, 124–25

Sesame Semolina Bread (bread machine), 435

Sesame seeds

Byzantine Easter Bread, 378–79

Cheddar Cheese Bread with Toasted Sesame Seeds, 142–43

Cracked Wheat Bread, 88–89

Honey and Seed Bread, 58

Pancetta-Onion Gruyère Ring, 200–201

Semolina Sesame Seed Twist, 124–25

Sesame Burger Buns, 170–71

Sesame Semolina Bread (bread machine), 435

Sesame White Bread (food processor), 398

Sesame Whole-Wheat Bread, 82–83

Sesame Whole-Wheat Long Rolls, 172

Sour Poppy Seed Rye, 134–35

Vienna Bread, 126–27

Seven-Grain Buttermilk Waffles, 239

Seven-Grain Honey Bread, 114–15

Shallot and Poppy Seed Bread, 196–97

Shortcakes

making, 181

making, in a food processor, 183

Old-fashioned Shortcake Biscuits, 186

Slicing, 31

Snails, 160

Soda breads

Irish Soda Bread with Caraway and Drambuie, 191

making, 181

Whole-Wheat Bran Bread with Dates, 193

Whole-Wheat Irish Herb Bread, 192

Sopaipillas, Yeasted, 274–75

Sour cream

about, 292

Blueberry Gingerbread, 354

Blue Corn Bread, 346

Fresh Apricot Gingerbread, 355

Green and Red Pepper Corn Bread, 347

Hungarian Sweet Cheese Bread, 390–91

Plum Crumb Cake, 308

Sour Cream Apple Muffins, 330

Sour Cream Braid (food processor), 412–13

Sour Cream Buttermilk Waffles, 238

Sour Cream Raisin Bread (food processor), 413

Vanilla Sour Cream Coffee Cake, 293

Sourdough breads. *See also* Starters

Farmstead Sourdough Bread, 118–19

Sourdough Farm Bread (bread machine), 453

Sourdough Pancakes and Waffles, 240

Sour Four-Seed Rye, 135

Sour Poppy Seed Rye, 134–35

Sour Rye Bread (food processor), 406–7

Suzanne's Sourdough Pizza (bread machine), 457

Special Diet Crêpes, 247

Spelt, 39, 81

Spice Crumbs, 281

Spiced Applesauce Muffins, 333

Spiced Brown Sugar–Pecan Coffee Cake, 288

Spice Filling, 424

Spinach

Spinach Calzone, 222–23

Spinach Popovers, 257

Torta d'Erbe (Italian Green Tort), 206–7

Spirits, distilled, 321

Sponge method, 18–19, 127. *See also* Starters

Squash

Cream Sherry–Pumpkin Bread, 320

Glazed Zucchini Bread, 322

Indian Pumpkin Bread, 320

Pumpkin Brioche, 286

purée, 165

Refrigerator Squash Cloverleafs, 165

Squash Cloverleafs, 164–65

Torta d'Erbe (Italian Green Tort), 206–7

Zucchini Madeleines, 336

Zucchini Pancakes, 253

Squaw Bread, 106–7

Squaw Bread (bread machine), 446

Starters

about, 19

Bread Machine Sponge Starter, 448

Classic Sourdough Starter, 120

Sourdough Starter from a Commercial Sourdough
Strain, 120

Steamed Applesauce Brown Bread, 325

Steamed Brown Bread with Dried Blueberries, 324–25

Steamed Pecan Corn Bread, 323

Stollen with Dried Cherries and Pineapple, 362–63

Storing, 31

Strawberries

Grand Marnier Strawberries and Crème Chantilly,
187

Orange Savarin with Berries, 388–89

Strawberry Blintzes, 249

Stromboli, Garlic and Mozzarella, 202–3

Stuffing, Savory Corn Bread, 345

Substitutions

cocoa powder for chocolate, 358

for eggs, 67

honey for sugar, 41

Sugar

honey substituted for, 41

Scented-Geranium Powdered Sugar, 365

Sugar Glaze, 384–85

Vanilla Powdered Sugar, 303

Vanilla Sugar, 303

varieties of, 295

Sun-Dried Tomato and Bacon Popovers, 257

Sunflower seeds

Bran, Molasses, and Sunflower Bread (bread
machine), 437

Bran-Molasses-Sunflower Bread, 92–93

Celeste's Sunflower-Oatmeal Bread, 156

Everyday Maple Bran Muffins, 334

Four-Seed Whole-Wheat Bread (food processor), 408

Quinoa Whole-Wheat Muffins, 339

Three-Seed Honey Whole-Wheat Bread (bread
machine), 432

toasting, 375

Whole-Wheat Irish Herb Bread, 192

Super Whole-Grain Buttermilk Waffles, 238

Suzanne's Sourdough Pizza (bread machine), 457

Swedish Rye Bread, 100–101

Sweet breads. *See also* Coffee cakes

Alpine Easter Bread, 376–77

Alsatian Kugelhof (food processor), 414

American Chocolate Bread, 383

Bohemian Sweet Rolls (Kolacki), 366–67

Bread with Three Chocolates, 392–93

Byzantine Easter Bread, 378–79

Cinnamon-Walnut Sweet Bread, 306–7

freezing, 32–33

Hungarian Nut Roll (Diós Tekeres), 372–73

Hungarian Sweet Cheese Bread, 390–91

Italian Anise Easter Bread, 370–71

Maple-Blueberry Whole-Wheat Braid, 298

Maple Pecan Bread (bread machine), 459

Mexican Chocolate Bread (bread machine), 462

Orange Cinnamon Swirl, 300–301

Pernod Panettone, 360–61

Pernod Panettone (bread machine), 460–61

Portuguese Sweet Bread with Honey, 368–69

Raspberry Braid, 297

Saffron Bread (bread machine), 463–64

Saffron Bread with Scented-Geranium Powdered
　　Sugar, 364–65

Stollen with Dried Cherries and Pineapple, 362–63

Sweet Swirled Breads (bread machine), 424–25

Sweet Yeast Dough, 294–95

tips for, 356

Whole-Wheat Sweet Yeast Dough, 298–99

Sweeteners, 41

Sweet Potato Biscuits, 184

Sweet Vanilla Challah, 66–67

Swiss chard
　　Torta d'Erbe (Italian Green Tort), 206–7

Swiss cheese
　　Brioche with Cheese and Walnuts (bread machine),
　　　431
　　Eggplant, Pepper, and Artichoke Pie, 208–9

Syrups
　　Lemon Syrup, 312
　　Orange Syrup, 388–89
　　Rum Syrup, 465

T Tangerine Bread, Carrot and, 319

Tarts. *See* Tortas and tarts

Techniques, 17–33
　　baking, 29–31
　　baking at high altitudes, 470
　　for bread machines, 416–17
　　cooling, slicing, and storing bread, 31
　　deflating the dough, 27

for food processors, 394–97

forming the loaf, 27–28

freezing bread, 31–33

freezing dough, 24

glazing, 28–29

kneading a yeast dough, 21–23

leavening and fermentation, 18–19

mixing the dough, 19–21

reheating bread, 31

rising the dough, 24–27, 28

Teleras (Mexican Flat Rolls), 163

Toasts, Olive, for Hors d'Oeuvres, 147

Tomatoes, canned
　　Deep Dish Pizza with Sausage and Mozzarella, 218–20
　　Eggplant, Pepper, and Artichoke Pie, 208–9
　　Tomato-Basil Sauce for Pizza, 215

Tomatoes, sun-dried
　　Cornmeal Brioche with Sun-Dried Tomatoes, 77
　　Italian-Style Herb Bread, 204–5
　　Sun-Dried Tomato and Bacon Popovers, 257

Tortas and tarts
　　Deep Dish Pizza with Sausage and Mozzarella, 218–20
　　Eggplant, Pepper, and Artichoke Pie, 208–9
　　Onion Tart, 210–11
　　Torta d'Erbe (Italian Green Tort), 206–7
　　torta rustica, 208, 212

Tortillas
　　about, 227
　　Blue Corn Tortillas (Tortillas de Maíz Azul), 230
　　Corn Tortillas (Tortillas de Maíz), 228–29
　　Flour Tortillas (Tortillas de Harina), 232–33
　　Low-Fat Flour Tortillas, 233
　　making dough in a food processor, 233
　　Mesquite Flour Tortillas, 233
　　reheating homemade, 229

Traditional English Muffins, 268–69

Tuscan Peasant Bread, 50–51

Tuscan Peasant Bread (bread machine), 449

Tuscan Peasant Bread with Olives, 51

Tuscan Peasant Bread with Olives (bread machine), 449

V Vanilla Belgian Waffles, 245
Vanilla Egg Glaze, 66–67
Vanilla Powdered Sugar, 303
Vanilla Sour Cream Coffee Cake, 293
Vanilla Sugar, 303
Vanilla Whipped Cream, 386–87
Verheiratesbrot, 104
Vienna Bread, 126–27
Vital wheat gluten flour, 39, 420
Vitamin C, 421

W Waffle irons, 239
Waffles
  Beer Waffles, 244
  Buttermilk Waffles, 238
  Buttermilk Waffles with Rice, 238
  freezing, 33
  Lemon Buttermilk Waffles, 238
  Seven-Grain Buttermilk Waffles, 239
  Sour Cream Buttermilk Waffles, 238
  Sourdough Waffles, 240
  Super Whole-Grain Buttermilk Waffles, 238
  Vanilla Belgian Waffles, 245
Walnut oil, 150
Walnuts
  Brioche with Cheese and Walnuts (bread machine), 431
  California Walnut Bread, 150–51
  Cinnamon Rolls with Irish Cream Glaze, 270–71
  Cinnamon-Walnut Sweet Bread, 306–7
  Country Bread with Raisins and Walnuts (bread machine), 440
  Cranberry-Orange Bread, 318
  Fig-Walnut Scones, 189
  Fresh Apple-Walnut Loaf, 264–65
  Glazed Zucchini Bread, 322
  Hungarian Nut Roll (Diós Tekeres), 372–73
  Italian Walnut-Raisin Whole-Wheat Bread, 86–87
  Prune-Nut Filling, 425
  Sour Cream Apple Muffins, 330

Sweet Swirled Breads (bread machine), 424–25
  toasting, 375
  Walnut Rolls, 151
Warm Lemon Sauce, 291
Water Rolls, 169
Wheat, cracked
  about, 40
  Cracked Wheat Bread, 88–89
  Cracked Wheat Bread (bread machine), 436
  Four-Seed Whole-Wheat Bread (food processor), 408
Wheat germ, 38
Whipped Cream, 388–89
Whipped Cream, Vanilla, 386–87
White breads
  about, 42
  Buttermilk Honey Bread, 54–55
  Buttermilk Honey Bread (bread machine), 430
  Cuban Bread (bread machine), 422
  Farm-Style White Bread with Cardamom, 56–57
  French Bread (food processor), 400–401
  French Bread (Pain Ordinaire), 46–47
  Homestyle White Bread with Poppy Seeds, 52–53
  Honey and Seed Bread, 58
  Sesame White Bread (food processor), 398
  Tuscan Peasant Bread, 50–51
  Tuscan Peasant Bread (bread machine), 449
  Tuscan Peasant Bread with Olives, 51
  Tuscan Peasant Bread with Olives (bread machine), 449
  White Mountain Bread, 43–45
White chocolate
  about, 358
  Apricot and White Chocolate Fillinf, 425
  Sweet Swirled Breads (bread machine), 424–25
Whole-Grain Crêpes, 247
Whole-wheat breads
  Blueberry Whole-Wheat Croissants, 284
  Buttermilk Whole-Wheat Bread (food processor), 399
  Country-Style Whole-Wheat Pita, 234–35
  Four-Seed Whole-Wheat Bread (food processor), 408
  French Long Bâtard (bread machine), 454–55

French Nut Bread, 148–49

French Round Boule (bread machine), 454–55

Fresh Herb Honey Whole-Wheat Bread (bread machine), 433

Graham Bread, 90–91

Honey Whole-Wheat Bread (bread machine), 432

Italian Olive Oil Bread, 122–23

Italian Walnut-Raisin Whole-Wheat Bread, 86–87

Italian Whole-Wheat Bread (food processor), 404–5

Lemon Whole-Wheat Egg Bread with Nasturtium Butter, 68–69

Maple-Blueberry Whole-Wheat Braid, 298

Maple Whole-Wheat Johnnycake with Blueberries, 348

Old-fashioned 100 Percent Whole-Wheat Bread, 84–85

100 Percent Whole-Wheat Bread (bread machine), 434

Pain de Campagne, 128–29

Pain de Campagne (bread machine), 454–55

Quinoa Whole-Wheat Muffins, 339

Raspberry Whole-Wheat Croissants, 284

Sesame Whole-Wheat Bread, 82–83

Sesame Whole-Wheat Long Rolls, 172

Super Whole-Grain Buttermilk Waffles, 238

Three-Seed Honey Whole-Wheat Bread (bread machine), 432

Whole-Wheat Bagels, 180

Whole-Wheat Basil Bread, 140–41

Whole-Wheat Biscuits, 183

Whole-Wheat Blueberry Buttermilk Pancakes, 242

Whole-Wheat Bran Bread with Dates, 193

Whole-Wheat Croissants, 282–84

Whole-Wheat Irish Herb Bread, 192

Whole-Wheat Pizza Dough, 215

Whole-Wheat Pizza Dough (bread machine), 457

Whole-Wheat Prune Bread, 314

Whole-Wheat Sweet Yeast Dough, 298–99

Whole-wheat flour, 39, 81

Wild rice

about, 113

cooking, 113

Multi-Grain Wild Rice Bread (food processor), 410

Rice Corn Bread, 344

Savory Wild Rice Pancakes, 251

Wild Rice Biscuits, 182

Wild Rice Bread Sticks, 176–77

Wild Rice–Molasses Bread, 112–13

Wild Rice–Molasses Bread (bread machine), 452

Y Yeast

about, 34–37

active dry, 35

bread machine, 37, 419

compressed fresh cake, 35–36

instant, 36–37

proofing, 18

quick-rise, 36

Yeast cakes

Golden Rum Babas, 386–87

Grand Baba (bread machine), 465–66

Orange Savarin with Berries, 388–89

Yeasted Sopaipillas, 274–75

Yogurt

about, 292

Bacon–Blue Corn Sticks, 337

cheese, 292

Yogurt Corn Bread, 344

Yorkshire Pudding, Best, 258

Z Zucchini

Glazed Zucchini Bread, 322

Torta d'Erbe (Italian Green Tort), 206–7

Zucchini Madeleines, 336

Zucchini Pancakes, 253

TABLE OF EQUIVALENTS

The exact equivalents in the following tables have been rounded for convenience.

Liquid and Dry Measures

U.S.	METRIC
¼ teaspoon	1.25 milliliters
½ teaspoon	2.5 milliliters
1 teaspoon	5 milliliters
1 tablespoon (3 teaspoons)	15 milliliters
1 fluid ounce (2 tablespoons)	30 milliliters
¼ cup	60 milliliters
⅓ cup	80 milliliters
1 cup	240 milliliters
1 pint (2 cups)	480 milliliters
1 quart (4 cups, 32 ounces)	960 milliliters
1 gallon (4 quarts)	3.84 liters
1 ounce (by weight)	28 grams
1 pound	454 grams
2.2 pounds	1 kilogram

Length Measures

U.S.	METRIC	U.S.	METRIC
⅛ inch	3 millimeters	½ inch	12 millimeters
¼ inch	6 millimeters	1 inch	2.5 centimeters

Oven Temperature

FAHRENHEIT	CELSIUS	GAS	FAHRENHEIT	CELSIUS	GAS
250	120	½	400	200	6
275	140	1	425	220	7
300	150	2	450	230	8
325	160	3	475	240	9
350	180	4	500	260	10
375	190	5